First of the Year: 2008

First of the Year: 2008

Benj DeMott
editor

Routledge
Taylor & Francis Group

LONDON AND NEW YORK

First published 2008 by Transaction Publishers

Published 2017 by Routledge
2 Park Square, Milton Park, Abingdon, Oxon OX14 4RN
711 Third Avenue, New York, NY 10017, USA

Routledge is an imprint of the Taylor & Francis Group, an informa business

ISSN: 1942-5619
ISBN 13: 978-1-4128-0801-9 (pbk)

Contents

Acknowledgments

My deepest thanks to: my wife Mbayang Diouf for providing time, space and spirit as I thought through this book; Charles O'Brien and Armond White for giving life to *First* (and me); Eric Lott for giving our crew its first shot in the '80s and for hanging tight with us ever since; Stanley Aronowitz for taking us seriously when *First of the Month* seemed like a fantasy; Irving Louis Horowitz for proposing to publish *First of the Year*; the DeMott family for a legacy of love and imagination.

I'd also like to thank all the writers who have contributed to *First of the Month* over the past 10 years, including those authors whose work didn't fit into this volume.

Dozens of people have given generous help of many kinds as we produced and distributed issues of *First of the Month*. I've named some of them below in a list that lumps together individuals who have donated thousands of dollars to our newspaper (Pace Collier!) with others whose acts of faith have been more modest. Yet I believe I can get away with that because *First*'s friends realize there's no need to rank kindnesses. I'd like to say exactly what I owe to the folks listed here, but it would take another volume to do them justice. For now, I simply want to acknowledge that I'll always be indebted to: Zoe Anglesy, Amiri Baraka, Thomas Bender, Don Bigelow, Veronica Boen, Julian Bond, Robert Chametzky, Edward Chase, Kandia Crazy Horse, Feridoun Danesh, Ossie Davis, John Demetry, Rosemary DeCostanzo, Dorothy Desir, Ruth Eisenberg, Bill Epton, Robert Egert, Eric Foner, Carol Ferry, Herbert Gans, Lawrence Goodwyn, Donald Graham, Vonyaska Gee, Collier Hands, Wesley Hogan, Andy Hsiao, Zaharis Kalaitzis, Cindi Katz, Charles Keil, Hans & Kate Koning, William Kornblum, Jeff Kreines, Scott Andrew Lamb, Kim Laskowski, John Leland, Bongani Madondo, Carolyn Nordstrom, Max Palevsky, Danny Postel, David Quigley, Adolph Reed, Sonny Rollins, Robert Silvers, Steve Sleigh, Scott Spencer, Stephanie Spina, Randy Stiles, Taylor Stoehr, Steve Talty, Kathy Tebbett, Robert Farris Thompson,

Victoria Traube, George Trow, Kurt Vonnegut, Patricia Williams, Ellen Willis, Robert Wuillamey, Asa Zatz.

Lower Manhattan Cultural Council (LMCC) has been the major institutional supporter of our writers' collective since 1999. *First of the Month* would not have survived without LMCC's funding.

Part I

First Cuts

Much of what you'll read in *First of the Year: 2008* appeared in *First of the Month*—a "newspaper of the radical imagination" that our writers' collective started publishing ten years ago. But this volume isn't meant to be a Best-of *First of the Month*. The aim is to define the democratic imperatives and demotic tones that make our ongoing politics of culture matter. *First of the Year: 2008* is a template not a keepsake. We still believe what we said (per The Clash) in our first Call to writers and readers back in 1998: The Future Is Unwritten.

An annual *First of the Year,* though, seems to have been in the cards. There were delays when we were assembling the inaugural issue of our newspaper and I recall now I had to write the poet Philip Levine apologizing for having taken so long to publish lines he'd given us for the first *First*. Levine replied that maybe we should change the title of our newspaper from *First of the Month* to *Last of the Year*. He turned out to be a prophet though his foresight wasn't perfect as he allowed a few years on:

> Never thought *First* had a prayer. But it looks like there's an audience for it. I wonder how many people read the *Partisan* when it first appeared. Probably ten more than read it now.

Partisan Review hadn't folded yet, so Levine wasn't rubbing it in. And I surely don't mean to sound an (unearned) triumphal note. The truth is we're now trying to fail upwards. Our "audience" notwithstanding, *First of the Month*, never managed to become a monthly. It's been an occasional publication though we still hope to live up to our original name through the web where we post regularly at www.firstofthemonth.org.

We took that name from a rap song by Bone-Thugs-n-Harmony about welfare paydays that spoke to those in the struggle for happiness all over the world. BT-n-H's words were politically unconscious but this piece of ghetto music gave body to a soul-deep sense of solidarity. By echoing it

1

we evoked "black and going on" emotions while signaling our refusal to separate race from class analysis. We're still trying to walk with (what one *First* writer dubbed) "dis" people—"disenfranchised and disadvantaged, disaffiliated and disinherited, discomfited and discredited, displaced and discarded, discussed and discounted, dispossessed and dismissed."[1] But we've sharpened our conceptions of solidarity and duty in the post-9/11 era. Take this as one of our new *First* principles: *The underdog is owed sympathy; the mad dog is owed a bullet.*[2]

First means to be more than a literary launching pad. We'd love to blow your minds—to change the game by sublating the Liberal Arts ideal of "the self" (which Amiri Baraka once dissected—"no selves, except alone … no Us, no intimate whispering, no dancing, no communities of intelligence"). Conceived in opposition to flagship papers of smart sets in academia (*The New York Review of Books*) and bohemia (*The Village Voice*), our tab has tried to move beyond a *humanism of comprehension* toward a *humanism in extension*. Armond White's reach has been key here. His blazing commentary exposes the superficiality of the "executive summary" approach to Afro-American culture. But it's not limited to race matters. His film and music criticism resists the shills who are killing us while offering an alternative to "alternative" popcrit on almost every cultural front.

Alive to possibilities of (Brecht's) "sports audiences," *First* has never had a problem with argufying that asks a certain height of readers. A *Time Out* columnist once wrote that *First* was the "only leftist publication [he] could imagine being read at both Columbia University and Rikers." Early on, intelligent critics conflated our desire to get to the base of this society with slumming. (Meanwhile, gangsta-centric frat boys responsible for the exploitative hip hop magazine *XXL* tried to steal our thunder by naming their letters page "The Real First of the Month.") But our two main men, White and Charles O'Brien, were once working class boys and they know in their bones "there is no such thing as the common man." While there will always be pieces in *First* that shout-out our availability wherever streets are watching, we believe our readers may be the sort on whom nothing is lost. Unafraid of the word "better," we make literary (and other) judgments. That's one reason why world-class authors have joined our party of hope.

A recent take on "what's wrong with the American essay"[3] points to another reason. The author quotes editors of anthologies such as *The Norton Book of Personal Essays* and the annual, *The Best American Essays*, who spell out their aversion to polemics and provocations. They prefer writing that's "middle-aged," "gentle," "narcissistic … but in a harmless way." Essays must not have "too much tooth," according to these authorities. But *First* writers (and readers) are more appetitive.

The genteel culture of literate pablum co-exists with an alternate universe ruled by cut-ups who reduce politics to sound bites and passion to an ordinary word. *First* isn't made for either of these worlds. We give the slip to quietists *and* blowhards. *First* will always be politically engaged, but it will never be at the mercy of ideological enforcers. I'm guessing most *First* writers and readers sympathized with Senator Obama's exasperation about being abused on the campaign trail for acknowledging someone on the Right once had an idea (even if he didn't agree with it).

Our editorial crew has never had any use for the neo-liberal orthodoxy associated with the Clintons. At the tail end of Billary's original Age of A-List adrenalin, one of *First*'s elders rejected "Clinton/Blair babble" and gave *First* (too much) credit for creating "a new vocabulary for a real New Left." Word is bond; we're still here to cultivate the power of the powerless. Yet that old equation of Clinton and Blair doesn't quite compute now and *First*'s crew no longer shares the Not-In-Our-Name a prioris of many former New Leftists. *First*'s Charles O'Brien spoke for us on this score a few years back:

> Immediately after September 11, there was an extraordinary communal feeling here, at least in New York City. A left that opts out, that prefers its sense of its own superiority to fraternity is not a left.

What it is?

> A bourgeoisie that views "conscience" as a thing to accessorize with. Some people are prepared to offer blood sweat and tears. That left offers only snot.

First's crew won't stop looking to (un)cover a truly new left in America. We'll be all over the developing story of Obama's "movement." But, *First* things first. Seeing what's right in front of your nose hasn't always been a no-brainer. One of our favorite writers likes to quote Camus's injunction that we all need the courage "to imagine the real." The first section of this volume, "First Cuts," takes a stab at showing how our tab has kept tabs on radical imaginations who dare to go there. "First Cuts" hints at the range of fractious democratic sensibilities who have found a home in our pages. The authors, though, don't serve as representative men and women. It's not about who they are but how they (or their subjects) reach beyond the obvious to the true.

There are those who believe *First*'s reach exceeded its grasp when we published the now famous (notorious?) talk Kanan Makiya gave at a New

York University panel discussion on the looming war in Iraq in November of 2002. Makiya made a moral case then for American intervention in the course of explaining the fraught relationship between the Bush administration and Iraqi democrats. His remarks at NYU are now widely regarded as a key moment in contemporary public discourse. Journalists often quote bits from his talk and/or invoke the surround, but *First* was the only journal that printed all of what Makiya had to say on this occasion. The transcript of his talk ("Inside the Whale") is a piece of history, but it's in "First Cuts" because it's still an eye-opening inside story.

Greil Marcus's essay on the intellectual left's non-response to 9/11 is another oldie but newsy. Marcus's "Nothing New Under the Sun" peaks with a quote from Charles O'Brien's post-9/11 critique of the "Vichy Left" (see "The War" on p. 348 to read the whole thing) and Marcus cites another *First* piece by Fredric Smoler. But don't worry, you're not getting log-rolled. "Nothing New Under the Sun" is here because it shines a light on Americans in dark times.

Marcus is best known for his rock criticism. His capacity to think straight about 9/11 was probably nurtured by his pop life history of hearing sounds of surprise. *First*'s editorial crew are pop lifers too. Our country and our culture would seem pretty grim to us without the rivers of music that flow out of Black Atlantic tributaries and the American South. Open to everyday people all night long, those sounds are our nation's greatest national resource. We aim to make them sing on our pages. This volume opens with Robert Farris Thompson's reflection on James Brown's passing and there's plenty more music writing stitched into "First Cuts" and later sections of the book. Our crew may be middle-aging but our ears are still up. The music will keep *First* young.

But this volume isn't only for America's oldest teenagers as Ben Kessler's piece below proves. Kessler is a kid and it's been a lift to learn there are gifted younger cultural critics who suspect (as he puts it) "the only radical mission that matters now is to destroy the Culturebox and resurrect the *tabula rasa*." We look forward to running with Kessler and his kind in upcoming *First of the Year*s.

Generations mix it up in "First Cuts." There's a tribute to our elder Ellen Willis, a meditation on 9/11 by a World War II veteran, a prayer for Johnny Cash by a punk rocker and that opening bow to James Brown. Mr. Brown and Ms. Willis get more love in later sections of this volume. As rapper Chuck D says in his goodbye to J.B. a little on down the line: "our words and deeds are in passing, but the passing down and forward is so important."

I've added brief editorial notes to certain pieces of writing in "First Cuts" and in other sections (though the authors always speak for themselves). The tables of contents for each section indicate the date when writings were originally published or posted in *First of the Month*, at firstofthemonth.org or in this first *First of the Year*.

Notes

1. The line comes from John Chernoff's introduction to the first volume of his ethnography of an African bar girl, *Hustling Is Not Stealing. First of the Month* published excerpts from this work.
2. The phrase is Charles O'Brien's.
3. The essay was posted by Cristina Nehring at TruthDig.com on November 29, 2007.

The Message

Robert Farris Thompson

Sweat pouring down his face and neck, head titled back at the ecstatic angle, eyes closed in distant meditation, lips contorted in rage and majesty, James Brown goes on forever. Like his spiritual brother, Damaso Perez Prado, he was a master of non-verbal action. His grunts and his screams detoxified a nation. I remember ten years back when I was asked to talk about him for the BBC, I gave them a typology of James Brown screams. It was not what they expected. But boy was I honored to talk about Brown's sonic landscape. Once I saw a video in Brussels on the life and art of soul brother number one. They showed him singing for a Democratic candidate. Brown screamed. Brown got down. The white candidate stood still without a smile. I thought: damn, if he can't react to James Brown, he's gonna lose. He did. There ain't no past tense big enough to hold James Brown. The cat, as I said, goes on forever. Locked in his screams, pain purified to pleasure, is a message from Kongo to all of us: *mu diavwezwa mweti mena diansitusu!*—from humiliation stems grandeur.

Never Too Soon:
Oliver Stone Joins the Battle for Catharsis

Armond White

"It's Too Soon"—that cowardly phrase planted in the public's mind by the mainstream media—keeps Oliver Stone's movie *World Trade Center* from the people who might especially appreciate its value.

The phrase seems designed to control popular sentiment while Stone endeavors to particularize and analyze the huge mix of personal and political feelings that have mounted in the American psyche ever since the sad events of 9/11. *World Trade Center* is never so untrustworthy as an attempt at an "official" remembrance of that day. Stone (and screenwriter Andrea Berloff) make the admirable, intelligent decision to concentrate on the experiences of two Port Authority policeman and their families. John McLoughlin is played by Nicolas Cage and Will Jimeno is played by Michael Pena. The particular speaks for and to the universal.

Anyone who remembers 9/11 deals with it on a daily basis. (More 9/11 movie stories should be made.) To suggest that popular culture cannot link up with and express those memories is, actually, an insult to our sensibilities. Sufferers and survivors must assess and grow from experience. It is an ennobling process but today's cultural gatekeepers either don't believe in the people's capacity for nobility or simply insist that only empowered speakers and media wonks know best.

Consider that the vapid action-cartoon *Snakes on a Plane* was generally greeted in the media as a phenomena of smart marketing. Never too soon for that. GO SEE IT! hailed publications from *AM New York* to *The Nation* magazine's blog. In the latter, *Snakes on the Plane* was praised for being a 9/11 allegory by Richard Kim who invited readers to follow the hype and embrace the spectacle of Samuel L. Jackson—wild-eyed, vituperative and profane as usual—as he tasers reptiles on board a commercial passenger plane. It's a silly disaster movie premise, yet Kim takes it as an allusion to United Flight 93, the plane that went down in Pennsylvania after passengers fought back against a group of terrorists. *Snakes on a Plane* isn't a movie that inspires thought (neither did Paul Greengrass's dour, uninspired docudrama *United 93*). Instead, it provides an occasion for *The Nation* to propagandize for you (Kim launches into ridicule of President Bush and the Homeland Security alert system). In other words: It's Too Soon to think for yourself.

The bizarre difference in media attitudes toward *World Trade Center* and *Snakes on a Plane* reflect the change in public discourse that has taken place since 9/11. Movies that attempt to deal with the spiritual and ethical crisis of that tragedy—*The Manchurian Candidate, Cellular, Phone Booth, Red Eye, War of the Worlds, Munich, Chicken Little, Final Destination 3, Monster House*—are routinely misunderstood. Either their serious meaning is denied, or their serious effort is scoffed at. This isn't just the usual mindlessness of journalists who promote anti-intellectualism and Hollywood marketing, but an insidious form of cultural hegemony. Let the punditocracy and irresponsible Hollywood hacks trivialize 9/11 *their* way—always the ignoble way and one that furthers commercialism.

In *World Trade Center*, Stone creates one of the finest American narratives in modern pop. Storylines that alternate between McLoughlin and Jimeno trapped in a pit under the rubble of Tower One and the anxieties of their suburban, multi-ethnic families are terse and poignant. The interplay of these scenes prove that sentiment can be accessed without over-the-top emotionalism. What Stone elicits, in fact, is credible empathy. You'd have to go back to the unifying sense of public distress during World War II (and to movies like *Till the End of Time, The Best Years of Our Lives, From Here to Eternity*) to find examples of filmmaking that aroused a similar shared pathos connected with common hope. In *World Trade Center*, hope is not namby-pamby; it's informed by a desperation for the fundamental patterns of life that have been ruthlessly shaken. Stone restores decency to a culture that was mired in cynicism long before 9/11. Thus the inability of some critics to appreciate the archetypal quality of Stone's characters. His respect for the range of American personalities, exhibited in the behavior of various working-class folk (along with the respect from actors who live fully into their roles, seizing the rare occasion of representing the working-class) is so radical that it tends to unnerve those mediacrats who (since Vietnam? Watergate? Clinton?) have claimed authority over democratic virtues.

Now, even the best American filmmakers find it difficult to treat honor as a subject. Any modern attempt to do the right thing runs into opposition from some preening establishment. That's what happened to Steven Spielberg's great, complex *Munich*. Not even the impressive collaboration with Tony Kushner (*Angels in America*) escaped the censure of those whose political biases clashed with the film's thoroughly inquisitive spiritual drama. Upset their own positions were not simply upheld, they couldn't stand to imagine how others felt politically. So *Munich* was refused proper philosophical and political engagement and denied its place in the discourse of popular culture.

Refusing *Munich* (as rudely as Spielberg's pungent 9/11 allegory in *War of the Worlds* was refused), the left-liberal media soon found a comfy alternative. In the first American theatrical release of Jean-Pierre Melville's 1969 film *Army of Shadows*, pundits could relax all that 9/11 anxiety and bask in an anachronistic spectacle of the already-won World War II. This film from the late '60s also brought back nostalgia for the good ol' counterculture. Liberal moviegoers weren't stepping into New York's Film Forum with forward-thinking courage and commitment; they were retreating into Melville's grave via his tired, late-career blandness. *Army of Shadows* was exasperatingly colorless, featuring a cast of art-house icons such as Simone Signoret and Lino Ventura who were way past their prime, yet fondly representative of uncomplicated political issues. This wasn't snakes on a plane but totems in a reliquary. A film as uncompelling as *Army of Shadows* could only become a hit in an era where elite audiences are afraid of their most urgent feelings—afraid of the shadow cast by 9/11.

After all, as critic John Demetry noted, no pundits whined "It's Too Soon" about Michael Moore's *Fahrenheit 911*. The exploitation of 9/11 footage and the conning of soldiers and soldier's families in Moore's anti-Bush propaganda was okayed by most journalists. But when they didn't get the expected Moore-rebuttal from Stone, some even complained that *World Trade Center* wasn't political. "It's Too Soon" must really mean that only the approved perspective will be accepted. But keeping people away from this extraordinary film is a form of cultural treason; it keeps audiences from finding their own responses, keeps them from catharsis.

What can be said satisfactorily about losses that are unfair and criminal, or sacrifices made without choice? The 9/11 terrorists stole the liberty that comes with an engaged battle, forever leaving us in a state of mortified offense. There hasn't yet been a fully declared war to relieve this unique frustration, yet other events have moved in to distract our mourning and cast Americans into bitter ideological contradictions.

One benefit of pop culture is to take in and weigh these circumstance, which Stone's film does beautifully by choosing to interpret the McLoughlin and Jimeno experiences as spiritual trials. "Where are we?" McLoughlin asks when close to succumbing, with massive rocks weighing on his chest. "We're in Hell," Jimeno answers with the sarcastic, gallows humor instinctively developed by men in combat. Stone uses this to characterize and validate civilian-life shock-and-awe. The hell of stolen liberty forces the men to reconsider how they lived their lives, to painfully revisit their daily regrets.

World Trade Center's approach is not apolitical. Stone's post-Vietnam alarm is threaded gently throughout, yet it is respectfully held in check—which is a different kind of politics than pundits customarily understand; a different rhetoric, if you will. His rectitude is judicious; he realizes that that blue-sky, blue-collar day triggered a working-class sense of unity, including the agape that makes privileged secular commentators uneasy. As shown, the events of 9/11 illustrate a richer sense of possibility than that fearfully half-satirized in Stone's *Wall Street.* Here the will strains toward a world of love not toward worldly power or material gain. As the buried men struggle to survive, their wives (portrayed by Maria Bello and Maggie Gyllenhaal) fight for faith. Their endurance is never Norman Rockwell banal; the Catholic families all pray in ethnically distinct manners and the men accept their grievous, unequal portion: "I don't smile a lot," McLoughlin tells Jimeno. "That's why I'm not Lieutenant. People don't like me because I don't smile a lot." Stone carefully leavens his stories with an earned solemnity, not rah-rah demagoguery; it is the equivalent to not smiling a lot.

In the consumerist mania that has taken over film culture, that song from *The Wiz,* "Don't Nobody Bring Me No Bad News," holds sway. It is, ironically, a cynic's anthem. Feel-good pop narratives disrespect post-9/11 audiences, denying them the catharsis that comes with hard-earned deliverance. *The Village Voice*'s critics deviously ridicule this as "uplift." Their attitude reveals privileged-class decadence. They dismiss commiseration and fellow-feeling, ensuring factionalism and polarization.

At the end of the widely disapproved *Munich,* a discreet vision of the World Trade Center towers appears in the distance. It is breathtaking—a visual memory that accentuates the story Spielberg was telling. History reverberates from that vista. Memory collapses into sorrow, for the terrorist slaughter of the 1972 Munich Olympics and the 2001 attack that took down the towers. What we might have wished never happened reappears almost magically, as if in fable, but now and forever an image of terrifying realism. It is a wound we all share and must not be forgotten.

Admittedly, nothing in Stone's movie is quite that powerful or cautionary but he literalizes another trope from Spielberg's 9/11 trilogy: That avant-garde fade to black featured in *War of the Worlds*—a cessation of stimulus—also occurs in *World Trade Center* after the towers fall. But Stone follows it brilliantly, though maybe too obviously, with a close-up of McLoughlin's eyes. It is a symbol of shocked witnessing—from inside the chaos—appropriate for the ending of *Munich,* appropriate to worldwide experience of that September day. Those stunned, pain-filled, apprehensive eyes describe how we currently look at movies.

When additional rescuers arrive at the towers site, they're soon waylaid by clouds of debris and billowing smoke. A marine says "It's like God made a curtain of smoke, shielding us from what we're not yet ready to see." Film geeks might liken this moment to John Boorman's

Excalibur when the fog rises, helpfully obscuring the small number of King Arthur's army of shadows; it's part of Boorman's intelligent use of national mythology. Stone has dared not to distance himself from the immediacy of 9/11; he's willing to countenance contemporary histori-cal mythologizing, insisting that we are ready to see and assess the felt consequences of what's happened to us. *World Trade Center* reminds us, though in a less philological way than *Excalibur*, that movie culture has a commemorative and restorative purpose.

Audiences who come out of Stone's movie shaken, sniffling and teary-eyed experience a rare sense of community largely because they have not assembled for something trivial. (They are not contemptuously regarded as snakes on a plane.) The step-by-step process of catharsis can only be accomplished by the ritualistic variations Stone makes on the action film, the war film, the domestic drama, the love story, the social docu-mentary as alluded to by each scene in *World Trade Center*. (Consider how meaningfully Stone immobilizes Cage, the fatuous '90s action hero, how he puts Bello into a more humane context than the rabid *A History of Violence*—each choice a correction of recent pop mythology.)

Stone's most artful risk comes with an aftermath montage showing an empty, debris-strewn downtown, a vacant Staten Island Ferry, an un-peopled subway car, then a wall of hand-made posters that advertise the lost as missing. This existential vacancy is a very beautiful capstone, recalling the metaphysical ending of Antonioni's *The Eclipse*. But this isn't just an artistic flourish; it respectfully accretes familiar images of despair, converting them into towering forms that we, hopefully, are ready to see. Stone's ultimate ending is sorrowful yet vital. Because Stone's touch is perfectly deft, never cloying, the audience's tears come from understanding *for themselves* the tragedy that they deal with everyday. As they walk out, they walk forward. They cry righteous tears. Never too soon for that.

Locked

Benjamin Kessler

A recent *Slate* "Culturebox" feature contained responses by "novel-ists, artists, journalists, and other thoughtful people" to the question: "What work of art or literature has helped you make sense of the attacks and the world after them?" That question isn't just loaded; it's cocked and pointed as well. There's an assumed equivalence between America's response to 9/11 ("the world after them") and the attacks themselves.

All of these events, to *Slate*, are equally removed from "sense." Faced with such a question, a genuinely thoughtful person would put the lid back on this Culturebox. Nevertheless, it's instructive for the reader to listen to the noises coming from the Box, because the confines of this cage map the minds and hearts of our culture's arbiters. This lid stifles us all.

One of *Slate*'s caged voices belongs to fiction writer George Saunders, who states his belief that the 9/11 attacks "were just what they felt like they were—a reminder that chaos and hatred sometimes rear their heads and, temporarily, are ascendant." As a moral philosopher, Saunders shows himself to be one or two levels of sophistication below Yoda, who at least never said that the Dark Side would disappear with Darth Vader. Saunders' "chaos and hatred"—an irreligious substitute for Satan—needn't alarm us or call us to action. It's "temporarily ascendant," a passing craze. Ignore it, it'll go away.

Having reduced mass murder to a harmless abstraction, he proceeds to praise the artwork that serves as the engine of this delusion. "John Adams' symphonic work 'On the Transmigration of Souls' ... 'helped' me in the sense that I've been able to use it, periodically and sacramentally, to move myself to tears," he writes. (Is it unfair to say that Saunders puts the "psychosis" in "metempsychosis"?) I haven't heard "On the Transmigration of Souls," but the use to which Adams' work is put here equates art with pornography. The Adams is what shelters Saunders from the implications of experience. Imagine the distinguished author holed up in his study with his secret stash of symphonic works, shooting one last look over his shoulder—Are they all gone?—and then pressing Play. What soon gushes forth is evidence not of human horniness but rather of the author's sanctified, solitary superiority. In this sacramental moment, 9/11 is summoned, flickers briefly, and then fades from existence until the next time it is needed: fleeting, untroubling, unreal. For Saunders, the blood evaporates with his tears.

I don't mean to pick on Saunders; he's merely representative of the lack of love within the Culturebox. The Gray Lady's 9/11/06 editorial was equally illuminating. As with most *New York Times* editorials, every sentence in this piece has its own undertow of dishonesty that threatens to carry off the unresisting reader to ... we-know-not-where. Some moral wasteland, anyway. Consider this passage about the Iraq war: "Without ever having asked to be exempt from the demands of this new war, we were cut out. Everything would be paid for with the blood of other people's children, and with money earned by the next generation." Did you see that? More than 2,500 American mothers—"other people"—just winced.

Like Saunders, the *Times'* editors assume they hold the copyright on a communal suffering. This petulant assertion of privilege is couched in a narrative that sentimentalizes the period immediately following the 9/11 attacks, in which, apparently, "sorrow was merged with a sense of community and purpose." In this story, less saccharine emotions such as fear and anger are confined to a later time, beginning (one assumes) with the invasion of Iraq and encompassing the present day. Remember the smell that hung in the Manhattan air in the weeks after the attacks? To the decision-makers at the paper of record, that was the aroma of "community and purpose." Similarly, the Gray Lady groans at "an invasion that never would have occurred if every voter's sons and daughters were eligible for the draft." Uncomfortably aware of its current irrelevance, the *Times* casts a wistful eye at some of recent American history's worst moments—through a rose-tinted gunsight.

Before we replace the lid, let's reflect for a moment on what a post-9/11 "sense of community and purpose" might actually look like. If nothing else, the events of September 11, 2001 should have dissolved our misplaced faith in the social protections of privilege and privacy. Five years after the massacre, we should be able to admit that the expression of emotion—both public and personal—is a civic obligation. Citizenship in a democracy requires sustained agape, an openness to exigency that transcends social status. Without this childlike core, democratic sophistication collapses into sophistry. Five years after 9/11, the only radical mission that matters is to destroy the Culturebox and resurrect the *tabula rasa*.

What's Love Got to Do with It?

Mike Rose

There was a remarkable moment in former New York mayor Rudy Giuliani's speech at the Republican National Convention [in 2004], a moment I keep turning over and over in my mind. It had to do with love. About half-way through the speech—after praising George Bush's leadership in responding to 9/11 and before an affirmation of the Bush foreign policy doctrine—Giuliani offers the following scene.

Bush is visiting Ground Zero and is soon surrounded by "big, real big" construction workers. Their "arms are bigger than [Giuliani's] legs, and their opinions are even bigger than their arms." Using language that

Giuliani "can't repeat," one of the men begins speaking with deep feeling about the attackers to Mr. Bush, and then "embraced the president and began hugging him enthusiastically." Giuliani completes the moment by observing this was an act of love.

I don't know this worker, so I can only imagine what feelings must have been churning inside him, seeking some kind of meaningful expression. And suddenly here before him stands the president of the United States. At Ground Zero. Overwhelming.

What troubles me, though, what I can't shake, is the use of that moment by Giuliani—and similar moments by other Republican strategists and speechwriters—to certify George Bush's deep bond with working people. Giuliani describes the construction worker with genial humor, but if you think about it, the portrait is pretty stereotypical: the big, patriotic hard hat. Joe Sixpack. The working men and women I grew up with were strong, yes, and loyal to country, but they were much more. Smart and skeptical, for starters. Think, for a moment, of all that you won't see in these GOP portraits. You won't see the female cannery worker with injured hands or the guys at bitter loose ends when the factory closes. You won't see people, exhausted, shuttling between two (or more) jobs to make a living or the anxious scramble for minimal health care for their kids. And you sure won't see people organizing to improve their working lives.

What a funny kind of love it is that undercuts unions, erodes workplace health and safety regulations, opposes increases in the minimum wage, changes overtime rules. The invocation of love at Ground Zero—and the replaying of the image—mystifies things terribly. Emotion trumps fact: the awful Republican record on working America. God forbid that the fellow embracing Bush develops, as so many have, serious respiratory disease. He won't find the administration's policies hospitable to his plight. He'd better seek instead the much-maligned trial lawyer.

American workers don't need love from their government, especially this funky seduction. They need opportunity. They need an understanding of their struggles. They need an appreciation of the skill and intelligence they bring to their work. They need enough respect for that intelligence that they're provided with facts rather than emotion. They need the protections of the secure workplace, of the fair wage, of the union contract. They don't need a one-way romance, the administration taking the embrace, but returning a deadly kiss.

Reconstructing America

First of the Month

William Greider tries to "explain power in plain English" to American citizens. But he's always ready to learn from them as well. His book, The Soul of Capitalism, *draws attention to individuals whose businesses and working lives hint at how Americans might remake our society. It manages to be deeply—even willfully—optimistic without buying into the bottom-line of happy globalists. The following interview with the author (from a 2004 issue of* First of the Month*) provides reasons to look forward to the Reconstruction of America.*

FIRST: In *The Soul of Capitalism* you argue that Americans must re-invent the economic engine that's made America the richest country on earth. Tell us why you predict a change in Wall Street's core values is "likely to occur."

GREIDER: In an ironic way, Wall Street's crimes and excesses are more visible than the innards of corporations. People can read the numbers and see the reckless waste and other contradictions. *The New York Times* had a business-section piece the other day on global warming and took note of the fact that better social performance produces a better bottom line, with major corporate logos as evidence. These facts are not secret and there are numerous interests outside the big boardrooms that can act on them in their investing behavior. The disconnect between conventional business lore and practical reality will sooner or later force people to move, even if the big banks and brokerages wish to remain in denial.

FIRST: You allow that Americans are currently at the mercy of imperi-ous financiers who love liquidity not community, yet you propose that a kind of counter-culture is busy being born thanks to more conscientious venture capitalists, forward-thinking union officials, bootstrappers, en-viro-developers, et al. How is this trajectory related—or opposed—to the ongoing incorporation of the 60s' "cultural revolution" (what Tom Frank has dubbed "the conquest of cool")?

GREIDER: That's a very interesting question, but I think its approach to cultural change is too shallow. This is not simply about a softer focus or people changing their values. It is about people discovering their self-interest has been misdefined for them by the current system. I'm not sure whether that's cool or hot, but I know people act on it once they grasp that they are actually losing something of value in their lives.

FIRST: You point out that American workers have the potential to transform the nature of American capitalism through their pension funds. To quote AFL-CIO's Ronald Blackwell: "The capital that belongs to working people should serve their purposes and values; right now it doesn't. If this can be accomplished, I envision a labor movement that will step forward as an able critic of business as usual. Labor, which has frequently been seen as a narrow special interest, would become an advocate for real development and the whole community—and labor will have real money in its pocket to back up its advocacy?" Can you give us examples of union officials who are currently using pension funds to back up their advocacy for workers and communities? And would you allow that unions have been slow to exercise their power on this front?

GREIDER: The unions that have rediscovered ownership and its potential for the future mostly got there from necessity—trying to defend viable production the home office was prepared to jettison. Some of those early leaders like Lynn Williams of the steel workers always had a larger vision—an economy in which worker ownership is the general pattern—but it's damned hard to be visionary when your back is against the wall. Most of organized labor still does not see all the possibilities and many are still skeptical of changes that would complicate the bargaining position for unions. But I do think labor generally is ahead of the curve in understanding the potential power of their wealth holdings to force changes that go beyond narrow definitions of "economic gains." They are in the early stages of figuring out how to apply this power.

FIRST: Over 10 million Americans are worker-owners in some 11,000 employee-owned companies. In *The Soul of Capitalism*, you tell the story of an exemplary temp agency called Solidarity that's owned by the temp workers—many of whom are ex-cons and/or recovering addicts. How did you find out about their business?

GREIDER: The origins of Solidarity are far more complicated than I described in the book. It began with BUILD, the strong and enduring Baltimore community organization developed by the Industrial Areas Foundation, a network that originated with Saul Alinsky. The first objective was to develop a union for marginalized workers of many kinds—from crossing guards to Head Start aides—and ways to improve incomes for the working poor. That led, among other things, to the living wage legislation that was pioneered in Baltimore and has since spread around the country. The temp agency was launched as an extension of those efforts and I learned about it from friends who were active in the development. These same inner-city pioneers are now on the brink of acquiring a small bank, which will provide the kind of financial oxygen that all struggling small businesses need to survive and flourish.

FIRST: You celebrate "humanist-populist-capitalists" who are practical visionaries and introduce readers to John Logue—Director of the Ohio Ownership Center....

GREIDER: John Logue is not a capitalist himself—he's a political science professor at Kent State who had the nerve and stamina to develop the Center as necessary infrastructure to assist companies and unions make the transition to employee ownership. (That is—to provide experienced lawyers, accountants and bankers with the expertise to do the necessary business deals.) The "humanist-populist-capitalists" are the owners who on their own figured out why this transition could be good for wealth creation and quality as well as for the workers who become owners. They are not sentimentalists, but practical-minded types who, if pressed, will acknowledge that this also seems "the right thing to do."

FIRST: You recently heard Logue lead a workshop on what workers might want if they could create "an employee-owned industrial park." Tell us about that and why you found it inspiring?

GREIDER: The discussion among worker owners and their allies about a "Mondragon in Ohio"—an industrial park composed of small, employee-owned companies sharing assets and overhead functions—illustrates for me the open-ended nature of human possibilities, once people imagine beyond existing structures of control. It also explodes the usual stereotypes about what workers want. They want whole lives, they want more control over their destinies, they want practical, intelligent, self-interested collaboration with others. The present system not only discourages such creative thinking, it makes it impossible for most workers even to entertain new ideas. Given the advanced level of our development, this seems to me a criminal waste of human capabilities.

FIRST: You devote a chapter—"Consuming the Future"—to America's environmental crisis. While you allow that employee ownership doesn't necessarily guarantee a firm will challenge the narrow hegemonic logic of consumerism/materialism, you tell of a worker-owned firm—Blue Ridge Paper Products—that's been relatively responsive to environmentalists. What's the lesson implicit in this example of engagement?

GREIDER: What's happened at the North Carolina mills and processing plant illustrates why power is the crucial variable—ideally power located close to the operating realities of a company. This doesn't turn the workers or their union or their management into idealized visionaries. Quite the opposite, they now have the power to alter things within the flow of production—practical changes that will yield real-life benefits where they live. This is what I mean by well-informed self-interest. As the union veep said, "we live here too." From the other side of this great divide, environmentalists are now talking up-close with the people who have control and who vet all their recommendations in the practical setting of running a mill profitably. This does not lead to utopia, I repeat. But it brings the pressure points closer together and makes the trade-offs more visible to both sides. Human experience suggests this is a better basis for reconciliation than hammer-and-tongs confrontation or orders from on high by a few remote insiders.

FIRST: You recognize the power of corporations must be restrained ASAP and you focus on the resistance offered by citizens' groups (like the Program on Corporation Law and Democracy). What's the basic question that should inform struggles here?

GREIDER: The democratic question—who has power to decide, who is excluded from any meaningful voice? I am convinced that virtually all institutions within capitalism will perform better for society and for genuine economic gain if they undergo democratizing reforms. Some are simply too large and too concentrated in their power to be reformed in this manner. They will be replaced gradually by many, many smaller firms and those smaller firms will have to learn how to overcome the disadvantages of their size and scale through cooperative networks—shared functions, markets, expertise. This is doable but difficult. As I suggested in the book, it is actually a good fit with the new technologies and some well-established companies are already heading in this direction.

Other reformers would say that I'm TOO patient—that it's possible to achieve much greater changes much faster by confronting such issues as the corporate charter and changing it to require concrete social obligations alongside the profit motive in the behavior of companies. I am not opposed to that goal. I do doubt that it is politically attainable any time soon—especially before there are more obvious outlines of an alternative social reality, existing examples of successful reform that people and politicians can observe.

FIRST: While you acknowledge the "plain fact" that "reinventing capitalism is impossible without reformation of government," your own vision is marked by your clarity about the (relative) pointlessness of national party politics at this juncture. Would it be right to assume that you've pretty much bought out of disputes on the left between, say, liberal Democrats and Greens?

GREIDER: I deliberately avoided the ideological disputes in my book, partly because these tend to turn the discussion to large abstractions rather than toward concrete examples from reality. My strong feeling is that we are about to enter a new era of reform (something like the early 20th century) but it's a bit premature to try to define its outlines and contending forces.

Someone once said: let a thousand flowers bloom. We will learn soon enough which ones flourish and which ones wilt of their own contradictions. I am for radical change. I am for incremental change. I have an idealized notion of how things might turn out. I also have patience and tolerance for imperfect experiments that may be half-steps toward something larger. If you believe, as I do, that we really are at a new moment in history, you have to acknowledge that we simply do not know enough yet to describe what the future will look like with ideological certainty. This means we're on a longer, open road, but it holds true to what we say we believe about democracy.

FIRST: While you suggest that national party politics is a non-starter given that corporations rule Washington, you note that local and state politics are more promising venues for political reformers. I wonder if you paid much attention to what recently happened in Alabama where the conservative, born-again Republican governor tried to take on entrenched class power? Do you consider that battle to be an anomaly or is it a sign of what could happen (for better or worse) in the future?

GREIDER: I tried to write this book in a way that would speak to ordinary Americans. That approach assumes that underneath class and partisan labels, even regional and religious differences, there is a commonality. I believe some aspect of my subject should be available to most everyone, whatever their circumstances. That is wishful, I know, but that was my goal. It required me not to demonize any citizens as backward. I have found some confirmation for this approach in people's reactions to the book.

Thinking in those terms, the dilemma of born-again Christian Republicans, especially in the conservative south, is particularly acute. I hope my book pokes at their sensibilities too. The recent battle over tax reform in Alabama demonstrates how difficult it is to overcome class-determined cultural reflexes and self-injuries. People of modest means rushed to vote against their own interests, as well as those of their state and society in general. A pessimist would say these dividing lines are immutable. My life's experience—witnessing how the civil rights movement changed this country, changed all of our lives—tells me that cannot be so.

FIRST: Many of your exemplary capitalists are Republicans—David Stockman, Robert Monks. Do their counter-cultural business practices hint at the possibility of a significant realignment of our party politics down the line?

GREIDER: Yes, but don't ask me how. We have already seen currents shift over the last two decades as some who grew up affluent and Republican (myself included) found the liberal Democratic party more comfortable, while lots of working-class Democrats moved in the opposite direction, feeling abandoned or disrespected by the party of their upbringing. I can't read the future currents with any confidence because, frankly, neither party is yet prepared to embrace what I describe. Who owns the idea of worker ownership, for instance? There are a scattered few in both parties who advocate it now, but is this a conservative idea or a liberal idea? It's not easy to answer that question.

FIRST: It's been suggested (most recently by the journalist Christopher Caldwell) that liberty is the foundational principle of those on the right while equality is the key for people on the left. Would you elaborate on the idea that the examples of soulful capitalism you cite implicitly refuse this antimony?

GREIDER: I reject the long-argued view that those are polar opposites. I embrace both and so do most Americans. If we tinker with the words a bit, it seems clear that liberty and equality go hand in hand, especially in our modern circumstances. First, if liberty in fact means the freedom of self-realization, then most Americans cannot possibly become genuinely free without engaging in collective action. Second, in a society of great abundance where scarcity is no longer the main challenge, then equality must be based on something beyond material accumulation. It should be founded on the ability—the right—to live one's life as fully as one's spirit and energy allow. This is an old socialist conception, of course, but I do not envision everyone winding up with the same bank account. Or the same set of aspirations and talents (or the same level of money-seeking intensity). What I can imagine is a society in which every child feels a sense of entitlement (as Robert Coles called it). To go anywhere in this country and feel comfortable, if not at home. To pursue life's possibilities from a platform of material comforts and with the skills to participate fully in work that is self-fulfilling (also productive). To reach beyond one's inherited circumstances—or to remain comfortably within them. We need—someday—a new Bill of Rights. I am not sure I will be around for that happy moment, but it could be an empowering national goal—literally liberating for most citizens.

FIRST: *The Soul of Capitalism*'s sense of possibility may seem out of time at a moment when many commentators see the nation on the verge of a kinder, gentler fascism. Do the doomy analyses of the academic left confirm their distance from the dailiness of American life. (I'm reminded on this score of a well-known man of the left who ended what was meant to be a stirring address at a "Socialist Scholars Conference" with the following call: "Back to the libraries!")

GREIDER: There is of course a lot of brilliant analysis and I read it. I do think, however, that much of the left-liberal progressive side (but not all) is looking backward, not forward. Their most creative decades are way in the past and it's naturally hard for them to let go. One implicit purpose of my new book—never stated plainly—is to help younger thinkers break free of that past and see the present more clearly, more creatively. There is plenty of misery in our present circumstances, but it is not like the 1930s or 1890s and it is not going to be like those times. This sounds arrogant, which is why I did not state it plainly in the book.

FIRST: Your invocation of the need for "radical patience" reminds me of the lessons implicit in Lawrence Goodwyn's great books on the American populist movement and Poland's Solidarnosc. I know you appreciate those works. Tell us why they matter to you....

GREIDER: Goodwyn's books gave me the language of democracy—and the nerve—to write the kind of books I have written. He has also been my great teacher in person—rigorous and yet unbelievably generous. Whenever we talk, I feel refreshed and ready to plunge on. The core of what I learned from him is that the deeper politics of this country lies in the experiences and stored knowledge of ordinary people. It flows along mostly unnoted, like an underground river, and once in a great while it surfaces with force and changes the society.

When he explained this to me years ago, I realized this is what I had been hearing as a reporter for many years in my encounters with ordinary folks who lack power and influence, who have no credentials or even much book learning, but who know certain things—important verities that ought to be part of our democratic politics, actually some day ought to steer it.

This view offends many learned citizens, of course, regardless of their political persuasions. But I can listen to Goodwyn or listen to those ordinary citizens and realize that they are speaking for the core of our history. They should be able to speak for our common future. So I am on their side. I write my books in the hope that explaining power in plain English may help them find their voice.

One of Us

Donna Gaines

There's a mystical property that elevates an artist like Johnny Cash above the idolatry of celebrity cult status and confers upon him, immortality.

What was it about the Depression-era farm boy from Arkansas who toured for 38 years, recorded 1500 songs, still has 45 albums in print, won eleven Grammys, and a Lifetime Achievement award too?

But true greatness transcends the banal units of market shares, record sales or arbitron ratings. For some, it was Johnny Cash's cultural impact. Critics have credited him with "strengthening the bonds between folk and country music so that both sides saw their similarities as well as their differences." Johnny Cash "liberalized Nashville so that it could accept the unconventional and the controversial." He blow-torched country music's rhinestone glitz the day he showed up at the Grand Ole Opry dressed in flat black. Oh, and then there was his voice.

Bono once said. "Not since John the Baptist has there been a voice like that, crying in the wilderness—every man knows he's a sissy compared to Johnny Cash." Cash revealed America's brutal truth in the tale of a drunk found dead of exposure in a Pima reservation cotton field. The broken bag of brown skin and bones was once a man of valor; Ira Hayes, the Native American soldier who helped raise the flag at Iwo Jima. Johnny Cash also taught us the healing power of forgiveness. He spent so much time performing inside prison walls we assumed he'd done hard time—but he didn't. He went inside to heal the hearts of heartless men. Men like the one *who shot a man in Reno just to watch him die*. Cash taught us compassion. He understood redemption was possible at anytime, for anyone, even the most abject cold-hearted killer.

He talked it, but he walked it too, using his gifts to uplift the human race, to repair the world to honor his Creator, Johnny Cash petitioned us to feed the poor, save the child, forgive the criminal, help the drunk, and remember the forgotten. His magnitude was also reflected in his character—in his devotion to his "poor valley girl," his bride and soul mate, June Carter who died just last May. And in his spiritual generosity—in sharing his most personal truths; a soul-killing addiction and born-again salvation. He understood how human frailties defeated us, and how miraculously faith, love, family, work, and music redeemed us. It wasn't until the day he died on that perfectly clear, crisp Friday, September 12, 2003, that I figured out what made Johnny Cash my American hero.

Because you're mine I walk the line. I hadn't had a drink in almost seven years. But on that day, a familiar darkness closed in and I felt myself falling back. All I wanted was to be sitting on a bar stool again. Alone, holed up at some dusty old man's bar, staring into the bottles on the wall, drinking. Playing Johnny Cash songs on the jukebox, gazing at that familiar mirage of salvation found at the bottom of the glass. But God had another plan. My niece called.

"Auntie, let's go for a ride!" Raina Mae sings in a Rockabilly band, she sounds just like her idol, the born-again Wanda Jackson. Careening through the Bonac woods, North to Sag Harbor, Johnny Cash sang to us in that voice once described as "Locusts and Honey," praying for us through the speakers of Raina Mae's red '89 monster GMC Jimmy ... *I hurt myself today to see if I could feel.*

Last year, after I got baptized in the crystal blue waters of Gardiner's Bay, East Hampton, my friend Anthony said, "Now that you're a Christian, Johnny Cash will be your Bob Dylan." I didn't grasp what Anthony meant until almost a year later, on the day Johnny Cash died. Anthony is a fully tattooed power lifter from the Florida Panhandle, an atheist. But he was so broken up by Cash's death, he said, "I think I'll call my Mama today."

Like Bob Dylan, Johnny Cash is someone who's words make us feel a little less alone, with their equally creepy voices—alternately singing, crying, ranting, and begging us to be merciful and righteous. Both Dylan and Cash have loved God in their own way. They have reached out for light and brought back what they found in the cold wilderness. June helped Johnny through an early recovery and then she walked with him, arm in arm, right up to Jesus Christ. Dylan's startling born-again embrace of the Jewish Rabbi from Nazareth and his subsequent "Baal T'shuva" return to Judaism confused his fans—from Yeshiva boys to lefty agnostics, atheists, to secular humanists. Both men have transported us to higher ground.

As Anthony explained, where Dylan has traditionally ministered to well-educated, alienated intellectual, urban audiences, Cash served Los Olvidados [the forgotten ones] of rural America—the truckers, farm workers, nickel & dimed country moms, hapless convicts, honky-tonk habitués. Both men hurled us into the dark caverns of the soul, exploring both existential terror and social misery. They've exposed our collective lies and soothed our psychic wounds. Each has understood that faith is a difficult, non-rational, haphazard, solitary process.

And this I command thee, to love one another.... Where Dylan's road to salvation lies in the human connection, in the possibility of engagement, Cash's resides in a living, loving God, in the Lord Jesus Christ. But, my dear brothers and sisters, we are obligated either way. Whether we think of the body of Christ as a socially constructed reflection of the body social, or the body social as the body of Christ incarnate, we all do have to serve somebody.

Play Fuckin Loud

Charles O'Brien

Friends
inquisitive friends
are asking me what's come over me
"(I wanna) Testify"—The Parliaments

For all that a first guess would have seen Martin Scorcese, director of *The Last Waltz*, "presenter" of the PBS *Blues* series, compiler of many rock soundtracks as the obvious choice to do *The American Masters* Bob Dylan, the finished thing is, like *Goodfellas* or *Casino* or *The Last Temptation of Christ*, the work of Martin Scorcese, connoisseur of betrayal. At the time *No Direction Home* was broadcast, someone in *Slate* grumbled that writers of a certain age talked about Dylan as if he were strictly a '60s artist and ignored his later career, about 40 years worth. There's an easy answer, but it's a good point. *Bringing It All Back Home*, *Highway 61*, and *Blonde on Blonde* are landmarks, sure, but people that have followed Dylan over the years could as easily put together three mixed CDs of post-accident Dylan that they'd listen to a lot more. By the mid-'60s, Dylan had already recorded with a band and accompanied himself on piano, and rock—particularly the Beatles—was being accorded a previously unknown respect. Electric Dylan, that thin wild mercury sound, had no business shocking anybody. It shocked somebody; and that is the subject of *No Direction Home*.

The film opens with Dylan and the Hawks on stage, in color, playing—just a taste—of one of his older songs; and cuts to black and white, and the same song, solo and acoustic. Scorcese certainly knows how to let a song play out and provide the visual accompaniment. Here, he provides snippets. You know this one? Good. How much does he even care about folkie Dylan? He grew up in the same streets in the same years as the folk scene he shows here. He must have passed by many of these people all the time—passed them right by. Picture Michael, the loan shark in *Mean Streets*, spending an evening listening to Odetta. But even the electric material is doled out stingily. Scorcese likes Visconti better than he likes Dylan, and the music wasn't allowed to distract from the drama. But after all, you can get the music elsewhere (preferably not on the *No Direction Home* CDs), and the music in the film is still worth hearing. Michael Bloomfield is here, in his best days. Sam Lay and Jerome Arnold, formerly Howling Wolf's rhythm section, are heard—though not credited—on "Maggie's Farm," compounding the offense at Newport.

Dylan's own offense was not really a musical one. And it was not—except in a more diffuse sense—a political one. The new Dylan did not want to move into a fallout shelter, and he didn't think that William Zanzinger had got a raw deal. That he wouldn't say so was disturbing. 1964's *Another Side of Bob Dylan*, with its more private concerns—as if—was met with its share of grumbling, but nothing like the spite-fest to come—oh, it was reciprocated. The likelihood that "political" Dylan, that certain trumpet, was gone for good, one could resign oneself to it. Some commentary at the time even proposed that loculated protest movements could become a mass movement only by becoming mostly a youth movement, and that essential to that transformation might be the carrying over of the values of the "folk revival" into the newfangled folk-rock: the Big Beat needed recruiting. The cultural politics of the mid- and late '60s made such claims plausible. But then Dylan went around the world at the height of Vietnam playing rock & roll in front of a giant American flag. He said nothing particular, and probably meant nothing particular, about the American (and international) political scene. But as provocation, well, he couldn't hire Lyndon Johnson for his band.

Bob Dylan came to New York from Minnesota. There he settled into a little bohemia, the folk scene; he picked up a name and began a career; and on his way out the door, he blew the place up. What makes it even better is that he was right. Liam Clancy is shown, got up in a sort of ethnic cap, holding forth in a bar. Of the '50s and early '60s, he says, "Freedom only existed here in the Village." And while the Clancy Brothers may have been around the world any number of times, to look at Liam Clancy here, you'd swear he hasn't stirred from this room in fifty years. And the riches in that room—only a little larger, that was the folk scene—were quite finite, and for a Bob Dylan it would not take long to run through them. There is a sense running through this film, as there was in David Hadju's book on Dylan and Richard Farina, of Dylan as an opportunist, a hustler.[1] The charge is hard to take seriously. Part of the point of playing "folk music" was that the song came from someone else. Dave Van Ronk concedes that "House of the Rising Sun" wasn't really his. But no: it really wasn't his. The question is what you do with the song—and anyone can play. In *Mean Streets*, Robert De Niro tells Harvey Keitel, "You got what you wanted." Yeah, even if he did, what does that change?

The film shows a range of Dylan's musical used-to-be's. Here is John Jacob Niles, offered as the source for "It Ain't Me Babe." It looks like an outtake from *Nightmare Alley*. To get away from such an encounter with your reason, let alone a song, is an achievement. We hear from Izzy Young: earnest, generous and altogether unpunctual. Peter Yarrow (*Songs of Conscience and Concern*), Joan Baez, and Dave Van Ronk all talk, all somewhat wronged. All, though the film doesn't say so, "went electric" after Dylan gave them the idea.[2]

Has any other genre had its falsity so laid bare by a single defector? Pete Seeger is a vivid presence here. He poses with a banjo (I am a folk musician), and he wears a festive red shirt (Here all is jollity). And he is here to say that nothing is wrong, nothing was wrong. Did he try to cut the sound cables at Newport? No, but he was concerned about the sound. One thing Seeger says here is worth preserving. Who were the Communists, once so much spoken of? They were revolutionaries, the only revolutionaries. They were, in a phrase often used, dead men on parole. And how did all that work out? You may pass your idle hours reading the martyrologies of a Paul Buhle or a Victor Navasky, or get it straight from Seeger.

> Not 2 years later, instead of singing at the Waldorf Astoria or Ciro's in Hollywood, we were singing in Daffy's Bar & Grill on the outskirts of Cleveland and we decided to take a sabbatical.

When Seeger gets to "Waldorf-Astoria," he pronounces the first A with a broad a, like the first a in "sassafras," not the schwa a New Yorker would use, nor even the narrow a, as in the name "Astor." From Seeger's mouth, it is As-toria. Peter Seeger, untutored rustic, and tread carefully when a four-syllable word looms. Now, the 4th street Dylan was guilty of lots of fake yokelisms, and worse than Seeger's. But he was young; and subject to bad influences (Seeger's not least); and they were a product of awkwardness; and a sense attended them of shame. Dylan is a famous mumbler. Actually, he says cryptic things, and is soft-spoken, and sometimes does mumble. Pete Seeger doesn't mumble.

In the early '60s, 20-year-olds liked to sing:

> All my trials
> Soon be over

Bob Dylan had read somewhere that all his troubles in the world came from not being able to sit still in a room, and wouldn't they be worth meeting!

In Nick Tosches' appreciation of the blackface performer Emmett Miller, *Where Dead Voices Gather*, Bob Dylan's name is brought up a few times, and each time, he is praised in the highest terms. This is puzzling. Dylan is an icon of the '60s. And Tosches' books include biographies of Dean Martin, the anti-Beatle, and Sonny Liston, the anti-Ali, and *Unsung Heroes of Rock and Roll*, and *Country: the Biggest Music in America*, both assaults on that sunny image of that sunny child of the sunny '60s, rock.[3]

No Direction Home helps solve the puzzle. As much as any individual, Bob Dylan invented The Sixties; as much as any individual—and at the same time denounced The Sixties.

Greil Marcus used the phrase "the old weird America" (for one thing) to describe the Harry Smith anthology. But the phrase is very much in the spirit of the various things Dylan himself has said about "folk music." Think again of Liam Clancy in that barroom. The old, weird America was not there. But you could hear about it there, maybe even get a glimpse of it there. Past a certain point, there was no point hanging around. Freedom only in the Village? Freedom was always available: in the old weird America, among Tosches' desperados, in pulp and noir. Claiming it, though, might cost your life. Village freedom was, by comparison, a straitened thing, virtually an oxymoron.

Dylan's world, ca. '65-'66, wasn't the old, weird America, either. It couldn't be. If not "old," it was—especially relative to most other pop of the day—rooted. And if not "weird" in that older sense, it was, at least, free to roam. In the film, we hear reactions from English ex-fans after Dylan and the Hawks have played: he "went really commercial;" he's "prostituting himself;" he has an "incredibly corny group." It is tempting to call such claims demonstrably false. But these are, after all, questions of taste; and someone who has let it be known that he can't realize his aesthetic vision without the drummer from "Secret Agent Man" must have known what was coming.

There is a shot early in the film of some record charts. Peter, Paul and Mary's cover of "Blowing in the Wind" is highlighted. That is at #2. Number 1 is "Fingertips, Pt. II"; Elvis Presley's "(You're the) Devil in Disguise" is #3, and "Wipe Out" is #4. If any song fails to transcend its period, it is Dylan's. The film shows the Byrds, briefly, playing "Mr. Tambourine Man" before a roomful of screaming teenage girls. Dylan is heard disclaiming any knowledge of "folk-rock." But put the Byrds' version of "Chimes of Freedom"—Beatles guitars, Fender amps, bridge appropriated from Donovan, Jim M'Guinn's awe-struck vocal against

Dylan's original with its world-weary vocal and bare-bones accompaniment. Dylan had just put himself into a more challenging place. A daughter was born to one of the musicians at the 1965 Newport Folk Festival. Some of the old acoustic regulars, Seeger & Co., take the stage to say, "We're dedicating this festival to this new child … and this time she's going to grow up in." This, remember, was a child born into the second half of the '60s. If she needed a charm against the time, it would not come from men with banjos, but, with luck, from the Roman candle sounds Dylan had embraced.

The first night of *No Direction Home* ends with the 1963 Newport Folk Festival. We see Dylan and Joan Baez on stage doing harmony. We see the two at a workshop, Dylan offering pleasantries as he tries to tune his guitar. The pleasantries are received as jokes. The guitar does not get tuned. The second night, and the movie as a whole, ends with footage from 1966 and some inter-titles. The inter-titles tell us that he had a motorcycle accident, was laid up, returned to touring. They don't tell us—we know already that he had since released album after album, tried out many different sounds, different bands, even different voices, has collaborated with the most improbable people has traveled the world almost without a pause, has taken his older songs places they could never have imagined. The film we see is this: footage, without sound, of people on an English street, in daylight, lined up to get in to see Dylan. Then we see Dylan backstage, strapping on his telecaster, talking half to himself, half to the camera. As he heads for the door, he says that he's "back from the grave." Well, not quite, but never far off. Then the screen goes black, and we see the subtitle, "Judas." We see him, lights up, onstage with the Hawks, and we know the rest of that exchange from *Live 66*. What's not on that CD is the visuals. Dylan is bouncing from the mike to the band and back, totally at the mercy of this music that hasn't started. He's not happy exactly, happy is not the point, but giddy to be kicking free, someplace else from the people right in front of him who wanted more of what they had already had.

It isn't here, it isn't there, it isn't anywhere you went looking for it.

Notes

1.   Hajdu sets Dylan and Farina off against each other, and he leans toward Farina. John Leonard, commenting on Hajdu, and offered that choice, goes with (this is John Leonard, after all)—Joan Baez. There but for fortune….

2.   The Bruce Langhorne interview segments are high points of the film, although we're given no idea of his significance. In the mid-'60s, to say that someone had "gone electric" usually meant that Bruce Langhorne had a new record out, and usually meant that he was the most memorable thing on it.

3.   Nick Lowe's "(What's So Funny 'Bout) Peace, Love, and Understanding" was
       the lost song on Elvis Costello's *Armed Forces*, following such numbers as "Two
       Little Hitlers." If the song had any meaning, it came from the context of a time
       and musical culture where invocations of "peace" and "love" and "understanding"
       were suspect—a little "funny," a little off. The song has been revived in the past
       few years, that context scrubbed clean. It's, as they say, as if punk never happened.
       It's become "Kumbaya." There's one way left to enjoy it: picture Nick Tosches'
       face as the song comes on.

Safe American Home

Benj DeMott

Drive-By Truckers' double CD *Southern Rock Opera* is the most daring and developed expression of rock and roll attitude since the Clash's
Sandinista.

The subject of the Truckers' *Opera* is the "duality"—their word—of
life in the land where blues began. Like (Rhythm &) Blues people, white
folks in the South feel they're different from mainline Americans. Their
country and Southern Rock musics have celebrated that difference and
registered the Great Shame of the South as well. All those cheating
songs hint that white Southerners knew they were guilty a generation
before the Civil Rights Movement. Though they weren't trying to hear
that unless they'd had a drink and even then their favorite singers had to
slip around the truth.

Which was never the whole truth. White southerners were mocked
as arch-bigots by the rest of country at a time when their racial attitudes
weren't much worse than those of most other white Americans. And the
society's moral condemnation of them was often polluted by culture
vultures' less-than-righteous contempt for "backward" populations below the Mason Dixon line. In the mid-'60s, Okie country rocker Buck
Owens sang right back at all the icy people looking down at him from
El Norte.

> You don't know me But you don't like me
> Say you care less how I feel
> How many you that sit and judge me
> Ever walked the streets of Bakersfield
> I walked a thousand miles upon it
> I've worn blisters on my heels
> Trying to find me something better
> Out on the streets of Bakersfield

I once heard Dwight Yoakam sing a cover version of "The Streets of
Bakersfield" live a couple years ago. I was sitting behind a white country

boy with a crew cut who'd been up dancing—shaking a leg like a little Elvis—through most of the show. When Dwight sang "Streets," the kid turned around and wailed the chorus back at all the sophisticated New Yorkers sitting in the balcony. "You don't know me, but you don't like me!"

A scene in the documentary *Elvis 56* helped me understand the root of southern boys' defensiveness. Elvis is being interviewed by a '50s tv personality named Hy Gardner who once sold his audience on an urbane mix of venality and hauteur. (Think Cindy Adams crossed with Philippe de Montebello). As the writer George Trow has explained, Gardner was a figure in '50s Café Society—a representative of the reigning paradigm of New York Rules. Gardner's tone in the interview makes it clear that he thinks Elvis is—and Trow rightly apologizes for using the phrase—"white trash." The subject of Elvis's movie career comes up in the course of the interview. And Elvis is supremely modest even though he had to know what kind of mimetic talent he possessed. He indicates he's off to Hollywood to LEARN. And he wasn't lying. When Elvis arrived on the set for his first movie, he had memorized not only his own part, but the whole script. He quickly found out, though, that no one, as Trow puts it, "was going to address his needs as a learner."

I don't know that Elvis ever talked back to the Hy Gardners of this world. While Buck Owens surely did, he ended up selling himself out on *Hee-Haw*—the '70s tv show that ridiculed country people.

Drive-By Truckers won't end up playing themselves. "Proud of the glory, stare down the shame"—they're not about to roll over for anyone. But they've also learned that pride is never enough. And they're not about to end up walking tall down dead end streets. Their *Southern Rock Opera* is a testimony to their continuing education. These lifetime learners have realized the democratic promise—everyday people teaching themselves—that once made millions believe rock and roll was the only culture that mattered. The Truckers worked on their *Opera* for six years—"brainstorming, writing, learning, playing and recording." (They even recruited a folklorist and expert on recent Southern history into their creative community—a fellow musician who, as they put it in their liner notes—"was actually in the Civil Rights Struggle as a reporter for the *Birmingham Post Herald*.")

Drive-By Truckers want their listeners to know white Southerners weren't/aren't the only racists in the country, but they're also aware that no one has hurt the South harder than men like Alabama's governor George Wallace who pandered to the region's segregationists in the '60s and '70s. (The Truckers treat Wallace's life story in the course of their *Opera* and their final judgment of the man who stood in the schoolhouse door to prevent black kids from going to integrated schools is worthy of Richard Pryor: "When he met St. Peter at the Pearly Gate/I'd like to think there was a black man standing in the way.")

I wouldn't blame you if the notion of a Rock Opera in 2002 seems dead-dog-dead to you. It wasn't exactly a Start-Me-Up to me when I first heard about it (from a black rock critic named Kandia Crazy-Horse who likes a lot of Southern Rock bands that I think are for the birds). But the wonder of this record is precisely that it comes rolling in from nowhere (just as Democratic art should). Drive-By Truckers churn up a mean old highway of the mind that runs from Bakersfield to "Zip City" where

> Your Daddy is a deacon down at the Salem
> Church of Christ
> And he makes good money as long as the Reynolds
> Wrap keeps everything in this town wrapped up tight
> Your mama's as good a wife and Mama as she
> can be
> And your Sister's putting that sweet stuff on
> everybody in town but me
> Your Brother was the first-born, got ten fingers
> and ten toes
> And it's damn good thing cause he needs all
> twenty to keep the closet door closed

Drive-By Truckers are ex-punk, hard-rock pussy-boys who knock down doors, throw open the windows and let the funk out. While they're not above lost cause myth-mongering and rockism, their chords cut right through their own hot air. There's always a musical bridge out of their bombast. Their own entrance on *Opera* defines a certain kind of quintessentially American daring. Talk about young lions. These guitar cats let their Gibsons ROAR. And there's nothing hoary about that sound. It takes the Truckers about 10 seconds to rock out the difference between sleepy classic rock verities and their own everything-old-is-new-Southern Thing.

Opera is dedicated to the rock group Lynyrd Skynyrd (who lost their leader—Ronnie Van Zant—and other key members of the band in a plane crash in the late '70s). But it isn't overly solemn. It begins with a Southern Gothic horrorcore joke about one of Skynyrd's most famous songs. Patterson Hood—the Truckers' lead vocalist and high idea man—raps about how his classmates invented a soundtrack for a car crash that killed two students the night before their high school graduation. "Everyone," he recalls, said that you could hear Skynyrd's "Free Bird" playing on the crashed car's stereo, orchestrating the screams and the sirens. And then Hood draws out the punchline…. "You know, it's a very loooooong song."

Hood allows in his liner notes that he didn't much like Skynyrd when he was growing up in north Alabama. It wasn't until he left the South for a few years that he began to dig the band. His Truckers keep coming back to—and blasting off from—the changes in Skynyrd's "Sweet Home Alabama." As they turn that band's story into their own *Opera* they go deep into Southern history and their own pop lives.

Hood allows he never saw Skynyrd play but in a track called "Let There Be Rock" he name-checks other Southern bands and arena rock acts that he did hear as a teenager in the '70s. The song's tale of drugging and drinking and driving and puking seems to have no particular place to go. Until Hood crashes into a memory of a rock group that actually rocked: "I sure saw AC/DC with Bon Scott singing LET THERE BE ROCK." A local history of wasted youth culture suddenly maps a majestic community. It's a lifting, left turn that the Drive-By Truckers are always looking to make. One that puts them on the road with that "race of singers" who have aimed (in Walt Whitman's words): "to endow the democratic averages of America with the ranges of heroism with which the Greeks and feudal poets endowed their god-like or Lordly-born characters."[1]

Whitman's prescription, of course, might be bad medicine for blowhard rockers. But the Truckers—"a little more rock and less cocaine"—have roots that keep them grounded.

They pump up America's democratic averages by turning up the volume to Tornado and heroicizing the half-remembered Lynyrd Skynyrd. "Life in the Factory" tells how this "bunch of fatherless boys" practiced "seven days a week" in a shed with no windows back in the Florida swamps, 100-degree heat radiating off the tin. That's why, Hood sings, they never broke a sweat when they went on to play summer festivals as part of a touring schedule that included 300 dates in a year. Skynyrd were always ready to play ferociously because they knew "Rock's the only thing to save them" from steel mills or Ford plants. The Truckers' clarity on this score hooks them up with Bruce Springsteen who once recorded his own song called "Factory" on *Darkness on the Edge of Town*—the album where he came into his own working class consciousness. But the Clash and "Sway" sound of the Truckers' "Factory" is a truer evocation of suppressed fury all down the line.

Southern Rock Opera is, in a way, the follow-up to *Darkness* that Springsteen himself never really managed to make. In part, because he couldn't quite cross over the color line. The Truckers down home truth telling about the burden of Southern History beats Springsteen's approach in a song like "My Hometown," where he sings about the racial problems that jumped off when he was growing up in Jersey. "There was a lot of fights between the black and the white/there was nothing you could do." Which won't quite do.

Drive-By Truckers don't throw up their hands—or pull their punches. They begin their *Opera* in earnest by invoking the Church bombing in Birmingham and immediately link their heroes' tale with one of the defining moments in American cultural history—that sequence of events in the mid-'60s that led first Wilson Picket and then Aretha Franklin to head down to Muscle Shoals, Alabama where they made the soul music that soundtracked the progress of the Civil Rights Movement. The Truckers remind their audience that white Southern musicians were playing behind Wicked Pickett and Aretha when those singers were out front embodying Freedom. Patterson Hood hears Skynyrd's "Sweet Home Alabama" as a tribute to Muscle Shoals where the band went to record a few years after Pickett and Aretha. Skynyrd met a lot of good people there, he sings, "not racist pieces of shit." His readiness to spit out that hard line hints why Drive-By Truckers are a little farther up the road than Bruce Springsteen who seems softer on racism even when he's singing a protest song about Diallo.

Drive-By Truckers impulse to take racism personally not only makes them model southerners. It makes them exemplary American Artists.

Their *Opera*'s last track should speak to all Americans now. "Angels and Fuselage" puts you inside a plane that's about to crash. Written before 9/11, it's taken on a new resonance in the aftermath. As the Truckers guitars hum and drone, Hood sings out his mortal fear of being "strapped to this projectile." Then the chords die down—"the engines have stopped now." Hood dreams of a last call for alcohol and faces up to the no-future:

> I'm scared shitless of what's coming next
> I'm scared shitless, these angels I see
> In the trees waiting for me....

There are no voices in the last couple minutes of "Angels and Fuselage." Just white noise with shards of melody out of "Layla" and Hendrix. And then, in the midst of the static and guitar dischords, strange little sprinkles of piano. The first time I heard them I thought of a child trying tentatively to get a tune out of a keyboard. Now the spray of notes reminds me of a rainbow—the sounds evoke the out of time/tune piano that finishes off the Rolling Stone's trippy '60s classic "She's Like a Rainbow." "Angels and Fuselage" is a about a bad trip. But the grace notes in that shattered soundscape bring it all back home to me—beauty's always being born somewhere in America's grand mess.

Note

1.   See Stephen Garbedian's review of Bryan K. Garman's *A Race of Singers: Whitman's Working Class Hero from Guthrie to Springsteen* (XCP: Cross Cultural Poetics. #9).

Nothing New Under the Sun

Greil Marcus

Marcus gave the following talk at Peninsula Temple Beth El on February 28, 2002.

I came here tonight to talk about the response of American intellectuals to the events of September 11—and I use the neutral, meaningless term "events" to start off right where any intellectual response begins, with an attempt to name what took place, or to avoid naming it.

We are all familiar with the words that quickly turned into buzzwords, or evasions. Some of these I'll take up later: "tragedy," "crime against humanity," "major atrocities." Some are now just shorthand: "9-11," "September 11." "Terrorist attacks" was somehow too much of a mouthful. Some names that seem to me the most weighty—enormous words that force the speaker or the listener to confront what they mean, where they came from, what ground they share—have been used by a few and have then disappeared, never entering the common conversation at all: "massacres," "mass murders." Intellectuals are supposed to care about words, to respect them, to understand their power to deprive public talk of meaning, or their power to block clichés. But intellectuals are also afraid of words—afraid not only of what they can do, but of how they can make one who uses them appear. Who wants to look like a fool, unserious, as if one doesn't know what to say? *The New York Times* on September 12 caught me right in the throat with its headline, a headline, I realized the instant I saw it, that I had been certain I would never see: **U.S. Attacked**.

The country itself. The idea of the country. Its territory. Its citizenry. Its past and its future. "U.S. Attacked." But after that, use of language as a blunt object dissolved into logos, each one, you could imagine, immediately trademarked by whatever news organization was using it: "America Under Attack" on CNN; "America Strikes Back" on Fox News and MSNBC; "A Day of Terror" and "A Nation Challenged" in *The* New *York Times*. That sense of shock, of the sudden recognition of a truth, that I'd gotten from the first *Times* headline had somehow been returned to the conventional, to the predictable, to the manageable, until I saw the headline on the satirical weekly *The Onion*. It announced the truth, but in words intellectuals wouldn't use as their last words: "Holy Fucking Shit." Against this, my favorite certified intellectual attempt at naming, far beyond composer Karl Stockhausen's "the greatest work of art ever ... the greatest work of art for the whole cosmos:" novelist Rick Moody, best known for *The Ice Storm*, beginning a mid-September essay by throwing his hands in the air—"The Attack—what else can I call it?"—and then proceeding to use his hands to smooth the paper before him: "'The Attack, '" Moody said, "—is a web of narratives."

Words used in that manner—that kind of naming, that kind of instinctive intellectual work—are an insult to whoever is unlucky enough to hear them. They laugh at your confusion. They mock your fear. They look down at you. They parade their confidence, their certainty that there is nothing that can't be folded into the language of the day before, their refusal to entertain the possibility that something might have happened that never happened before.

The acknowledgment that something can take place in the world that never happened before might be the starting point of any real intellectual activity. Acts can be taken, events can occur, that demand a whole new way of being in the world, of looking at the world, of speaking about the world. It may be the most common instinct, in the face of the new, to flee to the old: to analogies, to precursors, to whatever old name can be used to cover up the need for a new one, anything to avoid having to say "I've never seen anything like this before"—"Holy Fucking Shit," in other words—which means having to say, "I don't know what to say." So one says what one knows how to say. One says that this it not so new as it appears, not that surprising, not that shocking—and, doing that, one takes one's place in Bob Dylan's greatest protest song, "The Lonesome Death of Hattie Carroll," from 1963, with its saddened, angry chorus naming "those who philosophize disgrace, and criticize all fears." Those who claim to know what to say in the face of something new precisely criticize the fears of those who sense in their bones that something new has taken place—and who realize that they no longer know precisely what their place in the world might be. "'The Attack'—what else can I call it?—is a web of narratives."

My idea of an intellectual is Hannah Arendt, a German Jew who found her voice in the United States after the Second World War. As a scholar and a professor she was also always a student—a student of what she called the human condition. Her books—*The Origins of Totalitarianism, On Violence, On Revolution, Men in Dark Times*—were often attacked as ahistorical, or even anti-historical. That was because, to many, the stories she told—and she was most of all a storyteller, like a guide in the catacombs of history—were set less within a solid frame of reference, where every seemingly new event has its analogy, than they were anchored—anchored by the Athenians, the philosophers and the dramatists, more than anyone else. And Arendt was often condemned as antihistorical because she knew that sometimes anchors come loose, and that the ships they were meant to hold to solid ground go adrift. "Thinking without a ground" is how one student of hers characterized her work. She is best known for her 1961 book *Eichmann in Jerusalem*, where she wrote these lines which, to me, anyway, sum up her idea of what the human condition is made of.

> It is in the very nature of things human that every act that has once made its appearance and has been recorded in the history of mankind stays with mankind as a potentiality long after its actuality has become a thing of the past.... Once a specific crime has appeared for the first time, its reappearance is more likely than its initial emergence could ever have been.

This may seem like a truism, but in fact it goes directly against the grain of what, in most times and places, intellectual discourse takes itself to be—against what it most often takes its purpose to be. When confronted with what might seem like something new, most intellectual discourse says that what appears new is not: that to the contrary it fits into familiar categories, can be described, explained, and analyzed with familiar concepts, can be fixed with familiar words. Hannah Arendt was on the other side of the mirror. *Between Past and Future* was the title of one of her books, and the title spoke for her understanding of how the world works, what the human condition is. There can be a breach between past and future, and if there is such a breach, the future must be something new. It may be terrible, formless, incomprehensible, even mute, but it will be new—in truth, every time there is such a breach between past and future, a new event has taken place, for no such breach can be the same. "Originality," Arendt wrote in 1953, "is horrible, not because some new 'idea' came into the world, but because its very actions constitute a break with all our traditions; they have clearly exploded our categories of political thought and our standards of moral judgment." The past floats away like an unmoored, unanchored ship. We remember it; like a Spanish galleon loaded with Peruvian gold, as it drops over the horizon it carries off our treasure, our memory. As the ship disappears, we can imagine ourselves on it. We can even name it: the Flying Dutchman.

Feeling herself living in the space between past and future—feeling herself, if not the philosopher of that space, its storyteller—Arendt actively sought what had never been before. Listen to her language: "Every act that has once made its appearance and been recorded in the history of mankind"—it is a philosophical assertion that an act that has not been made before can be made. What the Nazis did, she argued at the end of *Eichmann in Jerusalem*—and, really, everywhere in her work—was something new: they altered the limits on human action. Now, crimes that heretofore were literally unthinkable—for which the conceptual, philosophical, legitimating apparatus did not exist—were, by the very fact they now were facts, easy to think. More than easy: it was impossible not to think such crimes. It was impossible not to imagine what the Nazis had done to the Jews in Europe in the 1940s being done to anyone else, anywhere else, at any time.

Arendt looked for the new, for what was making its appearance in the history of mankind. She found it in totalitarianism; she found it in the American revolution. And she wrote with such grace, seductiveness, and force because in such an intellectual quest, so much was at stake: the chance, which might not come again, to identify, in that gap between past and future, what the particular opportunities and dangers were—the opportunities that had never come before, the dangers that had never come before. As she wrote in *The Origins of Totalitarianism*:

> Comprehension does not mean denying the outrageous, deducing the unprecedented from precedents, or explaining phenomena by such analogies and generalities that the impact of reality and the shock of experience are no longer felt. It means, rather, examining and bearing consciously the burden which our century has placed on us—neither denying its existence or submitting meekly to its weight. Comprehension, in short, means the unpremeditated, attentive facing up to, and resisting of, reality—whatever it may be.

Almost immediately after the fact, I found out that the mass murders perpetrated in the United States by Arab terrorists—that's one of the things one can say instead of "the Attack"—might lead to very particular breaks between past and future: they could lead to breaks between friends. It came at a Yom Kippur dinner when I found myself shouting at an eighteen-year-old who had said that what had happened was more than anything "a cry for help." It came when a friend said on the phone that he was trying to come to terms with "who was really culpable here," by which he meant the degree to which the United States was culpable—"How about the people who hijacked the planes?" I almost yelled at him. It came when a British friend, a professor, said that "Anti-Americanism was a necessity" in any attempt to come to grips with "the Attack" and I instantly found myself on the far side of a great divide, in another country from the one we had both inhabited a second before, one in which I imagined that I was at home, and imagined that my friend was not, and didn't want to be.

Friends aside, the recognition of such a breach can be liberating. The first premise of intellectual work, of thinking without a ground, is to trust your first response—and my first response to reading the leftist intellectual Noam Chomsky's first statement on the massacres was disgust. "The terrorist attacks were major atrocities," he said on September 13, as if this was something that was in doubt—or a line that had to be laid down before what was really important could be said. "In scale," Chomsky went on, "they may not reach the level of many others—for example, Clinton's 1998 bombing of the Sudan with no credible pretext, destroying half its pharmaceutical supplies and killing unknown numbers of people."

What caused the bile to rise in my throat was not the formal accuracy or legitimacy of the particular things Chomsky was saying—Chomsky, an eloquent speaker in the movement against the war in Vietnam, a defender of Holocaust denier Robert Faurisson in the 1980s, today a relentless critic of American power everywhere at all times. It was the assumption of simplicity, of obviousness. It was the absolute denial of surprise.

Chomsky's words were those of someone who had seen all the way around the major atrocities even before they happened. There was no possibility that they contained, that they signified, anything new. Rather, they were a confirmation that, as President Dwight D. Eisenhower once put it, "Things are more like they are now than they ever were before."

That Chomsky's statement was an act of bad faith—less as a citizen of the United States, who has the right to say what he likes, than as an intellectual, who has an obligation to words and ideas—is borne out in the interviews he gave after September 13, and which he collected in a book he titled *9-11*. The fact that, to impress upon people that he was appalled by the acts of terrorists, he did not bother to put his own thoughts in his own words, but again and again quoted the reporter Robert Fisk to that effect, meant, "Get this out of the way so we can talk about what matters." "I mentioned," Chomsky said on September 21, "that the toll of the 'horrendous crime' committed with 'wickedness and awesome cruelty' may be comparable to the consequences of Clinton's bombing of the Al-Shifa plant in August 1998"—and so on. In other words, Chomsky's earlier "major atrocities" was not serious. What he really meant was this: In the context of the world order as established by American power, what happened on September 11 was an ordinary and not even particularly egregious action by people resisting that power by those means left to them. It was of a piece with Robert Fisk's own insistence, in his position as a veteran Middle East reporter who had himself interviewed Osama bin Laden several times, that the thousands of deaths were "a crime against humanity." This sounds impressive—serious—until you find out what it means: "policemen, arrests, justice, a whole international court at the Hague if necessary." In other words, *The New York Times* headline "U.S. Attacked" was hysterical. Rather, "Humanity" was offended. The United States has no right to respond. There was no war—except, as the book in which Fisk's statement is collected titles it, *September 11 and the U.S. War*—a book which, with its cover, in four photos, demands that one acknowledge an idiot symmetry: smoke rising from the World Trade Center, smoke rising from a target in Afghanistan; Ground Zero in New York, a bomb site in Afghanistan.

I am not going to spend any time tonight taking apart Chomsky's comparison of the New York, Washington, and Pennsylvania mass murders and Bill Clinton's attempt to retaliate against Osama bin Laden's bombings of American embassies in Kenya and Tanzania. Others have done it. What I want to talk about is the way in which American intellectuals have seized on the unprecedented acts of last year as an opportunity not to think—and I should say now that when I say "American intellectuals," I mean left-wing intellectuals. That is because I think leftist intellectuals come out of, and must necessarily draw on, a tradition of open inquiry in which neither questions nor answers are fixed in advance. It doesn't matter if the ancestors one chooses were, in some real sense, conservatives. In 1831, when he published *Democracy in America*, Alexis de Tocqueville was a conservative intellectual. So was Hannah Arendt. Their sense of gravity drew them to the past, even if they knew it could never be recovered. As intellectuals they were Robinson Crusoes, scavenging whatever could be rescued from the shipwrecks of their place and time as they tried to navigate in an altogether unfamiliar world. But like Karl Marx, Sigmund Freud, Albert Camus, or Edmund Wilson—all, in their way, deeply conservative thinkers—they understood that they were, in some significant sense, ignorant, deaf, blind, and mute. To make sense of a new world, or the gap between a past and a future, they would have to ask questions that had never been asked, and consider answers that to their ancestors would have made no sense at all. It may be that my inability to take right-wing intellectuals seriously as intellectuals is nothing more than my own lack of imagination—but as far as I can see, right-wing intellectuals in America today are propagandists before they are anything else. They speak and write not to ask, but to answer. They are literally bought and paid for—in so many cases, their titles awarded, their salaries paid, and their publications subsidized by the Hoover Institute, the American Enterprise Institute, the Heritage Foundation, the Olin Foundation, and the racist, eugenicist Bradley Foundation.

In the wake of the mass murders, leftist American intellectuals spoke again and again of the need to resist the attempts of the Bush administration and other right-wing powers in American life to use the excuse of war to do things they might otherwise not be able to do: to "hijack" the war, as people are beginning to put it, in favor of the curtailment of civil liberties, new tax cuts for corporations and rich Americans as part of an "Economic Security Act," drilling in the Alaskan Wildlife Refuge as part of an "Energy Security Act," and the like. But there is no chance to even begin to talk about what is right about a war and what is wrong about it, what is right about the United States and what is wrong about it, when leftist intellectuals no less than right-wing propagandists speak the same language—the language of flattery. If most right-wing intellectuals write to flatter those who pay them, so many left-wing intellectuals, who may be paid nothing to write, write to flatter themselves.

An international Gallup poll conducted in late February—"face-to-face interviews with 9,924 residents of Pakistan, Iran, Indonesia, Turkey, Lebanon, Morocco, Kuwait, Jordan, and Saudi Arabia"—determined that "sixty-one percent did not believe Arab groups carried out the September 11 terrorist attacks." The first I heard of such a notion came not from the Middle East, but from Berkeley, on September 12 or 13, when an anonymous e-mailer sent a left-wing thread my way: "Who has the most to gain?" one person asked, and immediately answered: "Mossad." Though within a week it would be plain that it was George W. Bush who had the most to gain from the mass murders—and who has, as a skillful politician, gained the most—no one suggests that he carried out the massacres. But the confluence between Arab public opinion and leftist intellectual analysis is quite stunning. Arabs are often quoted to the effect that Arab terrorist groups are incapable of the acts of which they are accused—technically incapable, imaginatively incapable, of insufficient intelligence, it's never spelled out. American intellectuals seem to proceed from the assumption that Arabs are incapable of defining their own destinies or making sense of their own actions.

To read through the writings and interviews of Chomsky and so many like him is to be told that everyone and anything the United States was or might be attacked by is in fact the direct creation of the United States. The Taliban. Osama bin Laden. Al Qaeda. The Pakistani secret service. Saddam Hussein. Leftist intellectuals from Chomsky to the scholar Michael Parenti to the *Nation* columnist Katha Pollitt to the social commentators Barbara Ehrenreich and Vivian Gornick to the historian Howard Zinn write as if to say, if America did not literally plan and carry out an attack upon itself, it might as well have. As Robert Fisk puts it, most crazily, if not really outside the boundaries of the common discourse: "Our broken promises, perhaps even our destruction of the Ottoman Empire, led inevitably to this tragedy." This tragedy—a terrible occurrence, in its formal definition, brought about by the arrogance, by the overweening pride, of he or she on whom the terrible occurrence is visited. A terrible occurrence, in its commonplace, everyday usage, that just happens, and for which no one can really be blamed. In either case, neither a crime nor an act of war.

It has been said by revolutionary theorists that it is the duty of every revolutionary to explain his or her actions. It was said by our own: "When in the Course of human events, it becomes necessary for one people to dissolve the political bands which have connected them with another, and to assume among the powers of the earth, separate and equal station to which the Laws of Nature and of Nature's God entitle them, a decent respect to the opinions of mankind requires that they should declare the causes which impel them to the separation." But one of the many things that was new in the astonishingly successful, staggeringly symbolic, overwhelmingly physical act of war committed against the United States last September was that, as an act, it was without speech. There was no manifesto, statement, or justification addressed to the opinions of mankind, let alone those who were to be killed—implicitly, anyone and everyone within the borders of or holding any allegiance to the United States. It was as if the reason for the murders was, in the next phrase of the *Declaration of Independence*, "self-evident."

But for so many American intellectuals, this was not sufficient. When one makes one's living speaking in public, nothing can be self-evident; otherwise, some people would be out of a job. So one learned, again and again, that the acts taken against the United States were the result of crimes the United States had committed against others—against Guatemalans, Chileans, Nicaraguans, Philippines, Japanese, Angolans, Serbians, Sudanese, Iraqis, Iranians, Afghanis, Saudis, and, most of all, most deeply and most hideously and most proximately, Palestinians. It was the United States, through its client state Israel, and the client state's general Ariel Sharon, one read, who was responsible for the massacres of Palestinian refugees in Lebanon in 1982—and the death of every Palestinian man, woman, or child killed by Israelis since. That by the same logic one could say that the United States was responsible for the death of every Israeli man, woman, or child killed by a Palestinian was not remarked upon; that from a different logic one might wonder why it is only the United States, or Israel, that is held responsible for the 1982 Lebanon massacres, and not the Lebanese Christians who in fact carried them out, was as far as I know mentioned only by Fredric Smoler, a professor of literature and history at Sarah Lawrence, in the leftist New York tabloid *First of the Month*.

"Responsibility for violence lies with those who perpetrate it," the novelist Salman Rushdie wrote in 1990. He was speaking, most specifically, of the fatwa issued against him by the Ayatollah Khomeini—the death sentence passed on him for his supposedly blasphemous book *The Satanic Verses*. What he meant, I think, was that should he be murdered, as the leader of the faith had commanded that he be, the person who killed him should be held fully responsible. That person, Rushdie was saying, would have made a choice. He—for only a man would have been considered worthy of the act—would not have been impelled by, and could not be justified by, any religious belief or historical necessity. Men and women make their own decisions, and rightly suffer for them. The greater cause only exculpates; only the individual can take responsibility. But this was not a notion that one has much heard from American intellectuals. Not only had the United States, as a world power, or a military apparatus serving as the protector of American capitalism, created the attack on itself; as good Americans, American intellectuals were obligated to explain and justify it. And this was only one more of the many things about the beginning of the war that was new.

There were many exceptions, and they were drowned out, or appeared in relatively obscure or specialized publications. In *First of the Month*, co-editor Charles O'Brien wrote from the heart, condemning Noam Chomsky and others as "the Vichy left," and saying, finally, more than anyone else was saying, right or left. The left always speaks in terms of its "task," its "duty;" almost mockingly, knowing who he was up against—that is, most of those who might be reading a leftist New York tabloid—that was the language O'Brien took up:

> It is the duty of the left in this time not only to be a party of war, but to be the maximalist party of war. Hostilities must extend not only to Iraq, Sudan, etc. but to the supposed friendlies, the darlings of so many on the domestic right: Saudi Arabia, the [United Arab Emirates], and Pakistan. We can do no better, to use Chomsky's phrase, than, first to disregard Chomsky utterly (along with such organs of disinformation as *Z* and *Counterpunch* as well as the more genteel *Harpers*, the *LRB* and the *Nation*). But more important, we can do no better than to emulate revolutionary France: which, with audacity, without indulgence, summoning up the people, carried the war, across whosever borders, to the enemies of the republic.

In *Artforum*, Homi Bhabha, a professor of English and African American Studies at Harvard, and as an intellectual most distinguished for his translation of the political concept of "plausible deniability" into literary discourse—putting every word of potential meaning in scare quotes, to indicate that he does not accept any meaning anyone might attribute to it—as in, "putting every 'word' of 'potential' 'meaning' in 'scare' quotes"—wrote a piece with only three such quotes: and rather than provide meaning, or explanation, simply merged himself with the event, which he somehow saw as a crowd of men and women climbing up and down on Jacob's Ladder. With startling eloquence he spoke of something he called "the Unbuilt." "Gardens of solace and towers of regeneration may heal the wound," he wrote:

> But the Unbuilt that haunts the space is the spirit of those, firefighters and rescue workers, who climbed an endless ladder, descending into the circle of death, to do their duty to those who had to escape. In that movement there is a sense of "making progress," step by step, without a transcendent form of progress. And in that action there lies the un-utopian ethic of the Unbuilt. There are no available images of this act of ascent; progress here is a lateral or adjacent move toward the stranger as toward the neighbor.

But those were oddities. The insistence on America—which is to say Israel—which is to say Jews—as, on the level of deepest truth, the true author of the massacres, was so pervasive, and often so automatic, that when I read the following—"The attack on September 11 was certainly not about people hating our freedoms. It was purely in response to America's foreign policy; and it was primarily about our monetary and military support of Israel"—I barely thought to look for the byline. It was American Nazi and Ku Klux Klan leader David Duke, but it could have been any number of people on the left.

All of this is summed up nowhere so well as in Susan Sontag's instantly notorious short comment that ran in the "Talk of the Town" pages in the September 24 issue of the *New Yorker*.

Sontag, since the 1960s the most ambitious, respected, controversial, and politically engaged of New York intellectuals, was surrounded in those pages by many voices. There was the repulsive, epicene eyewitness account of the destruction of the World Trade Center by the novelist John Updike, watching from Brooklyn, searching for words that would divert attention from the event itself and toward his ability to gild it: "We clung to each other as if we ourselves were falling. Amid the glittering impassivity of the many buildings across the East River, an empty spot had appeared, as if by electronic command, beneath the sky that, but for the sulphurous cloud streaming south toward the ocean"—I can't read any more. There was the novelist Jonathan Franzen, author of *The Corrections*, imagining, as a novelist is supposed to do, the possible contours of life and death: "the scene inside a plane one moment before impact. At the controls, a terrorist is raising a prayer to Allah in expectation of instant transport from this world to the next, where houris will presently reward him for his glorious success. At the back of the cabin, huddled Americans are trembling and moaning and, no doubt, in many cases, praying to God for a diametrically opposite outcome. And then, a moment later, for hijacker and hijacked alike, the world ends." One of the bombs planted in Franzen's sentences may not go off right away: "huddled Americans," from the "huddled masses" emblazoned on the Statue of Liberty, in the moment reaching out to the huddled few flying over it, as if, somehow, huddling is an American condition, our version of dust to dust.

In this context, Sontag's few words were imperious, unsurprised, impatient, and ice-cold. It was nothing she hadn't seen before—not really. When Sarajevo was under siege, she had traveled there again and again, to direct a play; she was, as she wrote in 1995, "a veteran of dread and shock," "comfortable," after her experiences, only with "those who have been to Bosnia, too. Or to some other slaughter—El Salvador, Cambodia, Rwanda, Chechnya. Or who at least know, firsthand, what a war is." She knew. So it was no problem for her to cut through the shock and dread of virgins—of those who, unlike her, had never seen anything like this before, who had never imagined anything like this before—who, even if they had imagined the destruction of the World Trade Center, which, since it was built, many people casually have, had never remotely experienced in their imagination the reality of what they imagined. Sontag had already been there and gone. She could speak like Ronald Reagan talking about redwoods: "Seen one war, seen them all." What happened, Sontag said in her first sentence, was simply a "monstrous dose of reality"—and I think one can take the "monstrous" as a grace note. Like Chomsky's "major atrocities," it translates into "ordinary events," and even more quickly: "dose of reality" takes you where she means to go. You have been living in a dream world, Sontag said; now, you have been forced to wake up. There is no mystery, there is nothing to wonder about.

Sontag wrote to close questions, not to open them—and as if hers was the only voice brave enough to say what had to be said: "Where is the acknowledgment," she wrote, "that this was not a 'cowardly' attack on 'civilization' or 'liberty' or 'humanity' or 'the free world' but an attack on the world's self-proclaimed superpower, undertaken as a consequence of specific American alliances and actions?"

Again, the bile rose in my throat, and for the same reason as when I read Noam Chomsky's first interview. "Specific American alliances and actions"—there was apparently no need to say what they were. It's the language of the hipster: If you have to ask, you'll never know. But certainly the writer, the thinker, did not have to ask. It had all happened before—that is, to those who understood, the event had happened even before it happened.

In a questionnaire Sontag responded to in 1997, she wrote that "You have no right to a public opinion unless you've been there, experienced firsthand and on the ground and for some considerable time the country, war, injustice, whatever you are talking about." Forget what the response of Sontag, or anyone, would be if the government, or a right-wing propagandist, were to say the same thing: "You have no right to a public opinion unless." There's no unless in the Bill of Rights, anyone would say. But that is not the point; establishing one's superiority to any event, and to any of one's fellow citizens, by denying the existence of anything that one's conceptual apparatus cannot enclose is the point.

Or rather the point is that real intellectuals admit that it is in the nature of the human condition that it will inevitably, at unpredictable times, in unpredictable ways, produce events that leave every conceptual apparatus in ruins, and that real intellectuals value nothing so much as the chance, which comes only to a few, to do their work there.

Inside the Whale

Kanan Makiya

Kanan Makiya's speech at an NYU panel discussion on November 22, 2002 was a turning point in post-9/11, pre-"Shock and Awe" discourse on the future of Iraq. His case for Democracy Now! galvanized some liberal intellectuals. (Last year, The New Republic's editor, Peter Beinart, ruefully allowed that when his puzzled wife asked him how he'd ended up supporting the invasion of Iraq, he had a simple answer: "Because Kanan Makiya did.") The interest of Makiya's "electric" remarks, however, went beyond his eloquent argufying for a humanist politics in the Middle East. His talk exposed "the lack of trust—the foundational political disagreement" that existed between Colin Powell's State Department and the office of the Vice President. A rift that would have heavy consequences after regime change in Iraq. Makiya's remarks are reprinted below along with an exchange between him and Mansour Farhang, a former Iranian ambassador to the UN who was forced to flee Iran after Khomeini consolidated power there in the early '80s. Various other panelists (Todd Gitlin, Michael Walzer, et al.) have recalled with satisfaction their own "answers" to Makiya that evening, but it was the call and response between the two Middle Easterners that was most telling.

I'm going to strike a discordant note here by arguing that when you look at the coming war from the point of view of those who are going to pay the greatest price—namely the people of Iraq, my compatriots—these people want this war.

Let me begin by giving an account of recent developments within the Iraqi opposition because this has not gotten all that much coverage. I'd urge you to consider that the US administration—whatever its deeper motives—is a very active player in this opposition. And it certainly at this time does NOT have a unified position about what it wants to happen after a regime change.

The military planning is far more advanced than the political planning. And that means there is room for directing the debate in one direction not the other. So let's begin by talking about the Iraqi opposition.

A row has broken out among Iraqis about a Conference that is expected to take place in December. And that row pits democrats and independents on the one hand—loosely organized or represented by the Iraqi National Congress, an organization that was established in 1992—against the traditional organized parties of Iraqi politics. The row has broken out over the two most important components of any conference (1) the agenda (2) who will attend. I'm going to begin with the latter issue....

The origins of the problems here go back to the August 9 meeting between representatives of various Iraqi groups and the Vice President—a meeting that represented a kind of anointing of the Iraqi opposition. All sides agreed they were envisioning a democratic future and everyone pledged then that they would hold a Conference that would carry that vision forward.

Following that meeting, the process agreed upon by the six parties to organize that Conference became blocked over the issue of who should attend. The four traditional parties wanted a small number of attendees—some eighty people—distributed among the parties according to a formula of percentages. For instance, the Supreme Council For Islamic Revolution—an organization that is based in Iran and is really an extension of the Iranian intelligence services—was to be given 40 percent of the delegates. The Kurds would have 25 percent and so on. There was no room left for democrats and independents outside of a very small percentage of seats allocated to the Iraqi National Congress. When the democrats raised objections—the four traditional parties eschewed attempts to reach a consensus and pressed ahead in an effort hold the Conference on their own terms on November 22. But we blocked it. It's now going to take place on December 10. And it will be an open Conference—the attendees will not be determined by the old formulas/percentages.

So how did we come to this state of affairs? Here, the US administration is very much implicated. All of the four parties were once upon a time inside the Iraqi National Congress (INC), which has long had the best program—it has called for democracy, rule of law, human rights and supports the Kurdish demand for a federal state in Iraq. But through the efforts of the State Department and the CIA, in particular, these parties were prised out of the INC. Their various activities were supported and they were given to believe that the future would fall to them since the INC was no longer a functional organization. (Which had the effect of allowing democrats and independents to claim the INC in recent years, though it had lost much of its clout.)

We now face the very strange paradoxical fact, which people like myself have to deal with—the strongest support that Iraqi independents and democrats get today comes from precisely those circles that have been the most attacked here—namely Wolfowitz, Rumsfeld, and the VP's office. The strongest supporters of the traditional parties—whose program is (at best) a reformed military dictatorship or a system where the parties entirely dominate any kind of semi-parliamentary structure that might be set up—comes from the most "reasonable" people in the administration who assume or imagine this is all that Arabs are capable of. Above all the traditional parties are championed by the CIA, actively with funds and with their units, which are functioning right now in Northern Iraq encouraging the parties to keep out of the INC.

The other key pre-Conference issue was the Agenda. Here, democrats and independents succeeded in hoisting the State Department on its own petard. Let's go back to the time before the word democracy crept into the discourse of the American administration; before Condoleezza Rice gave her important interview to *Financial Times* where she talked about the reconstruction of Iraq, nation-building and democracy not stopping at the borders of the Arab and Muslim world; before the VP gave an important speech in August talking about democracy in Iraq for the first time; and, obviously, before Bush's speech on September 12 (welcomed enormously by Iraqis because it was one of the very few occasions in which they featured prominently in the formulation of American policy). Before all these things occurred, the State Department started something they called their "Future of Iraq" project. Now, as this project was initially conceived, it had to do with everything but the future of the state of Iraq. They were, for example, interested in questions of public health and environment on the day after a war. (Which, incidentally they have been assuming will take place for a very long time now. I think the decision to go to war was made in some form or another back in December, but that's a moot point.) The position of the State Department was rather smart. They jumped on the bandwagon and initiated this "Future of Iraq" project to focus on very technical matters. They asked me to participate. I refused because they weren't addressing the structural political questions. I don't know anything about collecting the garbage the day after a big war. I could say something about the kind of political system I think is workable. I have views on that....

But after the August anointing of the Iraqi opposition, as I've said, democracy became the word. And a workshop was assembled called the "Democratic Political Principles Workshop." It was originally called the "Political Principles Workshop," but after pressure from Congress, the VP's office and people like Wolfowitz and Rumsfeld—it was changed to underscore "Democratic Political Principles." I've found that these are the kind of games that go on all the time since I've been heavily involved in this business over the last five months. This workshop was originally intended by the State Department to merely collect together 32 Iraqis of their choosing, representing what they considered to be a spectrum of opinion. Democrats were in a minority—there were six or seven of us very strongly committed to a radical transformation of Iraq in a democratic direction. The rest were representatives of the traditional parties—not the top echelon but the intellectuals and, ah, hacks—along with independent Islamists and some others. At the beginning, the idea was that people would go around the table and say what they thought on federalism, on human rights or various other questions. And somebody would make a checklist of issues that had been raised. But we succeeded in accomplishing something more. And I have to say that the way we succeeded is very revealing. It had everything to do with the lack of trust - the foundational political disagreement—that exists between State and the VP's office. They no longer trust each other. What happened was that the VP's office and the Department of Defense sent representatives to the workshop even though the initiative was hosted by the State Department. What we managed to do, with the help of these vice presidential and DoD aides, was force into existence a coordinating committee that has written a massive report on the "Transition to Democracy in Iraq." When we showed up with this report at the second of these affairs, which go on for two or three days, it stimulated a real discussion. Everyone realized that something important was afoot and they came back with comments. We integrated their responses into the document and now we have something that really matters.

This document represents quite a wide spectrum of Iraqi views, but it's driven and edited by democrats. And this document has emerged out of a process initiated by the State Department, though they never intended to produce anything like it. When all the parties fully understood what had occurred—and given that we had secured a promise that the document could become the working papers for the future Iraqi Conference—some people suddenly got very worried and began denying the validity of the document. It was now something over the top that had been produced by people out of touch with the Arab world because we were calling for things like a demilitarized state, democracy understood as protection of minorities and the rule of law—not simply majority rule, which is the usual understanding of democracy. Plus we were willing to postpone elections—until protections of the individual and minority rights were cemented—and establish a federal system, insisting that it is necessary to give up on the Arab nature of the state.

Now they're right—this is radical stuff if you're in Arab politics. This document argues that if the Kurds are to be a key pillar and component of the country—and not just the Kurds, but the Turkmens and the Assyrians and all the other national groups—the Arab character of the Iraqi state as it has been conceived should be done away with. This is dynamite!

So the document was ruled to be unsuitable for the upcoming Conference. Whereupon democrats made one hell of a fuss. They directed a letter-writing campaign amongst Iraqis that's been going on for two or three weeks. And they flooded the State Department with protests. Delegations were showing up at the Department. Iraqis were coming from England wanting to speak on behalf of democrats—asking why is the report not being accepted as the working document for the conference? Why are democrats being excluded? Why are these ridiculous proportions still in force? How could anyone imagine that the Shia in Iraq could be represented by the Iranians? Etc. Etc. The pressure had the following consequences. From 70 plus delegates, we're now well over 350 and we got this damn document to be the central focus of the conference. And throughout, we had the support of those arch-warmongers—Paul Wolfowitz, Secretary Rumsfeld, and the VP's office. These are the facts. This is simply what happened. They are the people who are interested in the document. Colin Powell is utterly uninterested and wants nothing to do with us. We are making his life difficult.

I wanted to say what happens when you view regime change from this kind of point of view. Notice first of all that there is absolutely no discussion inside the Iraqi opposition - among Iraqis generally—about whether or not regime change is a good thing. It is simply taken for granted that it is. Remember that after all, it is a war that is being waged in their name, on their turf and they are the ones who are going to pay the price for it more than anyone else in this room, right?

What this amounts to, what the whole phenomenon of the Iraqi opposition represents—inchoate, confused, anarchic, fractured upon itself as it certainly is—what it represents is something NEW in Arab politics. We have here for the first time in modern Arab political discourse—or at least since 1967—a population that has emerged which is clear that the be-all and end-all of its political world is its own homemade dictatorship. It's not the national question, not armed struggle, not anti-imperialism, not anti-Zionism—all the usual shibboleths of Arab politics for the past 35 years. This can be encouraged. Or it can be crushed. But think about what it means if you do that. What you're killing is something that would have extraordinary transformative potential throughout the whole Middle Eastern region.

Consider for instance the fact that this opposition arises from a seminal event. We talk about the 1991 Gulf War, but we often forget to talk about the uprising that followed that war. Here you have a situation in which dozens of countries participate in an invasion and you have the bombing campaign—the like of which no country has seen since World War II. And nonetheless, the population of the country that is itself the target of those bombs rises up and calls upon the very people who have been bombing them to help finish the war. (Now of course that wasn't what Bush, Sr. wanted. People like me hope it's what Bush Jr. wants, though that's a separate question.) In that uprising lies the possibility of something truly new.

Now if you go out there now and write letters to your congressman—demanding that the war be made in the name of democracy in Iraq, demanding that it be for a larger purpose—you would be nourishing that possibility. I submit to you that if there is even a sliver of a chance—a 5 percent or 10 percent chance—you have a moral obligation to do that!

MANSOUR FARHANG: You're really asking/expecting a revolutionary change in American foreign policy. I cannot imagine the US coming and trying to establish a democratic regime in Iraq—and maintaining Saudi Arabia, Kuwait, Jordan, United Arab Emirates and the rest of those states run by proprietors. The kind of commitment of resources and manpower such a project would require of the US over a period of five or even ten years in Iraq—and you know how fragmented that society is…. What bothers me about the scenario you are developing is that the Iraqi opposition has had an opportunity to create a democratic organization during the last 20 or 30 years in open democratic societies—and they haven't done that. (Now I could say the same thing about Iranians!) If they need Rumsfeld and Cheney to teach them the rules of democracy…. The idea that suddenly all these people are going to be transformed into democratic agents. You think the Ayatollah sitting in Iran sending his representatives to engage in this negotiation is going to be committed to democracy. No—what you're asking the US to do—any government, any governing system that is going to take that kind of responsibility would have a totally different attitude toward the underprivileged—the marginal populations in its own society. What you're asking is romantic—it's very desirable—but it doesn't have anything to do with the reality of international politics.

KANAN MAKIYA: There's another way of thinking about it. American policy-makers may have a more self-interested rationale. After 9/11, all the traditional pillars of US foreign policy in the Middle East have come down—starting with Oslo and working through to the key relationship with the Saudis. 9/11 demonstrated that it is an extremely unhappy and tenuous relationship. The political players that I've been speaking of are extremely hostile to the Saudis for that reason. You certainly couldn't even think about democratizing Saudi Arabia. That would be a pipedream—if you were to hold elections there today, Saudis would overwhelmingly vote for bin Laden. But Iraq provides an alternative. Think for a moment, Mansour, of the two revolutions that happened in the Islamic world. One was very noisy—of which you were a part in Iran. The other was very quiet, insidious and infinitely more dangerous. I'm talking about the export (after the oil revolution of 1973) of an austere little sect, which meant nothing to anybody and now today is Islam—substituting itself for a great religion and civilization, exporting hundreds and thousands of madrassas whose graduates become bin Ladens and al Qaeda. It's Saudi money that did all this.

Now look I'm pretending to be an American strategist. These guys know 9/11 wasn't about Afghanistan. That country was a poor fractured one that became a campground for Arabs. These are Arab problems exported to Afghanistan through Saudi money, which led to 9/11. The heart of the problem is in the Middle East. Something in this part of the world (since 1967 I'd argue) has gone terribly, horribly wrong.

To sum it up—what's apparent is that the Middle East needs a success story. In the Clinton years that was thought to be Oslo. But that's all finished for the time being. Iraq is being thought of by this of school of thinkers as an alternative. I'm just trying to say that they have a strategic design, a way of thinking about what they see as the root of the problem—namely a turn to democracy and an end to America's support for regimes like Saddam Hussein, or regimes like Saudi Arabia, which has been the rule for as long as I've been active in politics. It could be that that formula has finally proven itself to be a failure. That's what some of these people are thinking. (It's not what Colin Powell is thinking!) From their point of view, Iraq could be an alternative to Saudi Arabia. Its oil reserves are second to none. Iraq also has things that Afghanistan doesn't have—a developed infrastructure, a highly educated class. They have a sense that democracy could work in Iraq where it might not work elsewhere. I'll leave it there.

AN AFTERNOON W/AN AGNOSTIC

Of the sentence, if you read it to the end
The sentence, not words. A term of do, due, doing
        where the frills of ignorance can be shed,
The cavern of doo doo in yr head. I see, for instance,
This man over here. And he the head of state, of
        some entity
You hate. There he is. Fat wool face shirking
        humanity like bad air.
That's him, over there. See. Yeh, that's him. Now.
If you approach like in the afternoon. Just the two
A you. You might look unassuming, assuming,
        you can un-
Assume, and him, like he is, a blizzard of snail
        droppings
Shaped into a poison.

What's the first thing? Ask him to sing?
Naw, Ask him to do the "Boston Monkey," with his
        eyes closed,
And whirl into the pretty woman's arms. With a
Sly soliloquy which ends, the way
We know it wd.
Not that, well ask him to twirl his hat
Like Fred Astaire, on a cane … and while he's
Doing that, ten people live, who otherwise, wd not.
Is that closer to your shot?
No? Well What? Wd you say
If you cd address this dude that way?

You don'no?
I know. You ain't got no idea? Just ask him
his fucking name. And if he's insane! You can't do
        that? Well what is left but polite BS?
Like, "Oh, good day, my man? Is that a tan, you
        got, just an inch
Below yr skin? Make me think perhaps
We kin!"

You don't want to say that?
OK, say what you wanna say. Just silence?
No, Just a rumble in yr stomach
Like the eggs is attacking the ham. And you is
        slightly slower
Than you am. Then say what? Nothing?

Just the eyes you got. Piercing through the snot of
        his face. You wanna
Ask about race? About how he got to this place?
        About why he so ignorant, why a racist, why a
        murderer? Why a kidnapper? A child killer? A blood
        junky? A stooge for money. Ain't nothing you say
        gonna be funny?

But then he turns and walks away. Now what you
        gonna say? Just scream? What that gonna do?
        Just scream and call him names?
That ain't gonna get no change. Why you acting
        strange? Just holler? Make noise? Throw stones?
        Blow yrself up?

But then he keeps walking. Then just disappear. Next
        day he in the *Times*
Running a list of yr crimes. And the next day the
        same. This time he use
Yr name! What that mean? That you ain't agnostic
        as you seem.
It mean you actually believe in God,
And that was him, we bumped into. Dig that!

— Amiri Baraka

Editor's Note: Amiri Baraka sent AN AFTERNOON W/AN AG-
NOSTIC to First *around the time of the third annual commemo-*
rations of 9/11 (and after email exchanges about his campaign
to win back his position as Poet Laureate of New Jersey). This
white Anglo editor didn't get it at first, but the poet offered helpful
advice—hang with that first "sentence" and it will "open up."

Death from Above

Hans Koning

A contribution to a First *forum on 9/11 ("Five Years On") published*
in September, 2006.

The first truth about 9/11 is its uniqueness. That is to say that in the
early morning of September 11, 2001, it would be a new and unheard of
occurrence. It was a natural disaster.

The second truth is that this natural disaster was nonetheless planned
by human hand and mind. The way people died was unheard of—the

closest parallel is perhaps the sinking of the *Titanic*, that same fall from the warmth and order of daily life into nothingness. (This is also the reason that the *Titanic*, almost a hundred years later, is still so strong a part of our tribal memory.)

I cannot think, though, of any parallel where human thought has come up with a disaster of these dimensions. Ravachol, the French anarchist who was executed in 1892, and August Valliant who threw a bomb in the French Chamber of Deputies (which did not kill anyone) executed in 1894, are still remembered names in French politics. The assassination of Theo van Gogh in Amsterdam in 2004 still traumatizes Holland. It is not a matter of numbers only.

I find a chasm between the experience of the World Trade Center for the average New Yorker and for a veteran, any veteran, of one of the many wars of recent years. I know 9/11 only from a distance, but it has lastingly influenced me more than my time as a sergeant in the British Army during World War II.

Men died, we were shocked and aggrieved by this. Those deaths, though, still "fitted" into our daily lives, they were not an outrage against nature.

9/11, by its birth as a thought product of man, does not fit in anywhere. It shows human nature as a phenomenon which at its darkest denies all rules of life. It shows that, given the right circumstances, we will be able AND WILLING to destroy the world.

A Fascinating Fear of Fascism

Charles Keil

The author e-mailed First of the Month *a series of essays, notes and poems during, and immediately after, NATO's campaign to reverse Serbia's attempted ethnic cleansing of Kosovo. The following piece was one of those urgent communications. It's marked, like his other emails from this period, by his determination to keep thinking—and feeling—in the face of Serbian fascism. You can follow Keil's entire movement of mind at: http://www.firstofthemonth.org/archives/2000/01/kosovo_and_the. html.*

We all fear it in others. I don't know about you, but I fear it in myself. This deep, deep urge to be bonded, to be of one mind and body with kindred spirits, to feel righteous and strong in quantity of numbers and quality of truth, to have some shared beliefs you are willing to sacrifice for and even to die for if necessary, and ... and ... to kill for? Go to war for? No. Wait a minute....

What is a fasc? Just a fascis in Latin, a band or bundle of rods, twigs or straw ... "also crowd of people." Togetherness. Us-ness. We are all straw or grass or twigs together. Consubstantiation. Participation. Communion. Communitas. Solidarity. Diffuse enduring solidarity or love—what we live for and constantly search for, never more so than in an era of ever more profound alienations from self, body, labor, nature, society. We were born to bond and bundle, to stroke and be stroked, to groom and be groomed, to respect and be respected, to love and be loved. And everywhere we are foreign, alien, alone and trying to decide which commodity best relieves our oppression/exploitation/alienation. Mike soars across the screen and he says try Nikes. We do. Fascinating.

Add big victimage to alienation. The Germans thought they were the big victims after World War I. Reparations were Hitler's fuel for World War II. The Serbs think of themselves as big victims and justified in their new role as aggressors and executioners in Slovenia, Croatia, Bosnia, Kosovo—ask the survivors in Dubrovnik, Sarajevo, Srebrenica, Bihac and all of Kosovo what kind of victims the Serbs are....

How did a solid majority of those good, rational, intelligent, Mozart-loving, very civilized Germans become Nazis or Nazi sympathizers? Why do Serbs rally round Slobo instead of saying "guess we better stop butchering Albanians and burning villages 'cause 18 nations are finally saying that's a no-no in '99." Even more fascinating, why do 90 percent of Russians and 60 percent of Greeks side with the Serbian fascists and war criminals? How does that deep identification with the Serbs overlook the manifestly evil ways they have searched for lebensraum the past eight years? How does demonstrating against NATO bombing assuage Russian and Greek senses of alienation, victimage, powerlessness, wanting to belong, wanting to love. I haven't liked or trusted Mikis Theodoras ever since his music after "Song of the Dead Brother" got more mushy, sentimental, pseudo-folky, pretentious, but he seems an intelligent, creative man of left who calls Milosevic a butcher and monster in one breath, only to say that fascist Serbia must be defended in the next breath or all of Greek history and honor will have been in vain! Fascinating....

Since Roman times there has been an ax in the middle of the fasc. "Fasces—a bundle of rods, bound together about an ax with the blade projecting, carried before magistrates of ancient Rome as an emblem of authority." The power tribe…. How do we make the world safe for non-power tribes? How do we get the ax out of every bundle?

The most recent administrative massacres have been very low tech. The Hutu, using mostly machetes, were more efficient than the Germans! Slobo's thugs in ski masks use mostly small arms and their Serbian penises. (Those masks are very important; some shame or fear of being identified and taken to The Hague seems to exist. Progress?) It might be too hard to stop the Hutu or the Serbs as they search and destroy in small groups. But superfast high-tech planes flying 15,000 feet and higher don't seem to be the appropriate technology to stop or deter cleansing and genocide….

We have never said "No" to the administrators of massacres or the leaderships who generate other genocidal events in the first place. Read *While Six Million Died* and realize that no one ever tried to bomb the railroad tracks to Auschwitz. Fascinating. We don't even know the names or recognize the faces of the men who masterminded, planned, propagandized, ordered, and executed the most efficient slaughter of innocents ever accomplished. Who wants to know? I don't. I went and got the names of the Hutu evil geniuses and then promptly forgot them. Long names. Funny names. Too many syllables. Always faceless. Fascinating.

Since there are no conclusions to these paragraphs. Fascinations but no findings…. I'd like to end by going over my only personal experience of fascism/racism/pogroms circa 1967 over thirty years ago in Nigeria.

My wife Angie and I could see, hear, sense the pogrom coming to Makurdi, the polyglot administrative center of Benue Province, feel the anti-Ibo racism rising, read about unpunished pogroms in other cities. The dozen or so white expatriates working for the provincial government didn't think anything would happen, the Tiv people we were working with denied the possibility, but we felt it was just a matter of time and a trigger. Only the town madman, Gypsy Fullstop—a.k.a. Lord Rolling Stone, R.G.T. Above (RGT the initials for Royal Government Tyrannical)—was clearer than we were about the impending massacres, bringing word salads each day filled with truth-telling phrases ("gangs of jealousy" and "jeopardy, jeopardous," signing himself "cruciferous" or more than crucified).

When the day came and elements of a Nigerian army battalion showed up to lead the mob, I thought about going down the hill to the market area and trying to stop it. White people were still respected, distinguished visitors, closest to distant authorities—it was not a completely crazy thought. But I was afraid. And what happens to my wife and infant daughter if my bluff is called and I'm killed or incarcerated? I stayed home and watched the dust rise over the market from the hilltop. When we went across the Makurdi bridge by car the next day to see what the buzzards were circling over, to count the eviscerated bodies, to smell the most nauseating stench of rotting flesh in the tropics, to at least witness what had been done, we were greeted on the trip back by a Nigerian army officer at the bridge who cheerfully invited us to tea that afternoon and smilingly explained that we could discuss how important it was to rid the world of Ibos, what recent progress had been made in this area and what further progress could be expected. Chilling. The expatriates back at the social club, a few missionaries included, explained to us the next day that while indeed, it had happened, some had been killed, it was "just the riffraff," a few of the unemployed and hangers on, no one important. What I learned from this personal experience, and from the inability of Ibos and other "Eastern Nigerians" to find freedom, dignity, justice, in an independent Biafra over the few years of struggle and starvation that followed, is that: 1) no one wants to see it coming, to be alert to signs of oncoming fascism and genocidal events, to send out warning signals; 2) few recognize it when it does come—this is not an exceptional crime, it's "just cleansing" the riffraff, just how things are "in Africa" or "in the Balkans;" 3) the fascists think they are doing themselves and the world a favor "cleaning" up a problem, and, 4) by and large, the world would rather agree than get over it's fascinating fear of fascism.

To find out what the hell is going on with humans in this whole us/them, class/scapegoating, nationalism-gone-crazy department, and then figure out ways to stop the most appalling numbers of bodies from piling up in the charnel house does not seem to be a high priority for many philosophers, many social scientists, journalists, policy makers, thinking citizens anywhere. I know I'm hanging on to Hannah Arendt's *Eichmann in Jerusalem* and an old article by Bernard Nietschman, "The Third World War" from *Cultural Survival Quarterly* 11(3) for guidance and information.... But where is the shelf full of analysis and imaginative suggestions on how to cope with crimes against humanity?

In My Lonely Room

Ellen Willis

The following thought experiment was inspired, or provoked, by [2002's] art scandale, the "Mirroring Evil" exhibit at the Jewish Museum;

and in particular by Roee Rosen's installation, which invites us to imagine that we are Eva Braun having a last night of sex with Adolf Hitler:

Imagine that the exhibit contains no actual art works, a fact that is carefully concealed from the public and the press. The catalogue, issued in advance, describes the supposed works and includes supposed photographs of some items. It announces the intentions of the show—to demystify and appropriate rather than memorialize the Holocaust, to probe the appeal of the oppressors rather than the suffering of the victims. It discusses at length, in a series of essays by curators and academics, the questions and reflections the exhibit means to prompt. (From the Foreword: "As offensive as such work may seem on the surface … is it the Nazi imagery itself that offends, or the artists' aesthetic manipulation of such imagery? Does such art become the victim of the imagery it depicts? Or does it actually tap into and thereby exploit the repugnant power of Nazi imagery as a way merely to shock and move its viewers? Or is it both…?")

Predictably, the catalogue attracts a double whammy of outrage, from the culture warriors who never miss a chance to heap contempt on what has come to be called (in various inflections ranging from total earnestness to dripping sarcasm) "transgressive" art, and from the keepers of the flame who see all representations of the Holocaust as guilty until proven innocent. It also inspires, or provokes, a *New York Observer* article by Ron (*Explaining Hitler*) Rosenbaum lamenting that the work, which he has not yet had a chance to see, has already been "contextualized" to death by the essayists. They have, he argues, "done the art and the artists a serious disservice, imposing on the work a naïve, one-dimensional, postmodern point of view … that frames it in a single rigid lens that substitutes a simplistic moral relativism for real engagement with the issues."

Arriving at the museum on the exhibit's opening day, visitors encounter a further barrage of verbiage explaining what we are about to see and how we ought to look at it ("This art is cautionary…. It warns us not to take for granted the symbols of oppression that pervade our outlets of news and entertainment. It conveys wariness about techniques of persuasion, including those we encounter in the marketplace" etc., etc.). Having run this gauntlet, we approach the first gallery. It consists of a large empty space with white walls. Disoriented, we at first think we're in the wrong place, but another large explanatory placard reassures us: the catalogue, and the debate generated by it, are the real point. Any actual images would simply narrow the range of thoughts and feelings the debate has elicited. Nazism is above all a state of mind that cannot be attached to any object.

We move on to a second room, whose entrance has a warning sign: "The contents of this room may be offensive to Holocaust survivors." This room is also empty, but is surrounded on three sides with wall-to-ceiling mirrors. The fourth wall contains an elaborate explanation of what the mirrors are supposed to signify.

To save time and avoid insulting the reader's intelligence I will pass over this explanation and move on to the third and final room, in which we can watch a video of the artists who supplied the descriptions and photographs of their "work" for the catalogue, along with curators, art critics, and Holocaust survivors, discussing the show and its import. Finally, in the museum gift shop visitors can buy miniature bottles of Chanel perfume in the shape of Zyklon canisters (inspired by one of Tom Sachs's "works"). LEGO blocks for building replicas of Auschwitz were considered (after Zbigniew Libera's imagined LEGO "concentration camp set" boxes) but were deemed too expensive to produce. The idea is not, as an extensive wall placard explains, to make money by selling these disturbing objects (all profits are to go to a fund benefiting survivors and their families) but to force people to contemplate the dark attractions of a commodified society through the actual act of buying or resisting the temptation to buy.

My point, as I'm sure you've guessed, is that the work displayed in "Mirroring Evil" is almost incidental to the issues raised by the show. (For the record, the catalogue and entrance-wall copy quoted, as well as the debriefing video, actually exist. The wall-to-ceiling mirrors and souvenir canisters ought to exist.) Ron Rosenbaum's generous hopes notwithstanding, the exhibit does not, by and large, transcend the limitations of its relentless preemptive commentary. What we have here is not critics and theorists projecting their half-baked ideas onto hapless artists but something more akin to a group of people who have organized a party and are determined to have a great time even though the guest of honor has failed to show up. The sheer volume of commentary—which extends to posted explanations for every piece; nothing is allowed to speak for itself—is no doubt defensive, prompted by anticipation of the inevitable outcry; but it would also seem to reflect intuitive abhorrence of a vacuum.

The conceit of conceptual art is that it makes aesthetic (or anti-aesthetic) experience of ideas. This means, on the one hand, that it eschews the aura of the transcendent, autonomous art object; and on the other that—since it's art, not argument—it need not supply evidence for its ideas, or come to any particular conclusions. Rather, its effect depends on the force and resonance and multidimensionality of its conceptions; it must be productive of thought, yet ultimately mysterious, more than the sum of its statements. When a piece of conceptual art is banal or reductive it is not only bad art, like an image that purports to be beautiful but is merely pretty; it also becomes dishonest, hiding behind its aesthetic pretensions (who me? I'm an artist; I'm supposed to raise questions, not answer them) to avoid responsibility for its (inflammatory? impoverished?) intellectual claims.

What are the ideas that govern "Mirroring Evil?" A number of pieces let us in on one or another version of the big news that fascism has aesthetic, even erotic appeal; that it has been glamorized in movies and pornographic images. Piotr Uklanski offers a Warhol-like lineup of 166 photographs of actors playing Nazi roles (your favorite—Marlon Brando? Yul Brynner?—is almost certainly included). Christine Borland, inspired by her discovery that some of Mengele's victims found him attractive, displays the work of sculptors she commissioned to make busts of the evil doctor based on her description (without telling them who it was). A video by Maciej Toporowicz intersperses images from Leni Riefenstahl films with clips of Luchino Visconti's *The Damned*, Pier Pasolini's *Salo,* and Calvin Klein ads—thereby embracing another prominent theme of the exhibition, a Frankfurt-School-redux equation of fascism with consumerism. In this vein, Tom Sachs's canisters wrapped in Chanel, Hermes, and Tiffany packaging and his model death camp mounted on a Prada box have deservedly gotten the most notoriety. (Placard: "Do we desire designer labels so much that we would accept anything at all that comes with them?") Is this what all the trumpeting about new perspectives on the Holocaust amounts to? The repetition of half a century's clichés about the sinister seductiveness of mass media and mass culture?

I suspect that the problem with "Mirroring Evil" is not simply a matter of some disappointing work by individual artists (perhaps to be expected, given the difficulties of a subject that is at once over-represented, inadequately grasped, and emotionally punishing). Rather, I believe it has to do with the stagnant political and cultural climate in which art is currently produced. When the pop artists invented the deadpan sensibility now hegemonic in the contemporary art world, they were reacting to a romantic utopianism that rejected a world of mass produced, mass communicated consumer goods and images. Mass culture, they aimed to show, had its own distinctive forms of beauty, pleasure and excitement, forms that were worth celebrating. They did not deny that our society had its problems, but they were, for the most part, political fatalists. They saw no choice but to separate the aesthetic from the moral: Andy Warhol's gorgeous silk screens of electric chairs said it all.

Like or dislike the pop stance, it was, at the time (the mid-'60s), a genuinely no-quotation-marks transgressive critique of the assumption, ubiquitous among intellectuals, that mass media and consumer culture were nothing but a means of seducing a sheep-like population into confusing compulsive shopping with happiness. For those of us who embraced the critique while rejecting the political fatalism, pop pointed the way toward a different kind of utopianism, one that allowed us to be both radicals and rock and roll fans. That was what post-modernism meant in those days. Now, paradoxically, the inheritors of pop use its language to resurrect the old anti-consumerist, anti-media ideology, with all its moralism but without the leavening of any sort of utopianism, romantic or otherwise, at a time when political fatalism is the culture's common sense. No wonder they look at Nazism and see themselves: the culprit is not "simplistic moral relativism" so much as the academicizing and, ah, decontextualizing of pop irony.

One piece in the show confounds these remarks: Alan Schechner's much-reviled "It's the Real Thing—Self-Portrait at Buchenwald," in which the artist inserts himself, brandishing a Diet Coke can, into a digital image of Margaret Bourke White's 1945 photograph of inmates at the camp. The catalogue does its best (in this case Rosenbaum has it right) to coopt Schechner's work for its anti-consumerist brief: "The irony of a robust Schechner among gaunt, malnourished survivors becomes embarrassing in the presence of a symbol of our culture's self-indulgent body consciousness. We are faced with the fact that we can extravagantly afford to produce purposely nutritionless products for widespread consumption.... The Coke can draws parallels between brainwashing tactics of the Nazis and commodification. Just as much of Europe succumbed to Nazi culture because it was the dominant paradigm, so does our contemporary culture succumb to consumerism."

Of course it's starvation, not robustness, that ought to embarrass us, and the parallel between Coke-drinking and genocide is not exactly self-evident, but never mind. Schechner's image manages to elude this ideological meat-grinder and transcend its own rather glib juxtapositions of hunger and diet drink, Holocaust victim and privileged American Jew, to achieve something richer and more unsettling. The Coke can is alight with what looks like a halo: a radiant, holy object. The inmates appear to be staring at it. The artist frowns. Unnervingly, he seems to become a stand-in for the Allied liberators, offering up to the survivors an icon of freedom. And then, as I continue to look, the scene breaks away from its moorings: it becomes the devastated people of Europe facing toward the beacon of post-war prosperity; the Third World gazing at the symbol of the American dream and of corporate globalization; the perplexed American Jewish artist, representing this dual legacy, willy-nilly in the middle of it all.

In contrast, the idea that Nazism is mirrored in American consumerism comes across as a form of grandiosity, the desire of middle-class artists and critics to see themselves as the fulcrum of history. For in truth, the mirror images of the Nazis, in our time, are not Calvin Klein and Prada but Bosnian Serbs and Islamic fundamentalists and, closer to home, white supremacist militias and assassins of abortion doctors. These, at any rate, are the images with which I would fill my imagined empty room.

Common Cruelty

Kate Millett

A contribution to a First *forum on the 2004 presidential campaign.*

Despite his little grin, his carefully built common man's appeal, there is something genuinely evil about George Bush. Consider how he treats his prisoners of war. The pictures from Abu Ghraib prison. It is significant that they have become their photographs, visual reproductions of what they once were, human beings caricatured by outlandish poses into a series of protruding arms and legs from a central core of buttocks. Or lying along the ground like a dog. Or squatting on a stool with electrodes attached to what were its arms, a hood over what was its face.

Bush and Rumsfeld have found ways to make everyone talk—to keep you naked and in the dark, for days at a time. To make the night hideous with screams. To do this to time, to pain, to consciousness and to do it not only in Abu Ghraib, but in countless unnamed and unlocated prisons throughout the region. Even to confining thousands of undocumented prisoners held in Guantanamo Bay for three years now in a living hell without any recourse to justice or law. These are not a few tormented by a handful. This is a deliberate policy arrived at wholesale.

This is not just an angry man debating on television, furious at being challenged by a far more sophisticated debater. Why has Kerry never mentioned Abu Ghraib prison? George Bush is not merely stubborn as a male driver miles from his destination clinging to the wheel with a heavy foot on the gas pedal—this is a criminal behavior. This is the crux of the matter.

For George Bush is cruel as well as incompetent. And it is not merely the careless cruelty of the rich and powerful who really cannot see those smaller and frailer and less well-connected. It is something we are almost ashamed to admit is our own now—it is official sadism. Something he has made American. Beyond bullying. Beyond macho insensitivity. It is something he espouses and if you don't like it you are unpatriotic. You're maybe not "normal." Maybe you're not even "Christian." He is indeed "God-driven." He has used 9/11 to make himself a dictator.

There's something perversely sexual about Bush's wars. These wars have a peculiar "gender specific" bent to them. Men in Iraq are tortured and photographs are taken so that others may know their shame. A sexual shame. One hears the voice of the army psychologist "explaining" the policy that Arab men are more the prisoners of macho myth than we are and how we can entirely humiliate them, complicating the humiliation by dragging Private Lindy England into the picture.

Does anyone remember that one of the reasons we went to war in Afghanistan was to stop the Taliban from butchering women who learned how to read? And now we collaborate with warlords who would have them raped on the way to school. The gender wars have taken a bitter turn in both countries. A turn towards the barbarous, the cruel. Mixed with sex, the perfect repressive formula. Puritanical. Complete misery. Cruelty for its own sake in the contorted photographs of our "enemies," the corrupt reports of our generals, the mean-spirited snicker of our President. It hides unspeakable things, crimes against the human spirit he feels perfectly at ease committing. He is a dangerous man. We would follow him at our peril.

World Body

Ann Snitow

The author wrote this in tribute to her feminist comrade, Ellen Willis, after Willis' death in 2006.

On February 17, 2005, Ellen Willis gave a talk at Take Back the Future, a group that meets on the third Thursday of each month for old New Leftists and feminists to talk about What To Do Now. The abortion situation was heating up; it really looked bad for one of feminism's most concrete victories, *Roe v. Wade*. And no one seemed to care; there was a war on.

In this situation one would expect Ellen Willis, one of the great, original voices, one of the founders of the modern Women's Liberation Movement, to say what she had always said: that abortion was key to our struggle, that without abortion there is no freedom and sexual pleasure is threatened, that freedom and pleasure are what we should want and what politics should be about. In 1977, when the Hyde Amendment cut off funding for abortion, hadn't we founded No More Nice Girls to say just that? Rather than trudge around in a circle downhearted, we made our demonstrations theatrical and flamboyant, facing down signs on the other side that said "Abortion is Murder" with our own message: "Sex for Fun."

What Ellen actually said that evening was that, in spite of all our efforts to keep the subject sexy and edgy, abortion wasn't an exciting or useful starting point for radicals anymore. Liberal feminists had taken it over and disassociated abortion from sexual freedom, apologizing for this awful need women sometimes have. At the same time, left-wing feminists had buried abortion inside "reproductive rights" campaigns that were as much about health and having children as about that stigmatized, nasty thing, abortion. Besides, Ellen said, we're on the defensive now, trying to protect a right, which can never be like fighting for something new that you urgently want. Backlash, she said, has mired feminism in ambivalence. How can you raise issues of sexual freedom through feminism in this compromised, self-deprecating condition?

Ever the critic of everything, she turned on herself: I usually say the left refused to take the culture wars seriously and that this is a serious mistake. But I, too, want us to turn our attention from this particular piece of the cultural wars, abortion. The New Right has cornered the market on passion about this one; let's do something else, something new to raise the issue of sexual freedom. The passion we can claim at this moment is internationalism. People are not used to the idea that women's rights are key to international affairs, but sexual repression is a basic element in religious totalitarianism. The feminist demand for sexual freedom could enter here. Here is a place for a feminist politics where we can talk about the fear of sexual freedom as a force in current world affairs.

Some in the room were stunned. Abandon abortion at home for international culture wars about sex? Yes, yes. Because Ellen was always moving beyond what we were currently saying and beyond herself. She was unpredictable because she was always seeking the burning tip, the place where political life is alive with desire, and that place is always changing. She had proposed at a left conference that fear of sex was a central motive for the bombing of the Twin Towers, and some had tittered. Surely, the great Ellen Willis had gone over the edge—or was she joking? She was always disappointed when the left refused to take psychology, and particularly sexuality, seriously. She was always seeking to keep radical ideas about freedom and pleasure alive and moving in the world.

For me, and for so many others, Ellen's intellectual leadership has been formative, central, enduring. As a political comrade, she was cranky and skeptical, and I did my political work while woven into a constant conversation—argument with her for thirty years. She threw light on absolutely everything. When she edited our writing, she pulled from us a kind of clarity about what we wanted to say and do that we now have to hope will last us our lifetimes—lifetimes we expected to lead in her luminous company.

Part II

Humanism and Terror

The late Ellen Willis, along with her domestic partner, Stanley Aronowitz, put up half the money for the first *First*, even though she was ambivalent about our crew's less than reverent attitude toward the cultural politics of many of her former colleagues at the *Village Voice*. Having said her own goodbye to all that in the early '90s, this originary radical feminist and New Journalist didn't want outside readers to conflate her own way of thinking through recent history with anyone else's.

Still, she realized there were things we carried in common. In the spring of 2006, when Ellen was battling the cancer that would take her life later that year, she emailed to say *First*'s pieces by O'Brien and Fredric Smoler on the Danish Cartoon Controversy were "good." (That was high praise from Ellen whose mode of approbation was the opposite of American idolaters.) Struck by how much those pieces "echoed themes" in what she'd written at the time of the Rushdie affair, she wondered if we "might be interested in reprinting the editorial I wrote in the *Voice* as a historical affirmation of the bad road we are going down...." The piece of the past that Ellen thought belonged in *First* lies at the heart of next section, which maps that road and proposes ways out.

Flayed

Nat Finkelstein

I first sailed to Tangiers in 1964, aboard a Kaiser-built concrete poured World War II Liberty ship operated by the Yugolinia line. From New York at 99 dollars for the passage: The Beatnik Express.

My lady friend and I rented a terraced apartment overlooking the northern end of Avenue de Mohamed V, a bit away from the expat/Zocco Chico beatnik set. Every day I would stroll a mile down tree-shaded trees through the European Sector, to the Café Paris to quaff a Citron, while observing the street action passing and learning the body language and pattern of sounds. Livin' the life, like Papa Hemingway doin' the Ol' Boul' Mich. I would then head for the Zocco Chico and the Café Central, to suck some Kif and mint tea with Little Mohammed, a young poet who was into Haiku. He had a cough, so we called him Consumptive Mohammed.

At the end of the day, I would stroll back home, enjoying the sights and sounds.

One day, while walking past a deserted stretch of road, I heard several loud, sustained screams: a child in severe pain. I rushed toward the sound and came upon four Moroccan young men, who having captured a hedgehog, were slowly, very slowly, skinning it while still alive. I wasn't a hero—I saw four guys with knives.

The next day I asked Paul Bowles what I should have done: yell, scream, what, WHY? Paul told me that the Moroccans most likely had captured the hedgehog for food and were dismembering it alive for fun. He then told me the legend of the Treasure of Banu Nadir, as described in the Sirat Rasul Allah, the oldest known biography of Mohammed, written by Ibn Isbaq in the eighth century. It seems that the Jewish guardian of the treasure, Kinana, was brought before Mohammed, but refused to divulge the treasure's location. Mohammed ordered Zubayn Al Awwam: "Torture him until you extract what he has." Burning coals were placed on Kinana's chest until he gave it up. After that, Mohammed chopped off Kinana's head.

The next time I arrived in Tangiers was for a few days in 1965. I heard that One-Eyed Moe the Englishman had been busted with a gun. The Moroccans, at that time preparing for war with the newly liberated Algerians, were more interested in placing the blame on one of their own citizens than on the American who had actually sold the gun. They hung Moe by his heels, beat him across the ankles and forced water down his gullet until he named a young Moroccan poet—"Consumptive Mohammed"—as the supplier. Before he died in police custody, Mohammed the poet confessed to being an Algerian agent. I was never certain about Moe's version until….

The last time I went to Morocco was 1975. I went with my then wife, Jill, and our two-year-old son, Gustave-Che, who had Down's Syndrome and was sickly. We shared a bungalow in a small beach resort south of el-Jadida with a couple of Canadians. Jill and I spent our time traveling to Marrakech and surrounding towns, where we purchased fossil imbedded marble tables and built the specialized crates needed to ship marble. We noticed that we seemed to be followed, and kept on seeing the same loiterer in every town we visited. We ascribed it to either racism or paranoia.

One day we picked up a friend at Casablanca Airport, had dinner and arrived home after dark.

They came in five cars, about ten of them. They parked about twenty meters or so from our house and pulled submachine guns from out of their back seats, charged up the hill to our house, pounded open the door and chambered their weapons.

I WILL STOP MY NARRATIVE AND STATE THAT FROM HERE ON, GUILT OR INNOCENCE IS NOT THE ISSUE. TREATMENT IS.

They leveled their guns at each of us and identified themselves as *Surete*. Jill pleaded with them to stop pointing their guns at our son, Gustave. I said to the captain: "There are no weapons here. We will not resist you." He signaled, and they lowered their weapons and frisked us. They found a small piece of hash in Jill's pocket and announced that we were all under arrest. They commenced to search the house, our quarters first. They were quite methodical and careful not to damage our collection of 17th-century Tibetan Statuary (which later disappeared). They found nothing. There was nothing there. They searched our housemates' quarters and found four pounds of hash. They told me that I was responsible and transported us off to the gendarmerie.

AT THIS POINT I WILL STATE THAT DUE TO THIRTY YEARS OF DISTANCE AND POST-TRAUMATIC STRESS, SOME OF MY DETAILS MAY NOT BE IN ORDER: MY FACTS ARE. SO, I MAY SKIP SOME DETAILS, BUT HERE ARE FACTS.

They threaten you with pain such as you never have felt before. They separate you from your companions, and throw you into an underground dungeon, and tie you face to face with a leper. That's to soften you.

Obligatory whacks across the back of your head (s.o.p). They let you know that this will be rough: that you will be hurt. You decide to adopt a strategy because what they tell you, human beings don't do to other human beings. You call their bluff, and then a pig in a uniform asks a question and you don't answer.... AND THE CURTAIN GOES DOWN *BLACK*. AND YOU GET A TASTE OF COPPER IN YOU MOUTH AND THE TASTE OF BLOOD AND PURPLE AND BLUE FLASHES CUT ACROSS YOUR SCREEN AND YOU HEAR SOMEONE SCREAM SCREAM *SCREAM* ... SOMEWHERE IN THE DISTANCE GETTING CLOSER AND CLOSER AND IT'S YOU.

Because they have stripped you buck naked, hung you upside down on a pole, wet you, hooked you up to a hand cranked generator by your ears and jolted your reality into one of pure pain. So, you change the strategy 'cause the last one didn't work so good.

The French used imported Moroccans to serve as torturers in Algeria. The two main procedures were L'Avion (what I just described), and Fallakah, in which the subject is hung upside down from a pole and beaten across the ankles with a truck fan belt wrapped around with copper wires (this is standard procedure for natives).

During the ten or fourteen days I spent in the gendarmerie, I underwent electric shock four times, and I lost the use of two toes when a pig climbed to the top of a desk and jumped on my bared foot. I was told that my son had died. I was taken into a clearing at night with a gun pointed at me and told to dig my grave. They kept on cursing at me in Hebrew hoping that I would respond and prove their thesis that all Jews are Israeli spies.

I could recount more of what I saw while in jail there (of course I confessed—everybody does). The Political whose eyeballs had turned backwards or the Political who went deaf. But I'll stop here. I'm sorry to have shared my pain with you, but it's about fuckin' time.

Hedgehogs, humans and Jews—it's all the same to them. In a culture where being right is the same as having the right, all who oppose them are meat.

Bliss

Charles O'Brien

Excerpted from a 2004 analysis of (what the author termed) "the foreswearing of argument" by those who equate criticism of Arab cultures with "ignorance" and/or "orientalism."

Some months back, Joan Didion published a truly regrettable essay in the *New York Review of Books*. It has now been published as a *book*. On page 12 at the back, Didion quotes a Steven Weber, who says, in part,

> The first thing you noticed was in the bookstores. On September 12, the shelves of books on Islam, on American foreign policy, or Iraq, on Afghanistan. There was a substantive discussion about what it is about the nature of American presence in the world that created a situation in which movements like al-Quaeda can thrive and prosper. I thought that was a very promising sign.

> But that discussion got short-circuited. Sometime in late October, early November 2001, the tone of that discussion switched, and it became: What's wrong with the

Islamic world that it failed to produce democracy, science, education, its own enlightenment, and created societies that breed terror?

And Didion herself attests, "Most of us saw that discussion short-
circuited."

Three things, then: books were sold, there was a discussion, there
was a switch. That books were sold and that there would be discussion
after September 11 were matters of course. Whether there would be a
"switch" and what that switch would be would depend on how much
the word "discussion" would have to carry. Well, quite a bit, and Didion
comes prepared. Weber could talk about bookstores and conversations
in New York because he was there. Anyone in that time and place could.
But Steven Weber, says Didion, is so much more:

> A member of [U.C. Berkeley]'s political science faculty, Steven Weber, who is the
> Director of the MacArthur Program on Multilateral Governance at Berkeley's Institute
> of International Studies, and a consultant on risk analysis to both the State Department
> and such private-sector firms as Shell Oil.

How could it not be true? Look again at the "switch" though...

> What's wrong with the Islamic world that it failed to produce democracy, science,
> education, its own Enlightenment, and created societies that bred terror.

"What's wrong," after all, is an impermissible enquiry when ...
everything's fine! But there *are* problems in the Arab Muhammadan
world and there are many questions that need asking. What are the
prospects for democracy in the Arab world? In Iraq, it once existed, but
it was brief, and fragile. In Lebanon, it existed, as long as a non-Arab,
non-Mohammadan ethnic group was dominant. In Algeria, it elected
the F.I.S. Elsewhere, nothing. And science? The next Nobel laureates
in physics and chemistry could very well be Arabs, but not if they
work in Arab countries. Education? Don't even mention Saudi-funded
madrassas (themselves substitutes for the inadequate schools run by
various governments) or the schools run by the P.A. What institutions
of higher education would Weber recommend? Not even, one suspects,
the American University in Beirut. In place of enlightenment, there is
a deeper obscurantism. And as to the "breeding of terror:" that was the
very reason for the "discussion."

The questions Weber objects to are all reasonable points, all pertinent,
all definitive of what the "discussion" was *not*. Didion herself goes on
to discuss the "discussion," and that will have to fend for itself. Weber,
in this excerpt, does not. No need. "Discussion" is the *ignorance* trope.
"Discussion" is the arduous voyage to where-I-am. It begins with the

reading of a book and continues with, really, the first thinking the Discussers have done.

How, though, does the reading of books lead to this discussion? Books on Islam, on Afghanistan, and so on sold in great numbers just after September 11. And sure, it's good to read books. But let's hypothesize another Steven Weber somewhere. This Steven Weber has a job that requires him to wear a "Steve" nametag. He has read exactly no books on Islam, on Afghanistan, on American foreign policy, on Iraq. It's not incuriosity, just other interests, need-to-know, and a wariness that much of what is available will only frustrate: who to believe? Still, if he has good sense and some knowledge of the world (as most people do), and he applies them, he will (a) know that certain things he simply doesn't know and so can't form a reasoned opinion on them; (b) have a pretty good idea of which factual claims are too implausible to be true; and (c) spot a faulty argument. As long as he *works* round what he doesn't know, he may get quite a lot right. The truly lost cause is the one who says, "I read a book about this." Shortly after September 11, on Canal Street, with the smoke from the Twin Towers overhead, the air hard to breathe, a heavy military presence, strict checkpoints, I saw an earnest type hurrying along by Church and Canal holding the *Howard Zinn Reader*. About the same time, I saw another earnest type on the subway reading Edward Said's *The Question of Palestine*. Two discussants! But what, one wonders, were they getting out of these books? Isn't it pretty likely that they were taking the scrubbing brush to the smut that had just landed on their picture of the world? Their reading, was it effort at all, or the refusal of effort?

Not long after September 11, there was an item in the *New York Times* about recent book-buying in the city. It was mentioned that books about such things as Islam, Afghanistan, American foreign policy, Iraq were all moving units: but that was not news, not interesting, and not what needed an Institute of International Studies-MacArthur-State Department-Shell Oil expert to report. The item's *news* was that a range of books was selling that suited a new emotional weather. Books about war in general—the *Iliad*; for example—had become best-sellers; and women and men were reading these books in equal numbers. Compare. That earnest soul on Canal Street with the Zinn in the crook of his arm was doing his homework, taking his part in the Discussion. And was he not using the Discussion to filter out everything around him? And the women with the *Iliad* was learning nothing directly about ... Islam, Afghanistan, America foreign policy, Iraq. But she was trying it out, learning what was in herself, and in the world.

Before the War

Ellen Willis

This piece first appeared in 1989 in the Village Voice. *It was reprinted in* First of the Month *in 2007.*

Make no mistake: Ayatollah Khomeini's call for Salman Rushdie's execution is not simply a piece of lunatic demagogy directed at an individual, but a serious act of political intimidation with far-reaching consequences. The Iranian head of state has declared war—quite literally—on Western secular, democratic institutions. He has rallied his international troops in his most daring bid yet to extend the power of Islamic theocracy beyond his own country, even beyond the Moslem world, by force. Do the people and the governments supposedly committed to democratic values have the will to fight back?

Already Khomeini has won a few battles. Rushdie can hardly be blamed for going into hiding, and perhaps it's too much to expect of his publishers that they go on with his book tour as a protest, with a video or audio tape of Rushdie taking his place. But Viking's craven statement that they never intended to offend anyone by publishing Rushdie's book and "very much regret the distress the book has caused" is inexcusable. So is the action of the Waldenbooks, the country's largest books chain in taking *Satanic Verses* off the shelves. (As the company's executive vice president, Bonnie Predd, sententiously put it: "We've fought long and hard against censorship. But when it comes to the safety of our employees, one sometimes has to compromise." (How about simply offering any nervous employee a few days off?) In France, Presses de la Cite, Rushdie's publisher, has "postponed" publication of the French edition (you remember France, home of Voltaire, but more recently the drug company that tried to scuttle the abortifacient RU 486 under pressure from anti-abortion activists). Nor will the West German house Keipenheuer and Witsch publish Rushdie's book as scheduled.

There is no indication that the world's governments are taking Khomeini's move as seriously as it deserves. Britain has made the strongest statement, which nonetheless falls short of declaring that officially putting a price on the head of a British author exercising the right to free speech in his own country is an act of war against Britain and will be viewed as such. The United States has confined itself to a routine condemnation of terrorism. Canada gets the prize for moral oafishness. Revenue Canada, a government customs and taxation agency, has temporarily banned further imports of the Rushdie book, pending an investigation of the possibility that it contains "hate literature" (the ban was announced the first day of Canada's National Freedom to Read Week). Will Britain, the U.S., or anyone else move to bring this issue before the United Nations? If they do, is there any chance the UN will vote for meaningful sanctions against Iran? And if not, will those Western nations that call themselves democracies get together to impose sanctions on their own? The last two questions are, I'm afraid, rhetorical.

The attack on Rushdie and the anemic response to it are not occurring in a vacuum. Democratic secularism is increasingly vulnerable to a religious fundamentalism that in all its forms—Christian, and Jewish as well as Islamic—is increasingly feeling its power. And Western governments, far from resisting anti-democratic absolutism, have been abetting it. The Thatcher government has enthusiastically pursued its own censorship of books and other media. The U.S. has, of course, been in bed with fundamentalist Christianity since the election of Jimmy Carter. The Reagan administration never got too exercised about violent attacks on abortion clinics, refusing to include them in its antiterrorist rhetoric, the political climate surrounding abortion has become so intimidating that no American drug company has been willing to test RU 486, much less market it. Our government also supports, on the grounds of the right to freedom and self-determination, the fundamentalist guerrillas in Afghanistan, who—if, as now seems likely, they end up in power—may make Khomeini look mellow. Is there anything left of the West's loudly proclaimed commitment to freedom that goes beyond such ironies? More and more that question, too, begins to seem rhetorical.

Stop Breaking Down

Fredric Smoler

One of the Danish cartoons which my local newspaper has refused to print shows two veiled women, their staring round eyes, all that can be seen of their faces, expressing alarm, while a bearded man, apparently the Prophet, with a bar obscuring his eyes, his features otherwise visible, radiates a chilling and furious certainty. It is a pretty good cartoon: it raises the question of who is blinded, and to what, and who has been silenced, and how. It does this with remarkable economy, and with compassionate if mirthless wit. As economical if mirthless jokes go, it isn't a patch on the one represented by the editors, academics and politicians who claim that reproducing that cartoon is a mistake more or less equivalent to threatening to murder whoever drew it.

This claim generally involves what someone once called the Mucius Scaevola school of argument—there is an awful lot of on the one hand, on the other hand. On the one hand, bad to provoke and offend, on the other, bad to threaten murder and commit arson, to seek to destroy liberty of expression, to impose one's taboos on everyone, everywhere, with threats of massive violence. Sometimes the claim is not so even-handed: the recklessness and cruelty of the first act was frivolous and inexcusably stupid, whereas the second act was moved by powerful principle and honest moral passion. In the *New York Times*, the reliably contemptible Stanley Fish opined that insofar as a commitment to free speech, "an abstract principle," is a moral commitment, one that differs from the sterner morality of those who wish to murder heretics and blasphemers, "the difference … is to the credit of the Muslim protesters and to the discredit of the liberal editors."

It is not always clear—it is rarely clear—precisely what Fish is arguing; the sneering itself usually seems to be the point. In the *Guardian*, Ronald Dworkin argued that "The British media were right, on balance, not to republish the Danish cartoons … the public does not have a right to read or see whatever it wants no matter what the cost.…" But Dworkin boldly alleges that it would be improper for a government to suppress the republication of the cartoons: we have a right to see them. It is not wholly clear how we are to exercise these rights when editors, in Dworkin's view prudently, bend to the threats of murderous mobs, but an ability to consider things separately when they are inextricably connected is the wag's definition of the legal mind.

Fish, hilariously, is a professor of law, as is, less hilariously, Dworkin. The *New York Times* and the *Guardian* are newspapers. The Chinese, who possess neither academic freedom, nor a free press, nor the rule of law, nonetheless possess a useful proverb: never smash your own rice bowl.

Weapons of Criticism, Criticism of Weapons

Charles O'Brien

Most times, the words, *he's got a gun*, will redirect the conversation pretty effectively. Not this time, it appears.

The uproar over the *Jyllands-Posten*'s cartoons of Muhammad has been framed as a free speech issue. The real issue is force. People have recalled the Salman Rushdie fatwa, from almost twenty years ago, and it's worth recalling. Since Rushdie is still alive, many people think the fatwa never went beyond threat. But Ruhollah Khomeini's death sentence extended to all those "involved in [*Satanic Verses'*] publication who were aware of its content." The translators and others connected with the book who were killed all over the world were not killed as spillover, misunderstanding, rogue operations, frustration. These killings were exactly what the supreme lawgiver for the Islamic Republic of Iran had ordered. The Rushdie fatwa was not a free-speech question. An Iranian in Iran shot for blasphemy by the government of Iran is a free-speech issue. A Salman Rushdie sent to prison under Tony Blair's proposed blasphemy law, recently defeated by a hair, is a free-speech issue. The Rushdie fatwa was about sovereignty. Do subjects of the United Kingdom, resident there, get to live under the U.K.'s laws? Hundreds of millions answered no. To sentence a novelist, of all things, to death for a book you haven't even read will strike us as *small*. In truth, the enemy was thinking big. And the enemy still stands uncorrected. People were killed because of the fatwa, that assertion of dominance over the entire world. Most of the dead, you'd think, would be Iranian officials. Their death toll stands at zero.

The earlier hostage crisis also involved a question of sovereignty. The exiled Shah was dying of cancer and was admitted to the United States for treatment. The new Iranian order was sure that there was a plot to restore the Shah, and so the American embassy was seized, and its staff kidnapped. It would have been prudent for the United States to say before the world,

> There is no plot. It is as we say. We have no interest in restoring the Shah—we just got through ushering him out—and he's too far gone for political aspirations. You may ask that he be extradited, but we, like every other country, will say no. He—or anyone—may face justice, but not in your Iran. He is here with our permission. Borders define countries. We, and not you, control our borders. Deny that, and you deny our sovereignty, you deny our right to a national existence. You are arrogant. You are intolerable. In the name of not only America, but all humanity, we will cut off this "Islamic Republic," this chimera, at its birth.

It didn't happen. Instead, the Shah left his American hospital—better for everybody, it was supposed—bounced briefly around among countries, and was soon dead. Iran, with its trademark absurdity, said, "The death of the Shah changes nothing," and continued to threaten the hostages with death. The fact that Iran had gone to war against the United States and was in occupation of American soil was overlooked. The hostages' release was bought, and the embassy building abandoned to the enemy.

In war, soldiers taken prisoner are counted as casualties. It is expected that they will be protected by the applicable conventions. If they are not, any feasible attempt at rescue should be made, and failing that, the captors should be hunted down, at the end of hostilities, and killed. The lives of protected persons are not legitimate counters for the enemy's political purposes. Iran's atrocity was rewarded. And it paid no price, as it paid no price for the Rushdie affair.

Salman Rushdie was taken unawares. He was an adept of the Standard International Style. His writing was *ordinarily* transgressive—and then *this*. He had every right to wonder, with Nancy Kerrigan, "Why me?" The fatwa looked then like singularly bad luck. And where are we today? The Rushdie oddity has become the general rule. The sword is over everyone's head. At the Durban Conference, the week leading up to 9/11, a sign held up by a participant said, ISLAM WILL DOMINATE THE EARTH. Will?, you wonder, how'd that weasely word get in there? (And then you realize, ah, this was a moderate Muslim.)

It's not helpful to see the cartoons as just free speech, although they're also that. Some—few—have championed them as free speech. (Honor to the staff of *New York Press*, who walked out as a group in solidarity with the Danish cartoonists.) Others have been grudging—"They're not very good cartoons." (How many political cartoons are good?) But often, the talk has been of "provocation," "offensiveness," "responsibility," "lit matches." Bill Clinton—in Qatar!—called the cartoons "appalling" and "totally outrageous." I write what I like? Not this day and time.

Let me add my two cents of criticism. Here's how the cartoons came to be commissioned. A children's book, a biography of Muhammad, was written by a Danish author, Kaare Bluitgen. He wanted pictures for this children's book. Nobody could be found to do it. In a Europe so noisily proud of not having a death penalty, illustrators went in fear of their lives. Since the cartoon news has broken, we have seen that, for instance, pictures of Muhammad do exist, pretty uncontroversially, done by Muhammadan hands, and the twelve Danish cartoons were published without comment a few months ago in an Egyptian newspaper. It is not qur'anically forbidden to portray Muhammad.[1] For Europeans, and probably for Americans too, it is a capital offense. The sword is out, and there is blood on it. Against this regime of terror, with bodies piling up regularly, *Jyllands-Posten* commissioned a page of cartoons. Here, then, is my criticism: the cartoons are, for their purpose, inadequate. It's not the cartoonists' fault—they have no armies, and their call for support has gone largely unanswered. And apart from the nine deaths the cartoon war has—so far—produced, there are many people in Europe either in hiding or under heavy guard.

Blogger Hugh Hewitt, enamored of expediency as any Leninist, has condemned the cartoons. They are distinctly *unhelpful*. Where do they leave a Musharraf? Well, first, Musharraf is our "ally" only faute de mieux. Second, Musharraf had to be threatened into cooperation after 9/11, and any putatively worse alternative to Musharraf would be subject to Bush's refusal to take no for an answer. And third, how does a Western hard line hurt Musharraf's position? The plug uglies in Pakistan who want to take over have an idea of the world, that to yell a lot is to get your way. In the long run, that isn't true. Musharraf knows that, but to convince them, he could use evidence, facts in the ground. Those who have so heedlessly drawn the sword should be shown, and quickly, the unfunny things that happen in the final panel.

Note

1.   To gauge the "pain" and "outrage" caused by the portrayals of the "Prophet," we should recall Mel Gibson"s *The Passion of the Christ*. Before the movie could be shown in the Gulf States, it had to get past the censors. The problem was that it portrayed a prophet on screen. Such a portrayal is deemed *shirk*, kin to idolatry and polytheism. But if a film might add to the store of Jew-hatred in the world, what's a little polytheism? When the lights went down, the idol stayed in the picture. The justification offered was not the struggle against Zionism, but—free speech!

And of course, the notion of Jesus as one among the prophets strikes Christians as heretical at best, and the notion of Jesus as precursor to Muhammad is repugnant to them. But objections—let alone noisy demonstrations, burnings, lynchings—would be *unseemly*.

With Friends Like These

Benj DeMott

Victor Navasky wrote a letter of objection to First *after this piece was posted online at Firstofthemonth.org in 2005. His plaint and my response follow this article.*

In the midst of *A Matter of Opinion*—Victor Navasky's affable account of his professional life in journalism—*The Nation*'s publisher tells a tale about a libel settlement that dishonors a smart set who have trashed efforts to mobilize resistance to the Muslim World's Ku Klux Klan.

Navasky, though doesn't seem to recognize he's revealed the worst about some of his magazine's "best friends." His no regrets pose and narrow focus on process (legal and otherwise) make you wonder about his ethics. But this isn't personal. The deals at the heart of *A Matter of Opinion* are everyone's business. If you want to help stop the bleeding from the War on Terror you need to be on Navasky's case.

His pre-legal war story begins back in 1993 when he agreed to publish an excerpt from Kanan Makiya's *Cruelty and Silence*. Makiya's first book, *Republic of Fear* (1989), had called attention to the horrors of Saddam Hussein's Baathist regime before the Gulf War (and before Iraq invaded Kuwait). *Cruelty and Silence* confronted the broad realities of tyranny in the Middle East and exposed the failure of Arab (and "pro-Arab") intellectuals to condemn the slaughter of innocents.

The Nation excerpt placed Middle Eastern women inside "landscapes of cruelty of silence," citing instances of state-sponsored rape and honor killings. Navasky doesn't remark on the continuing relevance of Makiya's perspective at a time when Janjaweed militias employ rape as a genocidal technique in Darfur and Shiite extremists execute prostitutes in Iraq, but he credits Makiya with "powerful reporting and analysis."

Too powerful for at least one of Navasky's *Nation* colleagues who alerted Edward Said—"the preeminent Palestinian intellectual in the West, *The Nation*'s opera critic and a friend of so many of my friends that I thought of him as a friend myself." Said called Navasksy to urge him to kill the piece claiming Makiya was a "mischief-maker" who wrote "false (and libelous) things about Arab intellectuals, including not least Said himself."

Navasky acknowledges it wasn't "ideal" to have an (unnamed) *Nation* colleague collaborating with Said in an effort to suppress Makiya's piece, but he's too easy on these would-be cultural commissars. And his ease gets harder to take when he provides the back-story of his own relationship with "Edward." (Navasky, by the way, is never on a first name basis with that mischief-maker "Makiya.")

Back in 1981, Navasky had the sort of inspiration that justifies an editor's existence. Aware that Israel was a relatively open society with an active Peace Now constituency, Navasky realized he should encourage Palestinians to explore Gandhian modes of non-violent resistance, "substituting civil disobedience for terrorism." He also recognized (as a "New York Jew") he couldn't issue the necessary call for non-violence: "It needed a Palestinian, someone with the stature, prestige, credentials and intellect of a Said." So Navasky raised the subject with Said who was skeptical at first, asserting civil disobedience by Palestinians hadn't been effective in the past. Navasky emphasized he wasn't talking up any one tactic but calling for a non-violent movement: "Edward liked the idea and we went our separate ways."

A few weeks later, Navasky received an article on Israel/Palestine/America from Said that was "learned, nuanced, contextual, combative, and persuasive." But: "The clarion call for civil disobedience, for passive resistance, for Gandhian nonviolence was nowhere to be found." When Navasky "gently" asked why Said had put aside their original idea, he responded:

"Didn't you read the piece?" he asked with genuine puzzlement. "It's all there on page 8."

Said had written a sentence that might be read (by those familiar with the rhetoric of Palestinian officials) to mean he was ready to accept the existence of the State of Israel. But the notion of a Palestinian protest movement dedicated to civil disobedience, in Navasky's words, "got lost in the shuffle." (Over the years, close readers got used to that Said—"the time for speaking clearly has come"—shuffle.) No one could complain if Said had acknowledged that he wasn't ready to call for non-violence. After all, that might have been a dangerous thing for a prominent Palestinian to do (as Navasky notes). But Said's claim it was "all there on page 8" defines intellectual dishonesty.

Though not to Navasky who leaves it at: "So much for my brilliant idea." And then rushes to his next brush with celeb-intellects—"Now, 12 years later Edward was calling about Makiya." Maybe Navasky is in a rush to avoid judging the actions of his late Palestinian friend. But even if forbearance lies beneath the slick surface, his segues are bound to set off bullshit detectors.

Navasky recalls how he laid it on thick as he explained to Said why it would be "inappropriate for us to quash [Makiya's piece] as a favor to a cherished friend of the magazine (which I told him I knew was not what he was asking for)." Though, of course, that was precisely what Said was asking for. Navasky assured Said *The Nation* excerpt from *Cruelty and Silence* wouldn't focus on Arab intellectuals and warned that killing the piece would lead to a "minor" scandal that would "embarrass everyone involved:" "Edward took the point."

Navasky's remembrance of his own finesse is less than winning. Especially since he ends up conceding he asked Said to recommend reviewers for *Cruelty and Silence* though the man had announced his bias against Makiya's work. Said proposed (among others) one of his very best friends, Eqbal Ahmad. Navasky's narrative gets twisty (and windy) as he tells how Ahmad got the gig.

> I would like to be able to confess that the fix was in. It wasn't. Elsa Dixler, who very much has a mind of her own, invited Eqbal Ahmad to review Makiya's book, not because his name was on the list I passed on to her (it was) …

Eqbal, who was a friend of the magazine and of mine personally, was an anti-war visionary Pakistani radical ... one of those rare scholar-activists who brought his own global vision and original perspective to any issue he tackled. I always learned something new from Eqbal's writings. And when Elsa mentioned to me that Eqbal would be reviewing Makiya, I thought I could predict more or less what he would say.

Navasky's puffery ("visionary ... who brought his own global vision") and compactions of self-contradiction ("It wasn't"/"it was"—"I always learned something new from Eqbal"/"I could predict more or less what he would say") belong to the discourse of modified, limited hang-out. And the contradictions keep coming. Navasky expected Ahmad would defend Said while allowing Makiya was right to argue Arab intellectuals (especially those in the West) ought to speak truth to power. Instead Navasky's "visionary" turned in a "hatchet job." Ahmad insisted Makiya's case against state terror in the Middle East was worthless and "took a swipe" at *The Nation* for publishing an excerpt from a book that "treats documents carelessly." Ahmad upped the ante by suggesting one of Makiya's key sources was under investigation for embezzling billions of dollars.

But Ahmad misidentified that individual who threatened to sue *The Nation* once the review was published. Navasksy was forced to publish a correction and settle the case before it went to court. While he was trying to beat this potential libel charge by offering evidence of *The Nation*'s "lack of malice," Ahmad ("friend of the magazine") proved to be full of himself:

[Eqbal] refused to believe there was more than one al-Sabah: "The man's a liar," he insisted. "It will make me very unhappy that I had any dealings with *The Nation* if you print a 'correction' of any sort." ...

I explained that our libel insurance policy included a $50,000 deductible and the magazine couldn't afford it. Eqbal offered to indemnify the magazine—anything in order not to allow this "liar" to win....

Over Eqbal's vociferous objections, he argued it was Makiya's responsibility to prove his friend wasn't an embezzler [!], we published a correction.

Navasky elaborates on how *The Nation* came to make this correction (just as he goes on about how he handled Said's censoriousness), but he misses the import of his own story. His account of his friends' behavior bolsters Makiya's critique of their circle of "pro-Arab," "anti-imperialist" intellectuals—that "community of conscience and understanding" tenderly invoked by Said in a commentary on 9/11 in *The London Review of Books*.

It's instructive to compare Said's response to 9/11 with Makiya's. Said opened his *LRB* piece by noting the aftermath had been an "unpleasant time" for Muslim and Arab-Americans. After focusing on "the palpable air of hatred directed against the group as a whole," he allowed "official bellicosity" against Arabs and Muslim had "slowly diminished" in America—"catastrophe and backlash" preceded "backtrack" in his interpretation. He concluded that "long-term hope" rested on dissenters' capacity to spark a "decent reconsideration" that might lead eventually to "changed policies on Palestine, or a less crazy defence budget, or more enlightened environmental attitudes."

Makiya called for a different sort of "reconsideration":

> As I wrote in *Cruelty and Silence*, citing the 1930s Iraqi alter ego of Tom Lehrer, Aziz Ali, Da' illi beena, minna wa feena: "The disease that is in us, is from us and within us" ... Muslims and Arabs have to be on the front lines of a new kind of war, one that is worth waging for their own salvation and in their own souls. And that, as good out-of-fashion Muslim scholars will tell you, is the true meaning of jihad, a meaning that has been hijacked by terrorists and suicide bombers and all those who applaud or find excuses for them. To exorcise what they have done in our name is the civilisational challenge of the twenty-first century for every Arab and Muslim in the world today.

Makiya backs up his talk. Based in Baghdad, he heads The Iraq Memory Foundation—the most comprehensive archive of Saddam's crimes. Makiya's Foundation is digitalizing its extensive records to enable Iraqi citizens to find out for themselves all the information available on those who were disappeared by the Baath Party between 1968-2003. Intent on reaching the next generation of Iraqis, Makiya wants to ensure the murderous history of Baathism becomes a central part of the curriculum in Iraq's schools. His Foundation will help shape a new Iraqi sense of national identity:

> Identity is Memory. And Memory is Identity. People whose identities are cobbled together from half-truths, or from distorted memories of who is to blame and who is blameless, are prone to commit new transgressions.

The Iraq Memory Foundation aims to teach each ethnic and confessional groups in Iraq that Saddam's regime committed crimes not just against their kind, but against all Iraqis and against humanity. It seeks to sublate the psychology of the blood feud; to model an alternative to the mentality of our terrorist enemies. As Emrys Peters, anthropologist of the Bedouin feud has written, the feud is eternal.[1] And the War on Terror will go on until the will-to-kill-and-be-killed is exorcized from within.

Makiya and the other Arab and Muslim humanists who have taken up his "civilizational challenge" ought to be embraced by anyone who longs for an end to the War on Terror. But the heart of *A Matter of Opinion* hints friends of *The Nation* are more likely to slander Makiya than support his radical history project. Navasky's revelations are a symptom of a larger moral failure on the Left that Brit journalist Nick Cohen has nailed:

> What we have witnessed is a sinister attempt by liberal opinion to deny legitimacy to the very liberals, feminists and socialists who have a right to expect support. The authentic Muslim has become the blood-crazed fanatic rather than the reformer. The authentic liberator has become the fascist rather than the democrat. This is a betrayal on an epic scale which casts doubt on whether it is possible now to have a decent left.

Cohen made his statement as he was explaining why he's signed a petition against terrorism that began circulating on the Internet after the London bombings (http://www.unite-against-terror.com/). Other signers include Kanan Makiya and Omar (of the Iraq the Model website)—the Sunni Muslim who has been the strongest voice of Iraqi democrats in the blogosphere. No friends of *The Nation* have signed the petition yet. I don't believe Edward Said or Eqbal Ahmad would if they were still here because the statement accompanying the petition explicitly rejects the notion that terrorist violence is a response by Muslims to injustices perpetrated upon them by the West. Perhaps Victor Navasky will take the lead here, picking up on the inspiration that moved him back in the day to imagine a humane future for Palestinians (and Israelis).

But I wouldn't bet on that. Navasky seems stuck on the notion the Said/Ahmad/Makiya episode in *A Matter of Opinion* counts because *The Nation* had to pay somebody some money. When David Frum asked him about it on a CNN book-chat show, Navasky even denied it was an error to have Ahmad review *Cruelty and Silence*. Going back on his first interpretation, he insisted the only "mistake" was *The Nation* "ended up running through our libel insurance policy."

Such bottom-lines probably help him connect with a certain class of people who are certainly a presence in *A Matter of Opinion* (which might be retitled—*Meetings with Remarkable Rich Men*). They like Vic because he's not a prick. But also because his lite-righteous tone and esteem for authority ("stature, prestige, credentials and intellect") meld with their own way-of-dealing-in-the-world. A passage from a dreamy review of *A Matter of Opinion* (in *The Common Reader*) is on point here. The reviewer (another friend of Navasky) offers this story to explain why *The Nation* matters:

> *The Nation* had sent two young journalists to South Africa to report on apartheid. I asked if I might bring someone from GM to meet them. The head of public relations

at GM was John W. McNulty, former fundraiser for New York's Lincoln Center project, speechwriter for Lyndon Johnson, and friend of Bill Moyers. McNulty, the executive vice president, the general counsel of the corporation, and I went to the offices of the *Nation* to listen to the young journalists. On the way back to midtown Manhattan, the general counsel said to McNulty, "Jack, we have to get out. You have to tell Roger [B. Smith]."[2]

"Me?" said Jack. "You're the general counsel, you should tell him."

I heard nothing more for about a month. Had they dared to carry a message from two kids at the *Nation* to Roger Smith? And then one evening, after dinner in New York, standing on the corner of 57th Street and Sixth Avenue, McNulty said to me, "Roger's going to announce that we're getting out of South Africa. He's made an agreement with his pal at IBM. They'll announce their withdrawal two days later. Can you have a memo on my desk with your ideas about how we should withdraw?"

"Jack, it's the end of apartheid." I said.

He could, on occasion, be the tallest leprechaun. With a tight-lipped smile, he said, "Yeah."

I doubt Navasky shares his fan's fantasy that apartheid ended one evening "after dinner in New York." (As Charlayne Hunter-Gault once murmured to herself after a '90s screening of a Hollywood flick starring daring white men in struggle against apartheid—"God save us from white liberals.") But Navasky presides comfortably over a magazine that advertises its own elitism—"THAT'S WHY SO MANY SOMEBODIES READ *THE NATION*."

Which might be old news but *The Nation*'s in-crowd mentality is more problematic now than ever before. E.M. Forster famously wished he'd betray his country before he'd betray a friend. And many of *The Nation*'s writers and readers shared his values back when the magazine was solidarizing with Communist Party people or Vietnam-era draft resisters. There's always reasons to resist the patriot game. But in our post-9/11 era, the old antimonies are almost out of time. It's no longer about choosing between the state and your buddies. The choice now is between humanism and barbarism, between feeling and the jihadis' stone-cold absence of emotion—"I don't feel your pain" said the faith-based murderer in the Dutch courtroom to Theo Van Gogh's mother.[3]

Old New Leftists find it hard to get their minds around the new facts of feeling. One Ivy League revolutionist/cartoonist recently insisted in an email that soldiers in Iraq share the attitude of Vietnam era draftees—"The more fraggings the better, from my standpoint. As in Vietnam: a reasonable alternative to going out and murdering the civilian population." Ask this tenured member of the "community of conscience and understanding" which side in Iraq is defined by its commitment to murdering civilians and he slips the question—"It ain't THEM. They don't have to be admirable. It's US." But jihadis in Baghdad (or Amsterdam or London or Cairo or Bali or Madrid or Nairobi or New York) aren't simply—or even chiefly—anti-U.S., they're at war with this worldly world.

A *Nation* contributor predicts *First of the Month* writers will soon be claiming the war in Iraq failed because "valiant Americans were betrayed by the Left" as hawks used to argue after Vietnam. But it's our critic who (implicitly) amplifies the farcical notion that Iraq's right-wing Sunni death squads are morally equivalent to the North Vietnamese Army. And he's the one locked on class-bound oppositions between Left and Right that cover up a shared insensibility. The Ivy Leaguer who can't wait for the fragging to begin or the fantast on 57th Street who imagines Roger and he ended apartheid are brothers under the skin of Bush administration officials who ended the State of Iraq without preparing Americans for what might happen on the day after. Clarity about the mindless Left's THEM vs. U.S. bias doesn't mean you excuse the administration's multiple failures of imagination and candor. Dick Cheney's recent happy talk (on *Larry King Live*) forecasting the "last throes" of the insurgency is more likely to kill the American people's will to struggle in Iraq than doom-mongering on the Left. Dick and Co. *and* friends of Vic all live the surreal life.

Back from the frontlines in Afghanistan and Iraq, Austin Bay reported (in *The Weekly Standard*) U.S. soldiers in the field wonder at the vice president's beamishness (just as they're mystified by *Nation*-style negativism). "What in the hell is going on back there?" asked a Navy officer. Bay rightly criticizes the administration for refusing to confront Americans with the case for a long hard slog, pointing out Bush "failed to tap the great reservoir of political willingness 9/11 generated ... Administration officials did preach a bit, but the sermon was too cheery." Bay followed up his *Standard* piece at his blog by printing a marine's comment on the inadequacies of the Bush administration's political arguments for the war in Iraq: "[We're] watching the most important symphonic performance of human history without a conductor and no program."

The absence of a "conductor" is daunting. And not just for Navy officers or marines or *The Nation*'s wannabe "thought-leaders." But radical democrats who want to see history made from below or on the margins must respond to this challenge. If Bush's "you're either with us or against us" line left you cool, try this,

Which Side Are You On?

Notes

1. Thanks to The Belmont Club/Tech Central Station for the steer to Peters' work.
2. The Roger in *Roger and Me*.
3. Austin Bay called attention to this ad-lib.

Cruelty & Irony

Victor Navasky

Navasky's response to "With Friends Like These."

I write to thank my friend Benj DeMott not only for calling my book, *A Matter of Opinion*, an "affable account" and me personally "not a prick" (memo to Tina, my book publicist: Do we have a blurb here?); but more significantly, for his instruction in the higher media ethics. However, although I have read his good piece ("With Friends Like These" July, 2005) three times I am so morally obtuse that I still can't quite figure out exactly what my sins are.

Okay, I've now read it a fourth time and even though I still have trouble understanding the basis of Benj's various indictments, I know they must be important. Why else would he write early on "If you want to help stop the bleeding from the war on terror you need to be on Navasky's case"? Not only that but further on, much further on, Benj reminds the reader that "Navasky's revelations are a symptom of a larger moral failure of the left."

I want to help stop the bleeding from the war on terror. Who wouldn't? And although from where I sit it's hard to see The Left as a single, united entity, if "it" has a moral failure, large or small, I want to know about it. Needless to say I'm humbled to think that getting "on Navasky's case" can help bring an end to the death and destruction.

Here I apologize to the reader for perhaps telling you more than you want to know about pp. 321-328 of *A Matter of Opinion* (which are the only pages Benj has singled out for his exegesis) but it's the only way I can think to explain my culpability so that I may begin to make my amends.

The background: In his essay, Benj focuses on the seven-page section of my book where I reflect on the fact that "whereas I thought I had left the law for journalism, as *The Nation* became enmeshed in covering the increasingly acrimonious extra-national political and cultural conflicts of the late 1980s and 1990s, at times it felt like I had never left the law at all." As a case in point I tell the story of how *The Nation* got sued after publishing an excerpt from the Iraqi dissident Kanan Makiya's new book *Cruelty and Silence*, which documented the failure of the Arab intelligentsia to condemn Saddam Hussein's brutal massacres and human rights abuses of Arabs and Kurds. In my account I relate that we published the piece despite a request that we not do so from Edward Said, *The Nation*'s long-time contributor and friend. After the excerpt appeared, I continue, our literary editor subsequently recruited Ahmad Eqbal, the Pakistani radical, to review Makiya's book. Eqbal (who revealed in his review that he was a friend of Said) ended up (a) attacking Makiya and his book (b) attacking *The Nation* for excerpting it and (c) attacking Makiya's key (pseudonymous) source in the book. Unfortunately for *The Nation*, Eqbal misidentified the source he attacked, confusing him with another person with the same name and profession and living in the same place, London. Makiya's source ended up suing *The Nation*; and we chose to print a correction and an apology and to settle a lawsuit that our attorney, Floyd Abrams, assured us we would probably win, but which could have cost us $50,000 out of pocket.

Space precludes me from doing adequate justice to each and every one of Benj's ethical injunctions, but the gist seems to be that I (or *The Nation* or the left in general) am/is/are morally lacking for having Eqbal review the book in the first place, but more importantly for our failure to support Makiya, a strong opponent of Hussein and a strong supporter of the Iraq war.

As evidence of my bias I am accused of calling Said by his first name, i.e., "Edward" whereas "Navasky ... is never on a first name basis with that mischief-maker 'Makiya.'" Benj is right I am, indeed, guilty of calling Edward Said, whom I had known for 20 years, by his first name and Kanan Makiya, whom I have yet to meet, by his last. I guess friendship got in the way of my ethical antennae here. I won't let it happen again.

Second, Although Benj notes that the excerpt *The Nation* published from Makiya's book, *Cruelty and Silence*, focused on Arab cruelty towards Arab women, including state-sponsored rape, he adds "Navasky doesn't remark on the continuing relevance of this perspective." I plead guilty not only of failing to mention the continuing relevance Makiya's piece but also the continuing relevance of most of the other *Nation* pieces I referenced in the book. I am grateful to Benj for his suggestion, since a less generous reviewer might point out the book is long enough as it is.

Third, Benj writes that his "bullshit detector" was triggered because, after I report Said's request that we not run Makiya's piece, I move too quickly to my explanation of why we turned down Edward's [there I go again!] request. Here I am baffled as to what is bothering Benj. It's clearly not the ethics of a magazine running a review which attacks the magazine for having excerpted the book, since he doesn't mention that. Surely he is not suggesting that we should have killed the Makiya piece? Enlightenment please.

Fourth, Benj reports that when I explain how Eqbal Ahmad came to review Makiya's book my narrative is "twisty and windy." Here I am pleased to concede guilt, especially to such an expert on twisted windyness.

Finally, Benj instructs us that our dilemma in the age of terrorism comes down to an update of E.M. Forster's famous hope that given the choice between betraying a friend or betraying a country he would betray his country. Rather "in the post 9/11 era" Benj helpfully explains, "The choice now is between humanism and barbarism...."

Hey, like Benj, I'm for humanism and against barbarism. Maybe I'm not such a moral reprobate after all. But I still don't understand why Benj, who is anything but an old-fashioned Red-baiter, feels it necessary to make his point by comparing the new choice to the bad old days "when the magazine was solidarizing with Communist Party people or Vietnam era draft resisters...." Is he accusing the magazine of once again "solidarizing" with an evil crowd, in this case, terrorists? Explanation *por favor*.

Happily, Benj hasn't given up on me. There is, if I read him right, ethical hope for me yet if I will "take the lead here" by signing a petition which he says is making its way on the Internet and which he assures us that neither Edward Said nor Ahmad Eqbal were they alive, would sign. This he tells us is because the petition "explicitly rejects the notion that terrorist violence is a response by Muslims to injustice perpetrated upon them by the west." All terrorists? Some terrorists? Are the injustices said to be the sole cause or one among many? Is the response alleged to be justified or unjustified? What does this have to do with a section of the book whose main subject is how lawsuits have, alas, intruded on the editorial process? He doesn't tell us or rather me. So I remain grateful, affable, not a prick but perplexed.

He Ain't Heavy, He's My Brother

Benj DeMott

My response to "Cruelty & Irony."

Victor Navasky's new streamlined cover version of the Makiya/Said/Ahmad story is blander—and less revealing—than the original narrative in *A Matter of Opinion*. (Trust the tale not the teller.) But I'm happy to have his forthright acknowledgement that Kanan Makiya's *Cruelty and Silence* documented "the failure of the Arab intelligentsia to condemn Saddam Hussein's brutal massacres and human rights abuses of Arabs and Kurds." That exact assessment is credited to Christopher Hitchens in *A Matter of Opinion*. Given that Hitchens no longer writes for *The Nation* because he believes the magazine is soft on Islamo-fascism, it's odd to find his words coming out of Navasky's mouth now. But—what the hey—in this case that's progress.

When Navasky speaks in his own voice it's all about tone—the high empty sound of his irony. While Navasky sees himself pissing from a great height on penny-ante pieties, his facetious shtick brings home his own lack of moral clarity: "Is he accusing the magazine of once again 'solidarizing' with an evil crowd?" If Navasky has to ask, he hasn't been reading his own journal. When the murderous misogynist Moqtada al-Sadr and his Mahdi army battled the American military (and terrorized civilians) before and after the handover of sovereignty in Iraq last year, *Nation* columnist Naomi Klein repeatedly made the case for Sadr. One Klein piece, headlined "Bring Najaf to New York," urged the American left to take their cues from Sadr's militia. Thanks to the independent journalist Stephen Vincent, we can find out what that new model army has done for us lately:

Outraged at the sight of [700 young students in Basra] picnicking, listening to music and freely intermingling—worse, many women were not wearing hejab—between 20-40 of Sadr's blackshirts attacked the fete with guns, sticks and heavy electrical cables, injuring and robbing several, hauling at least 10 away in pick-up trucks.

The assault triggered several days of protests by students and their families, who demanded an apology and the disbanding of the school's morality police. Surprised at the public outcry, Sadr's office issued an apology—of sorts. "There was a mistake in our execution, but we had the right to intervene," said Mr. Jabari.

Vincent's parsing of these events beats the hell out of *The Nation*'s "nuanced" approach to evil in Iraq:

Oppression thrives in secret; exposure to the light of public scrutiny reveals the true face of illegitimate power and constellates perhaps the most potent and revolutionary reaction to its brutality—*revulsion*. No doubt many Basrans and Iraqis view Sadr's actions as necessary, if not admirable. But most, I'll wager, interpret the sight of masked armed men publicly beating helpless students—helpless female students—as despicable, contemptible, pathetic. The noble and strong do not act this way; the craven and cowardly do. Cravenness, cowardice—these are taboo, psychic stains to be avoided. Despite being armed with guns, truncheons and public sentiment that was hostile to civil rights, the reactionaries lost on the day that Bull Connor unleashed his dogs on peaceful marchers of Birmingham. Moqtada al-Sadr has taken another step into the barren wastes of Connor Country. It will take time, but he, like the Alabama sheriff and his ilk, will shrivel and die as well.

Navasky has not been responsive to efforts to apply lessons of the American Civil Rights Movement to situations in Iraq. (Vietnam, of course, is the preferred template at *The Nation*.) But Stephen Vincent is beyond anyone's ironic dismissal now. He was murdered last month on the streets of Basra after writing an op-ed piece in *The New York Times* exposing assassinations committed by Sadr-ites and other Shiite extremists who have infiltrated that city's police department. Vincent wrote for a number of American publications including *The Christian Science Monitor*, *National Review*, *The Wall Street Journal*. He never published in *The Nation*. His heroic reporting (like Kanan Makiya's journalism) wouldn't have fit. He was outside *The Nation*'s (the enemy is U.S.) consensus.

Navasky is an inside guy but when he tried to encourage Palestinians to explore Gandhian modes of nonviolent resistance, he was 20 years ahead of *First of the Month*'s outsiders. [*Editor's note: See our attempt to catch up on p. 79 of this volume.*] I hope he finds his way to the margins again, but I doubt he'll get Out because he takes it so light. Consider his response when he recalls in *A Matter of Opinion* how Said stiffed him after promising to make the case for civil disobedience to Palestinians: "So much for my big idea." It's just something to laugh off. But (pace Brecht) "he who's laughing hasn't yet heard the bad news."

The need to cultivate non-violent political action in Palestine and Iraq and throughout the Middle East is no joke (especially in a post-9/11 context). But a good tease can push the program. There's an effective one in the film *Divine Intervention* (2004)—an absurdist comedy about everyday life in Nazareth and Jerusalem. High-flying female Palestinian ninjas face off against the Israel Defense Forces in a scene that implies revenge fantasies come with occupied territories. But director Elia Suleiman, a Palestinian who describes himself as an "absolute pacifist," isn't going for catharsis when his levitating women start catching bullets in their teeth and the IDF goes up in smoke. His bloodless fantasia mocks bloodlust. Though that was lost on one angry white man in an aisle seat at the screening I attended. He solemnly clapped for the ninjas—signifying his support for the glorious armed struggle of the Palestinian people (and wishing a few more of them into their graves). Victor Navasky edited a satirical magazine in his youth and I'm sure he'd get Suleiman's hard goof. But that fool at the movie was carrying a copy of *The Nation* when he left the theater. And with friends like him....

A Palestinian Gandhi?

George Lakey

Mubarak Awad is a Palestinian Christian psychologist who organized a nonviolent resistance movement against occupation of Palestinian lands at the end of the 1980s. Israel expelled him to the United States where he currently runs an NGO based in Washington D.C.—Nonviolence International.

Awad has allowed that Palestinians had little use for nonviolent strategies before the first intifada. Gandhi, for example, was not a popular figure in the Muslim world because he was against the creation of Pakistan. Awad set out to try to develop education programs on nonviolence in Islam a generation ago. He went to India to find Abdul Ghaffar Khan, an ally of Gandhi's, who brought the Pathan people into the Indian anti-colonialist struggle. Awad wrote a book about Khan and he tried to update Khan's message for contemporary Muslims. (Sufis were immediately responsive.) Awad started the Palestinian Centre for the Study of Nonviolence and went to schools, cities, clubs—to anyone who would hear him, telling them they could get rid of the Israeli occupation through nonviolent means. Nonviolence, according to Awad, was about refusing the authority of those who occupy you. He taught Palestinians how to turn up the pressure by turning the other cheek. He recalls how "tough it was for Palestinians not to look somebody in the face, not to argue with them, not to fight them. I went to political meetings and gave a training for the PLO people in Tunis about how nonviolence can work. They thought I was crazy."

Awad eventually wrote a position paper that was published in a Palestinian magazine spelling out 120 ways in which the Palestinians could use nonviolent struggle against the Israelis. (Including driving on the wrong side of the road!)

*Once an old man came to him whose land been taken by the Israelis.
Awad told him to get 300 or 400 people from his village—children, young
people, old people—anybody who wanted to come take down the fence
the settlers had put around the land. But he insisted that if the Israeli
army came, not a single person should throw a stone. They should sit
in, instead, and refuse to fight back even if they were attacked. The old
man and his community successfully took back his land back from the
settlers. That moved many Palestinians who started coming to Awad's
Centre instead of to the PLO. He also began connecting with Israelis
and Christians who joined in nonviolent acts sponsored by the Centre.
Awad focused in particular on bringing Palestinian and Israeli women
together. One of his chief objectives was to teach Palestinians not to be
afraid of Israelis—"taking fear away from people and replacing it with
courage is the essence of nonviolence."*

*Awad began the following 2002 interview with George Lakey (a
longtime proponent of nonviolent direct action) by acknowledging the
"very unfortunate" fact that the Palestinians are now being "heard
more than any time in their history" because of the suicide bombings.
He allowed that there was an "ingredient" of sacrifice in those acts but
refused to connect them with past nonviolent protests by individuals who
immolated—or starved—themselves without harming others. He noted
the intifada of the 1980s was characterized, at least initially, by a kind
of resistance that was very different from that of suicide bombers....*

LAKEY: How would you compare the first intifada with this last one?

AWAD: The first intifada was all about convincing the Palestinians not
to depend on outsiders—depend on yourself. And to do that you had to
have activities that would let people see that they were capable of resisting
occupation. We got people not to eat or drink any product made in Israel;
we said don't pay taxes; if there's a letter sent to you in Hebrew, send it
back because you're an Arab and you should be proud to be an Arab. We
advised people to refuse to participate in official Israeli occasions. Or
even when the time came to change the clocks, we insisted on keeping
our own time. Just a complete rejection of the concept of occupation. The
activities were meant to show that the occupation was wrong and evil and
you have to resist it with your mind, your body, your heart and your soul.
And also with activities on a daily/weekly/monthly basis. Unfortunately,
in a cause where the armed struggle has been the thing for the youth and
the PLO—people have a difficulty understanding how a revolution could

be nonviolent. The first intifada was really an introduction to nonviolence and to what could be done with it. Later, unfortunately, people started throwing stones—and that becomes central to the intifada rather than the continuation of the earlier kinds of resistance. But for the first four or six months it was completely nonviolent.

LAKEY: The concept of the rejection of the occupation is very much like what Gene Sharp talks about—the power of nonviolent, non-cooperation. Isn't that right?

AWAD: Yes that's right. But the second intifada is really such a different thing. The second intifada became a very religious one rather than a political one. Because of the fear of the Palestinians that Sharon is going to go to the mosque with all those soldiers—the fear that he would come one time to destroy the mosque to build the temple—I'm talking about the Dome of the Rock. On Al Haram Al Sharif. And then after that so many people were shot at and died in Al Haram to protect Al Haram—the whole thing became very Islamic, very religious. And there's always a difference in feeling between a religious and a political struggle. And now the intifada has stopped being mixed, because the religious people started the suicide bombing and the political types—Fatah and other people start using what Hamas is using because it is very effective.

LAKEY: So I hear you saying that as long as you conceive of the struggle politically it also becomes more pragmatic whereas when it's religious it's more symbolic and people may be more willing to do desperate acts of violence. Are there other examples of nonviolent tactics that Palestinians have used over the years either in the first intifada or more recently?

AWAD: Even in the second intifada, there have been many, many uses of non-violence. But the Israelis now under Sharon have 30 new settlements and nobody's thought about how to stop it. One thing that we used to do was go to land where there was going to be a settlement and plant olive trees on it. The Israelis have a law that if the land has olive trees—any fruit trees on it—they cannot confiscate it. So we used Israeli law to protect some of that land by planting the trees. And we did that on thousands of acres. We always pushed hard to ensure we included some Israelis in whatever kind of protest activity we were engaged in. It's logical for us because it lets the Israelis see the suffering of the Palestinians and what the government is doing in their name.

LAKEY: What are the prospects for getting Palestinians (and Israelis) involved in some of these nonviolent activities now?

AWAD: In the first intifada we were able to get a lot of people thinking about nonviolent struggle and asking if it could be done and could be successful. So now, nonviolence is not something strange to the Palestinians. People say they believe it might work. Or it might not work. Or maybe we should act on it. But it's not something that's now identified with American ideology—or with some Israeli group or American group that has seduced the Palestinians with notions of nonviolence. But the Palestinians must start debating it and accepting or rejecting it. It will become most powerful if it is a homegrown activity by the Palestinians with their own culture and ideology. It's uniquely suited to the Palestinians. In the midst of the new intifada, for example, the Israelis wouldn't allow a lot of people to go and pray. And so thousands of people went out to pray in the streets in front of the checkpoint. They were making a very strong nonviolent statement. They were saying: "We wanted to go pray over there and they're not allowing us so we're going to block the roads here and stop everything." And just recently in Ramallah, the Israeli army wanted to go into the hospital and the doctors of the hospital came and said no way—we will not allow you to come in the hospital. Many times people don't say "this is non-violence"—but that's the way they act because it's a necessity. People have to do something and this is what they do. And later on we could call it non-violence.

LAKEY: Can you think of any reasons why Palestinians might at some point use more and more non-violence?

AWAD: Well to me, it seems that the more blood is shed between people, the more time will be required for healing, for reconciliation. And in any struggle the less bloodshed—the fewer people killed—the faster the two sides can get together to work on their problem. I don't think that at this time the Israelis can have adequate security or can be trusted by the Palestinians. No one can trust each other now because of the killing and the destruction. If we use nonviolent activities in our efforts to achieve a Palestinian state we will be able to convince the majority of the Israelis that we are not trying to harm them, but we cannot live under slavery, under colonization. That's something that belongs to the past. They cannot destroy our nationalism, our aspirations to having a state of our own. And we could show it by having thousands and thousands of people in the street.

My last idea before the invasion of so much of the Palestinian land was to press for an election. Two months ago I was arguing that we needed to pour our energy into a democratic election. And it doesn't matter if Hamas wins or anyone else. Let's have the whole world see that we're interested in an election. And I was saying loud and clear that we should have all the refugees come home for it. We should start walking—we don't need permission—back to Palestine from Jordan, from Syria, from Egypt, from Lebanon, from anyplace. And the whole world would say: "those are serious people—they're willing to die." And they would pressure the Israeli government, the Arab governments and the international community to do something.

LAKEY: That's a very bold idea. The whole world's attention would be on refugees coming from various countries, asserting their right to return, putting their own bodies on the line. If at some point people agreed to do that—to take nonviolence on the offensive (and I hear you emphasizing the election as another kind of demonstration) then would you imagine there could be a useful role for these third party people from Europe and the U.S. who are even now showing goodwill by saying that we'd like to go over and perhaps provide some protection in an unarmed way by intervening and encouraging people not to use violence on each other? Do you imagine there being a role for such people in the scenario you're developing?

AWAD: Yes, definitely. Very much so. I think that when two peoples engage in this kind of a conflict, they don't see the humanity in each other. They have to look at someone else to really direct them in that kind of engagement—to tell them just sit back, look and see that this person is a father, a mother—has kids who want to go to school, want to get educated, want to ride a bike. The third party can help make the "other" into a human being. When we don't see that, all we can see is death and the other person has to die. That's when you need a third person who can say: "Look, look! Easy now, easy." You need someone to just sit with them, talk with them, engage with them. To have coffee with them and coffee with the other side. It's important. Third parties allow you to rethink.

Part III

The American Organizing Tradition

The prospects for Mubarak Awad's Gandhian politics in Palestine seem dim right now. Still, his effort to encourage nonviolent direct action among oppressed Arab populations should have resonance for anyone familiar with the American Civil Rights Movement. *First* has tried to cultivate clarity about the Movement's achievements. We published an excerpt from Charles Payne's *I've Got the Light of Freedom: The Organizing Tradition and the Mississippi Freedom Movement* in our first issue and the opening pieces in this section show how we've tried to highlight this pivotal sequence of American history. *First's* approach to the Organizing Tradition owes a great deal to Lawrence Goodwyn whose short piece here, "The Democratic Revolution," may be the most *useful* one in this volume. Goodwyn wasn't thinking about *First*—his subject was much larger and more urgent than our little effort to open up the cultural conversation—but he summed up our crew's aspirations when he spoke of the need for a "graceful and constructive device" by which democrats "might come together and in ways that enhance all parties, disagree." It was Goodwyn who directed us to Wesley Hogan ("The Politics of Patience") and she, in turn, linked us up with Bob Moses ("Back in the Day") and Jeanne Theoharis ("There Are No Accidents"). No one could confuse such connections with the human chain that led to the Southern Freedom Movement, but this *First* flow of contacts was informed by that tradition.

Back in the Day and Today

Bob Moses

Bob Moses was a field secretary for the Student Nonviolent Coordinating Committee (SNCC) in the early '60s. One of the first civil rights workers to go to the segregated South ("inside the iceberg" as he once put it), he became a legendary organizer who helped start SNCC's revolutionary voter registration campaigns.

Moses now directs The Algebra Project—a national mathematics literacy program he founded in the early '80s. What follows is a transcript of his remarks at a 2003 conference on "Remembering SNCC and SDS."

I learned from Ella Baker one important concept about organizing. And it wasn't something that she expounded on, it was something she did. She enabled the students who did the sit-ins to have their own organization, their own network, their own space. And what I learned from being in that space, watching that happen was one way to distinguish leading from organizing. Namely, that one way to organize is to help something come into being that you are not going to be the leader of. And Ella was true to that to the very end, to the days when SNCC was struggling to figure out whether it was really going to stay alive or not. She never intervened to make a decisive movement, to say "this is so important that I should step in here, and say which way these young people should go to try to save this organization." So that was an important lesson for me from Ella and from the movement.

Ella was the one who passed me on to Amzie Moore, and from Amzie I was passed on to C.C. Bryant. C.C. by the way is still alive, he's 86 years old. Just last Sunday I drove down to C.C.'s house and there was this huge dumpster in front of it. I had been out of Mississippi for 3 weeks so I didn't know there had been a fire in the house a week ago Monday. And C.C. and his wife Emma Jean have lived in that house for 60 years. Maybe we can work with people here to do something for them. Some of us are trying to work with the NAACP—the State Conference and branches—to help C.C. and his wife reclaim their house….

C.C. passed me on to E.W. Steptoe. And so from Amzie C.C. and E.W., I learned how to live a life of struggle in this country. Because they have lived that, and C.C. still lives that. What it came to mean for me is that there is a way to live in this country with integrity. It was seeing people live that life that made that concept meaningful to me. So that was the second important lesson I learned being a part of SNCC and the movement.

On Aug. 31, 1962, Amzie had recruited a school bus to drive share-croppers from Ruleville down from Indianola to register. And I was one of the SNCC field secretaries on the bus. As we drove out of Ruleville, there was a lady on the bus who began to sing. It was like she knew every song that had ever been sung in any black church [*Laughter.*]. That was Fannie Lou Hamer. And what we learned from Fannie Lou Hamer was about our souls and about our spirits and how to give voice to that. It was Fannie Lou Hamer who really epitomized another lesson that Ella taught us. Which is that there is leadership at the grassroots and that part of the work of the organizers is to keep mining those grassroots for that leadership.

So those were three things—the concept of being an organizer not a leader, the concept about how to live a life of struggle in this country, the concept about your soul and your spirit and the connection to the soul and the spirit that resided in grassroots black America.

In the spring of 1963, I was on the stand in the federal district court-house in Greenville. We had been conducting a registration drive in Greenwood, and Jimmy Travis had pulled a bullet, people had grease gunned us on the highway going from Greenwood to Greenville. And in response to that, all of the SNCC workers had converged on Green-wood to do the voter registration drive. Hundreds of sharecroppers had come down to register. A few of us had been arrested and jailed. And we were transferred to federal district court when the Justice Department intervened in the case (John Doar was our lawyer). Well the judge—I think his name was Judge Clayton—he asked me when I was on the stand—"Why are you taking illiterates down to register." We had thought about that, and had decided that we'd take down anyone who came to us to try to register to vote, regardless of whether they could read or write. We had also thought about our answer to the issue. And the judge was reminding us that the state had a literacy test, so why take people who can't read and write down to register. Basically our response was: Well the country can't deny a whole people access to education because of its political arrangements, and then turn around and deny them access to its political arrangements because they're not educated. We won that argument. When the 1965 Voting Rights Act passed there was no literacy requirement for registering to vote. [*Applause.*]

So illiteracy was the subtext of the Voter Registration campaign in Mississippi, along with racism as the out-front issue. This country, after the Civil War, made the decision that it would go into sharecropping. And the Percys of Greenville were instrumental in setting up the system of sharecropping. After the Civil War, the planters had land but no cash, the freed slaves had no land and no cash. So the agreement was that the ex-slaves would farm the land, clear the land, and this system of share-cropping came into being. Now along with sharecropping came what I call "sharecropper education." Which means that people at the bottom who are going to do a certain kind of work only get a certain kind of education. Sharecropper education reigned right until the 1960s when we arrived in the Delta.

In 1944, on the Hobson plantation, outside of Clarksdale, eight bright red machines hit the field of cotton. And Richard Hobson, the planta-tion manager, wrote a letter to every plantation owner in the Mississippi Delta, and urged them to adopt the new mechanization of picking cotton because it would alleviate the Delta's Negro problem. And they did. And that began the refugee-ing of sharecroppers into every major urban area of this country. Five million black sharecroppers were refugee-ed between 1944 and 1970. It was bookend-ed by the mechanization of picking cot-ton, and (in the 1960) by chemicalizing the chopping of cotton—those little crop duster planes.

What nobody talks about was that the refugees brought their share-cropper education with them. Into every major urban area of this country. That's the legacy against which we struggle for school reform today. When they passed the Civil Rights Act in 1964, there was a provision in that act to investigate how black children were being educated in this country vis-à-vis whites. They gave that job to ETS—the Educational Testing Service. [*Audience response, some moans.*] They issued the Coleman Report of 1966. The Report said it was worse than anybody thought, but they didn't say what to do about it. The people who would say gathered at Harvard, the Graduate School of Education, in the aca-demic year 1966-1967. Thomas Pettigrew, and a person who just passed, Daniel Patrick Moynihan. Basically what they said is, "We are not able to fix these broken schools. Our problem is deeper than that." And they defined the problem in a way in which reporters once put the problem to me. [*Pause, handed paper.*] I've got two minutes folks. I'm gonna live up to that…. You know in the '60s every reporter came up to me with the same question: "Well Bob isn't the problem that your people are apathetic?" And what Daniel Patrick Moynihan said is that the problem is black children are dysfunctional. Now the apathy question vanished as soon as the sharecroppers were out there by the hundreds and thousands registering to vote. But the dysfunctionality question is with us to this day. And so all the programs that we have in this country now—charter schools, magnet schools, ABC programs, voucher programs, affirmative action—all of those are programs designed to rescue students from an underlying failing system. We need to end sharecropper education in this country.

The appellate court of New York State issued a verdict just last fall. They were looking at a case where a federal district court decision had said the state should give more money to New York City schools. And the state appellate court said that the state is responsible to see that its children have an education which allows them to serve on juries and to vote. They said an eighth-grade education is sufficient for that. Furthermore, one of the justices, Justice Lerner, said that there are a lot of low-paying jobs out here, and so people who have that kind of education can fill those jobs. Well, sharecropper education has moved to the urban areas of this country. [*Pause*]

We are currently raising serfs in our inner cities.

Just as the sharecroppers in the Delta areas were serfs in the industrial economy, the young people today are doomed to be serfs in this information economy with its technology of computers. So the work that we do with the Algebra Project, we view it as a continuation of the work that we did in the 1960s. In the 1960s we used the right to vote to get political access. We are organizing around math literacy for educational and economic access. Thank you.

There Are No Accidents

Jeanne Theoharis

Many of us watched with horror the national spectacle that unfolded to commemorate the death of 92-year-old Rosa Parks on October 24, 2005. The first woman to lie in state at the Nation's capital (and the 31st person overall since 1852), Parks who died in Detroit had first been flown to Montgomery for a service attended by Condoleezza Rice who affirmed that "I can honestly say that without Mrs. Parks, I probably would not be standing here today as Secretary of State." She was then brought to Washington DC accompanied by the National Guard and a bus trailing her coffin. President and Mrs. Bush "solemnly" laid a wreath on her coffin. Supreme Court nominee Samuel Alito went to pay his respects to Parks along with Senate Majority Leader Bill Frist who proclaimed that "Rosa Parks' bold and principled refusal to give up her seat was not an intentional attempt to change a nation, but a singular act aimed at restoring the dignity of the individual." Her body was then shipped back to Detroit for a massive seven-hour funeral celebration where a parade of speakers and singers from Bill Clinton to Aretha Franklin to John Conyers praised her, and thousands of people who had taken the day off from work waited outside to see a horse-drawn carriage carry Mrs. Parks' coffin to the cemetery.

Three months later, we were treated to a reprise when 78-year-old Coretta Scott King died on January 30, 2006. Her six-hour funeral was attended by Presidents Bush I and II, Clinton, and Carter—along with a slew of civil rights legends—and 10,000 people. But Harry Belafonte—longtime friend of the Kings who has been sharply critical of the Bush administration (as had King herself)—was not allowed to speak. King had laid in state in the Georgia Rotunda, the first woman and African American to do so. On the day of her funeral, flags were flown at half-mast to honor the "grace and beauty in all the seasons of her life (Bush II)." "In all her years," President Bush told mourners at New Birth Missionary Baptist Church, "Coretta Scott King showed that a person of conviction and strength could also be a beautiful soul.... This kind and gentle woman became one of the most admired Americans of our time."

But the women who emerge in these memorials bear only a fuzzy resemblance to Rosa Louise Parks and Coretta Scott King. Described by the *New York Times* as the "accidental matriarch of the civil rights move-ment," the Rosa Parks who surfaces in the deluge of political and media commentary is, first and foremost, "quiet." "Humble" and "dignified" and "soft-spoken," she was "not angry" and "never raised her voice." A similar image of a "kind and gentle" Coretta Scott King dominates the public media. An "obedient" "beautiful" King who was principally her husband's "helpmate" looms large.

An Accidental Matriarch? A Helpmate?

Where in this public spectacle is the Rosa Parks who helped organize around the Scottsboro case in the 1930s and voting rights in the 1940s, who was the secretary of the NAACP and attended Highlander Folk School, who worried when she was in jail about the women in the cell with her who were too poor to afford bail, who worked with Robert Williams and Malcolm X as well as Martin Luther King, who fought for racial justice in Detroit and throughout the nation for more than fifty years? One day noted rather than seven decades of activism.

Where is the Coretta Scott King who attended Antioch College and was active in the peace movement before marrying Martin Luther King Jr., who was an accomplished singer when she met him and whose talents helped raise money for the movement, who spoke up earlier and more forcefully against American involvement in Vietnam than her husband, who spent another three decades after King's assassination speaking out against poverty, working for peace and social justice around the world, for gay rights and attention to AIDS—not simply seeking to uphold her husband's legacy and agitating for a federal holiday for her husband?

Not Angry?

Why must Rosa Parks, a woman who spent her 70-years of adult life as an activist—who insisted that her most famous moment was not "accidental" but who also tried to push the conversation of the black freedom movement away from that December day—become an accidental matriarch in death to salve this nation's troubled conscience? Where is the resolve that compelled her to act—the righteous anger that Parks herself described when she wrote, "People always say that I didn't give up my seat because I was tired, but that isn't true. No, the only tired I was, was tired of giving in."

Where is the Coretta Scott King who at a march of welfare recipients in 1968 criticized a society "where violence against poor people and minority groups is routine." She continued, "I must remind you that starving a child is violence. Suppressing a culture is violence. Neglecting school children is violence. Punishing a mother and her family is violence.... Ignoring medical needs is violence. Contempt for poverty is violence. Even the lack of will power to help humanity is a sick and sinister form of violence." Where is the Coretta Scott King who saw her marriage as an emotional and political partnership and pushed to make it so, disrupting many prevalent conceptions of marriage in the 1950s and 1960s?

American Hero?

Where is a public accounting for the decades where these women were not treated like heroes? Of the economic repression visited on the Parks family (who was forced to move to Detroit when neither she nor her husband could find work anymore in Montgomery) and on nearly all black people who chose to resist discrimination, economic justice, and racial terrorism? Where was the National Guard or the FBI when the Parks and Kings—these celebrated "American heroes"—were receiving regular death threats? Why was it that instead the Kings were treated to near-constant FBI surveillance for "national security" reasons and an anonymous tape sent to Coretta Scott King herself by the FBI on the eve of her husband receiving the Nobel Prize?

Quiet?

Where is the critique of a society—and a movement—which has continued to keep these women quiet? From the first mass meeting in Montgomery in December 1955 to the 1963 March on Washington (where she was asked to stand up but not say anything), to the much-discussed visit of Nelson Mandela who had to recognize Parks on his own, pulling her out of the receiving line and chanting "Rosa Parks," (because she hadn't been asked to say anything), to Andrew Young's celebration of her quietness in his eulogy, what must be recognized is that her iconic status has rested on this determined woman having to be quiet. Similarly, where is the criticism of a movement that would render Coretta Scott King's importance singularly as Martin Luther King's wife—refusing to let her walk with Martin at the March on Washington—and of Martin Luther King himself, whose own views of women were too often to treat them as helpmates?

These public and publicized memorial celebrations seek to remind Americans of a set of interlocking truisms—that racial injustice was rampant in the South (but not the rest of the nation) back in the day, that Rosa Parks' individual act and Martin Luther King's individual leadership caused the civil rights movement, that the country then banded together and addressed segregation and now can unite and honor the "American heroes" of the civil rights struggle confident of our own righteousness. These interlocking myths deny the long history of resistance and widespread opposition to the black freedom movement which for decades rendered Parks' and King's extensive political activities "un-American." They spin a teleology of national progress toward a color-blind American democracy—all the more useful in a post-9/11 world where the United States seeks to trumpet its freedoms and democracy for all the world.

The images of these dignified women were used to cover up the travesties of Katrina, a shell game where the Jim Crow South obscures the Superdome, where an old woman on a bus distracts from the people stranded on rooftops, where the racial and economic injustices that seared our past are used to blind us to these injustices in our present.

At a time when the Pentagon has forbidden photographing the coffins of returning dead soldiers from Iraq, the myriad pictures of these women's coffins helps paper over 2500 Americans dead in a "volunteer" Army for an unjust War that has killed another 35,000-40,000 Iraqis.

In this post-civil rights moment, the nation needs this positivist retelling of the past—similar to the Reagan funeral—to evoke the power of remarkable individuals (so as to erase a history of collective action) and to affirm the distant reality of racial terror in the past to obscure the truth of racial injustice in the present. These memorials promote a children's story of social change so improbable (one woman sat down and the country was galvanized) as to diminish our ability to envision a movement today. And they consign Parks' and King's critique of American society to distant history when both women had continued to speak out and work for racial injustice in our own time.

The public circus around their deaths intersected with the real psychic and historical need to pay tribute to these women and the political struggles they waged—to honor their achievements and (implicitly) those of other women whose contributions to the civil rights movement have not been widely recognized. Indeed, we still need a memorial that honors these women not for their quietness and gentleness but for their courage and tenacity to take steps day after day after day—summoning the courage to stride out ahead and also to continue marching when many had decided the struggle was over. We need a memorial to demonstrate that political change is not individually-inspired or accidental. We need a memorial to women who understood that the movement was not a matter of one shining day but about individual acts of conscience bearing fruit through years of sustained organizing and collective action. We need a memorial that shows the "how" of the civil rights movement (by what tactics, strategies, and collectivities a movement is built and sustained)—a concept all but erased in the public spectacle that surrounded these funerals. If we understand how it was done, we can understand how it could be done again. And that would be the most fitting memorial to the legacies of Rosa Louise Parks and Coretta Scott King.

The Politics of Patience

Wesley Hogan

Wesley Hogan's "Many Minds, One Heart" (Duke University Dissertation, 2000 and North Carolina Press, 2007) is a riveting piece of scholarship about the rise and fall of the Student Nonviolent Coordinating

Committee (SNCC). The author is a natural-born democrat who fully comprehends the personal transformations at the base of SNCC's peak political achievements. But she also dares to explore why SNCC went down slow. Pressing beyond more superficial explanations that have focused, for example, on racial tensions within the organization, she tells an intense story of how a "structural" problem became moral one. "Many Minds, One Heart" is a historical narrative that should move anyone concerned with the future of democratic practice in America (or Iraq! or Cuba!).

We've reprinted Hogan's introduction to "Many Minds, One Heart" below along with a slightly adapted excerpt from her dissertation's penultimate chapter on SNCC's demise. Footnotes to these chapters can be found in the online version of this article at http://www.firstofthemonth. org/archives/2003/06/the_politics_of.html.

Sweat beaded on twenty-one-year-old Charles McLaurin's head as he opened the car door and got out. His stomach felt weak, his knees unsure. What he called "the fear" was upon him. He stood up as the three elderly women got out of the back seat and started toward the courthouse on a hot August day in 1962, "as if this was the long walk that led to the Golden Gate of Heaven, their heads held high." He stood behind them, watching the "pride with which they walked. The strong convictions that they held." The women had told stories of the years gone by in the car while McLaurin sat "with knees shaking, mouth closed tightly so as to not let them hear the fear in my voice." When they drove through Sunflower, Mississippi, one of the women said, "Won't be long now."

McLaurin's heart jumped, and then seemed to stop: "fear, so much fear, realizing what danger could lie ahead for us, especially me." The women, whose ages ranged from 65 to 85, "knew the white man and his ways, they knew him because they had lived, worked for him." At the courthouse in Indianola, McLaurin stayed by the car as each woman walked up to the white registrar and said, "I want to vote."

McLaurin spent the next four years "registrating." That is to say, in the majority-black Mississippi delta, he encouraged African Americans to exercise their right to vote. Eventually, those who registered and those who were stopped from registering combined forces to invent something entirely new in American politics—a party structure made up of "legal" and "illegal" voters. At the Democratic National Convention in Atlantic City in 1964, they would introduce their creation to the nation: the Mississippi Freedom Democratic Party.

Yet nothing in 1964 or later was the high point for McLaurin. Nor was any event later in the decade. His peak moment occurred when these three black elderly ladies had given him "the spirit to continue." So instructed on that day in 1962, he fixed in his mind how to live.

For subsequent observers, Charles McLaurin becomes an exemplar of where the movement stood at a critical juncture during 1965-66. He was a member of the Student Nonviolent Coordinating Committee (SNCC). Inside SNCC between 1960 and 1966, people learned to identify the specific nature of their grievances, and to act in a way that verified their own dignity. The young people of SNCC often felt like pioneers—"in a strange place and an unknown land," as McLaurin put it. They tried to provide "light," or follow a light, or perhaps even be a light that illuminated a New World of political activity. Drawing upon American traditions and Gandhian sources, they imagined and then put into practice fresh models of resistance—the sit-ins of 1960, and the freedom rides of 1961. Such dramatic innovations were not appreciated by the relevant authorities. Nevertheless, these activists managed to achieve a series of victories through their creative—and electrifying—protests. SNCC's assertions of independence from America's racial caste system—and the high drama of their efforts at self-definition—carried a recruiting power of its own. The movement's early philosophy and tactics were sympathetically greeted, if not fully grasped, by large number of young white Americans who adapted and experimented with the SNCC folkway of "acting as if you were free to act." The result was the "counterculture" of the 1960s.

The totality of these cultural transformations, both real and attempted, had the effect of generating inside SNCC an unstable combination of rising expectations and accelerating tensions. One of the great strengths of the civil rights movement had been the utter unpredictability that grew out of its experimental approach to inherited tradition. Within SNCC, this presence necessarily depended upon a genuine tolerance of error. Indeed, it was SNCC's faith in the lessons derived from experience (from failure), its seemingly effortless capacity for improvisation, that most dramatically stamped its style and also its appeal. If SNCC had anything to say about it, the new desegregated America would be generous.

Yet the acceleration of political resistance and police repression began to widen the gap between the political perceptions of the larger society and those of people in the movement. Lyndon Johnson's landslide victory in November 1964 did not resonate among either of the contending parties in the Mississippi delta—the hard-line segregationists anchored in the

White Citizen's Councils or movement activists like Charles McLaurin who had built the Mississippi Freedom Democratic Party. Despite some concessions by the President, the movement felt rejected by the regular Democrats. By the time Johnson settled into his new term of office at the beginning of 1965, SNCC was no longer riding some burgeoning tide of popular understanding and support. Quite the contrary. The movement turned inward, focused on internal recriminations and, in a remarkably brief time, lost its hard-won momentum.

By the late summer of 1965, McLaurin found the Greenwood project staff "divided and about to kill one another and the project not doing a thing." He soon got it back on track, determined to keep on "until more than 10,000 Negroes are registered to vote in LeFlore County." One of many who tried to deflect dissention in the name of preserving the movement's focus on organizing in the towns and hamlets of the South, he found the barriers to grassroots empowerment too imposing. The movement's cutting edge, its McLaurins working at the base of society, had been blunted. Things began to disintegrate. By the end of the following year, 1966, SNCC had ceased, in any programmatic sense, to exist.

Precisely how this happened has remained, for almost four decades, something of a puzzle. It is as if the civil rights movement became sacred ground, occupying terrain beyond reach, beyond interpretation, beyond analysis. A kind of sanctified mist hovers over this landscape. Doubting any movement pieties appears akin to correcting the grammar of the Gettysburg Address.

The result is profoundly destructive: the act of raising people to sainthood dehumanizes them. As the late historian Herbert Gutman vividly noted, it is not possible to honor people by romanticizing them. Today, forty years after the fact, young people are quietly skeptical of the idealized narrative they are often handed on Martin Luther King Jr. Day, or by Hollywood. Discussion of the movement is seen as just "old folks talking." Even those who don't know or care much about the inaugural dramas of the sit-ins and the apocalyptic freedom rides, or the tension and grandeur of the Selma March, can't grope their way to any sort of genuine historical understanding because they are, like everyone else, trapped within the aura of sainthood.

This is not to say that this book constitutes a dramatic break with tradition, because, simply enough, it begins and lives on this sanctified terrain. It must—and for a very elemental reason: In the 1950s, the rituals of a racial caste system rooted in three hundred years of lived experience persisted in the cities, towns and countryside of America. A scant ten years later those rituals lay shattered. The social relations of black and white Americans fashioned over the better part of three centuries had been consigned to historical oblivion. The ten-year achievement was profound; the cost for many people was severe; the long-term meaning still to be acted out on the stages of the nation's history. Nothing is settled. While segregation had been dismantled, the culture of white supremacy endures. Nevertheless, the movement's rise and fall remains one of the pivotal sequences of American history. Riven with agonizing contradictions, this moment is too rich in tragedy and rebirth to be sanded off, polished and then domesticated under a cacophony of churchly hymns.

What follows, then, proceeds from an undeniable premise: fallible human beings gave this epochal decade the shape it came to have. They did so with resolve, with imagination and while in thrall to grand dreams. They also, on occasion, proceeded in error. At their best moments, it appears they were ahead of where we are today.

It may be time to acknowledge that we cannot go much further up the road until we find a way to be precise about what they knew and what they had not yet learned....

What Do You Mean Revolution?

In the weeks following the Mississippi Freedom Democratic Party's betrayal and defeat in Atlantic City, SNCC staff struggled with the realization that the movement had gotten itself bogged down in some sort of impasse—at the very least a setback and perhaps something much broader and deeper, something approaching a crisis. SNCC was perceived to have "structural problems."

The answer offered by SNCC's Atlanta-based executive director, Jim Forman, was to put aside the movement's experimental style. He made very clear his view that the organization's decentralized structure was the causative factor in the aimlessness and confusion that beset the organization. SNCC needed to "alter the overall decision-making body within the organization, for the organization has been in limbo, because of the unresolved nature of this question." SNCC was much too leaderless and people continued to shy away from power, he said. SNCC needed a strong centralized executive structure. It was the only way to maintain internal cohesion and unity.

Yet Forman's proposed alteration of the movement's trajectory contrasted too markedly with SNCC's own traditions. From the very outset, the organizers deeply engaged in SNCC's most developed local projects did not support Forman's approach. Most prominent among them were

Bob Moses and Charles Sherrod. Many other well known local organizers, like Charles McLaurin and Hollis Watkins among them, also listened
respectfully, but did not rally to the views of SNCC's executive secretary.
Nonetheless, Forman proved tenacious. Participants discovered that we
was doing more than floating a trial balloon; when his sought-after support failed to materialize, he tried again. And he kept trying.

This impasse among the most compelling veterans of SNCC created
what can perhaps best be described as a problem in manners. No one
wanted to be seen participating in a public rebuke of Jim Forman. He
was a committed son of the movement. Yet his very unwillingness to
acknowledge the absence of support created an awkward gridlock....

Before the Waveland staff meeting—which, in retrospect, proved to
be one of the critical junctures of the movements of the 1960s—Forman
had tried to address the vacuum of power he perceived within SNCC by
introducing a Black Belt Program. He proposed that SNCC recruit black
students to fan out from Virginia to Texas, registering voters over the
following summer. For Forman, the Black Belt Summer Project could
"serve to capitalize on the momentum of the Mississippi Project, but
with our errors in Mississippi corrected, and [serve] to consolidate bases
in regional structure with national potential." There was no questioning
Forman's personal courage or dedication. Over the past five years, he
had faced down lynch mobs from Monroe, North Carolina to McComb,
Mississippi, and many places in between. To provide administrative support to those in the field, he had made countless drives on lonely country
roads, always wondering if nearing headlights signaled a mere passing
car or imminent death. He had stayed—and not bailed out of—jails in
Albany, Greenwood, and Atlanta. Once, in 1963, in Danville, Virginia,
he had personally challenged E.G. McCain, that city's malevolent police
chief, in order to give demonstrators time to get away from McCain's fire
hoses. Furthermore, Forman had tirelessly maintained the material base
of the organization since 1961, setting up an administrative structure to
fund-raise and communicate with northern supporters—all despite serious health problems which led to multiple hospitalizations.

Yet just as he admitted in his opening speech at Waveland, each SNCC
person could only know so much. "I shall attempt to write a personal
history of SNCC," he said on November 6, "because there are many
things about this organization which only I can write, just as there are
many things about the Indianola project which only Charles McLaurin can write, or just as there are many things about McComb which
only Jesse Harris can write, or Bill Hansen about Arkansas or Cordell

Reagon about Southwest Georgia." Forman had kept the Atlanta office functioning. He had traveled extensively in the field, spending a great deal amount of time in local projects in order to better understand and assess local needs—and convey these needs to northern supporters. In the aggregate, he had volunteered for a greater variety of undertakings than the vast majority of Americans, the vast majority of activists, and indeed, a goodly number of those present at Waveland.

There was one area of organizing in which Forman's level of experience did not set him apart from a large number of his movement associates. That activity centered around the slow and patient work in communities—the daily work that an old time labor activist once described as happening "at the base of society where people lived." And this fact associated Forman not with grassroots insurgency but with the political assumptions of all others persons, including activist intellectuals, who did not live "at the base." This happenstance kept Forman from a central movement insight—namely, the specific process through which ordinary humans acquired that most sought-after political attribute: "consciousness." It was not something that one learned by reading an approved text, or by following an esteemed leader. It was, rather, something one experienced through acting. And it was something that a large number (but not all) SNCC people learned through their own experiences at the base of society—people like Charles McDew, Diane Nash, John Lewis, Casey Hayden, Charles McLaurin, Hollis Watkins, and Charles Sherrod. Together with literally scores of other people who had lived in the movement long enough to see first-hand the process at work, these staff people learned (experientially and therefore in a manner that was reproducible) the specific ways through which self-activity generated consciousness.

Forman's work did not involve prolonged personal relationships "at the base of society where people live." He thus did not experience the process through which people moved from passive victims to active participants capable of saying (as the old lady in Indianola said to Charles McLaurin in 1962) "won't be long now." As a result, McLaurin possessed a different understanding than Forman did of how to give concrete meaning to such terms of political description as "revolutionary." The difference was graphic and unmistakable. This was why in 1964, Forman could not understand as McLaurin and Hayes did, voter registration as activity that could be transforming. "People going to the courthouse, for the first time. Then telling their friends to go down." When McLaurin expressed this at Waveland, he condensed into two sentences the monumental battles black Mississippians had experienced in their own minds of whether or not to go to the courthouse. They were lines that carried much more meaning for McLaurin and other voter registration staff than for those whose major experiences were in remote administrative enclaves. McLaurin called this activity—working to get people to think of themselves as citizens not subjects—winning the "revolution." It was not the revolution envisioned by Forman. Theirs was not so much an ideological disagreement; more accurately, it was an experiential gulf.

Moses, however, had shared McLaurin's work. Consequently, Forman's concept of revolution through simply increasing the numbers of black voters did not at all appeal to Moses. Students could not just come down and do the slow and respectful work of encouraging people to risk their lives to vote. They had to be trained by people like McLaurin. Yet this training took time and energy, and Moses felt "it was useless to try and go into another student project" when SNCC first needed to focus on its internal problems.

Forman elected to describe Moses' actions as a refusal to lead. It was clear to Moses, however, that he could not tell people what to do because he never in his own mind thought he had that right. "A basic principle in decision making in SNCC is that people who do the work make the decisions," Moses stated at the beginning of the summer. "Decision making should be geared to programs, not to hierarchy." He simply did not believe that telling others what to do was the way people learned to grow.

Forman, on the other hand, worked from a different understanding of politics. He thought the task was to "outmaneuver the racists ... hammer against the federal government ... consolidate our power and extend our influence." He felt that spending time in debate on how leadership was developed or decisions made within SNCC was an abdication of power—at the very moment in 1964-65 when SNCC might well be at its "peak of power and influence."

The gulf between Moses' and Forman's visions now widened. In fact, their philosophies and methods seemed so far apart that in hindsight it is difficult to envision how they appeared to work in concert for so long. A plausible explanation may simply be that a singular determination to register black voters had held them together prior to the Summer Project.

What would replace this working consensus? Two different modes of thinking appeared within SNCC at this point (although many people moved frequently between them). At one pole were people clustered around James Forman's driving question: how could SNCC create an organization which would survive and seek power? Forman and those who supported him felt that SNCC "had reached the point where it was necessary to become a revolutionary organization in every sense.... And an organization that is seeking revolution, and willing to use violence, cannot afford the fear of power. It cannot afford weak or vacillating leadership; it cannot afford liberalistic forms of self-assertion." At the other pole were those like Sherrod and Moses, who saw developing people at the grassroots to be their own leaders as the only coherent way to try to revolutionize society.

Forman was very clear on this point: "Most [in SNCC], in fact, did not see themselves as creating an organization which would survive and seek power, but rather as working themselves out of business as a result of community organizing efforts that would spin off other organizations. Most did not see SNCC building a revolutionary organization." What Forman did not acknowledge was that the two groups differed on how to define revolution: for Forman, it was building a revolutionary organization to seek power. Sherrod and Moses saw power emanating from building people at the grassroots, so they could articulate and achieve their own desires and needs.

Waveland

In later years, Forman considered those at Waveland to adhere around two factions, "Freedom Highs" and "Field Staff." For reasons that are not self-evident, historians and movement people alike then widely adapted this terminology. Yet it did not accurately describe the divisions at Waveland: it was not a matter of organizers on one side, and dreamers on the other. Everyone present was interested in organizing: they differed on what that meant. Some, like Moses and Sherrod, had come through the organization committed to the building of relationships that had emerged from the sit-ins and strengthened by their rural voter registration experiences. Forman labeled them "Freedom High." Subjecting his categories to the activity at Waveland, however, it is clear that those who were labeled "Freedom High" did not strategize together. They were not organizing for power within SNCC as an organization—they were searching desperately for a way to keep bringing people to civic life in local communities.

By the Waveland meeting, Forman said later, it was "revealed very clearly to me that we had a factional fight on our hands, and that it was necessary to organize in a way appropriate to such a fight." Framing his understanding through such conceptual terms, he found it impossible to work any longer within the group's democratic ethic. Forman now prepared for a battle, organizing against others in SNCC. In other moments he had advocated bringing criticisms of others—those whom he perceived as organizing against him—out into the open. Now he worked secretly to destabilize and overcome those he named Freedom Highs.

At a certain point a small rump group led by Forman began to believe that their analysis was more important than maintaining the group and holding it together. At this moment, some attempted to take control of SNCC to enact their agenda. Simply enough, people who wanted power took it. Goals become more important than process.

It was a circumstance repeated during the decade, most notably in the national SDS organization through the fervent Progressive Labor Party between 1967-1968, but one that also played out in hundreds of local activist groups as well as those of regional or national scope.

Long before SNCC evolved, other groups of Americans had experienced similar tensions between hierarchical and democratic forms. But SNCC workers had pushed their capacities to participate in public life to a new limit—for themselves, and for the local people with whom they worked. The range of issues that emerged within SNCC during the fall of 1964 had been developing for at least two years. The limit of the democratic terrain they had plowed for so long as an organization was reached at Waveland.

[Author's note: There would be one more SNCC moment of Democratic innovation—the Lowndes County Alabama organizing that took place in 1965-66.]

However, it is critical to note that even if no one had stepped forward to organize against others in SNCC, multiple impediments—disagreement on priorities, the lack of a process to make decisions or educate new workers, money problems, the central and undiscussed dynamic of racial identity, the questions surrounding nonviolence, and the lack of interpersonal trust—now had the cumulative effect of inhibiting both candor and mutual respect. This situation was noted by nearly everyone in the group at this point, and surely would have presented a crisis throughout the fall of 1964 and into 1965 even if factions had not developed. No individual can be saddled with the blame. It seems to be a strategic point in time reached by every voluntary organization striving for an authentic organizational form. At a juncture where the group has had enough success to attract many others, it then becomes too large to continue to depend on personal ties to hold it together.

Ella Baker had taught those at the center of SNCC the importance of a firm commitment to kindling these personal connections. But there was no longer enough interpersonal contact among all of the people within the group to maintain the interdependent vision possible through daily, shared experiences. Without this contact, some people, in Baker's vivid phrase, "ate on each other," harshly critical of their comrades in order to justify their own vision. Forman was the most visible—but certainly not the only—such critic. He characterized those who opposed his vision as infected with a "middle-class bias." Sometimes he distinguished them as too close to whites, or decried them for smoking marijuana, or cast them as people too tightly wedded to individualist or "liberalist" thought. Some, Forman said, lacked discipline or engaged in self-indulgence or elitism. Others, he alleged, were too close to SDS and its ethic of "participatory democracy." He characterized his colleagues as a "small elitist core of self-perpetuating organizers," who could not recruit masses of people into the organization. But Forman's style of argumentation never isolated the specific organizing methods that had to be guarded against—that is, the debilitating hazards remained undefined. Indeed, the prevailing reality was quite stark: the founding organizers of SNCC's two largest and most visible projects—its bellwether projects—were the Mississippi project initiated by Bob Moses and the Southwest Georgia project launched by Charles Sherrod. Among the many local organizers SNCC had across the country, none had more prestige than Moses and Sherrod. Both persistently declined to cooperate with Forman's centralizing objective.

Democratic Patience

Up until the 1964-65 period, respect and candor as modes of conduct had been the "radical" manners that structured the way people within SNCC were sanctioned to act with each other. The only way they had found to work successfully against all outside impediments—against the caste system itself—had been to band together and fight their way through to agreement, by compromise. As Dorie Ladner remarked at Waveland, "We have got to trust each other. If it takes all night, we should discuss [the lack of trust among us], to impress upon us all to be honest, a band of brothers we must be." Mike Thelwell agreed. "If one doesn't really trust someone in the organization, it is because we haven't taught trust here. We have got to find ways of creating trust and responsibility with everyone here." Absent these ways of being, the community faltered.

How did this happen? In their own way, the participants have been trying to tell us. John Lewis noted, in preparing for the sit-ins over the winter of 1959-1960, that the Nashville group knew they were "going to do something. But it's strange. We were very patient." It was a remark that meant much more to the sit-in participants than to those who later heard it. What did Lewis mean by "patience?" It was not the patience called for by southern authorities, needless to say. Nor was it "radical" patience. It was, indeed, not a call to be patient relative to the external pace of change. Instead, it was an understanding each workshop participant had to maintain while sifting through his or her own experiences, feelings, and possible future actions. It was patience with each other. Patience in the presence of their own errors. Patience with their predecessors in the older generation. Patience with larger African-American constituencies across America. It was a mode of persistent but calm behavior that allowed people to combine the ingredients necessary to act, and to do so with sustained poise. Looking back on the Nashville workshops, Lewis' comment defines a type of democratic act. His form of patience allowed people raised in a hierarchical and segregated society to go through a sequential process that prepared them to act as full citizens.

It would, in fact, be patience that Lawson-workshop participant Marion Barry would call for in his Waveland paper. "We want a world where people grow up learning to care for others and learning many different things they can do with their lives," Barry wrote. "We hope for this world, all of us (although we don't all believe it will ever really come about.)" Even though the programs SNCC developed "are sometimes dull, or ugly, or too impatient, the hope is beautiful," he continued. "Maybe we would be more patient with each other—and our organization would therefore become more democratic—if we remember that while we are all very different, we are joined together by a hope that is very beautiful."

But this idea of democratic patience would be hard to summon in the crisis period following Atlantic City. For most people at Waveland, their sole experience outside of the civil rights movement took place within hierarchical institutions—those of family, church, school, or business. In fact, few Americans had extensive experience with voluntary social forms. When the staff gathered at Waveland and put all of these matters on the table, it was difficult for most people to even envision, much less create, an efficient and non-hierarchical structure for SNCC.

Structuring Freedom

At Waveland, the staff discussed "program"—what to do next—for three and a half days. On Monday, Forman passed around a paper suggesting a new staff structure to grow the group into what he later defined as a "revolutionary organization in every sense." In it, the Coordinating Committee would meet three times a year to decide on policy, voting "very tightly and efficiently." An administrative body, the Executive Committee, would then form a Finance Committee to raise monies to disburse the budget laid out by the Coordinating Committee. An Executive Secretary "should be asked by [that] body to be the overall administrative officer of the organization." A single person—the Program Secretary—would be assigned to support people's work in the field. Even this was presented as more of an enforcer role than a supportive one: the role of the Program Secretary, Forman wrote, "will be to travel in the field to examine how programs are carried out and to report to the Executive Secretary his findings and to the Executive Committee."

The other two structure groups—one led by Francis Mitchell, the other by Casey Hayden and Maria Varela—presented alternatives to Forman's proposal to knit local groups through a tightly controlled hierarchy. In contrast, Hayden and Varela's group suggested a structure in which local groups could decide themselves when to draw together to show collective strength. Mitchell's group presented what amounted to a compromise between the decentralized and hierarchical models, instituting a "representative democracy" with an elected "interim committee" that met monthly and made decisions between full staff meetings.

On Wednesday, the second-to-last day of the retreat, each group presented their workshop's structure to the full staff at Waveland. When Hayden's turn came, she felt it difficult to make clear an organizational form that unfamiliar to people largely accustomed to hierarchies. She consequently drew a picture of seven or eight dots connected by a circle. Each dot, Hayden explained, represented a work group. Work groups consisted of people working on the same programs: a freedom school work group, a community center work group, voter registration work group, etc. Each work group would elect an administrator from the group, who would then talk to every other group's administrator, exchanging ideas, coordinating plans, and distributing scarce resources. She then drew a triangle to represent the hierarchy Forman's structure represented. The executive secretary would be at the tip of the triangle, and s/he would tell subordinates how to proceed.

But when Hayden finished, people laughed and booed. It was unclear why. In this rancorous environment, no clear resolution of SNCC's identity and purpose was possible. The three proposals by Forman, Mitchell, and Varela and Hayden both provided a strong framework for the organization, although the decentralist models were seen by some within the organization as "no structure," or "loose" compared to Forman's hierarchical structure. "That is inaccurate," Hayden later wrote. "Both are tight." Both, in other words, had the potential to hold people accountable and effectively distribute resources.

Staff members then discussed the possible drawbacks to each of the three structures. The Forman ("C" in the minutes) and Mitchell ("A") proposals would make SNCC an institution, not service a movement. The Varela-Hayden proposal ("B") could service the movement, but did not have a formalized channel to interact with the outside world, and did not have a check or balance on the personnel/finance committee. Structure B also assumed that people in the field had enough information to make decisions every day, but SNCC's communication channels were not efficient or dependable enough to provide such information. Structure A did not clarify responsibilities for personnel and budget decisions, and required work specialization. Structure C did not provide adequately for field needs.

All of the designs were sincere, legitimate structures for the organization, and in the tradition of SNCC, democratically generated by staff. Compared to traditional hierarchical models, the A and B structures offered SNCC a way to stay both "organized" and "accountable" to one another, without resorting to telling others what to do. B had flaws, but amounted to a decentralized structure, not anarchy.

In the absence of using consensus, Forman noted, they could not find a group solution "in an honest, thorough, collective way that would put problems in perspective and reduce frustration." Faced with this impasse, those at the Waveland conference ended on the decision to "remain with what we now have." Forman, Ivanhoe Donaldson, and Courtland Cox remained as executive secretary, administrative assistant, and program director respectively. Those interested in planning the next staff gathering were encouraged to meet.

Though nothing in the existing secondary literature reveals that Forman's plan was a "minority position" during the Waveland meeting, the minutes of the retreat make clear that a majority of those voicing their opinion were highly skeptical of centralization; indeed, two of the three proposals for a new SNCC structure rejected hierarchy, and Forman himself noted that his ideas were out of sync with most others in SNCC. "What kind of structure we are to have was left hanging," one staff member reported. Most later secondary accounts simply note that over the course of 1965, a hierarchical structure was implemented. South Carolinian and summer recruit Cleveland Sellers recalled that in this period, SNCC workers lost the "zip and enthusiasm that had kept us going in previous times."

SNCC persisted. Forman pursued the "Black Belt Project." Others participated in the Selma campaign in the spring of 1965. Out of this effort came SNCC's last major organizing campaign in Lowndes County, Alabama.

Outside of Lowndes, though, organizing now took a back seat to the traditional idea of leadership. The energy generated by the group who remained in the organization now came from the fundamental intellectual ferment that the SNCC leaders created amongst themselves in an immense struggle to reinvent black culture, the effort so powerfully documented by historian Clayborne Carson. Over the next two years, SNCC became an organization of leaders that told people what to think, rather than developing individuals' capacities to think.

The Democratic Revolution

Lawrence Goodwyn

Goodwyn gave the following talk at a City College Conference on the role of third parties in American politics after the 2000 presidential election.

I've been studying social movements for about 35 years and the more I study, the more I feel a distance between what I think I know and what is generally thought to be the essence of politics in this culture. And that distance keeps growing.

George Bernard Shaw once said that when people learn something profound that affects long-held beliefs, their first reaction is not elation but, on the contrary, a sense of loss. They lament the passing of their long-held belief. Such is the fate of people who study social movements. We bring to the study the assumptions of our time as to what politics is and what progressive politics is, what the word grassroots means, and then the movements we study contradict these assumptions.

In the case of Populism I looked at the cooperative movement for five years before I understood that it was an organizing—a recruiting—device. There wasn't anything in my culture that taught me that to build a movement one has to create social relations among people that would cause them to be in a room where politics is the center of discussion. I'd been taught that what mattered politically was what people said in the room. But the key question is how to get people into the room to hear—and respond—to whatever is being said there.

The Populists recruited two million people. How did they do that? They did it through the cooperative movement. As I say, it took me years to understand that was the point of the cooperatives. Eventually I came to see that "recruiting" is not a category of political science. It was not a category in my head. It was, however, in the heads of the Populists. I was able to make my intellectual contribution to understanding their great achievements only because I didn't go away during the five years that I was clueless about what I was studying.

This elaborate preface enables me to suggest that very little that I wish to say tonight will be what you expect to hear. Is there a device by which, when we come together on occasions like this we can find ways gracefully and constructively, and in ways that enhance all participants, to disagree? What would a democratic argument—or a democratic marriage, or a democratic classroom—look like? What would a meeting of democrats like this look like? Maybe it should be turned inside out. Perhaps the purpose of such meetings should be to bring together 100 people so they could talk to each other about the organizing problems they face, rather than hear wisdom from a panel. The only "wisdom" from a panel that would be permitted would be advice on how to organize. Discourse on visible injustices that undermine the credibility of those in power would not be cultivated because righteous exhortations or speechifying that doesn't bear on organizing produce a kind of politics that is programmatically empty. The words that are spoken might prove entertaining to some people in the room. But—sorry to repeat myself—what we need to be thinking about is how to induce people to come to the room in the first place. Where there exists no concrete plan of recruitment, there can be no organizing. And there will be no social movement. The historical evidence is mountainous; such movements happen only when they are organized. When people are required merely to appear but are not presented with a plan of collaborative activity in which they can participate, there transparently can be no activity that proceeds as a result of the meeting. No activity, no life!

The sinew of social movements does not come from "learned" people who bring clarity to the poor or "raise their consciousness." The poor know they're poor; they know who oppresses them. Their problem is not that they're ignorant of these facts. Their problem is that they don't know what to do about it. And neither do we. That's the crushing problem that we face as a people.

We can begin to address that problem here only if we accept that every person in this room by virtue of being in it has earned the credentials to have a major voice in how we organize our relationship with each other during this time we're going to be together. What functioning cultural assumptions would have been required last Wednesday and Thursday and Friday in order for us to come together in a new way, with new expectations that would lead to political activity? Revising our current assumptions is the beginning of the Revolution—the Democratic Revolution. It would surely put a lot of heat on speechmakers. Everyone's readiness to tolerate orators who go on and on would diminish rapidly.

In politics, it's my understanding that with respect to your opponents you have two options; you can either negotiate with them or you can shoot them. As an advocate of non-violence I come down heavily on the side of negotiation. Having a democratic conversation with one's opponent is not corrupting. Once we accept that politics is negotiation, and that the strength one brings to the table is a function of prior organizing, we can begin to have a serious conversation about recruiting. A discussion of radical networking or coalition building that's not tied to the problem of recruitment isn't going to address the looming historical task in front of us.

The Felt Quality of Autonomy

Paul Berman

Berman offered the following analysis of the 2000 election "mess" at a Columbia University conference devoted to Cornelius Castoriadis's intellectual legacy. His remarks are followed by a comment from the audience and Berman's response.

I had intended to talk about the shape and direction that has been taken by the American left, the influence that Castoriadis had or should have had…. But as I was listening to this afternoon's discussion of political questions in Castoriadis, I found myself thinking about the relation between those issues and the quandaries of the American here and now. So I've decided to veer off in another direction. Forgive if my thoughts tumble out in a slightly disorderly fashion….

I am very sympathetic to those speakers who noted a certain muddle in Castoriadis on the political question of direct democracy vs. representative democracy. I think that he's both wrong on this question and right to be muddled. The muddle arises from the fact that that when Castoriadis pictures autonomy, he does it in different ways. Sometimes he's quite clear that the shape and form of autonomy is going to be something like the

Athenian Agora or the medieval guilds or council communism.... Some kind of direct democracy. At other times, it seems not to be chiefly about a political arrangement. It's quite true (as Edgar Morin says) Castoriadis was not just a political philosopher, an economist, a sociologist—he was all those things at once. And he spoke with greater eloquence than anyone I can think of on the unity of these things in connection to the idea of autonomy. I find him especially moving and stimulating on the topic of Ancient Athens where he so vividly and lucidly explains that the insights of the poets, the historians, the philosophers and the politicians were all elements of a single thing, which was autonomy. That is to say, that freedom, which is not his word but the word I would prefer is not something that can be broken down into any particular set of institutions or relationships but involves every dimension of life.

Now I would say that freedom may refer to activities—to modes of participation—that have nothing to do with what's denominated normally "politics." It may mean running a business or opening a business. It might mean a trade union or a religious affiliation. It might mean any number of things—or perhaps the sum total of these things. So there's a subjective aspect to it—a citizen participates and feels either that his participation has meaning or is meaningless. And this feeling partly depends on the situation, but it also depends partly on how someone subjectively reads and responds to her own situation.

In short, it is a terrible muddle. And this, I think, is exactly the muddle that the United States is in right now. In the following way: the reason we have such a mess of an election is that there were three candidates instead of two. Had there been only two candidates it's fairly obvious that there would have been a clear and easy victory by one of them. The third candidate, Ralph Nader, proposed a series of points which were advocated with enthusiasm by his more articulate followers to the effect that the great problem facing the country is the power of the large corporations, the influence of big corporate money on the political system, the threat to American working people—and to the world—posed by the globalization of the economy. A series of fundamentally economic points derived from classic leftist analysis. I think it's quite easy to imagine how someone who began with a point of view heavily influenced by Castoriadis might arrive at a Naderite position. I am myself influenced by Castoriadis and I have not arrived at that position, but I think it's easy to see how someone could. Now Nader was supported by 2 percent or 3 percent of the electorate—with another 2 percent or 3 percent who agreed with him but finally didn't act on it. Let me add that voting for Gore—which would be the obvious alternative for a great many Nader voters—feels unfree or unautonomous if you hold the Naderite position. When you support Nader—you already feel free, you already have scored some kind of triumph, have achieved an autonomy for yourself because you are actively disrupting the system in some way, you feel that you've done something more than flick the channels on a television set. So it's already stimulating. The lure of that, I think was great for the 2 percent to 5 percent who were attracted to Nader's politics.

The other 95 percent of the electorate by and large saw things completely differently. And I think the other 95 percent had a fundamental agreement on what the election was about, which was never really articulated, but is this....

For 60 years now, the U.S. had been engaged in a single struggle, which is the opening up of an old American social system to include ever-larger new groups of the population. The 1930s were really the moment when the immigrants from the late 19th century finally were able to emerge into a situation where they felt they had political power. And from this unfolded all the series of reforms that have never come to an end—the Civil Rights Movement, the enfranchisement of blacks, the Women's Movement. An ever-larger series of reforms which were not just political but were social, cultural had to do with private life, had to do with every aspect of life. The reason the Democratic masses vote Democratic is because they identify with that long history of what feels like progress toward autonomy. Voting Democratic for them doesn't at all feel like watching TV, and doing nothing. Voting Democratic even for the worst and blandest of Democratic candidates such as we've had, feels like one more action in a whole range of behaviors intended to lead to the achievement of autonomy. Take the black vote, for example. (And I can imagine someone saying my qualifications for speaking for the black electoral masses are not as great as could be hoped.) Still, I can imagine quite easily why 91 percent of the black electorate voted for Gore. It had nothing to do with watching TV. Voting for Gore would feel like one of the thousand things one does to alter one's personal situation, to alter the situation of black America, to alter the shape of America as a whole, to change the shape of the culture.

On the Republican side, one might be in opposition to that whole thrust of events. Or one might say that the description of those events I've just provided is completely false—that what this entire tide of events has actually represented is the growth of government that's become more oppressive on the individual. But, at least, between these two groups, there was some consensus about what was at stake. And what's at stake was and is of immense significance.

So let's go back to the anxiety that was aroused in me by this afternoon's discussion about direct democracy vs. representative democracy. While that kind of analysis points us to what matters—which is the issue of ever-greater autonomy for millions and millions of people—as the same time, if we allow ourselves to be befuddled by the particular institutional forms which Castoriadis invoked when he described autonomy, if we tend to look for something like a workers' council, or if we tend to think of the corporation—or capitalism per se—as the threat and that we must make some great institutional rupture, we're likely to merely have blinded ourselves to the enormous and consequential social struggle that we actually have now.

A Comment from the Audience:

I was genuinely moved by your identification with black folks and that was a real reason to vote for Gore. I should say that I was going to vote for Nader, but I went to Barnes & Noble on election day and started reading a book about the Civil Rights Movement. I was reading about the great organizer James Bevel—and after that I couldn't go for Nader, because I knew black folks weren't. There was no base—no connection there. But, I just want to ask. Were you down with Jesse in 1988? (And I'm specifically not asking about the 1984 campaign.) Did you have the same feeling of identification? Because in 1988, Jesse was much more important—if you're thinking about self-creation, the virtues and values you associate with Castoriadis—to black communities. So were you down? If you were truly feeling it, you should've felt more for Jesse than for Al Gore....

BERMAN: I'm reluctant to get into the intricacies of the Democratic Party over the years. In 1984 and 1988, I was critical of Jesse Jackson for other reasons and I wrote at great, agonized length about it. I'll take the occasion to pile on once more on the Nader boom ... and relate it to Castoriadis in this way. One of the writers who influenced me along with him when I was young was his comrade C.L.R. James. In James I found a very striking passage where he said that "we who respect the working class—have devoted ourselves to it—must note that working class in its great majority sees its future in the Democratic Party." That struck me as having some truth to it. I would only like to say that during the 20th century the American Left has achieved wonders in regards to racial integration. The great protest and reform movements of the 19th century left were, with the exception of Abolition, almost totally white, overwhelmingly white. The 20th century Left—the socialists, the Wobblies and on to the Communists, who in spite of everything, had some very real achievements on this front—managed very slowly but with the force of inevitability to bring in black participation and to create finally a racially mixed—if not always integrated—reform, protest or radical movement in America. Which has had a revolutionary impact on the society. The Nader movement is not a 20th-century movement. It's a complete and total throwback to the 19th century—an all-white, or virtually all-white protest movement which describes itself as the Left.

Among the Believers

Tom Smucker

Lifeline, Iris DeMent, Flariella Records
The Way I Should, Iris DeMent, Warner Brothers
What's the Matter with Kansas?, Thomas Frank, Metropolitan Books
Spirit and Flesh, James M. Ault Jr, Knopf
American Jesus, Stephen Prothero, Farrar, Straus, and Giroux

What's the Matter with Kansas? is one of those books passed around and recommended by friends to explain the continuing rightward lurch of the USA, and Thomas Frank himself, funny in person as well as in print, appears to be the keynote speaker at all conferences to the left of the DLC. Besides the fact that what he's saying is true, Frank's thesis gains traction because he comes across as having genuine affection for the working class pro-life, creationist activists he profiles. Briefly put, Frank sees his native Kansas as the prototype for a nationwide right wing forged by the corporate class accommodating itself to anti-elite culture-issue voters kept at a boil since the Democratic Party abandoned economic issues that matter to working people. Kansans lose ground while taxes are cut, the rich grow richer, and ambitious politicians take the corporate cash and learn to use God-centric lingo.

I think it's a great book, short and entertaining enough to loan to a friend; not the kind of book that should be scrutinized for a tightly reasoned academic argument. But it does leave itself open to one line of attack: isn't this just a fancy new version of the old left "false consciousness" line? Isn't Frank saying that if the anti-evolution school board activists really knew what they really really wanted, they'd be joining the Communist Party, oops, er, um, reading *The Nation*?

Actually, Frank believes the working class of Kansas has been abandoned by the left, with nowhere to turn but activism drained of any economic interpretation, and suggests the anti-evolution activists may be Pentecostal Abbie Hoffmans, cooking up new ways to freak out the snobs. Still, there is a whiff of the false consciousness argument here, because Frank leaves the impression that religion is something people turn to when the role of business is removed from their politics. So right-wingers can dismiss him as just another secularist trying to reimpose his atheistic worldview on the faithful. *Kansas* is too good a book to allow that attack to succeed. In defense, I would offer the following CDs and books to elaborate beyond Frank's basic argument.

Iris DeMent occupies the same musical space between country and folk as her occasional touring and singing partner John Prine. Sometimes this is called Americana, or Roots music, and DeMent can out-rootsy anyone, but she has irked the taste police of this tasteful genre by lurching from old-timey backed confessional insight to folk-rock social critiques to a whole pile of old hymns (and one self-penned song about Jesus) on her latest album *Lifeline*. Folkies may recognize a couple of these from the Joan Baez repertoire; some are songs we sing with the words changed at my liberal Protestant church on Sunday. But DeMent achieves a kind of miracle. She skips the smug satisfaction and washed-out enervation of much white Christianity as well as the hats-off-to-mama obligatory nod of country stars' occasional sacred albums. Instead, she sings like her life depends on it, the Okie Aretha, with a desperation we usually attribute to black gospel music, as if the music is indeed a lifeline.

What's this got to do with Thomas Frank? Iris is on the left; check out "Wasteland of the Free" on her CD *The Way I Should*. Sample stanza: "We got CEOs makin' 200 times the workers' pay/But they'll fight like hell against raisin' the minimum wage/And if you don't like it mister/ They'll ship your job to some third world country 'cross the sea/And it feels like I'm living in the wasteland of the free." But she inhabits the same secular, well, wasteland as those anti-evolution activists in Kansas, with many of the same cultural reference points. As Iris sings it, the quest for meaning and personal grounding in a de-industrialized, globalized, brutalized consumer culture can turn to tradition without turning towards intolerance. "These songs aren't about religion," she writes in the liner notes. "At least for me they aren't. They're about something bigger than that."

This is doubly important because the secular white left sometimes "allows" African-Americans a spirituality considered out of date or out of bounds for Euro-Americans. Everyone from John Kerry to Alexander Cockburn practices this weird double standard, where a political position intertwined with religion is tolerated from blacks but not from whites. That's the open playing field George W. Bush runs in for his frequent touchdowns. If only blacks can mix politics and traditional religion on the left, then when a white person works that angle, they must be on the right. Not true, sings Iris.

This is dangerous terrain. With that cat out of that bag, we might have something in common with those anti-abortion activists out in Wichita. James M. Ault, Jr. explores this possibility in *Spirit and Flesh*, a description of his time spent researching a right-wing born-again Christian church down the Turnpike from his home in Northampton, Massachusetts.

There are a number of things to like about the book, besides the fact that it takes everyone seriously as human beings. For one, these Falwellites live and worship in ultra-liberal western Massachusetts; this red state is in the next town. For another, Ault lets you watch him shuffle between them and his post-modern academic buddies over at Brown. (Guess who comes across as the more intolerant?) By book's end, Ault, a lapsed Methodist has even been inspired by his born-again friends and becomes ... a liberal Episcopalian! Holy connection!

Ault parses out how the religion actually works in the working class lives of the congregation. For instance, the sex role differences backed up by Bible verses that seem retrograde to outsiders in the professions are used within the community to *increase* interactions between husband and wife. The emphasis on family sustains extended families that are the crucial safety net; the sexual morality is applied with more elasticity than the rhetoric suggests.

Taking this one last step in *American Jesus*, Stephen Prothero shows us the salesman Jesus, the Black radical Jesus, the reform Jew Jesus, the biker Jesus, the sexually ambiguous Jesus, the Muslim Jesus and suggests that something in our culture or political structure, (maybe the absence of a state religion), requires a mediating metaphor. If true, Thomas Frank's fellow Kansans are onto something, and it might be better to acknowledge that and work out the differences from there rather than jumping off from an a priori "Are you out of your f… mind?" Those of us lucky enough to experience inspiring political movements know that engagement can be fulfilling without being, to use the current phrase, faith-based. But trying to re-establish some sacred space in a world drained of meaning by corporate culture shouldn't be left to those who can only pull towards reaction.

Iris DeMent knows it isn't easy, but shows that it's possible, even necessary. The art of her singing manages to locate and highlight the psychological payoff inside the idiom of traditional southern white gospel music. But the urgency in her voice leaves an open question. Is this the sound of someone reclaiming a tradition, or the sound of a tradition being ripped away from the Left for good? Thomas Frank lays out what happened in Kansas. Is Ohio next?

Message from the Grassroots

Grace Lee Boggs

How will the 21st-century post-industrial city differ from the 20th-century megalopolis? These are the questions for our time. On one side are city officials who support and are being supported by outside developers intent on making huge profits with glitzy casino and sports complexes. Opposing them are grassroots people seeking to raise their children in healthy, just, and environmentally sound communities. These citizens have begun to imagine a 21st-century city as a collection of communities where human relations are enriched by multicultural interactions and the imperatives of direct democracy. Their struggle is a class struggle of working people against corporations and financial institutions. But it is also a struggle by citizens in neighborhoods against rootless elites who place themselves above any community. (Those who run the global economy are more at home on airplanes and in hotels than in real neighborhoods.)

Grassroots activists are re-inventing the idea of citizenship. They are determined to exercise their right to decide how and what cities should produce, how land should be used, how technology should be deployed. Their politics are informed by cultural and spiritual commitments. They are asking on behalf of the next generation: what kind of men and women do we want to produce? Do we want children to grow up to become passive consumers and spectators, living only for their own pleasures and self-gratification, at the mercy of momentary excitements? Or do we want them to become productive, self-reliant and self-determining citizens?

One of the most exciting aspects of the new urban movement is that it is spearheaded predominantly by working people of color—people who once tended to see the city as belonging to someone else. But now inner city-dwellers are ready to resist development schemes that threaten the health and safety of their neighborhoods.

The fight for the future of our cities takes place locally, but it's nation-wide in scope. And there is an international dimension as well because people and communities all over the world are struggling to create their own local economies. Asians and Africans and Latin Americans are all learning that globalization is a cover for a new form of colonialism that devastates neighborhoods and erodes native cultures.

One way to transform these local struggles into a self-developing national movement is by enlisting schoolchildren of all ages in community-building activities with the same audacity as the civil rights movement engaged them in the struggle to against Jim Crow. Classes from K-12 should be encouraged to take responsibility for planting community gardens, maintaining neighborhood streets, adopting neighborhood parks, rehabbing houses, visiting and running errands for the elderly, creating healthier school lunches, recycling waste, organizing neighborhood festivals, painting public murals, etc.

This is the fastest way to reverse the physical deterioration of our neighborhoods while addressing the deepening crisis in our schools. We need an engaged curriculum that nurtures the desire of children to be of service and offers those with different talents a chance to exercise them in the community. A curriculum that gives children a better reason to study than just to climb the occupational ladder is sure to get their cognitive juices flowing. Learning will come from practice, which has always been the best way to learn....

One of the most valuable lessons I've learned over the years is you have to go to the people to find out what's happening in the struggle. In the '30s, radicals helped build a labor movement because they went to factories where workers—no longer in thrall to bosses who couldn't solve the crises of the Depression—were struggling to control production. In the '60s, SNCC activists were able to develop a distinctive and imaginative style of community organizing because they went South where black people—energized by their experiences in World War II and by Third World independence struggles—were battling Jim Crow. In cities like Detroit, we were able to build the Black Power movement because urban blacks were fighting white power.

Today, in our multiracial cities, grassroots community people are struggling with developers and city governments, many of them predominantly black, to decide the future. If you're a radical seeking to stretch your own humanity and at the same time expand your vision of those engaged in struggle, that's the place to be.

Part IV

Metro Section

We're living through (what Adolph Reed terms below) "a moment of major metropolitan demographic reorganization." *First of the Month* has tried to chronicle it and *First of the Year* will stay on this story. The opening pieces in this section focus on new versions of "urban renewal" that rip up rooted minority and working-class neighborhoods. Irving Louis Horowitz's tribute to Claude Brown—author of *Manchild in the Promised Land*—takes a long view of the history of Harlem. Then we cut to poetry by an unrenowned writer from the Upper West Side and by a distinguished author from Detroit. Robert Farris Thompson provides a mid-century soundtrack and dancescape for four Black Atlantic cities, leaving off in NYC with memories of great Palladium days. "Metro Section" ends with Ellen Willis's rejoinder to *Arguing the World*—a documentary trumpeting New York intellectuals (who were something less than mambo kings).

Malign Neglect

Adolph Reed

Reed made the following remarks at a forum where he was "meeting his critics." He took time out from responding to a question about black urban politics to examine the practical consequences of a "mantra" promoted by influential sociologist William Julius Wilson.

We're living through a moment of a major metropolitan demographic reorganization on a scale than we haven't seen since urban renewal. These new low-income housing policies are at the heart of it. And I think this is one of the reasons why William Julius Wilson ... well, he pisses me off. Let's call a dog by its natural name.

I've been involved in two or three public housing fights in Chicago and Stanford, Connecticut. The principle mechanism through which this demographic reorganization is being conducted is HUD's Hope 6 Redevelopment program. Their mantra is this—poor people are concentrated in these alienating high rises where there's concentrated poverty. What we need to do is to replace these structures with mixed-income housing. What that means almost invariably in the Hope 6 program is the destruction of the stock of affordable housing that's available to poor people. For instance, the Cabrini Green case (which I know best), came down like this. There were 2200 units destroyed, 1700 built. All right, so already you got a problem. Of the 1700 that were built, half were for sale at market price in an area that abuts the most attractive and expensive area in Chicago—the Gold Coast and Lincoln Park. Market price meant three-bedroom townhouses starting at $395,000. Not many residents of Cabrini Green are going to move into them. Then another 30 percent was set aside for people of "moderate income." Which means people who make between 80 percent and 120 percent of the median income for the metropolitan area. The median income was $55,000. Not many former residents of Cabrini Green are going to move into those. So that leaves 20 percent that are set aside for low-income tenants. Well, it turns out low income starts at 50 percent of the median income for the metropolitan area. That gets you down to $27,500 household income. Nobody in Cabrini was making $27,500. Technically you could fill up all these units with nobody who had lived in Cabrini Green before.

So what happens to the people who live there? Well, they get vouchers for the Section 8 program. But there aren't new vouchers being cut so they get moved up to the top of the Section 8 list, pushing other people down. And the vouchers either put them in neighborhoods similar to the ones they were in before—but without what they had at Cabrini Green—the amenities such as transportation, commercial apparatus, proximity to the lake, proximity to the zoo, proximity to the greatest concentration of entry level jobs in the metropolitan area. (We're talking two stops away from the Loop.) Plus their new neighborhoods turn out to be the next stops on the train of gentrification. People were being moved from one neighborhood to another like this and then eventually to near-in suburbs—like Maywood. And that's what the substance of this demographic shift amounts to ultimately—it's a shift from what we've understood as the American model of dispossession where poor people are concentrated in inner cites—to something more like the European or—dare I say—South American or South African model they're sort of moved wholesale to the outskirts of the cities. But it's even worse here, because of dependence on automobile transit. So these other smaller cities become sort of warehouses for the poor.

Now, why do I defame Professor Wilson? Well I bring him up because every one of these Hope 6 applications that I've read—not just from the Housing Authority, but also from the private developers—runs his line about rectifying concentrated poverty. The Chicago Housing Authority proposals *cite* Wilson and invoke his theory about "when too many poor people live together bad things happen and you need to break them up." Now since this is a guy who, uh, has dinner at the White House and talks to presidential candidates and is sort of a public figure/policy spokesman, I would think that at some point somewhere in public he would say: "Wait a minute, I'm concerned about how my analysis is being used to conduct the equivalent of—or something close to—a cleansing of poor people in metropolitan areas around the country."

I mean this is getting worse and worse. They've torn down most of Robert Taylor Homes in Chicago. And since there aren't any new HUD vouchers being cut, where do people go? Well, in the Robert Taylor case, the Housing Authority admitted before they began demolition that there weren't enough Section 8 eligible units in the Chicago area to accommodate the people who were being displaced out of Robert Taylor. So their solution was to say that at least 50 percent of the vouchers would be good out of state. It's almost like they're saying—"just go back to Mississippi or Arkansas."

Stoptime

Tom DeMott

Columbia University is planning for a huge second campus in the West Harlem. The institution is buying up acres of property there, pressuring viable businesses to move out, and lobbying government agencies and elected officials to approve zoning changes that will facilitate its future schemes. Inside a cluster of high-rise buildings that would belong exclusively to the University, it intends to locate biotech labs where scientists will deal with hazardous materials that might put nearby residential districts at risk. But there's an alternative development plan for West Harlem. Working with respected city planners at Pratt Institute, com-

munity members and Community Board 9 have designed what's known as the 197-a plan that would protect longtime residents and businesses while nurturing a vibrant neighborhood life. That plan is fully available to the public. Columbia, on the other hand, continues to conceal aspects of its 197-c plan even as it pushes public officials to promote its implementation. The author of this October 2007 update on the struggle between Columbia and the West Harlem community has been in that fight for years.

The Reverend Calvin Butts of the Abyssinian Baptist Church had some tough words about Columbia University and its plans to expand into Harlem when he appeared recently on "Inside City Hall." In an interview with NY1 political anchor Dominic Carter, Butts said that it has been "a good long time" since he has spoken with Columbia President Lee Bollinger about the Ivy League school's expansion plans. "Columbia is sowing the seeds for another huge eruption in Harlem," Butts said. "It's an absolute fiasco. It's an explosion waiting to happen."

Last August, Columbia's consultant Bill Lynch—once campaign manager and chief of staff for former Mayor Dinkins and now cultivator/collector of politicians who vote as a block on the Local Development corporation (with the lone exception of State Senator Bill Perkins)—trotted out (Columbia's recently appointed) Professor Dinkins and Bollinger at the Community Board (CB) 9 Uniform Land Use Review Procedure (ULURP) hearing. They were supposed to provide some "non-partisan" star-power to sell the CU expansion/eviction plan for West Harlem to Board members.

The *Columbia Spectator* (9/4/07) reported on their appearance as follows:

> The meeting provided a chaotic battlefield for opponents of the University's plan to voice their disapproval. And voice it they did—at the meeting during which CB 9's ULURP committee voted against the 197-c application, former Mayor David Dinkins was booed and yelled at until he left the microphone. University President Lee Bollinger got similar treatment.

Some people found the booing rude, notably a few on the Local Development Corporation (the entity trying to negotiate a Community Benefits Agreement with Columbia) who don't seem to have the first clue about the University's history of power-plays and find gentility the attitude of choice when confronting a gorilla. Given the millions that Columbia is spending on public relations, their high stakes lobbying campaign and their strategic targeting (from above) of people in the community to sell this "absolute fiasco," the shout down response from the grassrootsy audience was a profoundly democratic expression of resistance to the expansion plan. (Hey, go to YouTube to view the diversity of booers: http://youtube.com/watch?v=g0JpF07SOo4.)

Now, no one in this game may own the press, but Columbia's PR machine certainly has people working 24/7 to damp down any stories of opposition to Columbia's underhanded tactics. But whether the press is on the story or not, we will stop the bulldozers. And if the elected officials don't follow the lead of Community Board 9's 32-2 vote against the Columbia 197-c plan, we will dog them in perpetuity.

We have done our best to participate over many years at every meeting and process imaginable. But if we are overpowered, by the powers that be, we ain't going to go easy. We'll stop the bulldozers, and we will do it for every borough in New York City where residents feel they are being forced to hand their neighborhoods over to big developers and gentrifiers. Elitist and racist (you can still actually use those words) real estate schemes are causing a rise in animosity in Harlem that is still hidden in plain sight. We will do our local thing together with workers, with students, business and property owners, artists, and homies from Harlem and all over the city.

And Bollinger, if you think this is bluff and bluster, we invite you to the West Harlem Coalition's 21st Annual Anti-Gentrification Street Fair on Tiemann Place. No you won't see us filling up sandbags; we'll be out on the block, enjoying live music, good talk and good chow. We have done it for 21 years, and we will be there for 21 more. Even if you continue your all or nothing nonsense. Hey, "to love is to fight" as Harlem's Skinny and Willie had embroidered on their jackets when they came for visits in my Columbia dorm room. And, yeah, they were armed but that was decades ago and a lost cause from the jump to think that had anything to do with organizing. We will win this with respect, love, faith, and even humor—the characteristics that allowed people to believe they could make a difference by standing on a damn soapbox on 125th Street.

Columbia is all about stonewalling, stifling and eliminating opposition, not about freedom and academic inquiry for the "good of humanity" as it claims. Why the hell was the 26th Precinct called to evict four members of the Coalition to Preserve Community (CPC) from Teachers College at Spike Lee's Levee Curriculum event where Bollinger held forth on the panel? The CPC worked long and hard on a curriculum of our own which we wanted to introduce into the discussion—a curriculum based on the idea that local development plans like "Hurricane Columbia" and their devastating effects on Harlem be considered in the post-Katrina analysis of urban America.

When four CPC members spread out in the audience ten minutes before the program and started to hand out the proposed curriculum, security guards came out of the woodwork. They led me out first, though I passed out 50 flyers on the way.

They sat me down in the stairwell in the front of the auditorium entrance, surrounded me with about eight guards and their boss (himself a familiar face from the 26th Precinct) and no less than three women administrators from TC approached separately to interrogate. Jeez, they all asked the same questions and all suggested that this was not the proper place for flyer distribution. I countered each one politely by pointing out it was exactly the right place because it was "Teachers" College, and because the event was billed as an occasion for curriculum development.

The capo de tutti frutti cop even told me it was a closed event, and the 26th Precinct was called when I argued with him that it had been advertised as open to the public. He just nodded, and then shook his head. In one funny moment, Nellie ("Manhattan Avenue") McKay—a fellow CPC member—stood in the hallway three feet behind all the interrogators, passing out a big stack of the offending fliers to all those who passed by.

Finally, after she distributed about hundred, McKay was told to join me in the holding pen on the stairs. After McKay's grilling, they told us they were kicking us out of the building. We got an escort to get our bags in the auditorium, but the program had started and we did not go quietly. I suggested loudly that audience members should check our curriculum's ideas about Hurricane Columbia and McKay let everyone know about the website, stopcolumbia.org. Sarah Martin joined us as we stepped out, holding up the flyer for all to see, urging everyone to get a copy, protesting we should not be prevented from passing it out. A fourth CPC member eased her way to the balcony and distributed more flyers. She ended up getting harassed by the same 26th Precinct cops who'd come to shut me down as she handed out the flyers on the corner of 120th and Broadway! The cops told her they had been called to stop the flyering, and she advised them firmly, "Well, you are not arresting me."

The talk that night of "impropriety" and "inappropriateness" is the same yakety yak we hear at all these Columbia "community" events. I heard it when Columbia's Ted Gershon told West Harlem Group Assistant's man to stop me from flyering at an event in Low Library I was on the list to attend. And I heard it again when Bill Lynch's Lee Chong complained when we passed out a flyer comparing the Columbia 197-c plan to the 197-a community plan at a recent Schomberg event featuring Lani Guinier, another PR deal arranged by Lynch to give Bollinger some Harlem cred.

But it is all about the gangsta. Why are they all so afraid of some words on a damn page? The trustees ought to take a look at this. They ought to read what Bollinger said after his first visit to Community Board 9 in April 2004 (when he made a completely deceptive presentation of the CU plan). He cried like hell then and you can see from his whining quote below that Pres and company have learned nothing in the 3 plus years since his first appearance at the Board.

Though Columbia claims it has "reached out to the community" and "heard them," this passage from a report in *The Chronicle of Higher Education* (October 2004) defines the University officials' unconscious and unconscionable attitude toward community input—in this case to questions following Bollinger's 2004 presentation to CB9:

> When he finished, members of the audience peppered him with pointed questions, revealing their skepticism about the project and the university's intentions. "I felt they were denouncing me and denouncing Columbia," Mr. Bollinger says of the meeting.

This is the way the elitist mindset works, and as universities become increasingly corporate in their structure and strategy, that mindset rules. Then, if there's resistance out there, strongman tactics are rolled out. But we will stop the bulldozers. Nick, Anne and Parminder ain't going nowhere. Mindy and Bob ain't either. Neither are Robb and Luisa, and none of the rest of us. Does the institution understand that many of its students love the neighborhood and are loved back and that lifetime connections are already established? You can't play that race card—condo white boy from Westchester BS—'cause we have all been fighting together for too long and we know who is standing up to Columbia.

So Columbia trustees, you ain't gonna play us. You want hell, we can provide it at the end of this polite land use process that we are trying to work with. So fire Lynch, dismiss Bollinger, start over, and respect Harlem, cause it ain't for sale and it ain't going away.

Never Grow Old

Irving Louis Horowitz

Reading the obituaries on the death of Claude Brown (who died of a pulmonary ailment on the 13th of February 2002) made me realize that such post-mortems can be cruel and careless and careless as well as comforting. One would think that what made *Manchild in the Promised Land* an important, even landmark work, was that it is—as one obituary put it—"the tale of a boyhood spent among killers, drug addicts and prostitutes." The same syndicated obituary speaks of the book as "evoking Harlem's astonishing culture of violence." Even the death notice of American Booksellers Association recounting the passing of Brown, speaks of *Manchild* being a "controversial book that exposed mainstream audiences to the stark realities of drugs and violence experienced by blacks in the 1940s and 1950s."

If these features are all of what distinguishes *Manchild in a Promised Land*, then it would not have sold more than four million copies in English and been translated into 14 foreign languages. Nor would this explain the continuing interest in the book. It is memoir that takes some liberties with realities. Brown uses pseudonyms for his characters, declaring that "all the names in this book ... are entirely fictitious." And he's not afraid to sound a note of ambiguity in *Manchild*'s final passage. He recalls that when he described to his father the cuttings and the killings he saw so frequently, his father in turn would raise doubts. "Dad would say 'Boy, why don't you stop that lyin'?' You know you didn't see all that. You know you didn't see nobody do that.' But I knew I had." Indeed, he had had. As the author of a memoir of growing up in Harlem, I can attest to the fact that children see a great deal more than adults imagine.

My own life in Harlem—from birth in 1929 to expulsion during the Harlem riots of 1943—preceded that of Claude Brown by nearly a decade, and in cultural terms by what seemed to be a century. There were differences as well as similarities. The biggest similarity was that life was lived in the streets, not the houses. The biggest difference was that the drug culture had displaced the alcoholic culture—and with devastating impact. I can attest to the essential accuracy of Brown's classic text.

Although he wrote a second work, *The Children of Ham*, Brown is strongly identified with *Manchild* just as Ralph Ellison tends to be associated with a single work—*The Invisible Man*. To read Brown and Ellison as authors "bookending" Harlem's special history is to learn much about black life as a whole, but even more importantly, it is to see American urban life evolving as a stratified mosaic. Sometimes the phrase African-American is employed as a shorthand assertion of a special culture and a denial of a mainstream existence. But, in fact, Ellison and Brown each tell an American story—not a pretty one, but an important one, and even a hopeful one.

The writing in *Manchild* is so stunning, so sociologically on target, that it merits at least a few extended quotations. Brown's observations rival those of an earlier generation of ethnographers, but he has a sharper eye for detail than, say, William Whyte had in *Street Corner Society*. Brown's evocative account of the explosion of drug use in the 1950s hardly needs commentary.

> It was a like a plague, and the plague usually afflicted the eldest child of every family like one of the firstborn with Pharaoh's people in the Bible.... People were more afraid than they'd ever been before. Everybody was afraid of this drug thing, even the older people who would never use it. They were afraid to go out of their houses with just one lock on the door. They had two, three, and four locks. People had guns in their houses because of the junkies. The junkies were committing almost all the crimes in Harlem. They were snatching pocketbooks. A truck couldn't come into the community to unload anything any more. Even if it was toilet paper or soap powder, the junkies would clean it out if the driver left it for a second.... Then money became more of a temptation. The young people out in the streets were desperate for it. If a cat took out a twenty-dollar bill on Eighth Avenue in broad daylight, he could be killed. Cats were starving for drugs; their habit was down on them, and they were getting sick. Harlem was a community that couldn't afford the pressure of this thing, because there weren't many strong family ties anyway. There might have been a few, but they were so few, they were almost insignificant.

Claude Brown was not exempt from all this. He was "cut out to be in jail" like so many other Harlem young people. It was a mark of manhood, of pride and security. Prisons were a good deal less dangerous than the streets. But Brown was also a product of the Wiltwyck School for Boys. It was there that the larger picture became clear. He was indebted to Eleanor Roosevelt, the founder of Wiltwyck, and absorbed in the life of Albert Schweitzer. In Aggrey House, he encountered supportive German Jewish immigrants like Mrs. Meitner, whose family had been destroyed in the Holocaust. Sociologists often mock the absence of scientific rigor in the work of social welfare personnel, while radical revolutionists think of social work as a dangerous palliative, as if any ameliorative approach to human suffering is worse than the suffering itself. It was Claude Brown's distinctive capacity to reject political and theological fanaticism of all kinds. His acceptance of life as a series of small steps forward ultimately defines *Manchild*, endowing it with a significance that transcends an incomplete life. Wiltwyck was not heaven, but neither was it the prison hell of Woodburn, "the Rock," or the Tombs. Those who have lived the "life" are less likely to fall prey to religious fantasies predicated on quotidian nightmares. They are also less likely to fall prey to chic sociological sophistries that hold the drug culture to be some kind of "recreational" reverie that can be readily "managed" by skillful users.

The secret of Claude Brown was precisely his analytic skills coupled with street smarts, or better said, a desire for self-preservation. There was "Billy Dobbs" and the search for a way out—first in the Muslim faith and then in the Coptic faith, in Ethiopia as the Garden of Eden. The street women showered their affections on Claude Brown, giving him a "little bit of tenderness." Claude's lasting "childhood" was that he could not "stand to see others suffer." His "manhood" is that he constantly had to "prove himself." The driving force in the book and in the life is the contradiction between childhood and manhood—hence the wonderful word "manchild." The dynamic was expressed in the larger life of the city; in Brown's migration to Harlem from the Village, and back again. It was a shuttle that permitted him to experience all kinds of people and do all kinds of things. But a shuttle is a moving object, and that was indeed what Claude Brown always remained, a moving object. His relationships with "Dixie," who was turning tricks in Harlem, and "Judy," the white, Jewish girlfriend, mirrored a man constantly "hiding out" from an uncertain environment. A man without dreams, but with fears. And here one feels the coming to life of Ellison's people.

If being a boy and a man at the same time was Claude Brown's contradiction, then the resolution was often attempted in his acute understanding of women. His writing on girls turned into drug addicts, whores and prostitutes revealed a side of Claude Brown that set him as a man apart.

Being soft, tender and sympathetic in fact resolved his contradictions on the ground if not in abstract terms. In an especially poignant moment, Brown writes, "even though I had been out there in the streets and had met all kinds of people, I hadn't learned to accept people, not really accept them." Epiphanies like this are one of the charms of the book. And Brown had many of them! Indeed, every time he traveled "uptown" he learned things: "The best way to look at Harlem was to be on the outside and have some kind of an in." And the "more I learned, the more beautiful it [Harlem] was." This is not a perfect book by any stretch of the literary imagination. People move in and out of the narrative in a wildly random fashion. They disappear only to reappear much later in the book. Stream of consciousness is not the best way to facilitate a flow of consecutive thought. Then again, *Manchild*'s form mirrors precisely the chaotic background of its author. His was an existence resolved far more in the death and wasting of friends than in a life of triumph or a career in public service. Harlem was not, is not, a moral playground of moving on up. Neither was it, or is it, a place of human degradation. Harlem is the capital of black America, where life is precious but tenuous, and ethics is chewed off in small pieces. It is not a place where "masses" constantly protest, and even less a place where "elites" gather to set national agendas. It is pure and simple, as Claude Brown constantly reminds us, a community—a sprit as well as a place.

In the final analysis, the success, nay, the worth of *Manchild in the Promised Land* was a function of Claude Brown's arrival as just a plain man in a turf not so much promised as full of promises. This in turn rested on a shaky foundation of racial consciousness that itself could never quite eliminate the worth of transcendent human consciousness. For in the last analysis, this is a book of hope built upon the sands of despair. I suspect that the book sold so well to so many because its author may been reared on the mean streets, but was himself a nice man, a reflective man, a caring man. He can now rest in paradise—where promises are fulfilled and everyone, from Greenwich Village or from Harlem, is treated fair and square.

"The City Among Us"

Robert Douglas Cushman

Douglas (as he was known to his New York pals) Cushman finished the final revisions on "The City Among Us" just before the disease that he battled for a decade showed him the Bronx where he died in a hospice in 2003. Douglas thought deeply about the design of his "City." The poems below represent it imperfectly, but I hope one day a publisher will bring the complete work to the public precisely the way the poet conceived it.

Douglas wasn't pious, but his book reveals he was a believer. It also shows how much faith he had in the City. Those of us who knew him had a clue there. I first met Douglas in the late '70s at the West End Bar where he hung out with my brother's crew. It was a New York bunch. South African exiles, Haile from Ethiopia—who jumped ship to swim to America knowing only pidgin phrases for food (chop-chop) and sex (zug-zug)—his Jewish wife Margo, her Dominican homegirl Maria, my brother's Italian- and Irish-American comrades from the P.O., my hometown buddies finishing up at Columbia who soon realized a chat with Douglas was worth a year with the professors.

A true intellectual whose mind couldn't be confined by any academic discipline, Douglas had a world-view—a stance that shaped his approach to language and life ("diminish yourself in what you see"). He was often intense but he could be easy too. Douglas was that rare Keatsian kind who lived for the sociable (not the glamorous) life without ever taking up all the air in a room.

When our West End crowd faded away. Douglas found new friends to invite to lunch at ungentrified Upper West Side diners where he'd (religiously) order a burger and a coke, buying the right to converse in public for hours. Over the years, his son Mathew inspired him to cultivate a thousand ways to be fully in New York (though it became harder for him to share his pleasure in the streets and parks and libraries and museums once he became ill). When Douglas realized he would have to leave his family and his City against his will, he faced the awful—that was one of his words and his poetry makes it sacred—truth. It's there in the last lines (appended to a note on the last poem) of "The City Among Us," which distance Douglas from his son Mathew and his playmates.

Tossing a ball,
Mathew and Dalton and Eddie
run farther from me.
And farther still.

Street Fair

A few of the women sat together
the last autumn they had the fair
One showed off her new calculator
from Japan,
another, shoes with the Italian label
hand stitched in Indonesia.

Now and then the oldest would rise to serve
a customer
from pots of beans in every sauce and color
each time folding up the blanket around her legs.
It was from home
but drained into a greeting card's design.
The threads, perfectly spaced,
were made of cotton and polyester,
no longer the lama hair on her mother's loom.

She set these things against
the rats scratching in the roof straw
the taste of the water
that killed her sister

and remembered late at night
the footprints in the frost
as shadows crept through the village.
Her mother wove them into the cloth.

Leaving Charlottesville

There is so much to keep me here.
My son would grow to love his grandparents
and learn something of their life
before they moved here.
His grandfather would tell his stories
as they walked by the pasture
on the way to the school bus.
He'd learn to trace a fox
Across leaves edged with frost.

The house on a small hill
seen in the travel ads,
focuses all that takes me away.
The simple lines,
the clock at the entrance,
the octagonal room
all show the designer's pared intellect.

But the man who listed slavery
as a reason for revolt
forced his slaves to live below grade,
not to be seen when he stood at the window,
to work in a tunnel,
not to be noticed when he passed.

The house is a painted lacquer box
that holds a severed head.
The place haunts us still.

Already snow is in the mountains.
Beyond the strip malls now
ancient trees line the fences.
Frost catches the morning light.
I will live fully in the city,
where my child sleeps.

The Forest of Nothing

Shh. Shh. I'll hold you
in the darkness
Don't be afraid.
There is nothing.

There is nothing
charged with creation,
a forest budding everywhere.

A curve becomes a leaf.
Lullay, lullay my new son,
lullay, lullow.

Brood over the city
as the cool night air
Lullay, lullay, son, rest thee awhile.

You'll fall as the late frost
that cracks the husks of strollers
and children in the park
and changes the germ into itself.

You'll fall as the late frost
and wonder how strange they are.
The workman feels the weight of the wrench,
but turning, it becomes his hand.

On the ferry, I'll put your hat over my ears —
Like mine as your mother accuses me.
Frightened at first by the spray,
you'll laugh seeing it freeze on my eyebrows

and laugh louder still as the cold drops
run off your face.
You'll surround the coasters at anchor in the harbor
and the storage tanks on the Brooklyn shore.
I'll name the bridges,
and you'll encompass them in your arms.

You'll treat the city with contempt
as if seeing it from a high place.

Almost to St. George, we'll watch
the light off the waters
and you'll begin to see
the generosity of creation.

One afternoon, after a rain, you'll find a leaf
the flesh washed away,
the veins remaining.
It will separate in your hand.

As you diminish yourself in what you see,
not to give up the world
but to know it plainly,
I hope you'll sense the net that is always there.
It is in the leaf that takes its form
from the geometry of roulette
and remains between us.

Shh. Shh. I'll hold you
in the darkness.
Lullay, lullay, child,
child rest thee awhile.

The Afternoon Light

After lunch we took our walk in the park
but soon found a bench,
me getting tired quickly now.

A young father set loose
his fierce stalker of pigeons.
Not far enough away, kids bumped and fell
in the trainwreck from their boombox.

We eavesdropped on a group of seminarians

disputing the prophecy of numbers.
One would find the mind of Providence
in a dandelion pappus,
a second in the secret sums of his text
and another by what He is not,
like the salvagers of Pompeii
who pour plaster in hollows of the stone
to discover a face.

A man shouted, his buddies moaned,
over the slap of a winning domino.

In the afternoon light, those around us
like the leaves, which had begun to brown,
seemed consumed by a continuing brightness.

We talked about her play and old movies
and Alan's book
and my seeing the Tiepelo drawings at the Morgan
with Janet and Joe

until I fell silent
hearing the voice of Mrs. Covington,
the mother of my boyhood friend.
I hope he's well.
Among different branches were the sounds
of father unlocking the front door
to fetch the morning paper.

His attendant wheeled off an old man,
not waking him.
As others sifted home, our cast of mind
came apart with the sustaining day.

My friend must buy a fish for Alan's dinner
she remembers.
Walking to her bus, we choke our buttons closed
and stiffen against the cold
that gives to the leaves
a severe beauty.

The Perfect Winter

Behind the Plymouth assembly plant
on East Warren, a clump
of tattered pin oaks and frail maples.
Sunday morning, late March,
the worshippers in dark groups
of two and three walked the long block
from the bus stop. Low clouds
dispersed, a watery sun rose
slowly toward 9 A.M. shedding
its light into standing pools
of stale water. Not far off
a river ran toward another river,
not far my father slept
his final sleep in a room
without windows. Spring punched in
right on time with iron bells
tolling from the bricked steeples,
wave after wave going out
over the acres of cars parked
in rows. I would give anything
to have February back, the perfect
winter of '37, the blanket
of snow unmelted, the dawn wind
trembling the house. My Aunt Yetta
comes back in a cab, her face
smeared, her silk hose safe
in the cracked leather purse
between her legs. Uncle Nathaniel,
not yet my uncle, rises late
but ready, knowing the nothing
he needs to know, and brushes
his teeth with beer. Outside
snow falls on the bare branches
of the black elm, it mounds
over each link of the back fence
and buries the early thorn
of my favorite rose, a single arched
blade waiting in the nameless waste.

—Philip Levine

Triumph Over Time:
Notes from the World of Mambo

Robert Farris Thompson

Mambo is mid-century music. It kept America dancing between 1949-1959. It bridged the gap between the modern jazz, an art music leaving Lindy in limbo, and the rise of rock dancing in the spring of 1956. In the process, it also revitalized the big band concept, which had languished in jazz, and inspired a distinguished and abiding body of music and choreography. The music lives on, in the special hard-swinging passages of a salsa or meringue tune called the *mambo* section. And the dancing does too, in venues like Orchard Beach in New York City, or La Conga in Hollywood, or virtually anywhere in Miami. Sample its history in this tale of four cities.

Havana

A brilliant composer and instrumentalist, Orestes Lopez working in the leading danzon orchestra of Cuba of 1939 had a brilliant cultural inspiration. As I noted in an article on mambo's musical innovators in the first *First of the Month*, "Orestes had observed local blacks devoted to the classical religion of Kongo (in Cuba) bring down the power of God and the force of spirits with special altar songs called mambos." He suspected that if singing *mambos* in the Kongo region brought down spirits, then singing mambos from a bandstand might similarly activate a strong and vivid reaction. Which was exactly what happened. First on the bandstand:

The syllables [of the word] first resounded in the clear, chanted strongly: *mambo! mambo! mambo! mambo!* Then transformed into orchestral mantras, the chanted syllables traveled deep into the musicians' minds, to re-emerge as strongly syncopated two-note riffs on violins, bass, and piano. The result: *staccato incandescence* (Thompson, *First of the Month*, No. 1, 1998 p. 10).

And then on the dance floor itself. Couples split in two. Apart dancing in the African manner took over. This, in turn, resulted in wonderful changes in lead. The woman was now free to dance around her partner and he was free to dance around her. She circles him. He circles her. She circles him right back. Mambo.

Guiding the entire orchestra into playing time, Orestes Lopez had achieved *nothing less than the Africanization of one of the deepest conceits of the West, symphonic music, and the splitting asunder of the Western couple dance.*

Very soon after other black composers, notably Arsenio Rodriquez and Damaso Perez Prado, were transcribing Orestes' violin riffs to trumpet (Arsenio) or to saxophone (Damaso). When Prado moved from Havana to Mexico City in October 1949, where he had one of RCA Victor's finest recording studios at his disposal, his rich and witty mambo took on a life of its own. It made him—and the dance—world famous by the spring of 1951.

Earlier, in Cuba, mambo caused continual excitement on the dance floor. One of the mambo-inspired dances of the '40s was "the Commando." It emerged c. 1943, as a danced response to the allied commando raid on Dieppe on the coast of then Nazi-occupied France. Dancers rapped out V for victory, in Morse code, performing the commando mambo.

Then, in 1947, came another mambo dance, the *botecito* ("the little boat"). Winthrop Sargeant, writing for LIFE (October 6, 1947 p. 157) introduced North Americans to the phenomenon: "as danced in the music halls and on the streets of Havana, [botecito] is a thing of regimental proportions … throngs of happy Cubans rock from side to side in a boat-like rhythm with hands on their hips." Havana had translated buoyant mambo riffing into mirroring swing-and-sway. In addition, the challenge of the music mix—symphonic+Afro-Cuban+jazz—was countered by sass and self-confidence, indelibly communicated with arms akimbo. Meanwhile, thrilled by all-black films of the early '40s—*Cabin in the Sky* and *Stormy Weather*—Afro-Cuban dancers in Havana were blending Lindy swing-outs and spins over the pelvic given of the rumba. That, too, was mambo. It anticipated what would happen in Lima, Mexico City, and New York.

By April 1951 *Time*, brash and patronizing, was reporting "a new dance—sweeping the hemisphere. Part rumba and part jive [i.e. jazz dance] with a strong dash of itching powder, the mambo had left unstormed only the tango strongholds of Argentina and the sambaland of Brazil. In all other Americas, dancers quivered and kicked to the mambo beat" (April 9, 1952, p. 38).

But mambo was not a spasm. It was a revolutionary return to eternally true phrasings of the spirit. In linking up with the protocols of the classical religion of Kongo, the music revealed its history and distinction. And then, when it traveled to Peru and Mexico and Latino New York, it entered places already culturally prepared for Afro-centered expressions.

Lima, 1951

In the capital of Peru Kongo-inflected pena music graces the night in certain small clubs in the barrios of Miraflores and Carranca. Here that ubiquitous Kongo hardwood box percussion instrument, the *cajon*, reigns just as it does in the traditional rumbas of Havana. Percussion-dominated dancing has in fact characterized Black Peru for centuries. As early as the 1790s, a watercolorist was documenting black dancers on the streets of Trujillo, north of Lima. He showed them moving barefoot, in time to a creolized descendant of the Kongo scratcher, the *munkwaka*, plus Iberian guitar.

Cut to a photograph of a young man and woman mamboing in the Lima, April 1951. Aware of the lindy, through film, and cognizant of bop mixed with swing in the Perez Prado style of mambo blaring from every Lima radio, they improvised appropriately.

The young man, whose face has the noble features of the Inca, "breaks" to the floor in rumba (ultimately Kongo) mode. At the same time, he wags his right forefinger in Lindy "trucking" style. He leans back, way back, with head erect, relaxed and limber, showing off athletic poise and flexibility. In the process, he had combined two black styles in one, breaking and trucking. Mambo.

Meanwhile his slim partner dances with widely spread fingers and open mouth. She initiates a crossover, entirely independent of the man. She mambos with arms before her, palms in the air, as if, in her ecstasy, she's high-fiving heaven.

Mexico City, 1948

Cut to Mexico City, three years before. The classic Mexican film of 1948, *Salon Mexico*, shows us clearly that Mexico City was aware of—and dancing to—the early danzon mambos of Havana, hits like *Almendra* and *Sopa de Pinchon*. You hear unmistakable mambo riffing on piano as the Son Clave do Oro orchestra plays *Almendra*. There are tantalizing close-ups of the footwork. High-heels flash and turn, in beautiful black and white.

Then something extraordinary happens. A trumpeter in the Son Clave do Oro Danzon orechstra "breaks" to the floor—like flutists in Kongo—playing his instrument lying prone. He rolls on the floor, still blowing his trumpet. Approaching the camera, he then slithers up, like Ka, the wise old serpent in the Alexander Korda films based on Kipling. He's dancing his mambo while playing it on trumpet, a deliberate mixing of roles recalling the performance traditions of Central Africa.

Cut to 1949. By this time the incomparable Cuban *sonero*, Beny More, and the superb Afro-Cuban composer, Justi Barretto, were living on Meave Street, the mini-Harlem of Mexico City.

There is a remarkable photograph from that year. It shows Justi and other black colleagues playing mambo on a stage in Mexico City. Beny More is with them. He points to a black Cuban, "Silvestre," who is suavely "breaking" to the floor. Silvestre deep bends his right knee, while shooting out his left with *prizhatka*-like assertion. Meanwhile, his partner, Amalia Aguilar, holds his hand and smilingly supports his footwork.

Who knew that in 1955, during the filming of *Mambo Madness* in New York, that the entire orchestra of Tito Rodriquez would "break" and play their instruments in the prone position. They took the culturally linked tendencies of Kongo, Lima, and Mexico City as far out as they could.

What these vignettes show us is that mambo clearly prepared the way for downrock (media term: "breakdancing") in hip hop. B-boyin' or downrock—the dancers' own terms for "breaking"—perennially reflect a certain aspect of Puerto Rican New York mambo. Just look at the names in hip hop choreography—Clemente, Molina, et al.

The New York Palladium: The Capital of Mambo in the '50s

But "breaking" was a single aspect. Many styles coalesce in New York Latino New York mambo, a logical consequence of colliding mainland black and Caribbean modes of motion. The masters were Cubans and Puerto Ricans who had lived in New York for some time, who were fluent in two kinds of language. Recall that Brancusi was Rumanian and Picasso Spanish. Both moved to Paris, learned French, and found their true expression in cultural mixture. Similarly, ambitious musicians, like Anibal Vasquez, trekked up from Cuba and Puerto Rico to New York to find recognition in the "city of ambition." Their mambo was mambo, the Latin dance supreme.

How fortunate that Anatole Broyard, the brilliant African-American writer, caught fragments of their early work. In Broyard's phrase, Cuban and Puerto Rican dancers taught New York how to "throw an arm around life and move with it."

Watching the dancers at the Park Plaza dancehall, Broyard sensed extraordinary release from uniformity and cultural constraint:

Everybody in the Park Plaza—and there must have been two hundred people there—knew how to dance. In Afro-Cuban dancing one dragged the beat, like postponing orgasm, withholding assent, resisting, buying time. Nobody danced on the beat—nothing was ever that simple. Here at the Park Plaza, everyone skillfully toyed with the rhythm and *it was exciting to see so many people triumphing over time* (*Kafka Was the Rage*, New York Vintage, 1993, p. 116—Italics by RFT).

In the process, Broyard saw a man "break." He thought the dancer had fallen, then noting an ending with a flourish, correctly noted that "he hadn't fallen at all."

Broyard's report shows the original sacred music that named and propelled mambo informed later manifestations of the dance. He witnessed a duet, between bongo and conga in Machito's great band. This caused some dancers to fall to the floor, kneel there, eyes closed in ecstasy, shouting out to the players, *no! no!*, begging them not to stop!

In 1950, all-out mambo moved from the Park Plaza to the Palladium at Broadway and 53rd. Mura Dehn was there in 1952 and pronounced it "the most glamorous popular dance hall in New York." She saw amazing concentric circles of class and cultural authority—an outer circle of rich visitors and celebrities seated at tables by the side of the dance floor, an inner circle of Latino and black dancing connoisseurs seated on the floor communally, and, in the sovereign center, the star dancers themselves. Such was the spatial logic of Palladium during Wednesday night contests and performances.

But even on Fridays, Saturdays, and Sundays, whenever the best dancers improvised in the "corner of the experts"—the southwest area reserved for the masters—African-like handclapping circles of appreciation spontaneously took shape around them. When and wherever these structures formed, they represented the ultimate accolade of mambo. "I am a circle-dancer, man," a Puerto Rican mamboist named Tommy Diaz proudly told me in 1959. He elaborated: "I mean when we dance they form a circle around us, me and my partner, clapping their hands, to drive us on more." Christopher Rand, in his book, *The Puerto Ricans*, wrote about the Palladium. He was impressed too:

> In general, I felt the Palladium had more gaiety and spirit than the run of New York nightclubs, and my partner on excursions there agreed. The Puerto Ricans dominate the place, but there is usually a sprinkling of mainland whites and a goodly number of mainland [blacks] (*The Puerto Ricans*, New York: Oxford, 1958, p. 28).

Rand came to the Wednesday night battles:

> Sometimes there was a contest, staged in dramatic spotlighting, and several couples take part in it. Each couple has only an instant to show their stuff. Then the master of ceremonies [Joe Piro] holds a handkerchief over their heads and the crowd votes by clapping or booing; and the next couple comes on lickety-split (Ibid. p. 29).

But the central attraction was not the amateur contests, but watching spotlit house stars perform their acts. They danced as couples, first together, then alone in consecutive solos, then together again as finale. These stars of New York mambo—the Mambo Aces, Andrew Jarrick, Cuba Pete and Millie, the Cha Cha taps, Ernie Ensley and Dotty Adams—they were the magnets for stage and film celebrities who turned up on Wednesdays. Brando came often. Later, in 1955, he showed off an over-the-hip spin of his partner, learned from Palladium stylists, in the film *Guys and Dolls*.

Kim Novak, another film star, insisted on dancing with the finest mamboist, Anibal Vasquez. Vasquez said yes. But first he chivalrously took the precaution of surrounding their mambo with bodyguards, lest someone cut in and embarrass her. Queen Soraya of Iran arrived one night in the spring of 1958. (The Shah had just divorced her on grounds of infertility.) I watched her dance with a strong, silent type. Someone shouted "well, *that* should take her mind off the king."

Black intelligentsia composed a loyal section of the audience—Amiri Baraka, Katherine Dunham, Geoffrey Holder, Harry Belafonte, and many others. In 1972, when I asked Baraka why he went so often to the Palladium, he replied: "Man, mambo was what was happening."

And what was happening on the dance floor mocked conventional wisdom about popular dance. It demolished the notion that "folk" styles exist in some sort of immanent state that transcends the individual (i.e., while everyone knows who Nijinsky was, mamboists dance without names); that "folk" dancing is utterly removed from "high" culture; that only in ballet do we have an art.

In actuality, New York mambo emerged out of the complex interaction of distinctive personalities who each contributed to the making of a classic style. Art history wasn't made anonymously at the Palladium. Nor did it amount to some vague overlapping of Western and Central African aesthetics. It reflected conscious choices, by named creative woman and named creative men, responding to deliberate acts by other creative individuals.

Mambo was a demonstration piece. In a forthcoming book, I'll retell its history and show what happens when a popular art gets on its feet. Here, for brevity's sake, I'll focus on a few mambo dancers to show there's no art without artists, no originary moves without masters.

The two most influential male masters were Anibal Vasquez, a black Puerto Rican, and Andrew Jarrick, a mainland black. Vasquez pioneered "the four corners" mambo that he called *la perfecta*. He marvelously mamboized flamenco stampings and postures by pulling down into the hips of the rumba. Hitting four corners with tightly webbed fingers, smooth as silk. His mambo *perfecta* by 1959 was danced by everyone. All the stylists knew who had invented it. He also mamobized mimes a la Chaplin and take-offs on the stance of Hollywood stars.

Andrew Jarrick began to attract attention around 1955. He was, and is, an incredible stylist. The movie *Mambo Madness* documents him in action, punching the air with his hands, carving out bas-reliefs, modeling King Tut, snapping on invisible currents of electricity. Indeed the electric boogie was trying to be born in his body. He would draw tiny circles, with the tips of his shoes, while counter-drawing with his arms and hands. He would swim, he would walk, he would grimace, he would freeze. Pope, it is said, was so talented he could write blank verse in heroic couplets. Jarrick, similarly, could write over box-steps with ballet and sports and mime in a personalized cubism that zooted his trunk and rocked his arms.

The Rosa Parks of mambo was Jackie "La Negra" Danois. This talented black woman broke the color bar in Broadway dance halls in the '40s. She opened the way for mainland and Caribbean blacks to come to the Palladium. "La Negra" danced barefoot, flaunting her roots, invoking barrio truths (decades before two American black athletes stood in stocking feet at the Mexico City Olympics to make similar points about history and authenticity).

Millie Donay, Italian American partner of Cuban Pete (Pedro Aguilar), had a gift for sensing how roots moved from various countries could fit into mambo. She fashioned *the tango fan*, a staccato version of the *quebrada* break of that Argentine dance. She was fluent in the language of gesture, especially the Kongo pose, left hand on hip, right hand forward. So was Barbara Boyce, a black woman from Brooklyn, who in 1962 was mixing mambo with the twist and the freeze, framing her face with her hands in poses that presaged voguing.

Teresita Perez found herself dancing one night at the Palladium with someone *antipatico*. She signaled to her friends on the sidelines (the story goes) to cut in and save her by drawing down, from time to time, an invisible window shade between her and her partner. Dotty Adams invented a similar move, covering her eyes with her right and pushing out with the left—the *get-outta-my-face* mambo. Adams was also famous for her signature leap into a shimmy. She too danced barefoot and in a classic photograph from around 1960 you see her reaching for the sky with a flamenco-like gesture while her partner Ernest Ensley, touches the earth with the palm of his hand in a break. Spain within Kongo within a twinkling of an eye. Mambo.

An important move in women's mambo was "the head"—a dancer stands in place, weaving one hand in space, then the other, while rattling her head in response to percussion. This is the move that announces the aura—the sudden coming of the spirit—among priestesses of the traditional religion of the Akan in Ghana. I have seen it rattle the heads of possession women in Agogo, in Northern Assante. Mamboists have a theory as to how it came to New York: "the head" may have entered mambo through Katherine Dunham's incomparable knowledge of African motion history. Several Palladium dancers studied with Dunham in the '50s.

But this was not the only link between mambo and black religion. Time and again I saw Tito Puente trace a circle around his head with his drumstick, only to be mirrored by a man on the dance floor tossing *his* hand in a circle around *his* head. To Anglos in the house this was "showmanship." But to Latinos it was self-purification in the name of God and the spirits.

Holes in the Argument

Ellen Willis

Call me a crank, but I've had enough of reverential nostalgia for The New York Intellectuals. My quarrel is not with neoconservatives who proudly claim *Partisan Review* and its intellectual tradition as their legacy (if anything, I'm dismayed that their loyalty to that tradition seems increasingly diluted by the more recent influence of free-market libertarians and the religious right) but with lefties and liberals who present their admiration as a disinterested tribute to brilliant thinking, whatever its ideological bent. Granted that the flowering of *PR*, with its convergence of radical anti-Stalinist politics and modernist aesthetics, represented an unusually rich and productive moment; granted too that my own style of political and aesthetic argument owes much to its influence, direct and indirect—a debt that no doubt lends an Oedipal edge to my irritation. What's pernicious about the "nonpartisan" brand of nostalgia is the un-admitted conservatism implicit in its uncritical endorsement of a certain kind of cultural authority. There were giants in the earth in those days, and now.... Well, now cultural authority is not only radically de-centered, its nature and legitimacy are a hot topic of conversation in intellectual circles; and in place of the center that did not hold, many people see only a vacuum. Thus Russell Jacoby, unable, to find the contemporary equivalent of *Partisan Review*, concluded in *The Last Intellectuals* that the enterprise of public intellectual had for all practical purposes ceased to exist—a suggestion that had many of us scratching our invisible heads.

The latest exercise in NYI envy—its advertising features *The New Republic's* Marty Peretz gushing, "A vivid evocation of an age when ideas truly mattered"—is Joseph Dorman's documentary film, *Arguing the World*. Dorman (characterized in an interview with the Bergen County Record as "a left-leaning Democrat") traces the political migration of Irving Kristol, Daniel Bell, Nathan Glazer and Irving Howe from their common starting point as boy Trotskyists in the '30s, hanging out in City College's legendary Alcove I, to their induction into the heady precincts of *Partisan Review*, to their traumatic marginalization by a new generation of student radicals. In reaction to the '60s, Glazer and Bell become neoconservatives and Kristol moves even further to the right, embracing the Reagan-Gingrich revolution, while Howe maintains a lonely commitment to social democracy until his death in 1993. Though my attention wandered toward the end—the story becomes pretty anti-climactic once Reagan is elected—for the most part I found the film riveting as a documentary, replete with juicy footage of the Lower East Side, the City College cafeteria, the student uprisings at Berkeley and Columbia, and so on. Insight, however, is in short supply.

Despite its billing, this movie is not really about ideas or the power thereof. We're supposed to take for granted that the gang of four, in the words of the same ad that quotes Peretz, "believe passionately that ideas can change the world ... especially *their* ideas." But the substance of those ideas is barely touched on—perhaps Dorman thought that in this post-intellectual age, the audience couldn't be expected to listen. In any case, far from being among "the century's leading thinkers" (that ad again), none of the four have minds as interesting and genuinely original as, say, Hannah Arendt or Dwight Macdonald or Sidney Hook. No, the real subject of *Arguing* is ideology, which is to say that it is more about how the world changes people's ideas than vice versa. Furthermore, Dorman is far more interested in the morality of those changes than in their intellectual content.

As the film tells it, the four protagonists become Marxists because they grow up in poor Jewish immigrant families and are exposed to the socialist politics of their Lower East Side and Bronx milieus. They become militant anti-Stalinists in response to Soviet totalitarianism. They begin rethinking their attitude toward the capitalist American government when it joins the war against Hitler; their revolutionary zeal further wanes as they enjoy post-war America's prosperity and their own success as academics and journal editors. In the '50s their anti-Communism leads all but Howe to be, at best, equivocal critics of McCarthyism. (Oddly, the complicity of various NYIs with the CIA, and in particular that agency's subsidy of the journal *Encounter*, which Kristol edited, goes unmentioned.) In the '60s, they are appalled at the new left's apparent determination to replicate the blindness of Stalin's American apologists by romanticizing China and Cuba; nor can they stomach the student revolt against the university, which they see as threatening the one institution dedicated to a free exchange of ideas. As a result three of our heroes turn decisively to the right; only Howe resists both SDS and neoconservatism. While the portraits of Kristol, Bell and Glazer are neither uncomplicated nor unsympathetic, Howe clearly occupies the moral high ground in the film-maker's estimation.

In focusing on the morality of these men's choices, *Arguing the World* manages an amazing feat of avoidance. It is virtually oblivious to the central issue that shapes their politics from beginning to end, but most dramatically in their confrontation with the '60s: the issue of culture. As the iconography of four white men, seen against the backdrop of their all-male and overwhelmingly white City College milieu, suggests (albeit without a trace of self-consciousness on Dorman's part), the American left of the '30s, Stalinist and anti-Stalinist alike, was culturally conservative. The influence of feminism, psycho-analysis, and anarchism, which had informed American radicalism earlier in the century, had been eclipsed by an orthodox Marxism that regarded class struggle as subsuming all other conflicts. Kristol, Bell, Glazer, and Howe may have been economic radicals, but their attitudes toward the family, sex, education, and cultural authority in general appear to have been entirely received and conventional.

In the post-war era, the social conformity, sexual repression and tyrannical domesticity of the emerging suburban middle class did have its cultural radical critics—some of whom actually appeared in the pages of *Partisan Review*—but Dorman's four were not among them. Having abandoned revolutionary Marxism, they could imagine no other choices but liberalism or a reformist socialism that was pretty much the same thing. What horrified them about the '60s was not only the authoritarian strain in the new left politics but the larger rebellion against cultural

institutions and mores. Neoconservatism was, in large part, a reaction
to black power, feminism, gay liberation, sex, drugs, and rock and roll.
Democratic socialists, Howe included, did their best to downplay the
insurgent social movements and their insistence that economic justice
was only part of the story.

Had Dorman explored this divide—inviting his subjects to discuss it,
letting some cultural radicals talk back—*Arguing the World* might truly
have lived up to its title. As it is, the argument is bloodless. Michael Walzer and Morris Dickstein, the film's chief commentators, are relentlessly
respectful. There are no feminists in the movie and few women; Kristol's
wife, the eminent historian and conservative polemicist, Gertrude Him-
melfarb, is conspicuously absent, as is Pearl Bell, also no intellectual
slouch. (On the other hand, in an amusing and unwittingly revealing
scene, Kristol describes being "trapped" on a couch at a party, hemmed
in on three sides by Mary McCarthy, Hannah Arendt, and Diana Trilling
conversing about Freud.) There are no blacks, of any political persuasion.
There are no ex-hippies. The '60s radical most vividly portrayed is Tom
Hayden, in a thoroughly repellent scene—and this time the effect is fully
intended—in which Hayden, recalling a rancorous encounter with Howe,
rants about the "decibel level" and "paternalism beyond Abraham" of
"these people," he might as well have come right out and complained
about loud overbearing Jews.

Arguing gets closest to the point when it interviews Glazer and Bell
about the Berkeley and Columbia revolts, capturing their pain and alarm
at the students' rejection of the institutions they cherish and, implicitly,
of their own authority. Bell, at least, recognizes that this is a conflict that
can't be resolved by brute force; he argues with a Columbia official that
authority must be earned not simply imposed. The cops are brought in
anyway, and Bell, disheartened by the poisoned atmosphere, soon leaves
for Harvard. But he never does understand why so many students failed
to see the university as a haven of freedom and enlightenment. Nor is
the film, which offers only one less-than-informative interview with a
Berkeley protester, helpful on this point.

I found myself wishing I could have talked to Dorman about my own
experience as a student at Barnard in the early '60s. One of the attractions of Barnard was supposed to be the opportunity to take courses at
Columbia, and I, as an English major, was naturally eager to take courses
with such giants in the earth as Lionel Trilling and F.W. Dupee. I was
told, however, that the English department faculty had a policy of not
allowing women in their classes because our presence would detract

from the seriousness of the learning that went on there. The shameless bluntness of this assertion—the absence of any impulse to obscure it with euphemisms—still strikes me as breathtakingly rude, even in a prefeminist context. Nearly as much as the discriminatory policy itself, it gets at what was corrupt about the authority to which the Trillings and their colleagues felt entitled, and why their horror of the student rebels' incivility rang so false. Any honest account of the New York Intellectuals must acknowledge that corruption and give the '60s cultural radicals their due; but this precisely what NYI hagiographers want to avoid at all cost. What Dorman's film comes down to, in the end is amnesia masquerading as history, myth standing in for debate.

Part V

The Margin Is the Center

The prominent sociologist Daniel Bell—one of *Arguing the World*'s Big Four—got roped into a correspondence with me after an old friend of his spoke up for the first *First*. I'd suggested to that mutual acquaintance (in the course of a conversation about how *First*'s angle on American culture would be different from New York Intellectuals') that NYIs had been MIAs when it came to American popular music. Bell wrote to correct me about that—"we all had records of Bessie Smith and Billy (sic) Holiday—on heavy 78's, some of which are still in our basement." Our correspondence started on that note but it developed into a broader disagreement that I sought to clarify in my last letter to Bell:

> Our disagreement is about the life and meaning and value in American popular cultures. I think educated citizens should care about what's fresh in pop life (while cultivating resistance to the opiates of mainline media). If my co-conspirators and I can find a way to keep *First* alive, we'll try to keep tabs on the best expressions of everyday people....
>
> But please don't understand me too quickly. Our disagreement is not (chiefly) a matter of taste. That's why I keep returning to Lawrence Goodwyn's history of American populism [*Democratic Promise*]. I believe there's a radical democratic promise implicit in America's authentic cultural traditions. It's the reality of everyday people moving—culturally and politically that moves me. Don't see a lot of evidence it moves you.

A busy Bell let me have the last word. Though he made it clear a few years on that he hadn't been won over by *First*. He was put off right away (no doubt) by Ellen Willis's piece on NYIs in our first issue (see her "Holes in the Argument" above) but he disdained the rest of our tab as well. In his correspondence, Bell didn't address arguments made by Willis or other *First* writers, but he did dirt on their characters—"[Baraka] sponged shamelessly off his first wife..." etc. Bell's contempt was capacious. It extended to writers we hadn't published. He'd heard I was a fan of C.L.R. James's books on cricket, Melville and American popular culture and he seemed to want to make sure his friend (who hadn't read James) wouldn't be tempted to try *Beyond a Boundary* or *Renegades, Mariners and Castaways* or *The Struggle for Happiness*. He offered the following anecdote to clinch his case for the irrelevance of James's "esoterica."

> I met James sometime in the 1950s. A City College classmate of mine, Saul Blackman, who was a member of the Johnson [James's American pseudonym] faction in Detroit came to see me—I was then an editor at *Fortune*—to get some help against the deportation of James. He gave me, with a smirk, a copy of *Renegades, Mariners and Castaways*, and said, you see, James loves America. I never fathomed whether the smirk was because this was a "maneuver" or true. He brought me to meet James at some apartment in New York. I remember a very tall, thin man with a high reedy voice who harangued me for the evening with the argument that "state capitalism" was the truer characterization of the Soviet Union than "bureaucratic collectivism," because it was Marxist. I wrote a letter to the Naturalization officials, but James was deported anyway, as you probably know. He then sank into obscurity until being raised again a few years ago by young leftists who need a fresh icon from the dead past.

Aware Bell's buddy would be reading our correspondence (since Bell had cc'ed him from the start). I added the following PS to my response to Bell's hit job on James (and *First*):

> Sad you caught James in rant as other accounts suggest he could be much more engaging:

> "James himself was one of the most delightful and easy-going personalities I have known, colourful in more ways than one. A dark-skinned West Indian Negro from Trinidad, he stood six foot three inches in his socks and was noticeably good-looking. His memory was extraordinary. He could quote, not only passages from Marxist classics but long extracts from Shakespeare, in a soft lilting English which was a delight to hear. Immensely amiable, he loved the fleshpots of capitalism, fine cooking, fine clothes, fine furniture, and beautiful women, without a trace of the guilty remorse to be expected of such a seasoned warrior of the class war. He was brave. Night after night he would address meetings in London and the provinces, denouncing the crimes of the bloodthirsty Stalin until he was hoarse and his wonderful voice a mere croaking in his throat. The communists who heckled him would have torn him limb to limb if it had not been for the police.

> If politics was his religion and Marx his God, if literature was his passion and Shakespeare his prince among writers, cricket was his beloved activity…. He was a demon bowler, and a powerful if erratic batsman. The village loved him, referring to him affectionately as 'the black bastard'…."

A year or so later, Lawrence Goodwyn gave me a fresher view of James whom he met at a university conference in the early '70s. The conference theme was "The Year 2000" and the hall was filled with academic stars who sat up front in a sort of inner circle. Goodwyn was placed in the back and his sense of distance increased as he listened to the certified "geniuses." He wasn't all alone, though, as he found out when James scribbled a note to him suggesting the only thing the assembled mandarins knew about 2000 was that each hoped to be president of Harvard by then. James kept quiet for the first day or two of the conference. When he finally opened up in public, he began by recalling modern instances when striking steelworkers destroyed machines in British factories and farm-workers in Trinidad fired cane fields that provided their livelihood. He wondered aloud if such expressions of deep alienation might be worth a thought or two as conference panelists tried to project what life might be like in the next millennium. There was a pause—the silence resonated promisingly until ... the discourse picked up where it had left off before James posed his question. Goodwyn caught James's eye and they walked right out of the room to the nearest bar. (I'm recalling just now that Goodwyn told that story as he was having a beer with *First*'s crew after he gave the talk reprinted here in "The American Organizing Tradition.")

One more for the road (from the past): you may have noticed I stole James's phrase "the struggle for happiness" earlier in this volume, treating it as part of *First*'s useable past. It's not a first offence. I also used James's line a decade ago in a fanfare announcing *First of the Month*'s appearance. That rip and a tweak of an (unacknowledged and unrecognized) phrase of W.E.B. Du Bois's helped get *First* some play in the local press. The Du Bois line was his definition of African-American culture as an oasis within "a dusty desert of dollars and smartness." A few weeks after the first *First* dropped, I heard Ossie Davis quote that same expression at a panel on black theatre. (The panel's organizer savored the phrase—repeating it so everyone could appreciate Du Bois's lucidity.) Out in the crowd, it felt to me like Mr. Davis had paid *First*'s debt to an Ancestor. I sent him a note thanking him for invoking (and crediting) Du Bois and we kept getting away with it. He wrote back with a projection he knew we could use: "*First of the Month* is spirited, stimulating and controversial in the best sense of the word." We've tried to live up to Mr. Davis's words. And we managed to fulfill a tiny bit of our obligation to Du Bois when we published a transcript of David Levering Lewis's authoritative lecture on his life and times. An excerpt from that talk opens this next set of pieces, which offer alternatives to consensual wisdom about America and the world.

I hope the left turns near the top here inspire radical imaginations. Though "Into Africa's" final passage celebrating Kenya's democratic upsurge is now shadowed by the recent civil unrest there, the story of how that country's polity surprised Western experts segues into Lawrence Goodwyn's streamlined account of the rise of Solidarnosc (which, years after the Polish August, still seemed unfathomable to one candid Polish intellectual: "I thought it was impossible; it was impossible; I still think it was impossible"). Goodwyn's piece on the workers' movement that presaged the end of the Cold War leads, in turn, to Armond White's protest against the "Black Curtain" that now separates black youth from other Americans: "Who knew the fall of Communism would coincide with a new, homegrown Balkanization?"

The last segue in "The Margin is the Center" may be a stretch. But it seems worthy of C.L.R. James's sensibility. (Pace Mr. Bell.) A tribute to Martin Glaberman—a comrade of James's who dropped out of Columbia University to become a "colonizer," a radical doing industrial work—precedes a celebration of Richard Pryor who went to street people to become America's king of comedy.

Majestic Alienation

David Levering Lewis

David Levering Lewis, author of the definitive biography of W.E.B. Du Bois, gave a talk on his subject at Boston University in 2003. What follows is the conclusion of that lecture.

Long before Du Bois lost his political balance to an otherwise reasonable conclusion that America's military-industrial complex was a threat to international peace after World War II, he had amended what he called his "pert phrase" about the problem of the 20th century being the problem of the color-line. For although it could never be said that Du Bois discounted race as one of the building blocks of the social universe, over time he did come to emphasize the maldistribution of wealth as the fundamental impediment to the expansion of human rights. The real problem of the century, therefore, was really the manipulation of race in the service of wealth, and a clairvoyant Du Bois greatly feared that the odds increasingly favored the manipulations by the rich. Had he lived until the end of his century, he would have witnessed the political center in America shift so far to the right that the legacy of the New Deal is now widely regarded as an anachronism. As William Greider conceded in *One World Ready or Not*, "the right has seized the revolutionary banner of the left." A strange triumph it must seem to some of us in which money trumps group interest and corporate royalists have captured Joe Six-pack's loyalty. In all likelihood, Du Bois would not be surprised to hear it said that all social problems have their solution in the unfettered operation of the market economy. Very likely, Du Bois would relish the cruel aphorism in Robert Katter's book *Everything for Sale*: "one thing market society does well," says its author, "is to allow its biggest winners to buy their way out of its pathologies."

As a historian and biographer, I should certainly resist the temptation to divine the what if judgments Du Bois would deliver upon the contemporary political scene were it not that he spoke rather precisely to these times in an essay composed a mere three years before dying. That tremendously pertinent essay, "A Program of Reason, Right and Justice for Today," could be reprinted in *The Nation* or *Progressive* without changing a word. "My friends note an election is coming up." So what? he asks:

> Whether a Democrat or Republican wins, it will be the same old gang. You will have no chance to vote for a meaningful third party. You will have no chance to vote for peace or war; for social medicine, housing or decent education. Why? We know the reason. It is because the United States is no longer a democracy. Most citizens know this well and do not waste time going to the polls....

> We are ruled by a minority armed with wealth and power. This usurpation we must resist.... Here is a program for those who have not lost hope and who yet believe in America.... Heal the sick as a privilege, not as charity. Make private ownership of natural resources a crime. Stop interference with private and personal belief by religious hypocrites. Preserve the utmost freedom for dream of beauty, creative art and joy of living. Call this socialism, communism, reformed capitalism or holy rolling. Call it anything—but get it done! Perhaps this is insane, but to me it is reason, right and justice.

In a real sense, the life of Du Bois is the site of the contested identities both of his people and of the modern national experience as the forces of progress and democracy have struggled and faltered over time against the institutionalized exploitations of race, class and gender. Du Bois's pronouncements may ring so oddly as to cause doubt as to his standing as one of the twentieth century's intellectual heavyweights—an entirely understandable predicament for a thinker who defended Japanese imperialism, who held fast to Soviet communism to the end, and who finally diminished the civil rights struggle in his homeland as a parochial, co-opted phenomenon. No doubt he was precipitous in totally writing off the market economy. Even so, it may be suggested that Du Bois was right to insist that to leave the solution of systemic social problems exclusively to the unregulated market is an agenda guaranteeing gross and ultimately unsustainable economic inequality. Surely, this is a Du Boisian critique that many sober commentators believe has more than a fair chance of trumping the votaries of the Lexus and the olive tree.

In the course of his long, turbulent career, then, W.E.B. Du Bois attempted virtually every possible solution to the problem of 20th-century racism—scholarship, propaganda, integration, cultural and economic separatism, politics, international communism, expatriation, third-world solidarity. An extraordinary mind of color in a racialized century, Du Bois's principled impatience with what he saw as the egregious failings of American democracy drove him, decade by decade, to the paradox of defending totalitarianism in the service of a global ideal of economic and social justice.

But what was the key to this sustained intellectual and political contrariness? What was it that nurtured an apostasy so profound that, in contrast to the lives of most men and women, Du Bois, at age ninety was more radical (and arguably more wrongheaded) than the great majority of the rampaging young of the Sixties? Part of the explanation lies in Du Bois's belief that the best possible United States—the progressive America emerging immediately after the Second World War—was forfeited in the turning-point election of 1948. But there is a deeper source of the majestic alienation that was ever present and increasingly controlling. And we should give W.E.B. Du Bois himself the last explanatory word as it was written in his second and final autobiography.

> Had it not been for the race problem early thrust upon me and enveloping me, I should have probably been an unquestioning worshiper at the shrine of the established order into which I was born. But just that part of this order which seemed to most of my fellows nearest perfection seemed to me most inequitable and wrong; and starting from that critique, I gradually, as the years went by, found other things to question in my environment.

Does that not say it all?

Into Africa

Stephan Talty

The following Q's & A's are excerpted from a First *interview with Aidan Hartly (author of* The Zanzibar Chest) *who was raised in East Africa and became a journalist for Reuters, covering many of the continent's fratricidal wars over the past two decades.*

TALTY: When there's a crisis in Africa, it seems ordinary Africans immediately call for a Western intervention. Do you think the "white-man-with-a-chopper" has become so ingrained that they can't imagine Africans solving their own problems?

HARTLY: You have a short-term reaction to a situation that outrages you, like the recent situation in Monrovia where you had people dying on the streets, you had rebels being supported directly by the U.S. through Guinea coming into the country and on the day that Bob Hope died, the flag flying at half-mast at the embassy—because Bob Hope died, when people within a stone's throw were dying of starvation. In a situation like that, the obvious reaction is: "Come here and stop this!" The "white-men-in-the-choppers" is another symptom of history. In Somalia, you have Italian colonialism that leaves not very much in 1960, then you have a cold war with Somalia getting weapons from the Eastern bloc and the West and then you have Marines coming in and getting shot with the same AM-16s that Reagan sent there in the late '80s. I mean, inevitably you have to have a peacekeeping operation. Basically, what has to happen in a country that has already gone off the edge like Liberia, you have to have African troops on the ground, an African-led multinational process, and the logistical wherewithal, the money, the expertise coming from the West.

TALTY: Can Africa support itself in terms of food?

HARTLY: The production of food out of Africa would be enough to produce a massive surplus, we can not only produce enough food for ourselves, but we can produce food of a higher quality because we've got an environment that hasn't been utterly fucked up. And this is something that should take up the lion's share of discussion about Africa, because Africans are by nature entrepreneurial.

TALTY: How do American and EU farm subsidies affect the average African farmer?

HARTLY: Let me give you an example. If you are a farmer in the EU, I believe the figure is that you'll receive a subsidy of $2 per day for your cow. A full-grown breeding cow in my part of Kenya costs $250. That's impossible to surmount. The subsidies that support farmers in the West, and in America in particular, have made it almost impossible for Kenyan farmers to grow maize. Kenya's literally being flooded with food aid and the U.S. calls this a policy. This is not a policy—it's a transfer of goods. How can you grow maize in the middle of America, ship it to a port, take it across the Atlantic and Indian Oceans, and have it at a price lower than a peasant who's grown it on his five-acre farm. It doesn't make any sense. We're supposed to have preferential access to the American market, but they can resort to other methods of stopping African imports, for example, on health regulations. Honey is produced in my part of Kenya—organic honey that is of such a high quality that it can equal the proceeds of the beef industry. But we can't export it to America because we don't have a pest control certificate, which would cost tens of thousands of dollars. It would be useful for aid agencies to assist farmers surmount those kinds of problems. The logistics are too much for the small man. And then we could be supplying Americans with the best honey in the world.

TALTY: Are you farming yourself in Kenya?

HARTLY: Yes, I wouldn't say I rely on my farming for my livelihood alone. People who are both smallholders and large owners in East Africa have an extremely tough life. In my part of Kenya, mutton prices have gone down by 20 percent in the last year. Farmers can't produce maize at prices competitive to the food aid, which is being imported into the country under U.S. laws that essentially transfer the entire crop of Nebraska wheat to the horn of Africa annually.

TALTY: You're starting an environmental news agency and website for Africa. Who is it aimed at?

HARTLY: I hope we can appeal to anyone interested in environmental issues in Africa. I think we can come up with best practices for people on the ground and on the other hand you might have a small NGO for a project but no idea how to fund it, and they could find funding through the website. I hope that we can embarrass and lead into better practices all those companies investing in Africa. But we don't need what's happening with Nigeria and the oil companies and that destruction of people's lives. Africa still has an environment that can be saved, and I believe that Africa's future is in many ways bound up with the health of the environment. It's going to be a long time before people in African villages become as wealthy as people in the West—and maybe that's not what they want, what we've done in the West.

TALTY: What's your view of Mugabe and his battles with the white farmers? Are the farmers victims or have they resisted a fair distribution of the land?

HARTLY: Look, you're dealing with some quite ordinary tobacco farmer who may or may not be racist, and he's not going to make any rational choices because this is his livelihood. This is something that should have been worked out by the British Commonwealth, the Zimbabwean government and the OAU years ago. It was mishandled, but it was mishandled from both sides right from the beginning. In the Kenya, at independence, there was a scheme called the Million Acre Scheme, which was quite successful at transferring substantial amounts of land from European farmers to the Kenyan government. It was supposed to go to smallholders, but what actually happened was that Kenyatta used it as a pork barrel to come to power. But it basically represented an orderly transfer of land. A similar thing was offered in Zimbabwe. The experiments that did take place were abused from early on, so the process was terminated. What Mugabe is doing is not about the white farmers, it's about the fact that he's at war with his own people. No one took notice when he killed between 10 to 20,000 people in Matabililand in the 1980s.

TALTY: How does the average black African feel about the revolutionary generation of Mugabe et al.?

HARTLY: This is a very serious question. In a large proportion of non-Zimbabweans, there is a respect for them. It's not necessarily a rational viewpoint, it's almost a sentimentality for an era when there was hope, hope that the rhetoric would become reality. More disturbingly, there is a sense of admiration for the guy who stands up against the West. I understand it, but it is very disturbing for ordinary Zimbabweans, who I think would disagree very strongly with middle-class friends of mine who have a grudging respect for Mugabe. There's a very good book called *Brothers Under the Skin* by Christopher Hope where he draws a parallel between the rule of Ian Smith and the rule of Mugabe. He talks about how dictators have the ability to take over the minds of their people—he calls it the "perfume of power."

TALTY: You had an election in Kenya recently. Do you think democracy is strongly rooted there?

HARTLY: I do. And I think the single largest reason is the development of the middle class. In the last 40 years, education has become the single most important thing to a Kenyan family. They're hardworking, dynamic, entrepreneurial people. They're coming up with new ideas—not just traditional industries. I hope we come up with a Bangalore situation in East Africa. They have a horror of the kinds of things Arap Moi was bringing to Kenya—the creation of private militias, the rampant looting of the country, with the help of international figures, the kind of big-man-in-a-suit politics—they were shocked and horrified by that. They surprised people in the West who had washed their hands of Kenya. If you walked into a Western embassy two years ago, the predictions for the elections would have been pretty grim. I don't think that anyone was quite prepared for the responsibility and the peacefulness of the elections. I believe it was the most significant election in Africa since independence. It was a euphoric moment—it was a real democratic competition. There was no real surprise in 1994 with the election of Mandela, though, of course, it was a high point. But in Kenya, we had nothing but bad things to look forward to—and then millions of ordinary Kenyans said, we just don't want this system anymore.

A Politics of Experience

Lawrence Goodwyn

This piece was prompted by a New York Times *obituary published on October 28, 2002.*

A 50-year-old Polish nurse, Alina Pienkowska, died last month in the Baltic coastal city of Gdansk, site of a 1980 shipyard strike that somehow ballooned into a passionate national movement that recruited well beyond half the adult population. Calling itself "Solidarnosc," the popular movement sustained itself through fifteen months of high drama before inducing a traumatized ruling Communist Party to roll the tanks and declare a "State of War." Unfortunately for the Party, the 1982 attempt to preside over a militarized national economy yielded a singularly unhappy result. Calamitous political and economic consequences over the next six years brought Leninism to crisis across the entire Soviet bloc. When these breathtaking events had finally run their course, walls of all kinds came tumbling down in Berlin and elsewhere. As the saying goes, "the Cold War came to an end."

We have subsequently had a great deal of trouble sorting through all the causal connections that produced these epochal happenings. In some elusive way, the Polish movement is understood to have exposed the rotten underpinnings of the "Worker State." But understanding opposition politics in Poland has proved tough slogging. The need to craft a suitable obituary for Pienkowska, the Polish nurse, affords the latest opportunity. Michael T. Kaufman of the *New York Times* has given it a try. "Alina Pienowska, a shy and soft-spoken nurse whose impassioned words turned a shipyard strike in Gdansk, Poland in 1980 into a nationwide and triumphant movement called Solidarity that ultimately helped to bring down Communism, died on Oct. 17th in Gdansk." After noting some shipyard turmoil, the author explains that a:

> dismissed welder named Lech Walesa climbed into the shipyard and proclaimed a strike. From the windows of her apartment, Ms. Pienkowska saw that a strike had begun. Rightly assuming that state security agencies would have cut phone lines from the yard in the hope of keeping the strike secret from the nation and the world, she called friends in Warsaw, who alerted Western reporters, making sure the news would spread through Poland over Radio Free Europe. But her greater contribution came two days later when she was with her fellow strikers in the shipyard. By then, many smaller factories and government establishments in the region had been struck, with their workers compiling lists of demands. On August 16, the shipyard management offered strikers there a considerable raise. The strike committee agreed, and Mr. Walesa announced the strike had ended. Thousands of jubilant workers headed for the gates and home. Mr. Pienkowska was enraged, realizing that as a result of the agreement tens of thousands of strikers at plants throughout the region were being left in the lurch. She found the voice and the courage to attack Mr. Walesa. "You betrayed them," she said of the strikers beyond the shipyard. "Now the authorities will crush us like bedbugs." She managed to shut one gate and pleaded for the strikers to stay and maintain the strike. Some lingered, but most rushed home to their families. But Ms. Pienkowska's message got through, and in many cases wives sent their husbands back; by nightfall, the shipyard was filling up once more.

Michael Kaufman's assessment of Ms. Pienkowska's causative role concludes, "The strike had been salvaged in the spirit of Solidarity, a word that would soon provide the free trade union movement with its name."

Unfortunately, this is not how things happened. Mr. Kaufman is not merely wrong, he is primitively wrong. *The New York Times* deserved a better performance than he provided, especially since John Darnton of the paper's European staff got things off to a knowledgeable start by capably describing the dramatic beginnings of the coastal strike in 1980. In any case, nationwide popular movements, particularly those in totalitarian states, do not happen because a passing worker phones somebody who phones a radio station or closes a gate with sufficient dispatch that she avoids being trampled by joyous but misguided insurgents. No, a 28-year-old nurse did not "turn a shipyard strike into a nationwide and triumphant movement" through such simplistic acts.

At the risk of seeming to report from another planet, it may be useful to offer a bit of background on the dynamics of popular politics in Poland that Mr. Kaufman passed over. Beyond his gaze was an elaborate worker formation assembled through three decades of organizing on the Baltic coast that generated germane political experiences for Poles or anyone else, including Michael T. Kaufman, who cares to be instructed.

In the course of bloody struggles in the 1950s, '60s and '70s, Poles had over time learned how to construct vast "occupation strikes" where thousands of workers united to take over coastal shipyards and protect by sheer numbers their own strike committees from immediate arrest. They had also learned to fashion worker demands that were structurally serious, that dealt with the animating grievance of the Baltic working class—the confinement of Polish workers in the party's official trade unions. The demands of shipyard workers were led by a call for "free and independent trade unions"—"free" of the ruling party because they were organized "independent" of the party. Activists in the coastal working class had also pioneered something truly innovative in the world of popular politics—an elaborate construct that they called the "Interfactory Strike Committee." As a striking blueprint for a general strike, it was to attain effective realization in the Polish August of 1980. It has not since reappeared anywhere in the world.

(Whatever else observers around the world thought of Poles, American labor organizers had, in the 1930s, borrowed freely from innovations Polish immigrants had introduced into the culture of the American working class. The "occupation strike" perfected in Poland in the early 1930s became the American sit-down strike, which at Flint, Michigan in 1936 materialized as the Great Sit-Down Strike at General Motors that brought the UAW onto the stage of national politics. The organizer of the Flint Strike had earlier learned about the occupation strike, and how to fashion one, from Polish co-workers at the White Truck Factory in Cleveland.)

Since the creation of the Eastern Bloc at the end of World War II, workers in Leninist countries had learned that their efforts at self-organization had to be huge because their intention necessarily had to be to organize against the State—not against individual bosses as in capitalist countries. But if most communist working classes around the world had experienced sufficient "democratic centralism" to be able to see the logic of such a large goal, none had the experience the Poles had amassed for themselves in 35 years of recurring insurgencies.

The most experienced of them all was a tireless activist named Lech Walesa. After coming in the 1960s to Poland's largest coastal workplace, the Lenin Shipyard in Gdansk, Walesa quickly associated himself with the "old militants" of the preceding generations who taught him the traditions of workplace organizing and warned him, as well, about the untrustworthiness of the party trade unions. So instructed, Walesa participated in the volatile politics of 1968. Two years later, he sat on the three-man strike presidium that led the tumultuous 1970 shipyard mobilization so seemingly militant that the party decided extreme measures were needed to put it down. Tanks and machine guns were deployed in the streets of Gdansk to beat back crowds of workers who had taken over the shipyard. When they began marching to the Polytechnic Institute to recruit students to the cause, the party leaders in Warsaw panicked and gave orders. The Polish army fired on Polish workers and blood flowed in the streets of the city.

The tense aftermath was fueled by a kind of pulsating popular outrage that cannot be adequately described in a brief article. Suffice it to say that workers on the Baltic coast never thereafter forgot the "December Massacre" of 1970. A dazed and defensive party did not help. Under immense pressure from impatient Soviets appalled by what they took to be the limp leadership of their Polish counterparts, coastal party officials were forced to do whatever proved necessary to reestablish party supremacy over the population. So many workers were forced to endure jailhouse interrogations, confinement, reassignment of workplaces, or combinations of all three that it took the party apparatus a good part of the next year, 1971, to restore order along the Baltic coast. Arrests mounted into the hundreds. But the transparent authoritarianism surrounding the inevitable judicial proceedings generated repeated occupation strikes up and down the Baltic coast. A political truth, totally unseen, lurked here: the social experience gained by thousands of coastal workers was unmatched in the rest of the country.

Walesa sought to cultivate that experience on the job where his energy level astonished everybody. His conscientious work made him a favorite of supervisors. As the best electro-motor mechanic in the shipyard, he was called upon to plug an ever-increasing number of holes in daily production. Getting "down engines" up and running eventually grew into fixing "down" systems of all kinds. Walesa therefore found himself moving with regularity to every shop section in the shipyard—precisely what he wanted to do as an organizer. Indeed, given the low priority that equipment maintenance possessed as a component of the Party's Five-Year Plans, engine breakdowns were such a constant function of life in the Lenin Shipyard that Walesa could frequently set up his daily work schedule based on his organizing needs. He could do this and still put in a productive day of work. The party hated him but plant managers loved him. As he subsequently explained to a western reporter who inquired how he managed to know so many workers in different shops, "I had the best job in the shipyard. It took me all over."

Walesa kept moving outside of his workplaces as well. In the late '70s, by some miracle of labor, ingenuity, and scavenging of parts, he was able to resuscitate an old Warszawa automobile. He obtained a driver's license, plastered copies of Poland's democratic constitution of 1791 over the car windows, thus creating a kind of mobile democratic exhibit that signaled, down every street he drove, the range of possible self-expression available to all Poles.

Walesa fraternized with groups of every political orientation. It seemed he could endure any amount of sectarian rhetoric as he counted the house and measured the utility of all those in view. Everything was subordinated to acquiring the ingredients necessary to the creation of the large-scale independent union.

His efforts on this front eventually led to his being fired from the shipyard (as well as two other jobs) and to over 30 arrests. All that he learned in the course of his unrelenting '70s outreach—and all that the Coastal workers had discovered during their history of resistance—was put to a final, climactic test when the party fired Anna Walentynowicz in August of 1980.

Walentynowcis was one of the better known and certainly the most visible of all the shipyard militants. For many years she had been a crane operator in an industrial setting in which the shipyard's huge cranes towered over every other structure in a city of half a million people. Not only was she widely known throughout the shipyard, the party's contempt for all workers was signaled by the sacking, coming short months before her retirement.

Movement printers were called, leaflets printed, and word passed to all the shop sections in the shipyard. Walesa spent the night of August 13th away from his apartment to avoid the security police, came to the shipyard the next day, climbed over a fence (since his most recent dismissal for activism, he had no job credentials anywhere), gathered among his many activist acquaintances in two dozen shop sections, staged a mass meeting, called a strike, and shut the shipyard down.

It was Thursday, August 14th the first day of what would become known as "The Polish August." The workers formed a strike presidium, drafted a series of postulates headed by the demand for a trade union independent of the party, delivered it to the shipyard manager and settled in for the struggle. The first object of attention was 15,000 shipyard workers whose participation in an occupation strike was essential to the protection of the strike committee. Done.

Friday, August 15th—the long years of movement building in the scores of plants and hundreds of offices throughout the coastal vicinity of Gdansk now came into play. Of all the coastal militants, the most strategically important was Henryka Krzywonos, head of the Gdansk transport workers. She needed only confirmation that the strike was on to shut down all public transportation. It was, and she did. Next came the sister shipyard at Gdynia that had a congenial name, The Paris Commune Shipyard. It, too, came right on line. With memory of the coastal massacre driving him, as it had for ten years, Sobieszek led Siarkopol out, as did Gwiazda and Lis at Elmor and Lewandowski at Gdansk Port. The enterprises whose workforces were too small in number to offer effective protection for a strike committee nevertheless had shop leaders who understood they had to support the shipyard's 15,000 for the reciprocal protection they could get in return for themselves and for everyone else. On this day, the workers of the Baltic Coast proved how long were their memories—twenty enterprises on strike and ready, when the time came, to elect delegates to an Interfactory Strike Committee. By nightfall, many thousands had affiliated with the Lenin Shipyard, precisely how many no one could yet be sure.

The city of Gdansk simply came to a standstill as Krzywonos directed her second job action of the month by the transport workers. The red and white flag of Poland, the first of what would soon become a vast civic display, appeared from the window on an office in downtown Gdansk. It signaled generalized support for the strikers by white-collar workers. The display of the national colors expressed their sense of the connection: they and the workers were the nation. The party was not.

By the simple expedient of looking out of his window, the shipyard director knew it, too. He spent much of Friday trying to convince Warsaw of the danger that was brewing. Reinstate the crane operator, Walentynowicz. Done. But, though allegedly the cause of the strike, correcting that problem was not enough. Walesa drew upon the lessons of twelve years. It was time, he told Gniech, to deal with structural matters. He said the magic words, "An independent trade union free of party control."

Crisis.

If, at the outset, the workers had brought more sophistication to the table than Gniech, the strike presidium, led by Walesa, soon discovered they were using up their accumulated experiential knowledge at a rapid rate. That Friday night, the best tactical minds in the Polish Party were put at work to devise a plan that would outflank Walesa's committee from the left. The task was not simple for the worker postulates were robust: in addition to the independent union; family allowances for workers equal to that received by the police apparatus; abolition of the special retail stores for party members; a 2000 zloty raise for all shipyard workers; and, finally, publication of the workers' demands in the government media.

Saturday, August 16. The party had given Director Gniech a new agenda. Before the party could feel secure about any settlement that was reached, the unrepresentative nature of the strike needed to be corrected by allowing each shop section in the shipyard to name four delegates to the committee. Walesa and his cohorts could find no way to object to the inherently democratic nature of this proposal, though the change dramatically increased the committee's size. The party then used its knowledge of the work force (Walesa, for one, had been gone for over four years) and also its muscle to elect a "soft" set of delegates. The Party then made so many concessions—including, a verbal acceptance of a free and independent union—that Walesa was unable to hold back the tide. The enlarged committee went for it, the formal vote having the effect of ending the strike. Gniech pointed out that it was now Walesa's turn. As chairman of the Strike Presidium it was his duty to announce the end of the strike. Unhappily, Walesa cast about for some expedient but could find none. The workers had voted and he was bound by movement experience and simple logic to respect their wishes. He did the best he could to preserve things for future struggles. "We have done a great thing, but we shall do still bigger things for the good of the shipyards and our motherland."

Gathered outside the door of the negotiating room were the most anxious workers in the place—the delegates from all the smaller plants in Gdansk who, of course, would be crushed if the shipyard workers settled. Henryka Krzywonos of the transport workers immediately took Walesa by the arm and reminded him, "Lech, we can't fight tanks with buses." She was aware as she spoke that both of them understood that the entire city of Gdansk had been paralyzed by the solidarity strike of the transport workers in support of the shipyard. Here was a way out and Walesa took it with dispatch: "We must respect democracy and therefore accept the compromise, even if it is not brilliant; but we do not have the right to abandon others. We must continue the strike out of solidarity until everyone has won. I said I would be the last person to leave the shipyard. And I meant it. If the workers who are gathered here want to continue the strike then it will be continued. Now, who wants to strike?"

This was the most awkward moment in the Polish August. All movements at some juncture are forced to confront contradictions of this kind. Things tend to fall apart or, to avoid that, a potentially crippling deception is introduced into the structure of advocacy the movement represents. At such moments, it is helpful if a movement has generated indigenous leadership with deeply internalized long-term objectives. The Baltic movement had. Walesa's reaction to Krzywonos was immediate and his explanation to the group effortless. Of course, the workers who wanted to strike shouted their approval and all those who wanted to go home were silent. The politics of the situation impelled both. The difficulty, of course, was that all who had been silent promptly voted with their feet to go home. As matters turned out, both the party and Walesa thought they held the trump card—the party because Gniech pulled the plug on the shipyard loudspeaker the instant Walesa's finished his reluctant acknowledgement and before he had time to triumphantly signal the strike's renewal. For a few moments, the party seemed to be right. The workers streamed home and, to all appearances, everything appeared to be over. But Walesa knew better, and so, too, did the veteran organizers who surrounded him.

The strike persisted over the pivotal first weekend, despite the absence of loudspeakers, because workers relied on alterative internal mechanisms of communication—electric trolleys. Militants used them to get to the key activist shop sections housing metal and electrical workers and to the hull sites of the "flyers" and the "temps" which also teemed with activists. Old Lenarciak and Stanislaw Bury successfully urged everyone to "stay calm and stay in the shipyard." About 300 to 400 did so. Walesa augmented this internal effort by taking an electric trolley to the far ends of the shipyard in the company of Ewa Ossowska with the same message to stay put; and Alina Pienkowska went to Gate #3 to carry a similar exhortation to departing workers.

All in all, something between five to nine hundred workers stayed through the weekend. They were the true "militants" of the coastal mobilization for they protected the Interfactory Strike Committee, which formed Saturday evening. The presidium was, simply enough, the formal gathering site of the activists of the Baltic working class:

Kryzwonos and Zdzislaw Kobyllinski of the transport workers but also such hardened veterans as Gwiazda, Walentynowicz, Szoloch, Borusewicz, Lewandowski, Pienkoska, Wisniewski and, of course, Walesa. This was the core group that presided over the tense negotiations with the government leading to the triumphant culmination of "the Polish August." They represented the lateral lines of communication that brought into being the "big union" that Walesa, in particular, had been working toward throughout the '70s. By Sunday night, they had recruited fifty thousand workers and within two weeks, the Interfactory Strike Committee would have over 700 affiliated factories representing more than 600,000 coastal workers—the structure that brought Solidarnosc onto the stage of 20th-century history.

For the militants of the Presidium, Monday morning was the decisive moment of the entire strike. Either some of the work force went back on the job, thereby undermining the basic integrity of the strike and putting a stamp of confirmation on the Saturday settlement, or the entire work force rejoined the occupation strike and thus solidified the movement.

Over the weekend, the full force of Leninist culture had been brought to bear on the strikers. The government media relentlessly chipped away at the integrity of the "anti-socialist elements" in the shipyard who restrained "honest workers" desiring to go home to their families. And even before the vanguard of the first shift appeared at the gates on Monday morning, Gniech had turned on the loudspeakers and initiated a litany: "On Saturday, we ended talks with representatives of all shipyard workers. We came to full agreement. Let's remember that we alone are responsible for the shipyard and for everything that happens here." The last line, needless to say, was an implied threat.

Walesa suddenly appeared, climbing up where all could see him. Many things had happened during his long years of recruiting and he called on that experience now. He surveyed the crowd, two crowds actually as they stood facing each other on opposite sides of the gates. Alone, in his loud distinctive voice, he began singing the national anthem, "Poland Has Not Yet Perished." Voices on both sides of the gate joined him. With a measure of solidarity to build on, he spoke in calm measured tones, reviewing the negotiations, and the help everyone in the shipyard had gotten from the transport workers and from all the supply enterprises ringing the shipyard. He briefly refuted the claims of the Party spokesman and then moved to the central Issue: The strike, he said, was for the defense of all workers of the coast, indeed, of all Poland. They were not quite done. "Don't hesitate to come in. We have to fight for what is rightly ours. Come to us, shipyard workers. There is nothing to be afraid of."

There was a pause—the gates were open now—and some strikers called for the others to join them. A vanguard of mostly younger workers came on in, to cheers of encouragement; then they all came, to prolonged cheering.

They were together. The strike presidium was protected against the security police. Nothing short of tanks could now prevent the formation of a trade union independent of the party. The Polish August.

Power, of course, never goes quietly. The government tried to conduct the negotiations in private. The presidium insisted on loudspeakers so all shipyard workers could hear. Gniech said the loudspeakers were out of order. Walesa, who knew about electrical matters, reconnected them himself. Security forces tried to prevent the Interfactory Strike Committee from adding affiliates by throwing a thick cordon of troops around the Lenin Shipyard. The movement countered by dispatching couriers to the other provinces. Many got arrested in this new war, which went unreported in a casually attentive world press. Couriers who got through explained to far away workers what an Interfactory committee was, how an occupation strike could be fashioned, and how to elect their own delegates to join the Gdansk strikers. The workers heard the couriers out, applied the lessons of self-activity to their own enterprises, learned quickly or slowly and then dispatched their representatives to Gdansk. Many of the new recruits got arrested, too.

As coastal militants had all learned in their own time, this sort of thing was all very educational. Party negotiators, led by a deputy premier of Poland, denied the government was arresting anybody, but the worker presidium was full of people who knew all about security detentions—of themselves in the past or of couriers at the moment. They told the government so. This form of dialogue—deception and rebuttal, new deception and new rebuttal—became a subtext to the formal negotiation. On August 31 the government capitulated and Solidarnosc came into being.

A struggle—not irrelevant to contemporary geopolitics—then ensued over a proper understanding of which Poles made the Baltic Movement happen (and which Poles should administer the important newly-formed institution called Solidarnosc).

During the Polish August, coastal enterprises as far away as Szczercin on the German border and Elblag near the Soviet Union had previously gone to school on their own actions and had also been taught by the savage response of the government in 1970. They therefore knew how to mount occupation strikes and how to affiliate with a distant Interfactory committee. A large number of enterprises on the Baltic Coast joined the Gdansk movement during late August of 1980, but enterprises in Warsaw did not and the rest of Poland did not.

Despite what the *Times'* Michael T. Kaufman (and many Polish intellectuals) would have you believe—hearing on Radio Free Europe that a strike had occurred somewhere did not instruct people in the relevant arts of movement building. Radio Free Europe's functionaries could not provide that information. It was not something one learned laboring in a media bureaucracy. Rather, the specific social knowledge needed had been slowly, painfully acquired by the veteran organizers of coastal enterprises.

It is fortunate for Poland and for the cause of democracy generally that people like Alina Pienkowska tried for a very long time to learn all they could about what they might be able to do to help those organizers. Not only did she man a shipyard gate and plead, successfully in some cases, for workers to stay on strike, she undertook over the ensuing two weeks to set up a supply system that fed 15,000 workers two or three meals a day. She earned her spurs in behalf of the Polish democratic movement. So did intellectual activists associated with the opposition group KOR, but Pienkowska's service was more centrally germane.

It was nice, of course, that she had a good bit of help in her labors. The final vignette in Michael Kaufman's obituary of Ms. Pienkowska in the *Times* reads: "In 1983, she married Mr. [Bogdan] Borusewicz, who was in hiding, in a secret ceremony. A year later, her husband, still a fugitive, attended the baptism of their son while disguised as an old woman. Mr. Walesa, a guest, unsuspectingly kissed his hand."

Had Mr. Kaufman been in Gdansk that day, he might have caught the twinkle in Lech Walesa's eye. But alas, Mr. Kaufman was not. He therefore failed to grasp yet another of the movement's fine moments of collective democratic striving under martial law.

CODA: After the Polish Party collapsed in 1991, many activists in the democratic opposition in Warsaw, others close to the Catholic Church and still others who grew up in the worker movement all contested for power. None were able to figure out how to resist the controlling influence over Poland's economy possessed by the International Monetary Fund and the World Bank. As a result, the post-Leninist economy proved to be a huge disappointment to almost all Poles. Inevitably, all the political figures who came to have some influence in the country fell victim to this imperial fact. Virtually every Pole mentioned in this article was such a victim. Even outsiders who care about democracy (and who have written about

Poland such as Mr. Kaufman and this writer) are also victims—to the precise extent they realize that economic relationships have a causative bearing on democratic possibilities in all societies around the world.

Tales from Behind the Black Curtain

Armond White

Now that hip-hop culture has become the lingua franca of international media and business, it ironically keeps a class of black Americans, especially youth, in isolation. That's how hip hop preserves it source—the engine of its innovation and perpetuation and commerciality. This conclusion is unavoidable after perusing educational statistics or watching many of the current Dirty South rap acts—Cassidy, Trick Daddy, Lil Jon and the Eastside Boys—whose language and behavior are a throwback to the socially-deprived manner and habits of black folks before the civil rights era. All varieties of social and economic progress seem to have passed by them. Only a few (Up North, West Coast, and across the country) stand to reap profit from exploiting their own deprivation. Yet the glorification persists. It's as if an iron curtain had descended between these black youths and other Americans.

This Black Curtain's divide is not economic or moral, but cultural. And unless one is sensitive to the deprivations black youth face, the Black Curtain is virtually invisible because the black youth behavior that popular culture frequently displays cannot be easily distinguished from what admirably, and naturally, defines black American lifestyles. Like the Iron Curtain Winston Churchill described at the end of World War II, hip hop's Black Curtain cuts off a real segment of the population, exerting influence and control over a group's aspirations. The habits and achievements of these children of capitalism are not autonomous; they have come to fit a pattern, reflecting the commercial conventions of the day.

Behind this Black Curtain, anything that pertains to black segregation is considered acceptable, whether it is an intrinsic style of speaking, singing, dancing, dressing—or unlearning or lassitude or fecklessness. Just ask a ruthless and wealthy entrepreneur like Def Jam/Rockafella's Damon Dash, a privileged spokesman for the marketable deprivations of black youth culture. The less-fortunated are perpetually teased by success such as Dash lives out. The myth of the American Dream is embodied—celebrated—by blackface revenants from Russell Simmons and P. Diddy to Queen Latifah and Eve. A generation of media consumers remains in the straits between their subculture and mainstream culture.

Hip hop's prominence results from a collision between prideful black nationalism and Reagan-era capitalism. Who knew the fall of Communism would coincide with a new, homegrown balkanization? Both the Civil Rights Era ideal of advancement through integration and the race man/woman's vision of black solidarity have been subsumed by avarice. "We Shall Overcome" has been replaced by the imperative "Do What You Gotta Do." This development was underscored by comedian Chris Rock while hosting the MTV Video Awards. Following a performance by Snoop Dogg and his mentor Don "Magic" Juan who hoisted a pimp's chalice in salute to the chorus line of half-clad, vixenish sisters parading in front of a global audience of viewers, Rock ad-libbed, "Isn't it wonderful to see Dr. Martin Luther King's dream come true?" Here are several recent moments in our hip hop era's waking nightmare.

I

Chris Rock's obnoxious performance at [2005]'s Academy Awards ceremony was what African Americans down South describe as "showing your ass." The mainstream media responded differently, praising Rock for being "edgy," because it was content with the liberal condescension to which Rock caters. Typically, Rock will angle his stand-up comedy routine to ridicule black culture and black behavior, justifying cultural stigma and racist stereotype. This has won him acclaim as "The Funniest Man in America" in a *Vanity Fair* cover story (a rare exception to its white cover conventions). Rock also received a featured profile in the *New York Times Magazine*; one of the story's anecdotes recounted how even white officers at a police precinct in the notoriously racist Staten Island proclaimed Rock as their favorite comedian.

The Oscars confirmed Rock's mainstream approval. His hosting gig was praised in advance as a social advance, elevating Rock from his neo-chitlin' circuit/hip-hop subculture. Fact is, Rock's precedent set back the progress of black performers by demonstrating how easily success in mainline culture can be had if one lacks principles. His presumed "edge" was to seem outside Hollywood corruption while simultaneously being all up in it. Rock's tactless, unfunny jokes (against left pariahs George Bush, Mel Gibson and box-office failures Jude Law, Colin Farrell) got great reviews from pundits because he displayed enmity for the incorrect and mocked momentarily disgraced celebrities.

Rock's comic specialty should be properly recognized as "punk"—not in the sense of British pop music rebellion but in the long-standing

American sense of bratty yet cowardly behavior. (He joined the Hollywood mob against Bush and Gibson and kicked Law and Colin at career low-points.) In the now unfashionable sense of ethnic accountability, this can be called: selling out.

In the most high-profile moment of Rock's career, he brazened "blackness" while misrepresenting it. The pretense of black folks' advancement further promoted by the Oscars' celebration of Jamie Foxx's performance as Ray Charles—is what's most troubling about Rock's new status. (In 1969, film critic Pauline Kael bemoaned Hollywood's exclusion of black pop performers: "Hollywood did more with Fats Waller in the '40s than it has done with Ray Charles and Aretha Franklin throughout the '60s." She pointed out the reality of cultural racism that has not changed despite the current heroicizing of Charles and Rock's recent ordination.) Selling-out means Rock can accept Hollywood's blandishments without having to reject its racism.

Rock's "progress" is facetious. He actually upholds cultural stigma. That was clarified by his disgraceful Oscar segment taped at a Magic Johnson movie theater in Compton, CA. Rock's shtick was to show the Oscars were out of touch with movies that "real people" (black ghetto folk) enjoy. But he manipulated the skit to show only those blacks who went to stereotypical exploitation films like *White Chicks*, *Saw* and *Soul Plane*. He left out blacks who went to *Million Dollar Baby* and *The Aviator*, as well as those whites (or any one else) who went to *Soul Plane* and *White Chicks*. Rock fostered the racist notion that all black folks think alike and enjoy the same dumbed-down entertainment. He appealed to white racist ignorance by excluding other ethnic groups (and their varied, surprising, democratic range of taste) from his jokey film culture essay. Rock's basic message—as usual—was: Yes, blacks deserve to be stereotyped negatively.

II

Tyra Banks' reality tv series *America's Next Top Model* is the best of the prime time shows that pretend documentary realism but are really sweepstakes contests. Banks offers her young female contestants the carrot of extending their 15 minutes of fame. But more importantly, she gives viewers a helpful look at the competitive nature of American big business (plus the insight that fashion and entertainment are indeed parts of big business). Producer-creator-host Banks—perfectly named—is one of the few contemporary black pop figures to balance her pride of accomplishment with social consciousness. She ensures that *ANTM* is also a civics lesson. The show's biggest revelation came in the episode where the most feckless black contestant declared: "My mother and grandmother are not ghetto, but I choose to be ghetto."

When the stubborn fashion-industry hopeful refused to participate in the show's games then laughed off her failure, Banks exploded. She berated the girl with the full indignation of the previous generation of African American strivers. Banks nailed young blacks who angrily defy social strictures without summoning the energy to accomplish worthwhile goals. P. Diddy's *Making the Band* series for MTV, by contrast, embraces those ingrates' attitude of entitlement. Diddy's show is built on arrogant tantrums, which he manufactures. While Banks' preferable program offered rare, raw proof of illiteracy and rascality (hip-hop era defiance) *chosen* as a kind of life-style option, *ANTM* condemns this dire social development; Banks instructs her young charges rather than exploiting them Diddy-style. Though glamorizing the competition for fame and riches, she manages to shine a light through the fog of caste.

III

Ossie Davis' funeral marked the end of the Civil Rights Era's Old Guard. This solemn occasion illuminated the existence of the Black Curtain more than even the controversy over Bill Cosby criticizing the failures of modern black parenting. Davis' passing was mourned by a retinue of elderly, unfashionable cultural figures, even a retired American president (Bill Clinton surprisingly quoting Nina Simone). It was a rare public demonstration of blacks and whites who shared a social vision that's fading. Actor Burt Reynolds' confession, "Ossie Davis took the bad part of the white south out of me," was humble, loving, familial—a startling contrast to the cartel-brotherhood modeled by Eminem, Dr. Dre and 50 Cent.

With each testament to Davis's now unfashionable political drive and ethical stance, the line of obsequies (from Attala Shabazz's personal memories to Alan Alda's professional recall), began to resemble a parade of shattered hopes. As a tv broadcast—indicative of America's consciousness—it seemed anomalous amongst the game shows and celebrity marathons regularly televised. Although it was "live," it was also sur-reality tv—and saddening for its evidence of social decline.

In black gospel parlance, a funeral is called a "home-going;" the perspective meant to revitalize mourners suffering through their time of loss. But a cultural leader's funeral marks a larger moment of transition;

it is more than a personal tragedy. The author of *Purlie Victorious* (the satire about an itinerant 1960s black preacher finally overthrowing the remnants of Jim Crow) and the man whose oration designated Malcolm X "Our black shining prince" demonstrated an awe-inspiring accountability to the future. Davis epitomized the '60s moment when activists not only had a sense of duty, but felt anxiety lest they fall below the level of achievement that would uplift their people, and move the whole wide world up a little higher. Davis believed in culture that edified and sustained his people, while affirming their claim upon society. But today the claim has narrowed into the covetousness that pop entrepreneurs now cultivate to tease—and delimit—their audience's aspirations. Laissez-faire capitalism and laissez-faire democracy are the bulwarks of the Black Curtain. Davis' funeral is the perfect moment to realize hiphop's confusion of doing well with doing good. As a result, hip-hop culture's demand for black folks' acceptance and prosperity *by any means necessary* has unwittingly become a barrier to their empowerment.

Mandela's Eyes

Don't play around the course he got the took
the rook the crook the snook all were
pasted upon him like a long vicious learning
there is all of Africa all of night all the
every trace of sweet hurt distilled like
cobalt turned into night the distant moon
a door to where no one wants to go Mandela's
face is naturally political like the disposition
of an Angel the smile a postage stamp of
verifiable desire Love glowing & objective
What amazes our enemies is that we all
fit into his suit so elegantly
                    and alive

– Amiri Baraka

Mr. Brown, May God Rest His Funky Soul

Chuck D

A response to First*'s call for reflections on James Brown's passing.*

Got the news Christmas Eve from Davey D on the Westside of the country; we'd just left there. Thus at 3AM in the East, it's too early and too late to call anybody like my man Kyle Jason who, together with me, did our damnedest to catch his tour three years back. I had heard things like Mr. Brown was pushing it real hard, defying gravity and time itself. I myself saw a seventy-year-old man wear an Atlanta stage out, as well as the crowd. It was good to see some black folks in the audience for a change, checking out our classic creator of funky soul himself.

Now this news. It makes one really understand that time is God itself.

Thus we shall praise God and cherish the time. James Brown is somewhat woven into my professional and entertainment regimen. In my travels on the tour bus from Sacramento to Spokane, I'd just picked up yet another James Brown CD—this one from Universal Millennium Masters, *James Brown and Friends*, for my drive time groove pleasure. In the hotel, the Blues Brothers were on AMC where JB did that scorching preacher scene in the church backed by the James Cleveland Choir. While everybody seemed to relish in the now of comedian Katt Williams on the long bus ride, I locked my DVD player and headphones to Mr. Brown's classic *Soul Train* and Paris performances. When talking music, JB was/is just part of the day, thank God for recordings. As a '70s B-boy I recall panic on the floors of hip hop while "Give It Up or Turnit a Loose" roasted off the 1969 *Sex Machine* Live LP transfixing the forming rap nation ten years later, as if it were a discovered oil well. While the rest of the disco and rock country had not a clue.

As barely a social hum registered at the recent passings of Atlantic Records founder Ahmet Ertegun and Atlantic Records star R&B artist Ruth Brown, I as a music student felt those losses. Good peer and buddy Gerald Levert's passing was a shock and largely just black folk's pain at the loss, like a family member … nationally only a few sentences because an Anglo-nation couldn't possibly understand. Now Mr. James Brown is entirely another magnitude, a seismic passing—the level of a KING, the Cincinnati record label he recorded on or a very funky president, the title of his 1975 political hit.

Recently I covered some ground being interviewed for a movie documentary his latest wife Tami Raye was producing. I myself felt extremely honored to have been asked to be interviewed for that and his prior *Soul Survivor* special and DVD. I promised myself to reach and do all I can when the legends callout.

I missed out on Mr. Ray Charles, wanting to catch any show during 2002, then I heard he got sick. The founders of rock and roll are still doing gigs—Little Richard, Chuck Berry, Bo Diddley, and we almost lost Fats Domino to Katrina. Jerry Lee Lewis just released a new album, and Ike and Tina Turner continue to defy time. Still Mr. JB is it for me. I have yet to meet Mr. Muhammad Ali, and only met Richard Pryor one brief two-minute period at the 2000 BET Awards in Las Vegas. I met Mr. James Brown. Backstage in the concocted green room looking at the screens—just me and another gentleman were checking it out. I was behind this man dressed in a bluish suit, but I could tell it was James Brown. Reading everything about the man beforehand I knew to address him as Mr. Brown. I tapped him on the shoulder and said "Hello, er, Mr. Brown" and introduced myself. He asked my name again and when I answered it must've registered, because he let out a "Whoa," and smiled with a hug. I didn't have a damn camera and asked him to hold on. When I came back a minute later he was gone, on stage doing his thing with singer Ginuwine. Off stage he left through another way … and that was the one time for me.

Man, no lie, whenever I see a frozen pond, I take myself to 1967 when us kids did the James Brown I Feel Good dance on any patch of ice. Global warming has somehow produced fewer patches of ice, just as soul loses a bit of itself every ten years. The sheer magnitude of *Say It Loud, I'm Black and I'm Proud* was an implanted, soundtracked theme into understanding that our minds, bodies, and souls were black and beautiful. Ali, Pryor and JB were our snap, crackle and pop from the transcendent, previously silenced black male in '60s-'70s Amerikkka. It ain't never left me. Never will. This is why spreading the word is our jobs as modern-day griots. I've had phone conversations with Huey Newton before he passed, Kwame Toure respected my works of words, and Minister Farrakhan and the Nation of Islam have introduced PE [Public Enemy] to parts of the darker earth where few like us had gone before. Yes time is God indeed, and all of our words and deeds are in passing, but the passing down and forward is so important. My children know Mr. James Brown's music, as well as Levi Stubbs of the Four Tops and Reverend Al Green (whereas it was a trip at the Scream Tour 5 in Madison Square Garden NYC hearing 16,000, mostly young black girl, teenagers finishing off singing *Lets Stay Together* during Young Joc's DJ set as if it was a Clear Channel hit).

In the fifty years of Mr. Brown's recorded music, since his 1956 hit *Please, Please, Please*, we, Public Enemy, head into our 20th year of existence with full dedicated honor to the fabric Mr. James Brown provided for hip hop's founders—Afrika Bambaataa, Kool DJ Herc, and Grandmaster Flash—to weave. Expect the utmost respect for the architect. Again I expect the executive asses of the record industry ashes to say little, and do less. The radio stations are eerie in their silence, proving there ain't no such thing as black radio, just robot fuel from white corporations who continue to argue that race ain't an issue. And in the end there will be folks who will dedicate and play 50 years of soul, that realize that black is important to say it loud and proud because Amerikka continues to discredit it and strip it away. But this should make us realize how lucky many of us are to have witnessed, experienced, and infused the work and pride ethics of the godfather of soul into our daily lives. For that alone we are all better for it. Probably the hardest working man in heaven right now ... but may his funky soul R.I.P ... Mr. Dynamite ... JAAAAMES BROWWWWN!

Shout Sister Shout!

Gayle Wald

In the yet-to-be written annals of stadium rock, the massive concert staged in Washington D.C.'s Griffith Stadium on July 3, 1951 ranks as one of the most extraordinary. That was the night singer-guitarist "Sister" Rosetta Tharpe, a musician and performer of arena-sized talent, married her third husband in a joint wedding ceremony-concert before 20,000 fans doubling as guests.

Those who made it to the stadium despite a city transit strike forked over between 90 cents and $2.50—or about as much as it cost to see the Washington Senators baseball team—for a program that opened with Tharpe's nuptials and climaxed (according to a front-page story in the Washington *Afro-American*) with a fireworks display featuring "a 20-foot, animated, lifelike reproduction of the famed Sister Tharpe, rhythmically strumming her guitar." Sandwiched between the pageantry was a gospel program that included Marie Knight, Tharpe's singing partner, and local talents the Sunset Harmonizers and Richmond Harmonizing Four. The indisputable highlight of the evening, however, was the bride herself, who regaled the crowd by playing her steel guitar from center field resplendent in white satin and lace.

The Griffith Stadium extravaganza was an audacious move even for Tharpe, a Holy Roller who had once appeared onstage at the Cotton Club astride a mule against the wishes of her first husband, a Pentecostal minister. Held on the eve of the annual celebration of national independence, it unabashedly flouted the boundary between religious ritual and show-biz spectacle, marrying solemnity with humor, the sacrosanct with the carnivalesque.

Decca Records released the Tharpe "wedding ceremony" in 78 and 33 formats, and *Ebony* magazine covered it exhaustively, down to the rumored cost of Tharpe's dress ($800) and the number of white orchids in her corsage (28). But beyond some tantalizing still photographs, we don't have any visual documentation of the show.

This absence stands out because of Tharpe's remarkable charisma as a live performer. Tharpe didn't just play the guitar, she *owned* it. Like a snake-charmer, she coaxed sounds out of the instruments, turning wood and metal into something alive yet completely under her control. Her contemporaries referred to this as making a guitar "talk." Sometimes, too, they said she played "like a man," as though a woman wasn't capable of projecting such command—or a woman-in-gospel conveying such palpable eroticism.

Since Tharpe's death in 1973, our window into her remarkable live presence has consisted of several mediocre concert recordings, mostly made in Europe late in her career, and a handful of filmed performances, including three 1940s-era soundies that find her acting the "girl" singer for the Lucky Millinder band.

All the more compelling, then, are the two brief and starkly different glimpses of Tharpe we get in [the 2004 PBS series produced by Martin Scorcese] *The Blues*. Both show her singing versions of "Up Above My Head," a church standard Tharpe originally popularized in a swinging duet with Marie Knight in 1947. In Charles Burnett's *Warming by the Devil's Fire*, Tharpe sings and plays electric guitar while sitting on a couch in what looks like a hotel room or a backstage sitting area. It's a quietly authoritative performance for a woman whose forte was the grand gesture, the theatrical move that would carry the saints home.

In contrast, Mike Figgis's *Red White, and Blues* contains footage of Tharpe from the short-lived variety show "TV Gospel Time" circa 1965. Against the backdrop of a full gospel choir, she turns in a guitar solo of heart-stopping brilliance. Viewing Tharpe tear it up on her white Gibson Les Paul, SG, you understand how she had the white New Yorkers attending John Hammond's famous 1938 "Spirituals to Swing" concert at Carnegie Hall "almost shouting in the aisles," in Count Basie's recollection. You feel how Tharpe used her guitar to sweet-talk the Holy Ghost and bring church-congregations to their knees. In the moment of witnessing a sanctified singer from Cotton Plant, Arkansas anticipate every move you ever thought belonged exclusively to Little Richard or Pete Townsend, you sense how everything you thought you know about American popular music—from the origin of the "duck walk" to the sources of rock 'n' roll—is now up for grabs.

Such is the power of these images of Tharpe that they prompt nothing short of a historical double-take. Yet, as is so often the case in *The Blues*, their eloquence in this respect competes with, rather than complements, the films themselves. In Burnett's episode, a semi-fictionalized coming-into-manhood story, Buddy, the ne'er-do-well uncle of the young protagonist Junior, instructs his about-to-be-baptized charge in the ways of the world. This primarily means blues and women. Yet where the former is transcendent—the latter, as Buddy explains to Junior, are elusive and not to be trusted. Women offer you sensual pleasures, but ultimately only to steal your spirit, as Junior's grandmother did to his grandfather before he was born.

Even though we know Buddy is a man of contradictions, an inveterate sinner who starts every morning with a prayer, it's jarring to hear him exhorting Junior to listen carefully to a recording of Tharpe singing, "Precious Memories." For one thing, as much as the film wants us to rethink categories, still it offers up a pretty standard narrative: that Tharpe, like other blues artists, "switched" from gospel to blues and then back again.

This seriously understates the degree to which Tharpe wasn't so much crossing boundaries as outright demolishing them, as her 1951 Griffith Stadium concert exemplified. "Blues is just a theatrical name for gospel," Tharpe insisted to English journalist Valerie Wilmer in 1960, in the process claiming priority for the church as the source of African-American secular music. In Tharpe's hands, a slowed-down version of the gospel song "This Train" (one of her earliest recordings) sounded like classic blues, while an upbeat "Strange Things Are Happening Every Day," a favorite of legendary Memphis DJ Dewey Phillips, was flat-out R&B.

Ultimately Tharpe forged a creative path that paid little attention to rules respecting genre or gender. Indeed, it wasn't Tharpe who played like a man but men who played like her. This is the story that Figgis' *Red White and Blue* might have told had it been more honest in its exploration of the role of African American musicians in the birth and development of British blues. Although "trad" jazz musician Chris Barber, a man of considerable influence in the British scene, first brought Tharpe to England in the late 1950s, their earliest gigs established that Tharpe's talents eclipsed those of her hosts.

Yet the Figgis episode, even after incorporating Tharpe's miraculous "TV Gospel Time" performance, manages to bury the question of Tharpe's authority over white male English musicians with an offhand comment about her taste for brandy and her "randy" offstage antics.

That's a shame, because as much as this quip puts Tharpe squarely in the company of the better known bluesmen—who were, after all, fully expected to behave badly—so it also dismisses her as a musician. This sort of move helps make *The Blues*—capstone event in the Year of the Blues—once again the story of "Men in Blues," as told by men. Not incidentally, none of the seven directors in the series are women.

The current revival of interest in Tharpe's career suggests that this history might yet be re-tuned. In late summer [of 2004] MC Records released *Shout Sister Shout*, a Tharpe tribute CD bringing together contemporary women rock, blues, folk, and gospel musicians. Three new compilations—*The Gospel of the Blues* (MCA/Decca), *The Original Soul Sister* (Proper), and *Sing, Sister, Sing* (Varese)—make Tharpe's work more accessible. And just a few weeks ago Roseanne Carter Cash told viewers of *Larry King Live* that her father Johnny's favorite tune was by Sister Rosetta Tharpe. No matter that most viewers missed the reference or that amid the volley of follow-up questions, Cash couldn't recall the exact song title. It was good enough, in the moment, to have remembered how much Sister Rosetta meant to her country brother-under-the-skin.

Squeezing Out Sparks

Bruce Jackson

John and Alan

In the 1930s, when most academics interested in folklore spent their waking hours in libraries looking for printed versions of the 305 ancient British and Scottish ballads certified as authentic 40 years earlier by Harvard scholar Francis James Child, John and Alan Lomax were ranging the countryside looking for people singing their own songs about their own lives. They recorded scores or hundreds of those Child ballads; they also recorded thousands of songs of cowboys, convicts, miners, farmers, railroad workers, hobos, cotton pickers and other folks none of those library-ferrets gave a hoot about. Millions of Americans first learned about the great range of American folk music because of their work.

When Alan died last summer, John Pareles wrote (in an excellent *Times* obituary) that "Mr. Lomax was a musicologist, author, disc jockey, singer, photographer, talent scout, filmmaker, concert and recording producer and television host. He did whatever was necessary to preserve traditional music and take it to a wider audience."

Alan was a huge presence in the American musical and broader cultural scene. His contribution to our heritage, to our understanding of ourselves, was incalculable.

Much of the music urban participants in the folk song revival of the 1960s played came from recordings Alan and John had made thirty years earlier, recordings published on red vinyl by the Library of Congress. The most important performers the urban folksingers in those years were emulating—Leadbelly, Woody Guthrie, Muddy Waters—had been recorded by the Lomaxes. Bob Dylan is indebted to the Lomaxes' work. So was John Lennon. If you've listened to the six-times-over platinum CD *Oh Brother, where art thou?* you've heard one of Alan's recordings from the 1930s: the very first song on the album, James Carter and a group of convicts singing "Po' Lazarus."

There was a time when, if you were out studying traditional music in America, you could not help but cross a path Alan Lomax and his father had blazed. You probably still can't.

"That Other Feller"

In the summer of 1964 I was recording traditional singers and instrumentalists in Saltville, Virginia, a small mountain town north of Bristol, Tennessee. Someone I met in Saltville's gas station sent me to see Alec Tolbert, who lived in a place called Poor Valley. According to my notes from that trip, you get to Alec Tolbert's house in Poor Valley by going out Route 91 about four miles to McReady's Gap, then you turn left at the red brick church, go three-quarters of a mile to the top of the hill, turn right, go about two miles to a little store. Then you go in the store and ask anyone where Alex Tolbert's house is. It was the most out-of-the-way place I had, to that time, been. Alec Tolbert and I talked for a bit and then he said, "That other feller had one a those machines."

"What Other Feller?"

"The one who had that machine like yours. He was here a while back. He was doing the same thing you're doing. His name was Lomax."

A few weeks later, I was down a red dirt road outside of Marshall, a small town in the Arkansas Ozarks, visiting Barry Sutterfield, a 73-year-old ballad singer, and his wife Nellie. The three of us sat on the porch talking for a while, after which Uncle Barry sang old ballads like "Cole Younger," "Barbry Ellen," and "The Little Rebel."

Then Uncle Barry said, "You know that other feller?" ....

"Which one?" I said.

"The one who was doing the same thing you're doing. Only he had a beard."

Alan Lomax.

In a very real way, I owe my academic career to Alan and his father, John. One of my earliest books was *Wake Up Dead Man: Afro-American Worksongs from Texas Prisons* (Harvard University Press 1972). That book never would have come about had it not been for the prison worksong fieldwork by the Lomaxes in the early 1930s: I heard and was entranced by their recordings, got interested in the music, went off to see what was still around, then moved from the studies of music to studies of prisons themselves, and from there to studies of the criminal justice process. A few years ago, it all came around when Alan's daughter Anna asked me to do the booklet for *Big Brazos: Texas Prison Recordings, 1933 and 1934*, one of the 150 CDs in the astonishing Alan Lomax field series being produced by Rounder. While annotating those recordings I realized for the first time that Alan and his father had recorded some of the same men I'd recorded in Texas in the mid- and late-sixties.

Newport

I met Alan when Pete Seeger got me elected to the Newport Folk Festival board of directors. We used to meet every month at jazz producer George Wein's Riverside Drive apartment to plan the four-day festivals that took place in July and to figure out ways to give away the money left over from the previous year's concert.

Newport was based on a concept developed by Pete Seeger, George Wein and Theodore Bikel. Their idea was that if people came to hear music they already liked, they'd also listen to music they hadn't known existed, and the way to make that happen that was to let the popular performers underwrite the unknown performers. So everybody got $50 a day. If you were famous, like Pete or Joan Baez you got $50 a day. If nobody outside your town or village ever heard of you, you got $50 a day. The Foundation rented several of the big Newport mansions and put everybody up in them. (A few people, like Peter Yarrow and Bob Dylan were fancy and stayed in their own suites in the Viking Hotel in town, but they paid for that themselves.) Most of the famous singers never collected their payments; they just performed for the fun of it. Everything that was left over each year was donated to folk music performers and to support folk music projects.

I remember Ralph Rinzler, Mike Seeger, Pete and Alan coming up with really interesting performers and projects. Most everybody was pretty calm, but Alan would often get really agitated if the rest of us didn't get

enthusiastic about some plan or project he thought was absolutely necessary. He'd tell us that if we didn't see the necessity for this or that we
could not claim to take ourselves seriously. Sometimes Alan's projects
were great, sometimes they were balmy. In my first year or so, when I
was new kid on the block, I'd mostly sit quietly while Seeger and Brand
and Rinzler worked it out with him. They were wonderful discussions
to watch and hear.

Resurrection City

In 1968, after Martin Luther King was killed, Ralph Rinzler got
the Newport Foundation to underwrite and help staff the music and
children's programs at Resurrection City, the tent and shack camp next to
Washington's Reflecting Pool. Resurrection City housed the participants
in King's last project, the Poor People's Campaign.

Ralph started setting things up and I went down to Washington to
help him. Alan heard about what we were doing and caught up with us
at a meeting we were having with Jim Bevel and other members of the
Southern Christian Leadership Conference staff. Ralph (who was later
founding director of the Festival of American Folklife in Washington
and was then the Smithsonian's Assistant Secretary for Public Service)
was one of the most tactful people I ever met. He was saying to Bevel
and the others, "Here are the resources we have. How can we help you?"
when Alan jumped up and gave everybody a lecture on the power and
importance of folk music, black folk music in particular.

It was a good lecture, but that was neither the time, place nor company
for it. Bevel and the others listened to Alan in polite, stony silence, then
went on to other business. When the meeting was over, Bevel beckoned
Ralph and me to the side of the room and said, "You guys ought to do
something about him."

"I wish we could," Ralph said. "He means well, and he knows a
lot."

"I guess," Bevel said.

That night was, I think, the first night of real activity Resurrection
City. A thousand or so of the six thousand people who would eventually
inhabit the place had arrived. Bevel and several others made rousing
speeches in the big community tent and Frederic Douglas Kirkpatrick
(one of the founders of the legendary Louisiana anti-Klan group Deacons
for Defense, and a Newport Board member) gave a great performance,
followed by some other musical groups.

Alan and I were standing at the back of the seats, listening to the music. When one group finished, Alan said, "Are there any academic studies of the high tenor in black male vocal music?" I said I had no idea. "I'm wondering where it comes from. Do you think it has to do with repressed homosexuality?"

He said that much more loudly than I would have liked. Several heads turned and stared. Another group sang. Alan tapped the shoulder of a woman in the back row and said, "Those boys sure do sing good, don't they, honey?"

I don't think he meant anything ill by it. It's just how he was. Several young men nearby had heard both his remarks and were looking at him hostilely. I was feeling more and more uncomfortable, and rather than have an argument with him about it, I just left the tent and started walking up the Mall toward the Capitol.

He caught up with me a few minutes later and said, "Why did you leave like that?"

"I didn't want to be there when you got them *really* pissed off."

"Ah," he said, seeming to find that a reasonable answer.

We walked along in silence, then I said, "Alan, why are you like that?"

He was quiet for a while. Then he said, "You don't know what it was like, growing up in the Library of Congress." For some reason, I thought I knew exactly what he meant.

I guess he *had* grown up in the Library of Congress. He joined his father in the pursuit of American folk music when he was 17, and that set the arrow of his life. Alan was a boy from Austin, Texas, who became the man who was more driven than anyone else I know for the world to understand and honor its own music. In the decades when academic folklorists in America and Great Britain were desperately seeking survivals from bygone centuries, Alan was insisting, "Listen to what people are singing now."

That night, walking along the Mall, the sounds from the tent fading out behind us, Alan talked about his early years in the Library, about being on the road with his father, about the thrill of finding and preserving bits and pieces of a musical world he knew was vanishing even as he recorded it.

I was staying at Ralph Rinzler's house, the other side of the Library of Congress. I don't remember where Alan was staying. I remember that when we reached the place where he went one way and I went another we stood there for a while, while he finished telling me something.

Nashville

I heard him talk like that one other time.

In 1983, Diane Christian and I were in Nashville for a meeting of the American Folklore Society. Saturday night we got on the hotel elevator to go downstairs for the plenary session, the big speechifying meeting of the Society. I think I had just been elected the Society's president for the following year, so I was supposed to be at that plenary session. In the elevator, we met Alan's sister Bess Lomax Hawes, who was director of the Folk Arts Program of the National Endowment for the Arts, which meant she was supposed to be at that plenary session too.

Bess said she was stopping at Alan's room to fetch him. "Come on along," Bess said, "and we'll all go down together."

I hadn't seen him for a while, so we joined her. It was one of those hotel rooms with two beds and one chair. Alan was sitting on one, talking on the phone, and all his stuff was on the other. There was an almost-full quart of bourbon next to the telephone. Alan motioned for us to sit down. We moved the stuff on the other bed around and one of us sat on the bed, one on the floor, one in the chair. When Alan was done with the call he said, "Let's have a drink before we go down." We all had some bourbon, which I hate.

Then Alan started telling stories. It was astonishing. I've known a lot of great storytellers but I remember no one ever doing anything like that. Alan talked for maybe three hours. Occasionally Diane or Bess or I said something, but almost entirely it was Alan, telling stories. Stories about working with his father, stories about people we all knew, stories about people only he knew, stories about doing the work. Three hours of it. It was just magnificent.

I remember one sentence out of all the sentences he said that night. He had gotten onto the subject of academic folklorists and he pointed down to the floor, toward the place however many stories below us they were doing their speechifying.

"They squoze and they squoze," he said, "and they produced another generation of pedants just like the generation of pedants they wanted to replace. But without the beautiful manners."

How can you not love somebody who can summarize a generation of ambitious and competitive pedants like that?

The four of us emptied that bottle of bourbon. None of us made it downstairs that night. After the bourbon was gone and Alan had wound down—or maybe it was we who had worn down—Bess, Diane and I went back to the elevator and went upstairs. Diane and I got off at our floor and Bess went on to hers. That was the best evening I ever had at an American Folklore Society or any other academic society meeting.

"They squoze and they squoze and they produced another generation of pedants just like the generation of pedants they wanted to replace. But without the beautiful manners." Goddamn!

P.S.: I received an email from the editor of *Journal of American Folklore* saying she really liked this piece [originally published online at Bruce Jackson's website] and asking permission for her to publish it in the *Journal*. I wrote back immediately saying she was welcome to reprint it. I didn't hear from her for a while, so I wrote and asked when it might appear. She responded that she wanted to thank me for submitting my article, but the editorial board didn't think it was appropriate for *Journal of American Folklore*. Why do you think the feet got cold? I bet anything it was "squoze" that did it. They never liked words with funny spellings, that board, not one bit.

Public Intellectual

Russell Jacoby

Under the headline "Loser-of-the-Year-Award" the last page of the periodical stated: "Having examined an incredible number of terrible journals, we have decided—without any hesitation—to give this year's Loser-of-the-Year-Award to a dark horse: the pompous piece of nonsense, *Cultural Hermeneutics*." This notice appeared in 1969 in an irreverent and scholarly periodical *Telos*. Its founder, soul, and long-term editor was Paul Piccone, who died last year after a tough battle with cancer.

No brief mention can do justice to Paul, a larger-than-life one-man publishing, editing and writing machine who championed an iconoclastic neo-Marxism. A good son of a solid Italian working class family—his English always sounded like Italian—Paul received a PhD in philosophy at SUNY Buffalo, where he founded in 1968 *Telos*, which started out as a magazine for graduate students. From the start bravado and bluntness marked Paul's style. At a *Telos* conference he ridiculed the first issue of his own magazine. "Besides being superfluous, since there were already too many journals around, *Telos* no. 1 was even inferior to the average." The magazine quickly abandoned its conventional origins and established itself as a free-wheeling vehicle for non-dogmatic radicalism. Already in 1969 its motto read: "*Telos* is a philosophical journal definitely outside the mainstream of American philosophical thought."

For both Paul and *Telos* this proved an understatement. No department of philosophy wanted them. For some years he brought the journal to St. Louis, where he taught in the sociology department at Washington University. Despite an illustrious record Paul was turned down for tenure, and never again found a regular academic job. He decided to move himself and the journal out of the "boondocks" to establish himself in New York, where he helped form a cooperative that purchased and renovated a collapsed building. Paul set up the basement as his editing and publishing headquarters. In the annals of publishing, *Telos* may simply be without precedent: a quarterly periodical chocked with lengthy articles on politics and philosophy, which was published for decades without any institutional support or affiliation. By dragooning friends and supporters to help, Paul managed to put it out year after year. It was a one man-show. *Telos* was Paul Piccone.

Paul himself linked *Telos* to several others international journals that were rediscovering an undogmatic Marxism such as *Praxis* (the former Yugoslavia), *New Left Review* (Great Britain) and *Les Temps Modernes* (France). For some American students intellectually finding themselves in the aftermath of the sixties *Telos* played an irreplaceable role. By its translations alone each issue provided an education in European Marxism: the Hungarian Georg Lukacs, the French Maurice Merleau-Ponty, and Frankfurt School figures such as Herbert Marcuse and T.W. Adorno all showed up frequently in *Telos*. Paul also published a series of *Telos* books that translated European leftists such as Lucien Goldmann, Antonio Labriolia and Jean Braudillard. Yet *Telos* was not just a journal of translations. Apart from original pieces on everyone from Beethoven to Gramsci, it contained spirited reviews, commentaries and reports. Weighing in at several hundred pages, *Telos* was a collage of scholarship, polemic and insights.

Paul was a restless thinker who approached everything from cooking to carpentry with elan and by the1980s he found neo-Marxism too limited. He tackled new subjects and thinkers. In *Telos* he fielded symposiums that reconsidered populism, new social movements, and conservatism. For a while he drew close to the historian Christopher Lasch, who also advanced an idiosyncratic leftism that tapped ideas on the right. For some of the original *Telos* associates, this new bent, which seemed to celebrate French and German conservative thinkers like Carl Schmidt, proved unpalatable; they dropped away. Yet Paul remained feisty, undogmatic and unpredictable till the end. The recent deaths of Edward Said and Susan Sontag occasioned much reflection about their lives as public intellectuals. Few would associate Paul with them, but it is fair to do so. That he is less known hardly constitutes a counter argument. Paul carved out a wholly exemplary life as an independent intellectual, neither in the university nor outside it. Not a large man physically his reach was long, his intellectual foot print vast. Without cronyism or favoritism he published for thirty-five years writings that helped an American left educate itself. Forthrightness marked his own writings as well. Paul wrote in what might be called academic street talk—footnotes, plain talking, and insults. He was one of kind—a tough, passionate, resourceful Italian-American intellectual, who could pour concrete as consummately as publish a world-class magazine. He is missed.

First You Strike

Staughton Lynd

Very few persons succeed in being both manual workers and scholars. Marty Glaberman was both. As a young man, he dropped out of a masters' degree program in Economics at Columbia University to become a "colonizer:" a radical doing industrial work. After twenty years as an autoworker in and around Detroit, he quit factory work and brought that experience to his distinguished political journalism, his teaching, and his work as a labor historian. He received a masters' degree from the University of Detroit and a Ph.D. from Union Graduate School. He taught at Wayne State University. Where George Rawick was a colleague and several of the men who formed the League of Revolutionary Black Workers were his students. In 1989, he retired from Wayne State University, continuing to teach part-time.

Marty Glaberman became a socialist at the age of thirteen, and was a lifelong Marxist who never lost faith in the capacity of the working class to emancipate itself and to transform society. About 1940, he associated himself with the West Indian Marxist intellectual C.L.R. James and with the Johnson-Forest Tendency (named for James who was "Johnson" and Raya Dunayevskay who was "Forest") within American Trotskyism. This small but enormously productive and influential group made the first translation into English of what came to be called the "early economic-philosophical manuscripts" of Karl Marx. They concluded that the Soviet Union was neither a "degenerated" workers' state nor a "bureaucratic collectivism," but a state capitalist society. They rejected the idea that elites were needed to organize social revolution, and specifically rejected the concept of a vanguard party. Members of the group saw in the Hungarian Revolution of 1956 a confirmation in practice of what they had projected in theory. The workers' councils of the Hungarian Revolution remained for Martin Glaberman the closest approximations to a genuine working-class revolution thus far experienced anywhere in the world.

In their marriage of over thirty years, Marty and Jessie Glaberman kept a house that was open to the world as a way station, a meeting place, and a refuge. In 1957 the Glabermans and a neighbor, Ms. Winifred Jenkins, started the nation's first inner city Little League. Marty acted as league president, keeping the bats and balls in the basement. After the tragic death of a couple in Flint, Marty and Jessie Glaberman adopted their children.

Marty's generosity also showed itself in his readiness to lead a discussion on Marx's *Capital*, anywhere, anytime. At the age of 80, he repeatedly drove from Detroit to Toronto and Youngstown, Ohio for this purpose. In Youngstown, a retired electric line worker, an inspector at a shop manufacturing metal drums, a tow motor driver, a steelworker and two lawyers, will never forget brother Marty glancing occasionally at his battered copy of *Capital* as he explained that Marx considered work under capitalism alienating for the worker "be his wages high or low."

I

I consider Marty Glaberman to be the most important writer on labor matters in the United States during the second half of the twentieth century. He is likely to be best remembered as an unrepentant advocate of workers' self-organization and the ability of the working class to govern.

One aspect of this theme is expressed in his 1952 pamphlet entitled, *Punching Out*. Scholars have termed the workplace regime established by the Congress of Industrial Organizations (CIO) "workplace contractualism," that is, the regulation of relationships between worker and boss by a collectively-bargained contract. What Marty pointed out was that in such a system even the well-intentioned union representative becomes an enforcer of the contract, including the no-strike clause. Even the former picket-line leader, chosen by his or her fellow workers to be their steward, becomes a cop for the boss.

I recall being handed a copy of *Punching Out* when my family moved to Chicago in the late 1960s. It turned my ideas about the labor movement upside down. Instead of seeing unions as "good" institutions that had inexplicably taken "bad" positions toward the Vietnam War and the Southern Civil Rights movement, I glimpsed the concept that the union in a capitalist society—even when its leaders honorably strive to establish certain minimum workplace conditions—functions in the last analysis to stabilize the status quo. (After twenty-five years' experience in which this concept served me as an hypothesis, I would now say that what is described in *Punching Out* is especially true of national unions, and that local unions may under certain conditions play a more creative and radical role.)

One discerns two sources for the provocative notions set forth in *Punching Out*. The first of course is his experience of the Johnson-Forest group.... A second source was Marty Glaberman's poignant personal relationship with Johnny Zupan. ("I recruited him," Marty recalled, "And I spoke at his funeral.") Zupan is described in his essay "The Left Wing Committeeman." He embodied the self-described radical who, without realizing it, upon assuming even the office of steward begins to drift away from the rank-and-file fellow workers who elected him.

As was the case with so many of Marty Glaberman's ideas, the analysis he expressed as a young man in *Punching Out* became part of a conceptual arsenal on which he drew for the rest of his life. He did not believe that the working class could make a revolution through trade unions, committed, as unions under capitalism necessarily are, to workplace contracturalism. In an interview with my wife Alice and myself in 1997, later published in our book, *The New Rank and File*, Marty said:

> What forms are available to the working class? The union movement is not a force for revolutionary change. I do not think it can be transformed. Mostly workers boycott and ignore unions: they do not go to meetings, they do not vote in union elections. Occasionally they will vote a contract down. They will occasionally, but rarely, participate in opposition caucuses. Whether the workers become revolutionary or not does not depend on what the union leadership does.
>
> This means that the course of future development in the workplace has to be sought outside the unions. Caucuses and factions will still be built and, here and there, will have temporary and minor successes. But the explosions that are to come are likely to have new revolutionary forms, organizations that are not simply organs of struggle but organs of control of production.

The belief that workers must and therefore will develop new forms of organization outside traditional trade unions was one of a cluster of related ideas that Marty Glaberman advocated all his adult life. Many of those ideas, it seems fair to say, were initially proposed by C.L.R. James and were adopted by Marty Glaberman, as well as by others in the Johnson Forest group. An idea more distinctively Marty's own was that *activity precedes consciousness*. The working class is shaped ("made" in E.P. Thompson's term) by the activity forced upon it in a capitalist society.

Working-class consciousness is best understood not by taking a public opinion poll, but rather by close observation of what workers do. Thus, Marty liked to say, a sociologist who took a poll in Budapest in September 1956 or in Paris in April 1968 could not have predicted the working-class upheavals that occurred a month later. Thus too, the path to revolution was not first to change workers' ideas, and then to proceed to revolutionary action. Quoting Marx, Marty insisted that activity would come first, and in the course of the activity consciousness would change.

This is the significance of Marty Glaberman's best-known published work, his study of the struggle within the UAW during World War II over the no-strike pledge. At the same time that UAW members, voting alone in their homes, recorded a majority for continuing the no-strike pledge, a majority of the workers in the Detroit automotive plants took part in unauthorized strikes. Which better revealed the workers' "real" consciousness, voting or striking? Marty thought it was the act of striking. He made the same point with a related homely example. Say you are working at your machine and see a group of fellow workers heading down the aisle in your direction. There are too many of them to be going to the tool crib. It is too early for lunch. Their procession can only mean one thing, so you turn off your machine, put your tools in your box and lock it, wipe your hands, and join the line on its way to the door. You punch out. Only when you get outside do you say, "What the hell is gong on?" and then, by your action, let other workers know whether you feel the wildcat is justified. The poem "Wildcat III" describes this process. It is also memorably evoked in a speech attached to the volume *Marxism for Our Time* at p. 197, where Marty sums up his description with the words, "the basic characteristic of the working class is that first you strike…."

The idea that action comes first is critical to understanding Marty's thoughts about overcoming white racism (a subject about which, at the time of his death, he was planning to write a book). He considered it a liberal pipedream to suppose one could *first* make white workers integrationists, and *then* launch a common struggle of both white and black workers for a better world. The Marxist approach, in Marty's opinion, was to believe that the conditions of life and work of the proletariat would ultimately force the working class to behave in ways that would ultimately transform society. As he explained in *The New Rank and File*:

> We're not talking about going door-to-door and making workers into ideal socialists. You've got to take workers as they are, with all their contradictions, with all their nonsense. But the fact that society forces them to struggle begins to transform the

working class. If white workers realized they can't organize steel unless they organize black workers, that doesn't mean they're not racist. It means they have to deal with their own reality, and that transforms them.

Finally, Marty went much further than C.L.R. James in framing an answer to the question: *If the Movement is not led by a vanguard party, how should it be organized?* He based his answer on the experience of the movements of the 1960s.

As compared to most "Old Leftists," Marty Glaberman responded with unusual generosity and tolerance to the movements of the 1960s. But his response was more than that. In the short piece "Student Unrest" he said that the worldwide student protests of the '60s were "revolutionary." Rebutting Hal Draper, he insisted in "The New Left" that the youth movement of the 1960s was more free of adult domination than the youth organizations that he and Draper had been part of. He argued that "the anti-war politics of the New Left is superior to that of the old." Even the notoriously inchoate ideology of the New Left was, in Marty's view, "far superior to the rigid stupidities that most of us held on to in the thirties and forties." The New Left's belief in the revolutionary potential of the American people was preferable to the "romantic vanguardism that characterized the movement in the thirties" and the "cynical nihilism of the old left," so Marty believed.

Of greatest importance were Marty's comments on New Left organization in the essay "Toward an American Revolutionary Perspective." Here is what he said:

When the NAACP proved inadequate to the needs of the civil rights movement ... it was not replaced by a new organization that represented the black community. It remained to perform its special functions. Instead, a host of new organizations appeared, some temporary, some permanent, some membership organizations, some loose coalitions and committees: the organization of the Montgomery bus boycott, SNCC, SCLC, CORE, local committees, ad hoc groupings, regional formations, and the like. When particular organizations outlived their usefulness or proved inadequate or could not accommodate themselves to changes in the struggle, they disappeared and were replaced. When the struggle moved from the rural south to the urban north, organizations like the Panthers and the League of Revolutionary Black Workers appeared to reach a new constituency and to put forward new tactics.

"Similar phenomenon appeared in the student movement, the anti-war movement, and, most recently, the women's movement," Marty continued. "This experience is clearly not the result of some secret strategy or some historical accident. It arises out of an objective situation and corresponds to the nature of that situation and of the times in which we live."

The crucial concept, he went on is "participatory democracy...."

The multiplicity of organizations and the ease with which masses of groupings of people can form or abandon them, reflects the control of the movement from below. It has been impossible for any single organization to dominate the left and to force strategies and tactics into a single mould, a mould which thereafter acts as a brake on further developments. The looseness and freedom of organization, on the other hand, has made it possible for varying kinds of "constituencies" to enter the political arena with issues and organizations of their own choosing. Students or workers, urban or rural, middle-aged or young, whites or blacks, can participate in political activity without the necessity of subordination to some over-all political formation.

As with all of Marty Glaberman's ideas, one can agree or disagree. That is what he would expect. What he asked is that these ideas not be evaded, but be squarely faced.

Running Buddy

Cecil Brown

Me and My buddy, we don't have no fallin out
We hip to women, we know what it's all about.
– Josh White

Berkeley, CA:
May 22, Saturday, 1971

Maryann mentioned to me that the comic Richard Pryor was trying to do satire, which is my thing so we went to see him last night. We had to stand outside the Mandrake in a long line that snaked around the corner of University and 10th Streets. Once we were inside the club, a stocky, middle-aged white woman guided us to a seat between couples not far from the stage.

"He might not be coming," she warned. While we waited, she asked Country Joe [lead vocalist of Country Joe and The Fish]—*a white dude with a long blonde hair and an apache headband—to entertain until Pryor showed up. Reluctantly, he got up and sang "Louie, Louie." The song took the audience by the collar and wouldn't let go. He shouted a phrase of the song at them, and they responded in kind.*

Then the white lady [Her name was Mary Moore and she owned the Mandrake] *cut Country Joe off: "Richard Pryor's here!" The audience broke into fervent applause. A slim shadow slipped on to the stage, and I took this to be their beloved Richard. He crossed the stage into the little spotlight and came out of the shadow.*

"Ladies and Gentlemen," the female MC announced: "The crown prince of comedy, his highness, Richard Pryor!" He was average height, almost skinny. He wore a green sweater, grinning, holding a cigarette. His face was open, sincere, and genuine. He was clearly a hip brother, and streetwise.

He stood, looking out over the audience. He glanced at me—I was one of the few blacks in the house—nodded and then refocused on the crowd. "Thank you ... Sorry I'm late ... Thank you, and good evenin"...

This was my first time seeing Richard Pryor. I'd missed him on the television programs he'd been on, *Merv Griffith, The Johnny Carson Show, Kraft Music Hall.* Born in Peoria, Illinois, in 1940, Pryor had gone to New York as a teenager, competed in and won an amateur contest at the Apollo Theater in Harlem in 1959, when he was nineteen. A few years later (1966), critic Phil Elwood saw him perform in San Francisco at Enrico Bertalucci's night club "hungry i" and reported that he was "unfunny and not original ... insecure and ill at ease, despite his projected hipness." Pryor had been so nervous—according to Elwood—he couldn't focus on his material.

But that night I saw him at the Mandrake, he surely wasn't nervous—and he was *very* hip.

"...I used to smoke weed," he started right in, "but I gave that up. It made me paranoid. Then I snorted cocaine. I had to give that up too. Cause I got so paranoid, I used to wake up my wife in the middle of the night and ask, you fucking the paper boy?"

The audience went nuts. "But comin' is cool. Comin' is real cool!—Especially if it's with a girl."

"...I think President Nixon's a lesbian!—And Agnew is his man!" The audience was now on the floor. He told jokes about getting laid: "In high school, I didn't get none." He told jokes about police brutality and show business: "I used to love getting arrested," he admitted, "because it was like being in show business."

We fell under the spell of Richard's voices. Next he added the Wino "who knew Jesus personally." "Jesus Christ? That boy ain't shit. He lives right down here on 3rd street. She was carrying that boy. She carried him low, that's how we knew she had a boy...."

The bits Richard did that night were from "the junkie and the wino" period—a time when Richard's genius unfolded like the larvae into the butterfly as he moved from the material he was doing on television to the riffs on his first records.

I immediately saw the relationship between Pryor and writers who used folklore to tell their stories. "The oral tradition is central to African American writers like Zora Neale Hurston, Richard Wright, and Langston Hughes," I'd said to my English classes at U. C. Berkeley where I was teaching at the time. I was impressed by Richard's use of voices. There was his own of course—the voice of the hip, black Narrator. There was the Racist Cop, Pryor's Father, the Black Policeman Who Has To Tom To Impress His White Partner. And when Pryor came to the "Line-up," he evoked all his usual suspects with unique voices. There was Allan T. Johnson, Bundy T. Wilson (anti-government agitator), Arnold T. Perkins, (child molester) et al.

Pryor also spoke in the voice of a Black Preacher who knows God personally, the Wino who knew Jesus Christ—and his moms and whole family—personally. Richard did women too. Girls who masturbated, but claimed they didn't. Girls who would give you some but make you swear you wouldn't tell.

I

I was one of the only blacks in the audience and Pryor glanced over at me through the entire routine as if I were a witness to what he was telling this white audience. "There was a time—not so long ago," he said, "when black was not beautiful." He paused and looked at me again.

"– In fact that was only a few years ago. Naw," he said, "Being black wasn't beautiful yet."

He pointed at me. I was wearing black leather jacket and a black knitted cap, and I had a "Free Huey" button on my jacket.

"He was dressed like you," he continued. "And he used to come by our house and tell people, 'be black and be proud.' My parents say, 'That nigger's crazy!'"

The audience could relate to that and rewarded him with more loud applause.

"Back before Black was Beautiful, the winos just want wine." "Now" ... He looked out at them—the white people (they knew who they were):

"Now ... them motherfuckers want more than wine now—they want justice!" "You used to give them wine," he said. "But now you have to give them some bullets—and a target!"

It was riveting satire. Maryann was right. Pryor's people are mine. And Juvenal's, Swift's, Twain's—all the great satirists!

I had my Nikon camera with me and I stood up from my chair to take a picture, but Pryor, seeing the camera out of the corner of his eye, turned away. Just as I was about to try again to snap the picture, he beamed his big black eyes on me: "Damn, nigger," Pryor said to me. "Take the damn picture!" When the audience laughed then, they looked at me. I was part of the show.

After the performance, I walked across the stage and followed Pryor through the back door of the club, which lead to a parking lot, where Rich was standing, smoking a cigarette.

"Hey! —"

He turned. I felt we had already met, especially since he had called me out in the audience.

"That was fantastic!" I extended my hand. He shook it giving me the black power handshake. Then, he shielded his hands over his eyes to kill the glare from the light shining through the door.

"How long are you going to be performing in Berkeley?" I asked him.

"I live here now." He said it like it was something to celebrate. "You can come by and hang out with me. I live about three blocks away."

Little did I know then that we would be running buddies for the next thirty years!

I visited Richard a couple days after his Mandrake show. He lived in a nondescript white house I was a bit surprised to find a white guy answering the door. I walked in and saw Richard lying on the sofa with a blanket pulled up around him, as if he had been using the sofa for a bed (which he'd probably given to somebody else).

After meeting other friends of Richard's, I learned that they'd also met him by going backstage to tell him how much they loved a show. Richard used his comedy act to recruit buddies. Going back stage to shake his hand could easily turn into a life-long cult trip. A Pryor fan named Allen was responsible for bringing the comic to Berkeley. Allen told me that he was traveling through L.A., and went back stage to tell Richard how much he liked his act. Richard asked him "Where you going now?" Allen said he was heading for Berkeley and Richard proposed, "Can I come with you?"

If Richard trusted you and you were accepted into the inner circle—you became part of a band with a shared satirical vision.

II

Richard Pryor's two years in Berkeley remind me of Shakespeare's vision of Prince Hal hanging tight with Falstaff's low-life crew. Falstaff— that "jovial, aging, witty criminal"—was the young Prince's tutor. Falstaff was a drunk, a liar, and a coward; he embodied the principle of misrule. By making Falstaff the young Prince's mentor, Shakespeare wanted to bring home the point that humor, and ease with everyday people are essential to leadership. When Pryor came to Berkeley I became part of a crew of low-lifers who circled around our Prince. While Shakespeare's Hal had Falstaff, a coward called Pistols, an "air-brain" named Mistress Quickly, a quick-witted whore called Doll Tear Sheet, we had Big Ass Bertha, John the Con, and various pimps to learn from.

I recently tried to contact some of these people in San Francisco and Sausalito. Whatever happened, I wondered, to John the Con, Jesus, Fast Freddie and All Well? It turns out many of them are dead, according to an anonymous source who knew most of the people who lived in the house Richard had shared with his crew.

"Whatever happened to the pimp Jesus?"

"Jesus who use to have all them bitches and that blue Rolls Royce?"

My source had seen Jesus a few weeks back, pushing a shopping cart. I was jolted by the idea that this FOR (Friend of Richard)—this formerly bejeweled pimp who once dressed in a sky-blue suit—was now a homeless man out on the streets.

In *Henry IV, Part 2*, young Hal sees Falstaff in the crowd during a royal procession just before he is to be crowned Henry V. Falstaff calls out to his old friend. Hal famously replies, "I know thee not old man."

When Richard Pryor became king of comedy he never turned his back on his old buddies.

In his early comedy, he pays tribute to them. When I listen to recordings of his stand-up routines, I hear their echoes in his characters and observations and tones. I hear them in his punchlines and pauses. And I see them in his gestures and facial expressions. They are laughing at this world along with him. The early Richard celebrated the common man struggling to survive on wit alone. Pryor didn't have a Falstaff, but "John the Con" was just as funny. There was no "Justice Shallow," but Pryor loved to fraternize with that fabulous pimp called "Jesus." John and Jesus and all the rest each contributed something to Pryor's satire—a word, a phrase, a gait, or an attitude that informed his comic genius.

Part VI

Wild Light

First wasn't conceived for lightweights, but we listened when one contributor advised us magazines of the left "need a massive dose of humor—they heavy!" Historian Thomas Bender, author of *New York Intellect*, over-praised our first issue, but he wasn't way over the top when he found in it a "sense of energy and fun, along with political seriousness." That seriousness is sometimes lost on those who can't place *First* because it's all over the map. One reader once called *First* "nutty." But that's cool. We mean to be *nutty*. Though (as per Richard Meltzer) "not nutty like Spike Jones, or *Hellzapoppin* or a Bugs Bunny cartoon; nutty like a miracle in the wilderness." Meltzer was evoking the sound of Dizzy Gillespie's "Salt Peanuts" but he could have been talking about his own nutty work, which is a thousand thought-miles away from tamer wack jobs. It's been a heady trip publishing Meltzer's stuff in *First*. A wild thing by him leads off the next section which illuminates *First*'s lighter side.

The late Kurt Vonnegut helped us get lit. His contributions to *First* went beyond the prose and poetry he faxed us over the years. Back in 1998, after he read the last article in this section, "Into the Summer Sea," in the first *First*, he sent us a $100 check and punchlines worth more than gold: "I was thoroughly demoralized by awareness that brilliant pro-bono writing was going on all over the fucking country. Now Claremont Avenue, for Christ's sake, checks in!"

211

Old Rasputin and Old Milwaukee

Richard Meltzer

Lest anyone wonder, Richard Meltzer confirmed "Old Rasputin is an actual beer. A good'un. Brewed in Mendocino.")

Here we are and here they are and now.

Between the ropes steps Emile Griffith, the Virgin Island Vanquisher, in his bluebird blue 3/4 robe with OLD RASPUTIN IMPERIAL STOUT block-lettered in powder blue on back. Soon he is joined by Lennox Lewis, the Williamsburg Walloper, in his blood red satin mini-cape with OLD MILWAUKEE scripted in gold & black.

Introductions by ring announcer Lou Donaldson, then the ceremonial stare-down—eyes of wrath and fire—as referee Art Skov blubbers the customary blah blah bla-bah-bah ... okay let's GO!

(Scoring by the 10-point "must" system.)

Round 1: Griffith jabs twice, Lewis once, they exchange hooks and Griffith rushes Lewis, backs him to the ropes but Lewis sidesteps, lands an uppercut right, Griffith ties him up, they exchange glancing blows at long range, clinch in mid-ring, Griffith tries a left hook, misses, Lewis wraps him up, Griffith connects with a sharp hook, Lewis jabs, Griffith misses wide with a right to the body, they clinch, Griffith a left to Lewis's jaw, Lewis two weak rights, both fighters miss in the final seconds. (Griffith's round, 10-9.)

Round 2: Griffith charges, they clinch, exchange hooks, Lewis's looks stronger, he jabs and lands a hard flush right, Griffith misses a wild left, Lewis lands a right to the head and a roundhouse left to the body, Griffith comes in under Lewis's jab and holds on, Lewis uppercuts him, Griffith jabs and follows with nothing, Lewis jab and a right cross, several more jabs and two very good rights, Griffith a lunging left hook, Lewis comes back with a crisp one-two, three jabs and an overhand right, Griffith is headed to the mat but grabs hold of Lewis at the bell. (Lewis, 10-9.)

Round 3: Griffith misses recklessly with a right lead, Lewis on target with two jabs and a left-right combo, Griffith misses long with a hook, Lewis flicks a half dozen unanswered jabs, Griffith has blood over his eye, Lewis continues jabbing, punctuated by an occasional uppercut, Griffith's punches fall way short, it looks like he's swinging at air, Lewis bangs two hard rights to the body, rocks Griffith with a huge hook, Griffith now a punching bag, Lewis snaps his head back with stiff jabs that bloody his nose as the round ends. (Lewis, 10-9.)

Round 4: Griffith backs Lewis up with a left-right-left, Lewis responds with a combination of his own, Griffith clinches and thuds a right to the ribs, misses with another as Lewis steps away, Lewis lands an uppercut-hook and a wicked right, Griffith's gloves graze the mat, it's ruled a knockdown and he takes a standing 8 count, Lewis slams home hooks and rights, Griffith holds on, more rights and hooks, Griffith misses long with a right, Lewis measures him with a left and uncorks a right that puts him

on his back, Griffith's face a mass of blood, he rises to a knee at 9 and tries to stand
but is counted out at 2:17.

Oh no how could it be! How could a watered-down pisspot lager like
Old Milwaukee beat the brawny and robust grand champion of hops, Old
Rasputin? By a kayo no less!

How (conversely) can anyone RESPECT a malt product you can
practically see thru? How the bleeping blip can swill like Old Milwaukee
be the "winner"?

If you're asking "me," well, I got no answer. You will hafta trust your
own nose and moth, I mean mouth, and firstmost your EYES. You've
heard of dark beer, well Old Rasp is black beer. It don't come darker. Dark
as Blind Joe Reynolds' blink … black as Roland Kirk's color chart. The
beer of night … of bleak winter midnights when all hope is hopeless!

And if you don' believe that's poss, pour yourself a snot, I mean shot,
in a shotglass. Don't let it bubble over. Allow it to set and you'll see:
brown head … black body: OPAQUE! Hope less no more!

Second you'll discover the pop—the punch—the pow of this elixir
as it downwarms your gullet and bounces your bottom to the canvas.
So strong it's almost black wine, this is the hard stuff—alcohol NINE
PERCENT—make no mistaking! Roasty and toasty, it is malty and
nutty and also tastes like … oh … like some kinda smoky earth thing or
things. The Good Earth.

Looks unrivaled and tastes unrivaled and is unrivaled for any manner
of intaking! You can swig it by the shot. Sip or gulp it from a 12-oz. mug
(or a 16). Athletes and cabbies should not but YOU go right ahead. Or
slug-a-chug it from the bottle and lettuce say a word about the bottle:

Verrrry attractive bottle. You will wanna keep flowers in it after-
wards.

To preserve the potency, don't dilute. Tho hearty as many cordials and
aperitifs, the secret is to drink it STRAIGHT. A Rasputin Highball mixes
fizzwater & ice with the pitch black potion. A Raspy Nail does same with
orange juice, crushed ice and a lemon wedge. A Last Rasp is O.R. plus
grenadine. Rasp La Rue (I just invented it!): O.R. and whip cream. But
don't mix, no, do not. No mixing! Straight or maybe with a sprinkle of
vodka. And M&M's. Share it with friends and acquaintings—sharing is
the "rasputin way!"

With or w/out saying, many in the beer & boxing field are up in arms
over the "loss" to Old Milwaukee. Many are inconsolable. May the
stinging gears of bitter defeat not throw a wrench into Old Rasputin's
boundless future!

You can't predict wrenches but I'll tell you one thing: imperial stout. Which means EMPIRE and empires strike back—so howzabout a RE-MATCH with Old Milwaukee?

Rematch! Rematch!

Never in the seamy corridors of injustice has a return match been more CALLED FOR! Rasputin-Milwaukee II is awaited in clamorous circles with anticipation. It's anyone's guess how many b.o. and t.v. records would be shattered.

But. But … calling and occurring are different horses. You can't always get what you don't. Try & not get your ropes in a lather. Sad but true: the mighty Raspa Far I may never in this lifeline receive its dessert. Sob, sob….

Sob be it.

Pour a double shot!

Death of Edgar Alan Poe in Baltimore, Maryland on October 7, 1849

Now a little more than a century ago
The world lost Edgar Allen Poe
It's a terrible thing for a man to die
But Edgar did—and this is why.

When the strategists down in Whig HQ
Looked to be short a vote or two
And like to take it on the chin,
They called the party faithful in
And told 'em "Boys, we're facing sure defeat
Unless we can get to the man on the street."

And those good old boys of Whig persuasion,
Moved by a sense of great occasion,
Swore that they'd as lief be reamed
"We got a ship of state to keep afloat
So we better haul ass and get out the vote."

So they sat and spat and bit cigars
Thinking on their patronage and power,
For when his party's in a jam
A man don't need a diagram
"Brothers," they cried, "we're gonna die like pigs
If we don't come out fighting like men and Whigs."

Than those stout-hearted men of Baltimore
Split up into teams of three or four
And armed with gin and laudanum,
They hauled in half the city's scum.
Then bored with bums, they picked up anyone
Too drunk or too old or too sickly to run.

And having divvied up their catch into handy
groups
They crammed them into rat holes known as coops
Which were a little weak on ventilation,
Elbow room and sanitation,
And they held them there without food or reprieve
For a full five days before election eve.

But when word came that the votes were needed
Friend, you can bet that word got heeded,
And off went those stiffs to the polls
Where there weren't no registration rolls,
And every candidate for a coffin
Was free to vote early and vote often.

Which is why they got dragged from ward to ward
While the early returns were being scored,
And friendly hands were always free
To mark their ballots properly.

But when word came that the foe was beat,
Why, every bum found himself back on the street
Which is where a doc found Edgar Poe that night,
Smelling like disease and out like a light.
They carried him off to the hospital
Where his fever raged and heartbeat fell,
Till one Sunday morning—an hour before dawn—
Edgar Allen Poe was gone.

Now don't wait supper
And don't hold your breath,
But Edgar Allen Poe—
He got *voted* to death.

– Timothy Mayer

Da Enron-Ron Hey Da Enron-Ron

(Tune: "The Doo-Run-Run") (The Crystals)

On Inauguration day I bought them stocks
Da Enron-Ron-Ron-Da EnRon-Ron
Bush & Cheney tol' me they were really hot
Da Enron-Ron-Ron-Da EnRon-Ron
& Whoa no dey didn' stand still
Yeah and I held them till…
And when they drop like a stone
The Bushies they run yeah they run-run-run

They knew what they were doin
When they backed our bucks
Turned out to be a buncha cheatin fucks
Da Enron-Ron-Ron-Da EnRon-Ron
O yeah they caught my eye
Now I am about to cry
Today I just lost my home
Da Enron-Ron left me all alone…

Yeah the Enron-Ron-the Enron-Ron
Fuckin Enron … Fuckin Enron-Ron
American capitalist son of a gun
Well fuck ya all with your Enron-Ron

—Tuli Kupferberg

Outsource This!

Dennis Myers

Of course you're confused. You're out of a job. What you need, aside from gainful employment, is advice. You can get some from us. We have *the* plan, a mother of invention of all employment plans. You must follow this plan and you must follow it exactly. No matter what. Or no job for you.

We've crystallized the best and the brightest counsel into one simple twelve-step program that will lead you to the job of your dreams. Ready to get started and win? Good.

1. Prepare and Bargain: Put yourself in a power position when the time comes.

You sense you're about to be laid-off. You walk the empty hallways, imagining a target on your back. (You know you're not paranoid, because they're coming after your colleagues too.) Now's the time to prepare. The best defense is a strong offense. When the smiling HR guy comes bounding into your cubicle, waving a pink slip like a flag of honor, sit back and let him have it. (Since most corporate layoffs are handled by email, you may have to schedule this meeting yourself.) Bargain! Strike a deal with him about the conditions for your quiet surrender. After all, it's the last time you will be able to exert any power.

If you have already been laid-off, please politely skip this step.

2. *Register for Benefits: Sign-up for unemployment as soon as (legally) possible.*

You'll sit in the middle of a beige and brown room, wallpapered in the late seventies style. The desks will be community college issue—uniform unimold plastic, and beige to match the wallpaper. You'll be surrounded by white middle aged, middle class, middle managers. All these middling faces look non-committal. And you will know that this is what the world is coming to: "I need all your forms."

3. *Network: Talk to colleagues, friends, office workers, secretaries, ticket-takers.*

Start networking quickly. After you get past the realization that you're unemployed, you'll soon find out that most of the people you know are unemployed, underemployed, or unhappily employed. And that anyone outside these categories aren't hiring anyhow. Even if no one can help you, at least you can draw comfort from knowing no one's happy. The Germans have a word for that kind of joy.

4.   *Understand the Job Market: Make it your job to figure out where the next jobs are and how to acquire one, even if it requires re-training.*

The government publishes lots of statistics. That's one of their jobs. Some of these statistics indicate where to find the next wave of good, solid, meaningful employment. If you had been smart enough to check these statistics, say, five years ago, you'd know that Information Technology jobs were, at that point, golden. This is why retraining line manufacturers into computer programmers was such an important government initiative.

Today, working as a surgeon or a litigation lawyer is right up there in terms of good pay. But, with your current resume, you may find these positions difficult to acquire. So you may want to consider taking a position in the high-growth fast food restaurant field, or perhaps working as a greeter for America's store, Wal-Mart. (You must forgo any alliances with union groups, of course.)

If you are not yet qualified to surf the next wave of employment opportunities, the State offers many re-training programs. Five years ago, for example, you could have trained for that high-performance job in I.T. Today, New York State proudly offers training classes in plumbing and elevator repair. Going up?

5. *Think positive: It may be hard at times, but it is important to keep faith in yourself.*

After a while, it's hard to believe that anyone will ever want to hire you. They did in the past, but, of course, you were younger then. And now your experience makes you an expert or a specialist and likely overqualified. Just because you've done an excellent job in fashioning blue boxes, that doesn't mean you know a thing about making green boxes, even if you're willing to take a cut in salary to do it.

To get the right perspective on things, you need to turn around. You'll understand your own self-image better if you understand the employer's perspective. Remember, they all have businesses to run. Right? You've been there; you understand. That should answer your questions about your self-image.

In an emergency, when you're feeling down, and life has passed you by, take an even higher perspective and recall that the President has a job and he believes in the future.

6. *Maximize your employment: Bargain from a position of strength.*

Follow this plan (precisely) and you will eventually get a job, which is a good thing. But how do you capitalize on the moment and get that really good salary that you deserve? The secret is to get multiple offers. Don't hop in the first taxi headed your way. Wait till you see a bunch of taxis barreling down the street before you stick your hand out.

Competition will let you set the tone. It's a supply and demand thing. Of course if only one potential employer is interested, then this simply won't work and neither should you.

7.–12. *Out source this:*

Like all good self-help programs, this surefire plan for employment success involved twelve steps. Six of the steps, however, were recently outsourced overseas.

You Must Choose

Robert Chametzky

There were people who wondered when Larry Bird was announced as the coach of the Indiana Pacers why Bird would want to be a coach. What suggests itself in answer is another question: why would the prospect of retirement around age 40 seem so attractive? Perhaps Baryshnikov's move in the '80s to being artistic director of the American Ballet Theater occasioned similar questions but it seems unlikely. There is some recognition that ballet may be interesting and worthwhile enough that a major practitioner might wish to continue in it even given diminished capacities and no obvious financial need to do so. But, basketball is also sufficiently interesting and worthwhile.

What makes basketball worthy is, in part exactly what many "serious" commentators deride it for—that it is, after all, a sport. Traditional rhetoric and current cant to the contrary notwithstanding, no one participates (long) in any sport to build character—though character is revealed—nor does anyone start and continue the hours and years of practice necessary for mastery to get rich. It is precisely the non-instrumental seriousness required for mastery that is the basis for the appeal of sports.

Sports also offer what ought to be a rather more obvious source of value, though one whose obviousness surely varies in accord with the wider culture. This is an experience of *comradeship,* which is evidently unusual in a society that seems otherwise to offer only the choice between interactions that are entirely personal and intimate or entirely public and pointless.

But such general considerations about value are only part of the story with respect to basketball. A comparison with cricket helps clarify what's unique about the game's address to the imagination. C.L.R. James, in *Beyond a Boundary*, argues cricket is a sport that provides unmatched drama. James claims a specific structural aspect of cricket sets it apart and above other sports (he explicitly compares it to baseball). In cricket, James explains, when the batter faces the bowler, no other members of the batter's side can affect the batter's success in scoring. Thus, batters, functionally, are more than representatives of their sides; they *are* the side. This, James continues, is precisely the sort of dramatic confrontation—an individual standing in for a collectivity against another standing in for another collectivity—which writers and story-tellers have long sought to create through their art—often without success. Cricket, then repeatedly and inescapably enacts that resonant conflict.

Basketball—especially NBA basketball offers a significant variation on this dramatic theme. The NBA disallows zone-defences, thus requiring that each individual defender guard an individual offensive player. This means each time the offensive team brings the ball into the frontcourt the player with the ball at any moment faces a dramatic situation that goes the cricket batter's one better. The offensive player *chooses* whether to confront the defensive player as the individual embodiments of their respective teams. The offensive player can give up the ball, and thus decline the latest confrontation (there are complications, of course, e.g., the defense can double or triple team the player with the ball, declining the individual confrontation in an admission of the superiority of the offensive player). This means basketball engages not only the dramatic structure James finds in cricket, but also the drama of a player accepting or declining the role of individual "hero." And this is no small thing.

Karl Malone, [1999] NBA Most Valuable Player had a memorable moment involving this dramatic situation in the playoffs of the previous year. With his team barely behind in the closing seconds, Malone had the ball on offense, in a high post situation. He passed. Malone, typically one of the NBA's leading scorers, easily the leading scorer on his Utah Jazz team, invariably voted to the First Team All-NBA team, picked as one of the "50 Greatest NBA Players" ever, passed. He chose not to embody his team at its most significant moment during his decade long association with it up to that time. This is interesting. This reveals character. Those who participated in this moment, either as players or observers, were perhaps less than shocked by Malone's difficulties with free-throw shooting in [1998]'s NBA finals.

Isaiah Thomas observed of Michael Jordan during [1999]'s NBA playoffs that what he admired most about Jordan was his "offensive mind"—that is, his mind in relation to playing offense. Thomas was emphasizing that a great player is not merely a physical phenomenon, but also a cognitive agent, analyzing and responding to the particulars of the current context. This, too, is interesting. It's characteristic of Thomas, who is known to stress that African American players do not "come dribbling out of their mothers' wombs," but rather develop their skills and capacities through thought and work. It also elaborates on the crucial role of choice in offense, in a way complementing a modified Jamesian analysis: where the latter presents a player choosing whether to confront *a* defender, the former presents *this* player choosing how to confront *this* defender.

Larry Bird's decision, and that of Karl Malone, and the decisions Michael Jordan makes repay scrutiny: a decision to work, a decision that reveals character, analytic decision-making by an African American male. What is extraordinary—and unfortunate—is that such decisions should need underscoring, surely a world in which they are normal is a more sensible one than the reverse. Basketball is more microscope than macrocosm, allowing examination of life under an alternative system, rather than reflecting the rules of the actually existing world order.

The Blueprint

Charles Planck

As Tamerlane, Count Metternich, Premier Tojo, et al., could have foretold, rolling out a grand new world-historical concept is never easy. Preventive Free Market Democratic Military Imperialism will face heavy going in certain quarters, as pre- and post-cakewalk carping at its inauguration in Iraq already shows. Nervous, fastidious nellies are never lacking. The Defense Policy Board and its spokesman (the secretary of defense and the president are the best) need a slam-dunk for the next application.

There would seem to be a shortage of perfect cases: Iran, while once attractively nasty, has the downside of currently lying low, being big and sounding a lot like Iraq. North Korea is gray, distant, and rather dull. Moreover, Kim Il Jong is mainly guilty of the old-fashioned crime of starving his own people. (Lots of countries have nuclear weapons and push drugs.) The Saudis, already sullied by September 11, would make a delicious target, but prudence argues for pausing until Iraqi oil comes reliably on line. Pakistan could be positioned as an unstable, treacherous ally, but we already invaded a country composed mostly of rocks. Latin America is passé.

Fortunately, for strategists willing to bomb outside the box, a perfect choice exists. The Israeli-Palestinian conflict features everything it is our duty to eradicate. Terrorism, both the state-sponsored and garden variety. Weapons from rocks to nukes. The flouting of countless U.N. resolutions. Subsidized, pathetic economies. Surreal religiosity. The region is a noisy disgrace to the modern world.

Repetitive relentless demonization is the first step. It might seem tricky to saddamize in the same campaign one so long in the tooth as Arafat and one so fresh an ally as Sharon. But the beauty of invading both parties at once is that we can simultaneously deploy each side's rich gallery of monsters. Consider just the short deck the Palestinians could play: Begin and the Stern Gang. Rabbi Kook and the Greater Israel Movement. Sharon and his Phalangist allies at Sabra and Shatilla. Baruch Goldstein mowing down worshippers at the Ibrahimi mosque. Boys like Faris Odeh and Muhammad al-Durrah dead at the hands of Israeli soldiers.

Equal indignation could be drummed up with Israel's trump cards. Constant infiltration by the *fedayyin* since the country's founding. Black September's killing of Israeli athletes at the Munich Olympics. The early suicide bombers of Hizbollah and their long line of copycats in Hamas, Islamic Jihad, and the Al-Aqsa Intifada. Arafat's ingrained duplicity. *Mein Kamph* on bestseller lists in Ramallah.

Best of all, both sides can be trusted to continue committing *new* perfidious acts. No need to pad intelligence this time. There are bloody shirts to wave in all directions.

With this wealth of outrage, molding opinion at home and collecting sidekicks abroad will be pushing on an open door. Publicly everyone already despises one side or the other. Privately, we can be sure, growing numbers—probably including the Dalai Lama—are fed up with both.

Bringing compassionate colonialism to Israel and Palestine will be great for the U.S. For years we have underwritten the Israeli military with little in return but continuous diplomatic flak and the gratitude of one small voting bloc. Scenes of American soldiers patrolling the Via Dolorosa or Mount of Olives would garner much wider support, especially from our largest faith-based community. Indeed, the old aspiration to make Jerusalem an *international* city is misguided. The nations of the world are a quarrelsome religious bunch, within and among themselves. The Holy City should be run by *America*, home of religious tolerance.

The land between the Mediterranean Sea and the River Jordan has no oil, but plenty of troubled water. To gain supremacy in the coming struggles over that waning resource, American industry needs new places to work out deals for its private control.

The contestants in Palestine have had their chance. It is time for a country with military might, democratic legitimacy, business smarts, and evenhanded decisiveness to set things straight. The Israelis are accustomed to being governed by generals and the Palestinians must learn. The world will thank us.

Fujiyama Mama

Lorna Salzman

The Society of Mothers for Self- and Offspring- Sacrifice (SMSOS) today attacked Suha Arafat, the wife of Yasir Arafat, after Arafat said she would readily sacrifice her son for the Palestinian cause.

The SMSOS group was particularly upset at her statement because Arafat, who lives in Paris, has a daughter, not a son, and did not offer her daughter's life for the cause.

"I am mortified that a woman of international prominence and prestige could dismiss the notion that women are not entitled to blow themselves up for a political cause," said Thana T. Opsis, spokeswoman for SMSOS. "This is an insult to those of us who have worked so hard to obtain equal rights for women."

Arafat is still living in the Dark Ages of pre-feminism according to Opsis: "Despite the efforts of female cultural studies professors to inculcate their students with the notion of honor that accompanies suicide for a political cause, Arafat still accords such notions onto to her son, not her daughter." Opsis noted approvingly that secular democracies allow all of those who reach the age of majority to choose suicide and that recent suicide bombings by young women in Jerusalem "show promise for a better future for Arab women."

Said a State Department official: "It is long overdue for the Arab world to award women the same status and prestige associated with suicide bombing as they do to their men. Only in this way can we achieve complete women's liberation and a true sense of pride and patriotism."

ALIENS GOT MY SISTER!!

aliens got my sister
in a UFO Cadillac
a real pavement blisterer
now she's got fins in back

aliens got my sister
in a family way
told her they couldn't resist her
but that's what aliens always say

my sister's been abducted
by some hunk from outer space
deep inside he's a monster
but he has a human face

he came dressed as a preacher
he was going to teach her her place
I found out too late to reach her
he was just a creature from outer space

he only wanted to probe her
then strand her on her own
on the sidewalks of another planet
8 billion light beers from home

aliens got my sister
they put her on so hard a pedestal
regular fellas couldn't keep her
from taking up with extraterrestrials

aliens got my sister
in the trunk of their UFO
the only reason you don't hear her screaming
is they turned up the radio

– Natalie Estrellita

she don't like my gospel music

she don't like my poetry
she don't like my shoes
she don't take me seriously
or the language that I use
she don't give a rat's ass
how I've paid my dues
think I better take it to Jesus
how about you

got my overcoat on inside out
my heart hid up my sleeve
seen too many Bibles to know
which one to believe
got a miracle in my pocket
where my soul is rubbing through
think it's time I took it to Jesus
what about you?

she don't like my manners
she don't like my views
she don't like my philosophy
or the metaphors I choose

she don't like me violently
with a zeal I can't excuse
think it's time I took it to Jesus
what about you?

– Natalie Estrellita

The Depths

I remember reading Williams' poem
"The Yachts" and thinking it was about yachting.
"No, no," advised the young professor.

"Nothing is what it seems. Everything
stands for something else." A simple poem
by de la Mere named "Snow" depicted

snow falling. "It's about falling snow,"
I had the lunacy to announce
to my freshman class. That whole year

I learned nothing. I read *Moby Dick*
as a great novel about whaling.
I got all the way through Dos Passos'

USA thinking it was about
my country. I did everything
badly. At the draft board physical

I read the eye chart perfectly
as though it were a competition
for most eligible to be shot

to pieces, and I wanted to win.
The huge illiterate heavyweight
who was 4F shouted "you fight

for the both of us," as he shadow-boxed
on the trolley home. I took a job
driving for Lucky Lottie Wolf

who owned a stable of race horses
and on whose advice I bet my whole
summer earnings on a sure thing,

Son of Tara, who broke his neck
in the starting gate. "Lucky Lottie,"
Indeed! In six months I'd be twenty,

Dewey would fall to Truman, Walcot
to Louis, day would turn to night
just as in the movies, and all this

without the least hint of irony.
Soon I could drink legally and smoke
two packs a day and become a man.

– Philip Levine

Head of State

Eric Lott

Adaped from a piece published in a Clinton-era issue of First of the
Month.

"I'm trying to stifle my natural impulses here:" as meet an autopsy
of Bill Clinton the pol as those other infamous tags ("won't have me to
kick around anymore," "I paid for this microphone," "Can a president this
well-hung be lying," etc.) were of the presidents who uttered them. And
Clinton's line to confessor Jim Lehrer came every bit as live and direct
from the unconscious. The problem is not only that Clinton would be a
lot better president were he on better terms with his natural impulses,
it's that we're all fascinated with his natural impulses and want to know
more about them. They make Clinton interesting—maybe tragic, probably just randy, but interesting in any case. What I'm saying is that it's
about time we had some word on those distinguishing characteristics.
No satisfaction forthcoming from displacements (grotesque John Wayne
Bobbitt's patched-together perp—now on video) or sidelights (Tonya
Harding and noisome hubby in their sportive video moment—not bad,
though) or substitutes (Frank Gifford coming too fast in the hands of his
plane pal—according to the *Globe*'s assiduous reporting). I seek details
of the presidential peter, and I think I'm not alone. More than half the
people who voted for Clinton believed he had "affairs" and other "natural" impulses. Am I dreaming or did we want presidential dick, men and
women both? What exactly are our relations with the head of state?

As Clinton sat absurdly face to face with Lehrer, fig-leaf hands in lap,
you could almost feel his dick straining the—we know now—briefs to
blow his cover. Is it huge? Uncircumcised? Roly-poly? Ever-hard? Flirta-
tiously moled? Eccentrically curved? Could it be—*pierced*? Searching
for answers to these and other question, Brian Williams on MSNBC

fiberoptically consulted everyone he could lay hands on, milking the porn from Clinton's legalisms: "there "*is*" no "im*prop*er" relationship, President Clinton says, and one wonders just exactly what those words mean." *Newsweek* deputy of dullness Jonathan Alter went for the zinger and missed the point: "The president spoke of trying to *stifle natural impulses*, presumably his anger, in responding to these charges, but in fact it appears that *other* natural impulses may have gotten him in trouble." *They want to see the dick*! And I do too. They speak for me who sometimes did me flee. Circling ever closer to the meat, commentators spoke feverishly of 20 hours of tape recorded by internal White House nemesis Linda Tripp (a Bush holdover) containing conversations she had with the twenty-one-year old intern Clinton allegedly bedded. This of course petered out almost upon utterance: we don't want to hear somebody talking about it, we want to hear them doing it. UNLESS, does she mention jimmy? Hey!

Nixon's Deep Throat told reporters to follow the money, Clinton's deep throats say follow the money shot. Butch bottoms of the press (and gallery) oblige, and their urge to peep may follow a more general political logic of attention to Clinton's body—its hair, its flab, its sexual habits. Clinton's is surely the most pondered straight white male body since Robert DeNiro gained seventy pounds for his role in *Raging Bull*. And no wonder. Citizens' relation to the state is always coerced, mystified, imaginary, distant. For much of the nineteenth century, just as Marx was making this clear, reserves of imagined community allowed presidents and legislators of prominence to seal the deal. By now the state stands in such naked, brutal relation to all but the most pleasure-domed of our eminent bourgeois that the only way to find any sort of link to the chief executive is by eroticizing him, if possible (and his wife if powerful). Hence, no one was interested in William Ginsburg's take on the situation: "if the story is true, then the president is a misogynist [go for yours, Mr. Ginsburg] and my client has been ravaged; if it's not true than my client has been ravaged by the OIC [Kenneth Starr's Office of Independent Council]." All too true, though this reading relieves his client of any intentions, desires, or designs of her own. Either way, nobody cares about *her*. Press Secretary Dee Dee Myers affirmed that yes, it probably was an "improper" thing for a married fifty-one-year-old to be shtupping a twenty-one-year old intern. Anti-choice crusader Henry Hyde talked impeachment ("*if* the charges are true," quoth he) as though it were a municipal ordinance regulating sexual behavior, which, in the dark place that is the mind of Mr. Hyde, it probably is. Holding forth so transparently, the commentators demonstrated the common-sense embodiment of civil devotion that finds men like me sucking William Jefferson Clinton's cock.

There's a racial tip here too, beginning with the various interracial buddy films of state involving first Clinton and Ron Brown, now Clinton and Vernon Jordan. These seem to materialize in moments of state financial or sexual crisis for reasons Leslie Fiedler could help you nail and Quentin Tarrantino could not. With Clinton and Jordan shaking hands over the prostrate form of Monica Lewinsky, could anything really be *so wrong*? The presidential dick thus vindicated if not authenticated, it's the perfect signifier, both vilified and loved, of freedom from the claustral routine of everyday life in Clinton, R.F.D.—a signifier straight men seem to need. It's far too long ago to remember the industrial ignominies Americans swallowed in exchange for their daily bread. Work-time as we know it was invented in a couple of decades' time about a hundred and fifty years ago. Natural impulses were sent packing. Shoved back into the recesses of consciousness, unruly desires are only safely indulged through the imaginary spectacle of others' enjoyment. Hence blackface, porn, gay "realness," whatever. Occasionally, an avid president has served the purpose of imaginary vessel of pleasure—and, therefore, necessary disavowal. Thomas Jefferson and his "alleged" slave concubine, Sally Hemings (and her kids), first aired in a Federalist screed against the president-to-be; Abraham Lincoln, Honest Abe, whom southerners lampooned as obsessed with mixed-race sex and called, in a racist sucker punch, "honest ape;" JFK, whose boner for bleach blonds put him forever in the company of Joe DiMaggio, Arthur Miller, Andy Warhol, and Norman Mailer, all white-ethnic boys romancing America in the form of Marilyn Monroe: imaginary desiring machines for the people. The First Cock has lately become virtually our only imagined connection to the nation-state.

But what if under the blessed trinity of Marv Albert, Marion Barry, and Frank Gifford, we could at last go to the videotape? The head dick is out of reach, we know that. Would the sight of it, though, spring open a state of passion, of "natural impulses"—frank with our fantasies, out for much more than the state, done with dominion in fact, through with a deal that makes us the subjects we are?

Ghazal of Twat

Lover, tell me what you see down there.
I tried a mirror, but it's hairy down there.

Jewel of many names—*lotus garden*
nappy dugout, yoni, down there

Lilith got bored with missionary.
Kneel and taste the honey down there.

Adam refused, *I need a woman under me.*
Besides you bleed and piss down there.

Shiny lips, real hair, but Eve is missing
something. Just a plastic V down there.

Men dream of women filled with teeth
and razor blades—an arsenal of weaponry down
                there.

On today's show: Pre-teen sluts confess to Mom
That ain't no cherry down there.

Tomorrow frustrated women teach their husbands
how to solve a mystery down there.

If a man cooks dinner, he'll expect
to dive into the sea down there.

Magazines push perfume, yogurt.
Take pains not to smell fishy down there.

Be creative—shave a stripe or heart.
Just don't go crazy down there.

Kick him to the curb if he forgets
your birthday or is lazy down there.

Scientists debate fidelity. Perhaps men aren't
                creeps;
they're drawn by DNA to seek variety down there.

Forget my MENSA mind and wit, my great legs.
You'll find the best of me down there.

I will know my true love by his eyes and when he
            says,
You're gorgeous Stone. I want to spend eternity
            down there.

                        – Alison Stone

What Salvation Must Be Like After a While

The late Isaac Asimov, a great science fiction writer,
was also Honorary President
of the American Humanist Association.
Humanists try to behave as honorably as possible
without any expectation of rewards and punishments
in an Afterlife.
I said at an AHA memorial service for him
"Isaac is up in Heaven now."
It was the funniest thing I could have said to the
Humanists.
They were startled,
and then they laughed and laughed.

Who would be mean enough
to wake up Isaac,
or any other dead person, for that matter,
except Adolph Hitler, maybe,
for bliss throughout Eternity?

                        – Kurt Vonnegut

Into the Summer Sea

Charles O'Brien

I remember reading somewhere in an article somewhere an account by
the author wherein his teacher one day leaned over and told him softly that
you should always keep *two* passports handy; and, the text went on in its
proairetic way, that teacher was none other than George Steiner. And I,
who do precisely that, that is to say, keep two passports handy, I wonder:
what's he yelling about? For George Steiner comes recommended.

Very. Steiner publishes, in books and in a variety of magazines, and
lectures prolifically. He has and has had numerous academic appoint-
ments. He is often spoken of as a *great* critic. His range of languages!
His prose! (his prose!) And what has he not read? The recent *Reading
George Steiner*, a sort of Festschrift with, up top, in lieu of the maraschino
cherry, "A Responsion" by Steiner himself gives the flavor. There we

are told of the "passionate seriousness," of the "puissant majesty of his oeuvre," and we learn that:

> A month after the second moiety of lectures began.... Steiner offered some fascinating reflections on modern music, especially on rock and acid house. (*So many* questions have been raised about this new dance craze!)

There often comes a time in the career of a writer who has over a while inspired doubts that these doubts get resolved against him. With Steiner, this book, *No Passion Spent: Essays, 1978-1995*, is that time. This is a poorer collection than his 1984 best-of, *George Steiner: A Reader*, which began with 1965's "To Civilize Our Gentlemen" (a title that at least had the virtue of unfailingly calling up a smile and the thought of a rope). But since nothing here is exactly new, it probably only seems that he's getting worse. Impressive from a distance, a long one, seen closely, the book is more than a little repellent. So much industry, what good can come of it? And Steiner's many celebrated gifts, will they come when he does call? Random quotation would be sufficient to show what is wrong, but would be more cruelty than justice. Let's look instead at a few passages—none unrepresentative—that cover the main problems.

From "The Uncommon Reader:"

> To accumulate paperbacks is not to assemble a library. By its very nature, the paperback pre-selects and anthologizes from the totality of literature and thought.... It is only when we know a writer integrally, when we turn with special if querulous solicitude to [an author's] "failures" and construe our own vision of his presentness that the act of reading is authentic. Dog-eared in our pocket, discarded in the airport lounge, lurching between ad hoc brick bookends, the paperback is a marvel of packaging and a denial of the largesse of form and spirit.... Can a paperback have seven seals?

The critique of the paperback is old as, no doubt older, than, the paperback itself, but this one is the most worthless I can recall. As an exercise in but-abandoning-oneself-to-it it is simply stunning. Where it is not flatly untrue, it is blithely beside the point. What, for instance, is a library? In this view, it is, really, the room that books do furnish. Would the library of Alexandria qualify? If yes, then only because it could produce references. Aleksander Wat, in his memoirs, talks about reading in the Lubyanka as a guest of the GPU. Books unavailable to the rest of the Soviet population were given, if haphazardly, to the inmates, and there Wat read, among others, Proust. Was that a library? Not by Steiner's standards (although it did have at least seven seals). Yet that is how reading, in the world, gets done and more "authentically" than with Steiner's fancied "querulous solicitude."

Steiner is one who, in Samuel Johnson's contemptuous phrase, *reads books through*. But he even wants points for what he hasn't read. Well who wouldn't want that. But nobody like Steiner:

> I have a dozen times slunk by [Paolo] Sarpi's leviathan history of the Council of Trent (one of the pivotal works in the development of western religious-political argument); or the *opera omnia* of Nikolai Hartmann in their stately binding. I shall never manage the sixteen thousand pages of Amiel's (profoundly interesting) journal currently being published.

Slunk by! (Where?) An even dozen times! Stay off the pipe! But if Steiner isn't—couldn't be—going anywhere with this, he's careful to cover himself. If he hasn't read it, he is willing to bet nobody else in the room has. What should be concession is further grandiosity.

From "The Archives of Eden:"

> The most voluptuous of central European chocolates is named after Mozart, the most seductive of steak-dishes after Chaateaubriand and Rossini. Such kitsch (!) pays tribute to a formidable recognition. Why are American streets so silent to the remembrance of thought?

Steiner has his facts wrong, and they are truest thing here. There are plenty of "American streets" with toney names—and let's not for a moment forget the Parthenon in Nashville, TN. And after pigging out on the weekend specials at a Frenchish restaurant that's seen better days, and a couple of Mozart candies (which are not exactly chocolates) we can crack open a bottle of Rembrandt mouthwash and—live a little!—rinse and spit. But even granting Steiner the facts, what could any of it matter? If scorpions lived on sense and logic, such an argument as this would be the carapace left behind. Is there anything Kantian about a street named after Kant? When Goebbels called Germany "the great country of Kant," what was that a "formidable recognition" of? What do Chateaubriand and Rossini, of all people, have to do, of all things, with "thought?" And is it any favor to Steiner to note the *possibility* of some lumbering levity in this passage?

From "What is Comparative Literature?"

> Labor as we may, bread will never wholly translate pain. What in English, French or Italian is Heimat?

Among the many claims made by/for Steiner is that he is so fluently multi-lingual, with, for example English *and* French *and* German as his first language. Such skills are certainly useful for a guide up the Amazon or a pimp in Berlin and indispensable for someone, like Steiner, whose fondest aspiration is to be the Peter Lorre of American criticism. But, what's in it for the rest of us? Steiner, having experienced, in English, the inexpressible, is here to tell us that it is inexpressible, that and no more. "*Bread* will never translate *pain*" stripped of the trivial and tautological, the little truth is that the place of bread in Anglophone cultures is not that of bread in French culture. But that is not an issue of translation. And anyone seeking to "wholly translate" a freighted word by its easiest pocket dictionary equivalent has not worked at all: how, then, does the phrase, "Labor as we may" apply? As so often in Steiner, underneath the sonorities, it's all arpeggiated fuck-ups. Note too, Steiner's insistence on italicizing foreign words as often as he can. Good English wouldn't; advertising does. There's more: the world is full of imperfectly multilingual people, not "wholly translating" from one language to another. The differences are not the situs of a problematic. Wise men and others, fish in those lacunas, and few people come away with nothing. Polyglossy is more commonly a pleasure than a sorrow.

From "Two Suppers:"

> Two deaths continue to characterize western moral and intellectual history. (Would that history have been markedly different, could there have been a steadier light in the landscape of western consciousness if the axiomatic events had been that of two births?)

Where to pick this up? The "two suppers" are the Symposium and the Last Supper. Hackneyed as the Socrates-Jesus comparison is, "Incomparable" Steiner, as he deserves to be called in Eighteenth-Century style, should have foregone comparison. One hint: a three-hour agony is observed; twelve days of Christmas are celebrated. What is there in what we know of Socrates to set against the Magnificat? What could an Angel of Philosophy have prophesied to his expectant mother that would not leave her groaning. "Just great! Another fucking lumpen?" The last 59 pages of this dismal book are devoted to these specific deaths, to those two, or any other births, part of one sentence. What steadier light is to be found here? Elsewhere in the book, Steiner pronounces, "It is a Socrates, a Mozart, a Gauss or a Galileo who, in some degree, compensates for man." Man may need redemption, or not, but not compensation; and compensation is not to be found where Steiner would send us looking. Whatever needs making up is to be looked for in the world, somewhere, as we may find it, and not in the greater retentions of [somebody else's name here]. Steiner, so much of whose work is an extra-long I'm-with-incomparable-genius t-shirt, is not to be trusted on matters of the everyday or the domestic. In a (favorable) review of Althusser's genuinely loopy, rather pathetic memoir, *I Want to Tell You*, Steiner observes, "There is something vulgar, almost absurd in the notion of Mrs. Plato or a Mme. Descartes, or of Wittgenstein on a honeymoon." I don't know, but as James M. Cain's characters liked to say, "You shoulda seen the other guy." There is an account of Elvis Presley, in the flush of his first fame, appearing in front of an audience, and before starting the first number, in that moment, pink and black, *spitting* on the stage. I don't mind that such a measure is quite lost on Steiner—let him mind—but he could have been expected to know such things as that the world must be peopled, and those people fed, and with something more nourishing than a spectral died of *pain*, seductive steaks and voluptuous marzipan bonbons.

From "A Preface to the Hebrew Bible:"

> Time and again, I have sought to imagine, albeit indistinctly, Shakespeare remarking at home or to some intimate on whether or not work on *Hamlet* or *Othello* had gone well or poorly, as the case might be. I can picture him, just, expressing satisfaction over Feste in *Twelfth Night* or the compactions of syntax (still unique) in *Coriolanus*. And then inquiring as to the price of cabbage.... What I am unable to do is to arrive at any thought-image, however naive, at any impression of literary technique of rhetorical transport, however masterful, when confronting the author(s) of God's speeches out of the whirlwind in Job, of much of the Qoheleth, of certain Psalms or considerable portions of "Second Isaiah." The picture of some man or woman lunching, dining, after he or she had "invented" and set down these and certain biblical texts, leaves me, as it were, blinded and off-balance.

What is not wrong with all this? "I can picture him, *just*, expressing satisfaction over Feste...." Why just? It is hard to imagine Shakespeare, working actor-playwright, shareholder, impresario, and presumably as gregarious as today's show-folk, *not* discussing the clown role with the company clown. *Hamlet* ... and the others would be similarly subject to discussion. A poet the very height of whose eloquence is reached in such lines as:

Never, never, never, never, never

and

      Pray you, undo this button: thank you sir

surely is more capacious than Steiner lets on. And *Coriolanus*'s "still unique" compactions of syntax, while we're at it, are a little less unique than those of *The Winter's Tale*.

Could someone write *Ecclesiastes* and then go to lunch? It is precisely the book of someone who has never wanted for lunch. These biblical texts are the very last ones to support the kinds of distinctions Steiner would impose on them. Erich Auerbach, who insisted on the *commonness* of Biblical style, writes:

> But what a road, what a fate lies between the Jacob who created his father out of his blessing and the old man whose favorite son has been torn to pieces by a wild beast!—between David the harp player, persecuted by his lord's jealousy, and the old king, surrounded by violent intrigues, whom Abishag the Shunnamite warmed in his bed, and he knew her not.

Here is a prose that, even in translation, communicates brilliantly, a prose caught up in the wonders it speaks of. It is also a prose that, for all it says about the texts it addresses, speaks achingly, but without so much as a sideways glance, of the actual situation to which its author, "really cast down," had been brought. Steiner, not really saying anything about his chosen texts, says nothing about anything else.

It is hardly worth quoting, but what was in the ellipsis in the above Steiner passage, that is after the Shakespeare and before the Bible, was a sentence about (or "about") Schubert and Einstein. *What do they have to do with it?* Chez Steiner, even those texts, the Bible and Shakespeare, that are most common property, that are most freely, sluttishly, accessible—and the better for it—are to be kept behind glass.

From "Two Cocks:"

> It is in Marxism that post-Christian western messianic hopes were invested, that newfound expression was given to the hunger for justice on earth. Both the Sermon on the Mount and *The Communist Manifesto* proclaim their origins in Mosaic teachings and in Amos. The downfall of the Marxist ideal may bring the final enfeeblement of Christianity, Wrestlers succumb to mutual exhaustion.

And this too the wind beareth away. Passion in here invoked not with passion, but with guesses, and mistaken guesses. In a similar context, Steiner speaks of "hope of hope." No comfort, and no such thing. If hope that is *seen* is not hope, neither is hope that is speculated on. Steiner is something of a diminished Ernst Bloch. He has long and very chastely flirted with Revolution (see, if you must, his book-length fiction, *Proofs*). Let's tease out Steiner's schema. "Marxism" supplants Christian messianic hopes. The "Marxist ideal" then falls. Christianity itself than succumbs. Nothing of this corresponds to anything that may be observed in the world. Aspiration has never been institutionally or textually bound. "Marxism" is, to Steiner, pre-eminently the Marx of 1844; and that is only a moment, and not a particularly big one in the history of the Nineteenth-Century workers' movement. The "Marxist Ideal," (confusedly), is far more the brainchild of Engels and Lenin. What specifically had a downfall is hardly the death of hope. As if the likes of Suslov and Markus Wolf worried their evil heads about love for love.

The presence of "post" and "exhaustion" are tip-offs. Steiner's reading of 1989 is, in essence, the standard rightist one: an engulfing capitalist order *defeated* Marxism. In truth, though, the Eastern European states fell in response to pressure almost exclusively from within and mostly from the left. The opposition there, far from being "exhausted," was audacious, sustained, principled, and intelligent. A good representation can be found in Adam Michnik's collection of essays, *The Church and The Left*, which covers the same ground that Steiner purports to. But how differently Michnik's honorable, somewhat messy book has wrestled with his subject. Steiner's posturing is so much easier and so without point. In a recent article on the killing of Aldo Moro, Steiner makes a passing reference to "Red Brigade covens." It is not only that this is the sort of lunacy you would expect to find in the *Congressional Record*, but for him not to spare a kind word for The Terror is to have labored in vain. Can such a "hunger for justice on earth" as some "messianically hopeful" corner of Steiner's being would claim, and so tiny a thirst for blood dwell together? Yes—but not often, and not easily. No Future can be gleeful; Steiner's is only enervating—and not even credible.

xxx

The single least agreeable thing about this book is reading it. It is as if the slogan, No poetry after Auschwitz, were a prescription for bloated prose. His style is vaguely Baroque, but waxy and overdressed, like a defendant or a corpse. It would be fun to make up a list of Steiner's tic-words—actually you've met a few—but "floruit" should not go unnoted. His adverbs usually come announced fore and aft, as if trying to capture the speech rhythms of Frank Costanza. He refers to the Jewish refusal to convert as *gran rifiuto*. Dante tells us nothing about the discussion, and the discussion tells us nothing about Dante. But I suppose Steiner had gone too long *without anything in italics*.

At some point, Steiner quotes a few lines from the first scene in *Hamlet*: They are, predictably, in original spelling. There is, of course, nothing wrong with unmodernized spellings and, in some cases, they will be preferable. Not here. Here, it is for effect, another flourish, such as are to be found in about every line in Steiner, and even when he shuts up for a few, and such as "when they seldome come, they wisht for come."

Steiner's manner is central to the Steiner effect. He comes with the face you put on walking into a wake or a job interview. As effusively as he offers praise, it hardly seems with any affection. Instead, it is court-ier-like, a duty done, and really no more. Steiner's suggestiveness, his implied lines of inquiry are the crabgrass of the graduate seminar. We know so little about, he says over and over, and so much work remains to be done on, but if we know anything, it is that the work isn't going to get done here. His most challenging inquiries, his star turns, e.g., why have the Jews refused conversion?, are worse than difficult, they are insoluble; and they are insoluble because, well, because they are dumb.

Steiner is perhaps most prized for his high seriousness. Adorno's *Aesthetic Theory* offers the right response, a stool painted by Van Gogh shows up the insufficiency of the "great," the "august" subject. Or see Adorno kicking Heidegger in the head—and loving it!—"a poesie concocted from Parmenides and Jungnickel," and then see with what owl-like solemnity Steiner always treats Heidegger. And it is not so much that Steiner is wrong and Adorno right. It is that Steiner couldn't be right. You can't get there from here.

The gloomy Steiner appears to suffer from the Soame Jenyns syndrome, a condition first diagnosed by Dr. Johnson:

> A head thus prepared for the reception of false opinions, and the project of vain designs, the [the malign gods] easily fill with idle notions, till in time they make their plaything an author.... Then begins the poor animal to entangle himself in sophisms, and flounder in absurdity, to talk confidently of the scale of being, and to give solutions which himself confesses impossible to be understood.

Reversing Dante's lines in Canto V of the *Inferno*, Primo Levi once wondered if perhaps there were no greater joy than the remembrance of pain in a later *tempo felice*. For him, it was a fugitive hope, as it turned out, but that he entertained it is proof of his integrity. There is, by contrast, a willed quality to Steiner's so frequent recursion to Auschwitz. Where you can come to be so at ease is probably not hell.

Steiner has lately, especially in *Real Presences* and also in a good bit of this book, acquired a reputation as a theologian of sorts. I am reminded, first, of the title of a book by Leszek Kolakowski: *God Owes Us Nothing*, and then of a news item Jay Leno once read on the air. Charles Manson had just been hospitalized after acid was thrown in his face by another inmate. The assault took place, said Leno, "during a religious argument." He added, "Now, there's two major theologians." Sure; then throw in Steiner, Dr. Cornel West, and a carton of cigarettes, and you will have one wicked game of whist.

It's hard to know just what the title, *No Passion Spent*, means. But, say, you're walking down the street, and you see a rubber half-unfurled. Curiosity might drive you to peer inside, to see if anything's there. On a good day, you'll think better of it.

Part VII

Forget U

I was tempted to include—in the "Wild Light" section or in the following set of pieces about higher ed—Charles O'Brien's *First* response to the Whit Stillman issue of *Intercollegiate Review*. It's still a hoot to read O'Brien on self-righteous doofuses who insist characters in Stillman's movies personify Old Right virtues:

> The dialogue, so finely crafted by Mr. Stillman, so sublimely dopey in his characters' mouths, baffles the criticasters of *Intercollegiate Review*. In *Barcelona*, Fred says that he's been reading (!) and coming across the word "subtext." And then this:
>
> Fred: But what do you call the message or meaning that is right there on the surface, completely open and obvious? They never talk about that. What do you call what's above the surface?
>
> Ted: The text.
>
> Fred: OK, that's right, but they never talk about that.
>
> In the claims of the *Intercollegiate Review*, Ensign j.g. Fred is opposing his good American plain talk and common sense to exegetic nihilism. But gentle reader: just watch the movie. [Actor] Chris Eigeman asked the question because he didn't know the answer, and when the answer turns out so obvious, he refuses to admit his ignorance. He is being in character: not too smart, and not too honest. In fine, everybody wins.

Stillman himself allowed O'Brien's piece was "pretty funny" (and his actors liked it too). A friend of the director, however, set O'Brien to rights about Stillman's own class origins. O'Brien had noted that Stillman once referred to himself as a social climber, but the director's class mate broke it down: Stillmans start at the top and float "like the pearl in the bottle of *Prell*." A pearl of a line yet one that hints why O'Brien's brief for *Metropolitan*, *Barcelona*, and *Last Days of Disco* isn't in this volume. Stillman(s) and his art films don't need a push from *First* (or anyone else). And his idolaters in the Academy are a threat to nobody but themselves.

There are university film cultists, though, whose blankness is catching. *Matrix*-mongers provide justifications for a pop phenomenon that contributes to mass cultural amnesia. Armond White resists what these intellectual enablers are promoting in his piece, "History Gets Lost in *The Matrix*." It leads off this section, which targets ahistorical mind (and grind) games promoted in the Academy. Closing pieces on the plight of adjuncts and the history of adult education in the UK affirm there are worthy academic traditions as well as empty ones.

History Gets Lost in the Matrix

Armond White

"Comprehension is not a requisite of cooperation."
—*Cornel West making his Hollywood film debut in* The Matrix Reloaded

More people—including black people—have seen *The Matrix* than have ever heard of Herman Sonny Blount. Blount was a pianist, composer, bandleader and sci-fi visionary born in Birmingham, Alabama, almost a century ago. Once migrated to the North, he took part in community action, developed a singular big-band musical style and then announced to the world an unprecedented theatrical cosmology under his stage name Sun Ra. Fancying jazz's relatively esoteric mid-century scene—and the license its artists took to originate and agitate—Sun Ra extended bebop intransigence into a personal political withdrawal from America's discrimination and disrespect. He intuited a space age myth about black people's history—and their future. This creative leap of imagination and self-edification used art—music—as a vehicle for escape and salvation the way others more commonly and frivolously used movies.

Performing in costumes redolent of ancient Egypt as well as Old World mysticism, Sun Ra looked upward and outward; alternately labeling his band Myth Science Arkestra or Solar Arkestra or Astro Infinity Arkestra. He acted as a jazzy-theological combination of Garvey and Noah and Ellington, providing a berth for such stalwarts of avant-jazz as Pharoah Sanders and Archie Shepp, but above all promising to take his listeners out of the mundane and back to the superior space from which they were spiritually, and perhaps literally, displaced. Blount's priestly musical mission seemed weird and ahead of its time until George Clinton grooved to it, concocting the '70s cartoon-ethos he and graphic artist Pedro Bell built around the Parliament-Funkadelic colony. Clinton made popular what Blount proudly would not (he had learned the need for intransigence from early work in progressive social organizations). It would take several decades for Blount and Clinton's vision of metaphysical entertainment to be popularized—commercialized—into *The Matrix* movie phenomenon.

Not simply a space opera like *Star Wars* or *2001: A Space Odyssey*, both *The Matrix* and its sequel *The Matrix Reloaded* derive from the hipster sensibility; awareness of black and Asian subcultures has turned into the basis for a new kind of pop consciousness. More hype than either George Lucas or Stanley Kubrick landmark, *The Matrix* movies demonstrate a timely fusion. They blend kung-fu martial arts spectacle with whatever resonance remains of the counterculture's old idea of racial intermingling and social justice. It's an underground ethos transmitted through youth pop (sci-fi, comics) and esoterica like Sun Ra (once a favorite of '60s radicals). Not only black intellectuals and buppies respond; *The Matrix* (with an ad campaign that combines computerized numerals with Asian ideograms) confirms the global consumerism to which African American pop culture is now insidiously pledged. The cooptation of Sun Ra's already baroque vision, cannily adds the speed and glamour of Hong Kong action flicks. Because discontented urban youth made a hero of Bruce Lee in the '70s—buying out of white western mythologies (though not altogether conscious why)—*The Matrix* uses the appeal of non-white mythology to bring pop culture back into the hegemonic fold. It flatters youth cult's need for heroic-identification by populating its story with black and Asian archetypes as if there were an authentic expression of African American hope in its metaphors.

Casting Cornel West as a member of an underground city's tribal council trying to determine mankind's fate shows that the creators of *The Matrix*, Andy and Larry Wachowski, are undeniably hip to the most fashionable currents of black pop culture. There's genuine conviction in West's bromides (he's not one of those shallow, noisy race hustlers like Michael Eric Dyson and gives a more credible performance than Samuel L. Jackson in *The Phantom Menace*) but it's not clear that the Wachowskis take West seriously because they keep things on a predictable, cartoon level. To see a new generation of black intellectuals embrace a form that bowdlerizes Sun Ra's unleashed dream of freedom shows how susceptible black pop culture has become, taking its cues from mainstream media rather than authentic black marginality. Black hipsters' esteem for *The Matrix* comes out of their unquestioned regard for the persuasive power of the mainstream (envy is, in part, what motivates the movies' characters). They're seduced by *Reloaded*'s calculated folk celebration. After Morpheus (Laurence Fishburne) urges his people to fight against the tyranny of "the machines," an orgiastic mating ritual ensues with mostly black bodies writhing and sweating, saliva dripping from their mouths. It's a cartoon of tribalism and paranoia: Spike Lee's "Da Butt" linked with *Gangs of New York*. Fetishing black sexuality this way (showing the masses in large-scale bacchanal) uses blackness as the Beats did, to vivify an unarticulated wish for human liberation. It is, in a word, exploitation.

Despite black intellectuals' usual reflex to distrust Hollywood offerings as Trojan Horses, *The Matrix* has been ushered into the center of contemporary discourse through the back door of structuralist race theory (and nationwide cultural studies programs). That's why Cornel West can unashamedly pop up in a cameo role. His key dialogue—"Comprehension is not a requisite of cooperation"—sounds like capitulation because it is. In West's quasi-apology for *The Matrix*'s nearly impenetrable plot, black academia has colluded with Hollywood—made it ok to buy a ticket—rather than pursue the more difficult roots task of resurrecting Sun Ra.

I

Funny how some black American film buffs and political geeks conveniently scoffed at the idea of a "white savior" as an excuse to avoid movies from *Mississippi Burning* to *Cry Freedom*, *Amistad* to *Rosewood*, and yet action-fantasy like *The Matrix*—which indeed offers a white savior—gets them open. Their racial anxiety latches on to the chimera of identity transcendence (black people as cosmological "viruses")—a crackpot bohemian notion recently distilled from Sun Ra in the sci-fi documentary *Last Angel of History* by the black British filmmaker John Akomfrah. This postmodern disaffection, garbed in New Age trendiness, repeats Hollywood's continued avoidance of the difficulties in real-life racial, political alliance.

In *The Matrix*'s plot "reality" has been constructed from computer software, tripping the clock forward one millennium and enslaving people to an artificial intelligence—a sham existentialism that replaces philosophy with the rules of Sega-Genesis. This Helmut Lang Terrordome suits the dystopic fashion but is primarily a power/race pantomime. That's why neo-black nationalists are *The Matrix*'s most surprising fans; they're thrilled with Laurence Fishburne as Morpheus, a black "underground" leader, teaching Keanu Reeves, as the putatively white cyberfreak Neo (anagram for The One), to save humanity—those Dionysian legions of the oppressed whom Morpheus calls "Children of Zion." Religious parallels are only decorative, race is the true currency of the Wachowski brothers script. They use race and ethnicity as dramatic ballast—from Morpheus' ebony skinhead and mottled facial contours to Neo's mercurial, Asiatic features. Aboard his cybership Nebuchenezzar (the Biblical allusion is meaningless unlike Sun Ra's witty Arkestra), Morpheus explains to Neo "The world ... has been pulled over your eyes to hide the truth. You're a slave in a prison to hide you from yourself"—making political fodder of mythological/sci-fi/fashion mag/Afrocentric aesthetics.

Follow the allegory: Morpheus trains Neo in vast, white virtual spaces recalling *THX-1138*, *2001*'s colonial room and TV commercial cycloramas in one. ("Welcome to the desert of the real," he half-quips.) Morpheus' lessons come down to a slave's truth: He warns against oppressors—whites dressed like *Men in Black*—who intend to exploit mankind's energy, turning people into batteries. (Slavery in post-Marxist metaphor.) Morpheus educates Neo about their enemy, warning that "many of them are so hopelessly dependent on the System they will fight to defend it." So he's a futuristic Frantz Fanon—but he acts as butler, too: "I can only show you the door, you must walk through." And the old white-negro concepts of black exotic efficacy characterize his advice: "Free Your Mind—don't think, do." Naturally, when tiny bad guy Joe Pantoliano jumps onto an incapacitated Morpheus' lap, he seems a buglike supplicant before a gigantic African idol.

Approved by Al Gore as "sophisticated," *The Matrix* compresses its racial allegory so completely few people can see it. After his lessons, Neo confesses, "I'm not the one," expressing temporary hollow faith. Yet, action-figure Keanu (a white man with a Bruce Lee aspect) achieves what mainstream action movies never allow black characters—a valiant rescue, thus the film's appeal to politically unconscious white viewers. It's shocking that not a single review in 2000 mentioned the film's racial games-playing. So much virtual reality has virtually canceled realistic perception. Yet those black intellectuals who latch onto Morpheus secretly dream that this multi-million dollar summer action flick actually has something to do with what they perceive as The Struggle. In *Reloaded* when Morpheus says "I am here not because of the path that lies before me but because of the path that lies behind me," it's familiar Afrocentric cant. The Wachowskis tweak the spiritual view expressed in *Amistad* where Cinque intoned "My actions at this moment were the only reason my ancestors were alive at all." *The Matrix*'s fantasy takes the onus off contemporary black behavior; it makes dreams of tenure sufficient unto itself, as the reward for the struggles of the past.

The spectacle of Keanu Reeves among the black underclass has gone unremarked not because critics are color-blind liberals, but because they are almost always inattentive to the significance of race in our culture. Black pop artists must sustain this diligence themselves—even in facile parables like the recent black motorcycle movie *Biker Boyz*—or else the alternative is vapid appropriation by hipsters like the Wachowskis. (Critic Gregory Solman has dubbed them "The Watch-Outski Brothers.") *The Matrix*'s evocation of soul-weary underworld blues looks music-video chic. Evidently the Wachowskis, like many boomers, have traded too many comic books, played too much Play Station and watched too much cinema trash to make genuine Afrocentric commentary. A cultural phenom, nonetheless, *The Matrix* is a Caligari machine, reducing contemporary moviegoers to zombies whose brains short-circuit from their souls (like Cesar in *The Cabinet of Dr. Caligari* who follows the orders of his titular mountebank master). Hollywood conditioning makes *The Matrix* seem a masterpiece to overanxious academics and children with overactive fantasy lives. The white hero and simulacra of the racist world provides a "residual self image" for embattled/benighted viewers. Mr. Smith (Hugo Weaving), the films' Big Brother threat, warns: "Your civilization—as soon as we begin thinking for you it becomes our civilization" (in other words, hegemony). The Wachowskis uncover anxieties about race and politics as if revealing society's hidden agendas, but then turn those fears into hallucinations—a big-screen game—so that audiences actually leave unenlightened. Not inspired or enraged but temporarily, foolishly sated.

Sun Ra knew better. Jazz historian Ted Gioia described how a Sun Ra concert offered more authentic and challenging entertainment: Sun Ra's coterie of fans came to expect the unexpected, and were seldom disappointed. The Arkestra lineup might include, on a given night, as few as ten musicians or as many as thirty. Dancers, costumes, slide shows, and other extras might be included with the price of admission. The Arkestra's music could be equally changeable. Elements of bebop, hard bop and swing loom large on the band's mid-1950s recordings. But over the next decade, the Arkestra would embrace an even broader palette: swirling layers of percussion, spooky electronic effects, disjointed echoes of rhythm and blues, hints of Asian and African music, dissonance, atonality, at times aural anarchy. Sun Ra's jargon-laden talk of the cosmos and interplanetary music may have sounded like a half-baked script from a Cold War sci-fi movie, but his appetite for the new and anomalous truly spanned a universe, or at least several galaxies, of sound.

But *The Matrix* and *Reloaded* are too much like meaningless sci-fi (rather than the highly metaphorical sci-fi of Octavia Butler and Samuel Delany) to do proper justice to black struggle. The Wachowskis' epic vision is too conventional and formulaic to approximate Sun Ra's dream. Except for Keanu, the films only sign of humanity not dictated by comics and video games comes from the late Gloria Foster with her sultry yet stentorian voice—one of the glorious sounds of American theater. Throughout her career Foster worked in the tradition of Sun Ra, demonstrating the fierce integrity of an enlightened black person expressing her intelligence against the odds (she gave legendary performances in *Nothing But a Man*, *To All My Friends on Shore*, Genet's *The Blacks* and Bill Gunn's *The Forbidden City*). But Foster's *Matrix* appearance went unnoticed by most critics. As The Oracle, ordaining Neo's quest and ascension, Foster, preposterously but poetically appears in a kitchen baking cookies, symbolizing an archetypal black matriarch. Yet Foster's the right punctilious, principled actress to give such a role distinction. Her wit seemed spontaneous: "No one can tell you you're in love, you just know it. Balls to bones." Calling Neo "Kiddo," she's flesh, style, education, weight—experience. Her light skin and blackheads, crinkled eyelids and careful coif exemplify a multi-racial conundrum (Toni Morrison in Octavia Butler drag) and she dismisses the villain's propaganda with a fillip that bespeaks no-nonsense black toilers—and describes the film's own pretensions: "Fate crap." Toni, Octavia, Gloria—take a bow!

Left to his own virtual destiny, Neo goes into action. But action-overwhelming character—what kids love most about *The Matrix*—exposes the genre's cheapness. Neo prescribes "Guns, lots of guns" setting up the film's famous "bullet time" special effect—but I prefer the moral bullet trajectories in Korn's video "Freak on a Leash" or Tracy Chapman's "Bang, Bang, Bang." Offering comic book violence as an answer to existential despair is mere placation. Sun Ra—and Foster—offered art that provoked. For all *The Matrix*'s extravagantly stylized fight scenes, the movie basically indulges the audience's sense of powerlessness. In this f/x-crazed era excessive retaliation should remind movie lovers why in the history of cinema Griffith superceded Melies; his climaxes were real-world-based and superior. *The Matrix*'s rope hanging climax, with Morpheus and Neo extending their hands in mid-air, takes the classic situation of *The Defiant Ones* then cheats its humanist point. *The Matrix* starts with race reversal of black/white social positions but, in essence, its "sophistication" gets so overdeveloped that moviegoers no longer discern reality in it. Unfortunately, they come to prefer comic book trivializing.

Seeking highbrow justification for this frivolity, the Wachowskis put Jean Baudrillard's *Simulacra and Simulation* in one shot. If there is a reference to Sun Ra I have not caught it but apparently nothing trumps an obscure black jazz artist like a European intellectual (especially for black academics). Using Structuralist chic to justify a $60 million teenagers' action movie—instead of analyzing and clarifying the way politics affect people's daily interactions—may be trendy but in the end it's also trash. Or to paraphrase debutant Cornel: You don't have to know shit to support the Hollywood system.

A Mighty Wind

Richard Webster

This essay is adapted from one that originally formed part of the manuscript of Richard Webster's Why Freud Was Wrong: Sin, Science and Psychoanalysis. *For narrative reasons it was omitted from that book. An extended version of this essay is available online at richardwebster. com.*

The career of Jacques Lacan is one of the most remarkable phenomena in twentieth century intellectual history. Until 1966, when, at the age of 65, he published his *Ecrits*, very few people outside of a small group of Parisian intellectuals were aware of his existence. Even with the psychoanalytic movement he was very much a minor figure within the psychoanalytic movement—an eccentric psychiatrist with a taste for surrealism who had made no significant contribution to Freudian theory and who was known, if he was known at all, for his stubborn refusal to conform to the therapeutic guidelines laid down by Freud. When, however, Lacan finally emerged from obscurity, he attracted not simply admirers but followers. As Elisabeth Roudinesco, his biographer, has written.

> Lacan's texts were sacralised, his person was imitated; he was made into the sole founder of the French psychoanalytic movement. Subdued, an army of barons spoke like Lacan, taught like Lacan, smoked Lacan's cigars…. If that army had been able, it would, like Lacan, have carried its head inclined to the left or had the cartilage of its ears stretched in order to have them, like his, stand out.

By the 1980s, Lacanian theory was regarded in much of the Academy as the only modern and ideologically correct form of psychoanalysis. For many literary intellectuals Lacan remains one of the greatest thinkers of the twentieth century. By some others the rise of Lacan is regarded as a shameful indictment of the intellectual standards which prevail in the Academy and an affront both to science and reason.

I

The "cornerstone of Lacan's oeuvre"—as Raymond Tallis has written—is "the theory of the mirror stage"—a theory originally developed by a French philosopher turned psychoanalyst named Henri Wallon. In 1931 Wallon published a paper in which he attempted to give an account of what he believed was a crucial stage in the development of the individual's sense of self. He maintained that children started to react to their mirror image at the age of four months. By the end of the tenth month he claimed that children actually located a part of their self in their mirror image and that they then imagined that their own body was split into fragments. The child now fell under an inner compulsion, so the argument ran, to unify its ego in space and in order to do this was forced gradually to subordinate the data of immediate experience to pure representation. The ordeal of the mirror eventually led, according to Wallon, to the child's entry into the symbolic stage of development.

Thinly based on a number of selected and heavily interpreted observations, Wallon's argument moved almost imperceptibly from a description of real events and reactions to an account of unseen processes supposedly taking place in a mental realm not susceptible to observation. In this respect it had something in common with psychoanalysis, but Wallon's theory of the child's relation to mirrors was a completely independent creation. Its content clearly had no relationship to the theories of Freud nor did Wallon himself claim that it did.

Wallon's paper was published in *Journal de Psychologie* in 1931 under the title "Comment se développe chez l'enfant la notion de corps proper." It might well have fallen into complete obscurity. In 1936, however, Jacques Lacan presented his first and only paper before the International Psychoanalytical Association at their fourteenth congress in Marienbad. His paper was entitled "Le Stade du miroir. Théorie d'un moment structurant et génétique de la constitution de la réalité, conçu en relation avec l'expérience et la doctrine psychanalytique." As this title implies, what Lacan undertook in his paper was the unlikely project of marrying together Wallon's mirror theories with the ideas of Freud. The complex, and at times impenetrable, paper which resulted appears to have made little or no lasting impression on the psychoanalysts who first heard it. It was not mentioned in Ernest Jones's brief account of the congress and received no public discussion.

Lacan, however, persisted in his unlikely project. In 1946 he gave a lecture in which he referred to the mirror theory as though it were his own without acknowledging the influence of Wallon at all. He adopted the same strategy in 1949 when he read a revised version of his mirror paper to the IPA congress in Zurich. Without explicitly claiming original-ity he leads his listeners by his opening words to assume that the theory in question is his own creation: "The conception of the mirror stage that I introduced at our last congress," he declares, "has since become more or less established in the practice of the French group."

Still closely following Wallon, Lacan argued that children are able to recognize their own image in a mirror from about the age of six months. This act of recognition, he claims, immediately leads the child to identify with its mirror image, which is not really its own self. This allows the infant to escape from a primal discord (a fiction invented by Lacan) into a kind of self-imposed alienation. An extraordinarily complex argument is then introduced by means of which the whole mirror ordeal becomes the basis of an Oedipal drama; the outcome of this drama in Lacanian theory is that the child "enters language" in the quest for a phallus or alternatively is "inserted" into language. This entry into language, which involves complex abstract and symbolic relationships with the child's parents, the mother's desire and the father's phallus, is described by Lacan in quasi-mystical terms:

> In the quest for the phallus the subject moves from being it to having it. It is here that is inscribed the last Spaltung [splitting] by which the subject articulates himself to the Logos....

> The fact that the phallus is a signifier means that it is in the place of the Other that the subject has access to it. But since this signifier is only veiled, as ratio of the Other's desire, it is this desire of the Other as such that the subject must recognise, that is to say, the other in so far as he is himself a subject divided by the signifying *Spaltung*.

It is in terms such as these, in which the illusion of meaning is created by technical terminology whose difficulty cannot ultimately disguise its vagueness, that Lacan demonstrates, to his own satisfaction at least, the compatibility of his mirror theory with psychoanalysis in general, and Freud's Oedipus complex in particular.

The possible objections to this theory are so numerous that an entire book would be needed to anthologize them. One of the simplest would point to the inherent implausibility of a theory of human development in which a child's relationship to a mirror is held to be more significant than its relationship to its parents.

More specifically this objection would point to the overwhelmingly intellectualist bias of Lacan's theory. It seems to be the product of an intellectual who hugely overvalues his own cognitive skills, and has become almost completely cut off from the world of ordinary human relationships. This intellectual can convince himself of his own normality only by elaborating a theory of childhood development which makes alienation into a norm, and subordinates complex emotions to simple cognitive acts. Lacan's theory, on this view, appeals to other intellectuals because it performs the same function for them. By obscuring emotional complexity and negating human vitality it helps to hide from them the depth of their own alienation, while offering the illusion that emotional integration can be achieved through intellectual effort.

A different argument has been put forward by Tallis, who points to the intrinsic absurdity of any theory which proposes an *accidental* basis for a fundamental aspect of human development:

> One measure of the value, truth or explanatory power of a theory is its ability to predict novel facts or at least to accommodate facts that were not taken into account when the theory was originally formulated. If epistemological maturation and the formation of a world picture were dependent upon catching sight of oneself in a mirror, then the theory would predict that congenitally blind individuals would lack selfhood and be unable to enter language, society or the world at large. There is no evidence whatsoever that this implausible consequence of the theory is borne out in practice·

II

Just as Lacan had reinvented psychoanalysis in the image of Wallon (modified by the philosophical mysticism he imbibed from Alexander Kojeve's famous 1930s seminars on Hegel), he gradually reconstructed his own version of Freud to make it appear either that Saussure was one of the founders of psychoanalysis or at the very least had provided a key by which the mysteries of Freudianism could finally be unlocked.

Lacan's decision to forge an alliance between his own traduced version of Freud and Saussure's structuralism proved to be one of the most effective of his intellectual maneuvers. It enabled him to attract supporters from outside the constituency of psychoanalysis. This proved indispensable to Lacan when his own idiosyncratic approach, and his increasing insistence on shortening analytic sessions to a matter of minutes (without any proportionate decrease in his fee), led to his expulsion from the International Psychoanalytic Association.

Lacan's turn to Saussure meant that he could draw support from both Marxists and structuralists. The most important of these coalitions was created in 1964 when Louis Althusser, already established as a charismatic Marxist ideologist, ended a period of immersion in structuralist thought by producing an article entitled "Freud and Lacan" in which he paid homage to the latter.

Now that Lacan's texts had received the imprimatur of French ideological Marxism, they were pored over by Althusser's students and colleagues at the Ecole Normale Superieure. Meanwhile Lacan's Paris seminar gained a sudden access of prestige and became in the words of one sympathetic commentator, "a glittering socio-intellectual occasion"—a kind of abstruse secular mass which those who saw themselves as intellectual revolutionaries, and who wished to be initiated into the deepest mysteries of structuralism, felt compelled to attend.

Perhaps the single most important factor in Lacan's success has been the extraordinary expository style which he developed over a period of some thirty years and which eventually became the hallmark of his disciples' discourse. His followers, will readily admit that they find large portions of his work unintelligible. As Lacan's English translator, Alan Sheridan, once put it, "Lacan doesn't intend to be understood.... He designs his seminars so that you can't, in fact, grasp them."

Behind Lacan's style there lies a conscious and deliberate rebellion against the traditional virtue of French language and thought—*la clarté*. The main justification usually offered for this rebellion is that human complexities, internal contradictions and injustices vanish away as reality is reduced to the hard, clear outlines demanded by conventional philosophical expression. When the problem is viewed in this perspective it is easy to understand why Lacan's discursive style should be represented by many as a contribution to the politics of liberation.

If the practice of obscurity were itself an effective rebellion against *la clarté* then it would be reasonable to regard Lacan as a major revolutionary. To adopt such a view, however, would be to allow oneself to be bewitched by words. For although "clarity" and "obscurity" may appear to be logical opposites, their relationship is, in ordinary usage, much more complex. When writers aspire to the precision and purity of style implied by the notion of clarity, they do not so much eliminate obscurity as renounce a vernacular or poetic richness. The language in which *King Lear* is written would scarcely be described as embodying clarity. Yet its lack of what the Royal Society once termed "mathematical plainness" does not engender incomprehensibility. Rather it enables a denseness and richness of meaning to be carried by the poetry.

While it is true that poetic writing may at times actively harness ambiguity, not all forms of ambiguity conceal a richness of meaning. In Lacan's style there is a compulsive attempt to pump up an artificial sense of richness and vitality, to use a convoluted surface in order to project the illusion of depth, but real poetic wealth is never apparent. The ambiguity of Shakespeare's poetry serves to convey something of the richness and complexity of human experience. The ambiguity of Lacan's prose serves only to convey ambiguity.

Unable to sense intuitively the voice of his body, Lacan attempts to construct an "unconscious" by disordering his intellect. The result is an alienated mechanical rhetoric in which a central emptiness of feeling is defended by a compulsive eccentricity and a deep philosophical confusion is masked by mechanical mathematical terms which tacitly claim for themselves technical precision and scientific objectivity: "synchronic system," "differential couplings," "modulatory variability," "non-cylindrical anamorphosis," "apodosis," "the primal dyad of the signifying articulation."

It would appear that the real reason that such abstract terminology is adopted is not methodological necessity but psychological comfort. For underlying such rhetoric we may discern a cultural compulsion towards purity inherited from our religious tradition. Just as the behaviorist psychologist B.F. Skinner has argued for the introduction of a new technical language on the grounds that ordinary language is "obese," so in the work of Lacan and elsewhere in structuralist writing, it would seem that ordinary language is rejected not because it is inadequate but because it is unconsciously experienced as unclean, gross, or soiled by usage. The language which many structuralist and post-structuralist writers offer us instead is not a language which any man or woman speaks, nor even a literary language, but a language which has been purged of ordinariness, a language in which the rhetoric of science is mixed with pseudo-technical neologisms and superficially spattered with a hodge-podge of personal oddity.

Beneath the obscure surface of Lacan's prose is concealed an intellectual project whose cruel reductionism is no less extreme than that of the most severe form of rationalism. For Lacan eventually reached the conclusion that psychological truths can only properly be formulated in mathematical terms or according to the model offered by the physical sciences. "Scientific formulae," Lacan once said, "must be expressed in little letters" and gave as an example $\frac{1}{2}mv$.

Lacan allotted an increasingly important role to his pseudo-algebraic formulae as time went on. Indeed, at one stage he virtually abandoned the complex and almost completely opaque rhetoric of his lectures in order to concentrate on discovering the formulae or 'mathemes' which he believed psychoanalytic truths could be reduced to. In 1976 Lacan's "Freudian school" held a three-day meeting on the mathemes where, according to the account given by Sherry Turkle, mathemes were brought to bear on every conceivable subject, from James Joyce to the structure of the complex knots.

> There was a matheme of perversion, a matheme of phobia, a matheme of the my-theme.... Equations, ratios, arrows, diagrams of knots and Venn diagrams covered the blackboard.... While some members of the audience were enthusiastic, other felt guilty at understanding nothing or very little of something that, as one of them put it, "everyone important seems to feel is so crucial."

III

The mathematical idealism which seems at times to constitute the very core of Lacanian psychoanalysis is not a twentieth century innovation peculiar to French structuralists. It develops out of the tradition of thought, beginning with Plato and continued in different ways by Descartes, Newton, Leibniz and Spinoza, according to which mathematics gives true knowledge either of physical nature or of the realm of essences. Due to the influence of Descartes this tradition of mathematical idealism has been retained by twentieth century French philosophers of science as it has in no other national intellectual culture. Althusser, for example, always conceived of Marxist "science" according to the model offered by mathematics, and made no secret of his repudiation of the value of external evidence or external processes of verification and disconfirmation:

> Once they are truly constituted and developed [the sciences] have no need for verification from *external* practices to declare the knowledges they produce to be "true," i.e. to be *knowledges*. No mathematician in the world waits until physics has *verified* a theorem to declare it proved.... The truth of his theorem is a hundred per cent provided by criteria purely *internal* to the practice of mathematical proof, hence by the *criterion of mathematical practice*, i.e. by the forms required by existing mathematical scientificity. We can say the same for the results of every science....

Althusser's words express well not only his own approach to science but also the epistemology of Lacanian psychoanalysis. It is ironic that Lacan's supposedly subversive science should have at its core a perfect, almost masochistic submission to the very repressive orthodoxy which has flayed and whipped the body of Western epistemology for centuries.

It is also remarkable that a number of influential commentators have discussed Lacan's style without even noting that the most distinctive feature of what has frequently been presented as a rhetoric of liberation is nothing other than its authoritarianism. Lacan wields learning like a scourge. To readers nervous about their own powers of intellect his habit of referring to arcane, idiosyncratic or personal theories as though they were familiar orthodoxies will almost certainly intensify feelings of intellectual insecurity. The intimidatory power of his formulations is heightened by the sheer obscurity of his prose. His writings convey the impression of an unremitting miserliness with meaning, as though any meaning conveyed to the reader would be a precious substance lost to the writer.

There can be little doubt that the fear of not being at a sufficiently high intellectual level, of having missed something which "everyone important seems to feel is so crucial" has played a very large role in Lacan's success. Lacan himself—apparently quite deliberately—played upon this fear. When he appeared in a two-part television special in France in 1974, he began the programme by announcing that "most of his audience were surely idiots, and that he was surely in error in trying to make them understand." Given his readiness to engage in such intellectual bullying, it is not surprising that he repeatedly encountered opposition.

The Italian Marxist Sebastiano Timpanaro, the author of a book on Freud, has spoken of Lacan's "charlatanry" and "exhibitionism" and concluded that "behind the smokescreen there is nothing of substance." In 1967 a former student of Lacan, Didier Anzieu, published an article in which he condemned Lacan as a danger because he kept his students tied to an "unending dependence on an idol, a logic or a language, by holding out the promise of fundamental truths to be revealed ... but always at some further point ... and only to those who continue to travel with him." Anzieu's criticism might well be placed alongside some words of Jacques Brosse, in his review of *Ecrits*: "The whole—let us say so immediately—is overwhelmingly impressive, because it is impenetrable.... It is above all to be feared that in the face of an obscurity this aggressive, intellectual snobs, who are masochistic by nature, will forge a success for J. Lacan without having read him."

Taken together the words of Didier Anzieu and Jacques Brosse come close to the heart of the Lacanian phenomenon. For the urge towards self-humiliation in front of an ineffable wisdom is one of the most significant elements in our religious tradition. In a hymn which appears in a section of the hymn-book entitled "Patience and Submission," we encounter precisely the pattern of dependence and the withholding of revelation which Anzieu describes:

My Father, it is good for me
To trust and not to trace
And wait with deep humility
For Thy revealing grace.

Lord, when Thy way is in the sea;
And strange to mortal sense,
I love Thee in the mystery,
I trust Thy providence.

I cannot see the secret things
In this my dark abode;
I may not reach with earthly wings
The heights and depths of God.

So faith and patience! Wait awhile,
Not doubting, not in fear;
For soon in heaven my Father's smile
Shall render all things clear.

Driven by his own fierce ambition and his simultaneous need to be loved, celebrated, and feared. Lacan eventually stumbled upon a way of exploiting this aspect of our cultural psychology. He did so by inventing an explanatory system which does not explain and a version of psychoanalysis which renders human nature infinitely obscure.

To understand something is to reduce it to human proportions; to allow something to remain incomprehensible is to let it remain mystically vast and potentially dominating. At his most extreme Lacan thus projected himself not simply as a messiah, but as an inscrutable God. The young psychoanalysts who were his students frequently referred to him as "God the Father" and one of his former patients, Danièle Arnoux, has even recounted how she sought out Lacan rather than enter into analysis with one of his followers on the grounds that "it was better to deal with God than his saints." While it is tempting to dismiss such talk as humorous exaggeration it is difficult to study the Lacanian movement for very long without realizing that, at one level at least, it is utterly serious. For Lacan, more than any figure in the psychoanalytic movement since Freud himself, ultimately pursued his own deep sense of messianic distinction to its logical terminus; he actually assumed the persona of a God before whose ineffable and ultimately impenetrable wisdom others would prostrate themselves.

To the extent that we have done just this, it is the sanity of our intellectual culture as a whole, and not only that of Lacan, which needs to be questioned.

Grossman-ism

Fredric Smoler

Lt. Colonel Dave Grossman (U.S.A. Ret.) is the author of *On Killing: The Psychological Cost of Learning to Kill in War and Society*, and now with Gloria De Gaetano, "a nationally recognized educator in the field of media violence," of *Stop Teaching Our Children to Kill: A Call to Action Against TV, Movie and Video Game Violence*. Lt. Col. Grossman, a former paratrooper who has taught psychology at West Point and is now a professor of military science in Arkansas, has Good News and Bad News to reveal. The Good News is the attractive and inspiriting proposition that most people have a powerful instinctual disinclination to kill other human beings, and under normal conditions, including their own presence on a battlefield in immediate proximity to homicidal strangers, will refuse to do so. The Bad News is that modern media culture produces an abnormal condition in which ordinary children are all too likely to become more effective killers than, say, a typical American GI facing the SS in Normandy. And Col. Grossman is supremely confident that he can prove both of these contentions. His attempts to do so, in these two fantastic and extremely dispiriting parodies of rational argument, are fascinating illustrations of the intellectual level of much contemporary American social science.

How does Grossman know that ordinary people are wonderfully disinclined to kill one another? He relies on the groundbreaking work of the S.L.A. Marshall, who published *Men Against Fire* in 1946. Marshall therein revealed his discovery about what ordinary human beings will do on a battlefield. By rigorously investigating behavior in combat, interviewing the men of at least four hundred American rifle companies in the European theater during the Second World War, Marshall had found out something of unparalleled significance: he discovered that in any given body of American infantry, no more than a quarter will ever fire their personal weapons at an enemy. The normal percentage willing to kill was even lower, generally around fifteen percent.

Marshall explained his "ratio of fire" in various ways, sometime with reference to general principles of human psychology, sometimes with specific attention to the psychology of civilized urbanites, who while not necessarily cowards, were strikingly unwilling to become killers. "These men may face danger *but they will not fight*." And why not? "The fear of aggression has been expressed to him so strongly and absorbed by him so deeply that it is part of the normal man's emotional makeup. It stays his trigger finger even though he is hardly aware it is a restraint upon him." Then again, at other times Marshall seemed to suspect most people were cowards, or at least shiftless: "In the workshop or the office, or elsewhere in society, a minority of men and women carry the load—the majority in any group seek lives of minimum risk and expenditure of effort." Similarly, since only a few of us are "forceful," since most lack "initiative," we "simply go along for the ride" and, "When the infantryman's mind is gripped by fear, his body is gripped by inertia, fear's Siamese twin."

Grossman inclines toward Marshall's more generous and optimist interpretation: he believes that inhibitions against taking another's life—against what the sociobiologist's would call "instraspecific violence"—are the source of the alleged refusal to fire. However, Grossman does not believe that only moderns suffer from this splendid inhibition: he believes that the military historian Paddy Griffiths has shown that it was present during the American Civil War, he approvingly quotes the classicist Arthur Nock to the effect that hoplite warfare among the ancient Greeks "was only slightly more dangerous than American football," he is impressed by Ardant du Picq's nineteenth-century researches into combat in the ancient world, on the strength of which he has decided that one of Alexander's battles, which he apparently takes to be a perfectly representative one, was "an almost bloodless pushing match." And he is much impressed by the military historian Richard Holmes's researches into infantry combat in the Falklands, where Argentine troops seem to have fired much less than British ones, a phenomenon Grossman interprets in light of his prevailing thesis: British troops are trained in such a fashion that life-preserving inhibition can be overcome, a process now pandemic in modern societies via the instrumentalities of video games and film.

So to recap the combined argument of these two books, human beings will not easily kill one another; in fact, they are almost fantastically unwilling to do so, even when their own lives are at risk. However, it is possible to extinguish this inhibition through training, training previously available only to those few modern armies which had profited from

S.L.A. Marshall's groundbreaking research. Horrifically, the process of disinhibition, chiefly via desensitization, is almost perfectly if unwittingly duplicated by video games, so that ordinary American children may now be on the moral level of the Waffen SS. The evidence: unprecedented levels of intraspecific violence are now pandemic in this country, and rising hideously quickly in all cultures exposed to modern media. The link between desensitization and violence is said to be demonstrated in studies conducted by vast numbers of social scientists—many of them apparently psychologists—each of them presumably as scrupulous, cautious and intellectually subtle as Lt. Col. Grossman. And if we doubt these claims, we are talking through our hats: decades of social science have *proved* these contentions, just as Marshall proved the original assertion. Or so Grossman repeatedly tells us. As it happens, Marshall proved nothing of the kind. By the late nineteen-eighties, Marshall's statistical argument for his "ratio of fire" had been debunked as a fantastic fraud. I should declare an interest. I was one of the people—by far the least distinguished, and certainly the one who performed the least original research—who discovered this fact. Although a lot of people have looked for it, no evidence has ever emerged that he interviewed a single rifle company in the European theater, let alone the four, or five, or six hundred that he at various times claimed to have interviewed. But Marshall had interviewed some in the Pacific, who had fought on Makin Island, and on Kwajalein, and my only real "research" involved finding a record of what Marshall had there discovered. As it happens, those men showed no striking refusal to fire—in fact, Marshall discovered that on Makin, at least, they fired far too much, as one might suspect would be the case with green troops. "Much aimless shooting by 'trigger-happy' men occurred.... In the early morning its volume increased.... A wave of shooting hysteria swept through the area and men started blazing at bushes and trees until the place was 'simply ablaze with fire' ... shouted orders to men proved ineffectual ... flat terrain and limited area made control of fire abnormally difficult."

If Marshall had invented the 400-600 "ratio of fire" company interviews—and the evidence of this is very strong—what else did he invent? Quite a lot: some family lore, a lot of colorful stories, much of his biography (Grossman describes Marshall as a combat veteran, but while Marshall at various times claimed to have fought with three regiments in two division in three countries, there is no independent evidence he ever fought, anywhere), even his name (he amended it to provide the additional letter which made his initials the more manly "S.L.A.M.").

Marshall went on to become a very good anecdotal military historian, writing books not undergirded by the spurious social scientific apparatus that originally made *Men Against Fire*, and its author, so famous, but what, if anything, had he actually discovered. It is hard to say. My guess is that he may have discovered—"intuited" may be the better word—that most men do not in fact fire their personal weapons in combat quite so frequently as popular film representations of combat suggest, although he grossly misinterpreted the significance of this fact by psychologizing it into a failure/refusal to fire. WWII infantry had a number of good reasons for not firing—to conserve ammunition, to avoid drawing fire, etc.—but Marshall's implied picture of combat in *Men Against Fire*—as essentially homogeneous—concedes no good reason for not firing, and ignored the fact that combat was in fact asymmetrical. "Being in combat" often meant being under indirect fire, to which one could not reply. When I began the research which was a small part of the collective enterprise of unmasking Marshall, I interviewed a single combat veteran, my father, and discovered that his eleven weeks of combat, for which he had been trained as a sniper and initially employed as a scout, included being a member of a platoon almost annihilated by tree-bursts, being overrun by tanks, mortared, fired on by machine guns and leading a lot of patrols, but that on none of these particular occasions did he fire a rifle. Marshallian combat in *Men Against Fire* is characterized by a uniformity of event, and is implicitly everywhere the same; real combat was startlingly various.

What about the rest of Grossman's "research," which we are told reinforces Marshall's original discovery? One cannot pronounce in advance of competent scholarly debate, and remember that it took forty years to unmask Marshall, but my first reaction is that Holmes's discoveries about Argentine troops on the Falklands may tell us more about the behavior of demoralized and badly trained Third World conscripts shipped off to a wasteland bordering Antarctica and subsequently abandoned by feckless officers and a brutal government, than it tells us about a universal human inhibition against intraspecific violence. I have not read Paddy Griffith's work on some battles of the American Civil War, but the universal claim Grossman seeks to bolster thereby runs afoul of what I do know about some Civil War battles. If memory serves, the C.S.A. troops entrenched at, among other places, Fredericksburg, do not seem to have shown this allegedly universal inhibition—was human nature oddly different there? Of the Napoleonic evidence, again, under some conditions many troops will find it impossible to fire—all but a handful of troops charging in column, for example—but this does not suggest a universal human instinct, it suggests a tactical shortcoming. And if soldiers in the ancient world suffered from an inhibition about intraspecific violence, it would have come as news to the Athenian prisoners blinded on Sicily, as well as to the six thousand Samnite prisoners slaughtered by Sulla's troops, or the vast numbers systematically disemboweled by Roman legionnaires following their standard tactics over many centuries.

Grossman is much given to psychologizing mono-causal explanation, with the result that many of his military historical dicta are absurd. Take a single example: "Gunpowder's superior *noise*, its superior *posturing* ability, made it ascendant on the battlefield. The longbow would still have been used in the Napoleonic Wars if the raw mathematics of killing was all that mattered, since both the longbow's firing rate and its accuracy were *much* greater than that of the smoothbore musket. But a frightened man, thinking with his midbrain and going 'ploink, ploink, ploink' with a bow, doesn't stand much of a chance against an equally frightened man going 'BANG! BANG!' with a musket." The traditional explanation of the decline of the longbow is less subtle: an arrow could not penetrate plate armor, whereas an arquebus ball could, and did, and gunpowder thus rendered the longbow thoroughly obsolete by the mid-16th century, around which time the last *Dialogue Between Hermes and An English Soldier* was published.

Grossmanism, then, is a compound of various forms of historical illiteracy, aggravated by a perfect absence of common sense. The assertion that video games have produced an ever-more violent American population runs afoul of the simple fact that rates of violent crime in this country have been falling for most of the last decade, precisely the period in which video game use has exploded. The argument that disinhibition of an imaginary instinct via immersion in violent visual imagery—an argument that is repeatedly shrieked throughout the chapters of *Stop Teaching Our Kids to Kill*—runs afoul of the fact that some of the cultures least exposed to violent visual images—medieval England, for example—had horrific levels of violence, while cultures immersed in staggeringly violent visual imagery—for example, contemporary Japan, where popular theaters featuring sadomasochistic burlesque do a land office business—have some of the lowest rates of personal violence recorded by modern societies. One could make a case for the proposition that exposure to massive quantities of violent visual images is inversely correlated with the propensity to commit actual violence: the Taliban, who look at no representational images of any kind, may be usefully compared to male Italian teenagers, who assimilate vast quantities of sadomasochistic fumetti but are nonetheless relatively shy about murdering women, or one another—oh, that the Taliban were so restrained. The American frat boys of my childhood, raised on relatively decorous horse opera, fought in bars, broke the hands of thieves, and were generally a great deal more violent than my own undergraduate students—who play the video games Grossman so dreads. Aztec children, to the best of my knowledge, did not play video games, nor did Zulu children, nor Assyrian children, nor Comanche children. The armies that conducted the Thirties Year war were not copiously exposed to pictorial violence, unless one counts representation of the Crucifixion. The contemporary American middle class, less violent than most populations recorded in all of history, is surely the most immersed in representations of violence, of any recorded culture. Once upon a time, psychologists usefully distinguished between the meaning of fantasizing a thing as opposed to doing it, but those days seem to be very long gone.

And yet Grossmanism, as a cultural product, despite its almost fantastic hysteria and silliness, is not restricted to these two slim volumes. Contemporary social science does indeed produce reams of "research" of this kind. Off of college campuses, it is, happily widely ignored. The interesting and indeed disturbing question is why gross parodies of reason are taken so seriously by groups nominally trained to revere rational argument. Brooding over this review, I was pondering Grossmanism with a friend the other day; "If you don't know any history," he remarked, "you don't know anything at all." That, I think, is indeed part of the story: a genuine ignorance of history is probably a precondition for this sort of warmed-over Rousseauvian sentimentality about the astonishingly violent human past, and contemporary American social scientists are pretty innocent of history, particularly of the range of historical evidence that makes historians intensely hostile to this sort of overarching claim; historians are by nature splitters, not lumpers. A reverence for quantitative methods is also part of the story: Grossman, after writing off the most recent evidence as indeterminate, proudly disdains data for American violence which predate FBI statistics, appearing innocent of the problem that the FBI started accumulating statistics fairly recently, and did so at the start of a long fall in American crime rates, followed by a long rise, so in essence two data points become the statistical universe for conclusions about allegedly fundamental human traits. Marshall, too, fell afoul of this reverence for quantitative methods, and as a result invented the statistics that would instantiate his claim. Finally, Grossmanist "thought" is wonderfully prepared to write off all of our ancestors' experience as unscientific—they are assumed to have perfectly misunderstood themselves, and the vast array of their art and literature and political philosophy that concerned itself with war and violence is readily written off as no better than fantasy. And thereby hangs the tale: Grossmanism is part of that very crisis of intellectual authority it subsequently bemoans. Eerily quick to ignore the millennia of thinking that predates his own, Grossman is subsequently astonished that hoi polloi ignore savants like him. The authority of the past, so scorned, is thus revenged, after a fashion—but revenge is proverbially only a kind of wild justice. A version of Gresham's Law dictates that bad forms of argument drive out good ones, and the left-liberal pieties expressed in these two volumes are no less scientistic, pseudo-rational and historically illiterate than the rightist pieties so enshrouded down the row at the bookstore. Bleak times.

Death by Cookie Cutter

Fred Kirshnit

"[Y]et he failed somehow, in spite of a mediocrity
which ought to have insured any man a success."
William Makepeace Thackeray, *Vanity Fair*

That eminent esthetician, Lisa Simpson, once remarked that she was indebted to her elementary school music teacher for demonstrating to her "that even the greatest concerto can be stripped of all of its soul and beauty." Leaving aside the shameful abdication of the American public school system for another day, it is instructive to look at the conservatories in the United States and their deleterious effect on the state of classical music at the beginning of the twenty-first century. The statue of Dante directly across from the entrance to Lincoln Center, home of the prestigious Juilliard School, often reminds me that they missed the boat in not including a sign over their portal: "Abandon all hope, ye who enter here!" Churning out faded clones shaped in the images of their own pallid faculties, themselves the product of the same incestuous system, the modern American musical institution is no more involved in the courageous propagation of art and culture than the trade school down the block.

The best evidence of the deterioration of the finished product is in the music itself. Let us examine for a moment the state of contemporary performance of one particular piece: Brahms' "Variations on a Theme of

Paganini." Written for solo piano, the Paganini "Variations" are a masterful set designed to present a variety of shapes and colors, all generated from the same core theme, the twenty-fourth caprice of the Italian violinist, composer and romantic figure of satanic debauchery. The genius of Brahms, in addition to a superhuman melodic inventiveness, is that no two variations have the same style, the resulting totality a marvelous survey of musical thought from the Baroque to the modern, from the concert hall to the salon, from the palace to the whorehouse (where Brahms himself spent his early years at the piano bench). However, most modern pianists, educated in the conservatory system, have little clue as to musical style or period and their resulting "variants" sound like so many repetitions of similar thematic material. Virtually all of the musical thought that Brahms put into this composition is lost to modern fingers (and, in time, to modern ears) and the resulting performances are tedious and bland (since the composer spent so much effort on the nuances of style, he keeps the music almost exclusively revolving around the same key of A Minor). Even the most adept at striking the individual notes leave out the most important element: the music itself.

Considering the anti-intellectual character of modern American domestic life, it is amazing that qualified aspirants are even able to line up for auditions at one of the big three northeastern conservatories. Most achieve the requisite level of technical skill through a rigorous regimen prescribed by overzealous and anally competitive soccer moms on steroids, bound and determined to prove that their progeny are more sensitive than those of their neighbors. Most who apply at the Juilliard School for their pre-college program at the ages of twelve or thirteen are used to many hours per day of mindless practice, the modern equivalent of Dickensian factory children, who have exchanged bobbins and spindles for keyboards and bows. Without a sense of their chosen craft's beauty and power—completely ignored by the parents and teachers—these automatons are bred only for the championship. Throughout their conservatory careers, they will be pushed to excel, to be better than their peers, to place first in competitions and earn first chairs in the orchestras. The practice room becomes the weight room, the music teacher the football coach, the parent a refugee from a little league nightmare (I have actually witnessed incidents of corporal punishment meted out for wrong notes). Art is forgotten; success is all. Except that, as Pierre Boulez has said, "music is not the Olympics."

The carbon-copy technician who eventually emerges from Juilliard, the Manhattan School or the Curtis Institute may very well be able to translate all of the dots and lines into sound, but seldom possesses any sense of the architecture, design, historical context, landscape or style of a masterwork. For this emerging cipher, music has been deconstructed into sharps and flats, crescendi and diminuendi, fortes and pianissimos. In a consummate irony of red, white and blue perversity, since seventy percent of these students are East Asian, critics, and therefore the public at large, have stereotyped artists with Pacific origins as being unemotional, even though their training at the hands of white Europeans has fostered this mechanical method. With no emphasis on music history, the modern conservatory robs its students of any appreciation of the religiosity of Bach or Bruckner, the supreme order of Haydn, the surprisingly contemporary angst of Mozart, the granitic power of Beethoven, the lyricism of Schubert. For these pubescent instrumentalists, Handel sounds like Schumann, Stravinsky like Wagner, Schoenberg, Berg and Webern (if played at all) not glorious revolutionaries, but rather theoretical academicians. Performers from these schools have little intellectual basis with which to make intelligent phrasing decisions and become part of a less informed generation of Stepford children, adding to a tradition that Gustav Mahler described as "simply the memory of the last bad performance." The litmus test is to ask recent graduates of these venerable institutions to name three operas of Verdi: if they weren't voice majors, most can't.

Finding a position with a solvent symphony orchestra these days is almost impossible. In a recent year, there was exactly *one* opening in the entire United States for a French horn player. Considering that a successful candidate for that one position must have about as many rigorous years of study under their belt as a physician, the competition is geared towards the surest path to acceptance. That path is the middle ground, the bunny trail taken by the bulk of music teachers in this country, a yellow brick road leading to the illusion that the traveler has reached a place of musical knowledge and serenity. Alas, the elusive wizard is indeed just a fake little man manipulating the machinery of ersatz culture, whose paycheck is probably signed by *Disney*. Contemporary composers are grist from the same run of the mill, hence the enforced popularity of the mawkish John Adams and the vapid Phillip Glass.

Of course, there are exceptions. Young kids imbued with the fire and passion of real musicians do survive their matriculation at one of these sterile institutions, but almost exclusively do so because they are already the products of nurturing environments wherein music is respected as the highest of all art forms, where the searing and searching glories of Bach or Messiaen lead to contemplations of the infinite, where the awesome power of a Shostakovich symphony is felt in their very marrow, where their own innermost thoughts and dreams are reflected in a concave mirror of notes and chords. Many of these noble souls would have prospered had they simply received private tutelage in their own home environment; for others, the interaction with a symphonic ensemble is essential. But those who can keep their head (and soul) while all around them are losing theirs are of a rare breed. As a critic and both a former music student and Juilliard parent, I have observed that many potentially fine musicians are ruined by this grinding system that emphasizes only the *appearance* of technical mastery. The most insidious factor in the entire process is its grandmotherly and "practical" emphasis. Students are victimized like Kafka's inmate in the Penal Colony, only the message carved into their backs is:

BE SAFE

Imagine if John Coltrane had been told that he should never go outside of his home key or embellish his improvisations with any personal embroidery, that he should always approach his art as a vehicle only for straightforward explication of melodic material (actually, he *was* told this early on and reacted in a sunburst of rebellion). His art would have not only suffered irreparable harm, but would have actually been rendered non-existent. A similar type of straitjacketing goes on every day in the American conservatory. The overwhelming atmosphere is one of conformity and caution. The creative juices of the acolyte are slowly boiled out of the stew, taking with them in their evaporation all of the nutrients. What is left is only a sickeningly sweet (but insidiously comforting) bowl of musical pabulum, the musical equivalent of fast food. This distillation process is accomplished at the conservatory level in various ways. Choice of repertoire ("oh no dear, you don't want to include anything *modern* on your recital program") is perhaps the most obvious example, but there are many others. Fingering is a tool used by these overprotective pedants to stifle individual expression. Leaps of intervals too difficult or dissonant for students are reworked for facility and smoothness, leaving the practitioner aware that the easier path is also the one that sounds more pleasing to the untrained ear of the audience; slowly the music changes form from the challenging to the complacent. This is particularly true of vocal music: aspiring singers today are trained from an early age to "cheat," that is, when a leap from one note to another is difficult, simply transpose the second note to one within your range, gliding the voice from one point to the next rather than enunciating two distinct tones.

These students grow into opera singers and eventually their pathetic shortcuts become accepted as the norm. The poor composer, long dead and unable to speak for himself, is lost in the shuffle. Excerpts from a recent review of a Juilliard concert winner performing Bartok at Lincoln Center are telling:

> [C]oncentrated exclusively on not making any mistakes ... neverapproached the essentially wild and primitive center of the piece. Even in the allegro vivace, a good old-fashioned country fiddler's section, he was shackled by his gingerly approach.

The overriding message from the teachers is clear: never mind the music, just don't screw up.

Recently, I attended a recital at Carnegie Hall by one of the most important musicians of our time. Midori had sailed along through half of the first movement of a Mozart sonata when she abruptly stopped playing and signaled her accompanist to do the same. Stepping up to center stage, she announced that she was not satisfied with the tuning of her instrument and begged the audience's indulgence while she tweaked it a semiquaver or two. Virtually nobody in that hall would have noticed this tiny indiscretion, but, for such a consummate artist, it was necessary to expose herself, warts and all, in order to serve the greater good, the music itself. I could literally hear her teacher, Dorothy Delay, the embodiment of the safe approach, turning over in her grave. The crowd was, of course, very impressed with her courage and greeted the decision with applause. But Midori had violated the first principle of modern academia: like the characters in Woody Allen's *The Purple Rose of Cairo*, she had recklessly crossed the line and involved the audience in the performance. For her, classical music doesn't belong in the museum but is rather a living, breathing entity. She is the same performer whose very public rejection of and resignation from the Juilliard system sent shockwaves throughout the art music world some years ago. Now herself a committed teacher, she gives a pessimist like me some hope for the future and the survival of a beloved art form assailed daily by the forces of cultural barbarism and, what is ultimately worse, the spineless enemy within.

Test Time vs. Dreamtime

Stanley Aronowitz

There's that scene from *The Sopranos* in which Carmela—against her religious principles—uses Tony's mafia status to strong-arm an influential graduate of Georgetown to insure college admission for his daughter. While Carmella hates to pull rank, in this era, a ticket to an elite college has as much value as a carton of cigarettes during the first days after World War II. Viewers who have suffered the anxiety surrounding college admission immediately resonate to Carmela's dilemma. The middle class has always sweated where their children will go to college but lately the pressure has intensified. Urban haute bourgeois types find it easy to identify with the Soprano family's school woes. And they're not the only group feeling heavy pressure and murderous frustrations on this front.

Working class folks are now told their kids *must* go to college too. There are simply no jobs for high school graduates that pay enough to permit a young adult to leave his or her parents' home. Thirty years ago it wasn't even necessary to graduate from High School. In New York City, for example, there were thousands of decent paying factory and construction jobs—many of which offered union wages and benefits. But as factory employment declined from a million in 1975 to slightly less than a quarter million in 2000, postsecondary credentials began to look more attractive to the majority of students. Even young people who wish to qualify for an apprenticeship program now need a diploma and a community college credit. For most kids, the lack of a high school diploma means being condemned to jobs in the largely minimum wage service sector and consequent poverty. Which means they have little choice but to stay in school and try to compete with middle class kids (who have the advantage because they've inherited much more cultural capital). Plus this rigged system has everyone running scared earlier and earlier.

While the higher ed establishment has been stuck on tests (SATs, GREs etc.) for generations, in the Age of Bush, purveyors of the given have successfully pressed for the establishment of national standards for educational attainment—standards measured by performance on a battery of tests administered at every level of the academic system.

Most school districts are now locked into a regime of testing and most teachers and kids have their collective noses to the grindstone right from start. A whole generation of students is absorbed for years of its collective life in the quest of competitive advantage in the race for economic security. The school system reproduces the notion that the bottom line is all that matters and, in the bargain, snuffs out the joy of learning. Students are discouraged from becoming seekers for vocation in the religious sense of a life-forming activity (which includes the modern sense of a trade). Instead kids are encouraged to follow the money; a path that, by definition, can be traveled only by a small minority. No wonder that teen-age suicide is reaching epidemic proportions. Kids, often break down under the pressure to succeed in the testing regime. A few lash out at teachers or their fellow students because you can't hurt the "culture" that makes them feel desperate. Some are despondent after failing to get into leading schools and fall into academic slumps, aggravated by drugs or drink. There is no space between high rolling and dropping out or back. Since mediocrity is not an option, perhaps a third choose another path than the grind. They fuck-up, rebelling by refusing to achieve (and then may spend the last year of high school trying to catch up).

For New York high school students, spring is test season. With various Regents, SAT and ACT obligations, some students may take as many as half-dozen major tests in the last two and a half months of spring semester. Those who are determined to do well will typically devote seven days a week to study for this period and try to deal with the accompanying anxiety.

Kids often try to purchase a leg up in the mad climb to college entrance. Some persuade their parent(s) to lay out $1,000 for Kaplan, Princeton, or some other preparation mill to help them score better on the SATs. What goes on there, of course, has almost nothing to do with learning specific academic content. The educational aim is strategic rather than substantive: test-taking is a skill that only remotely reflects what you know. It does not matter much what you retain after you take the exam; the point is that you have been willing to force yourself to ingest a certain quantity of material long enough to be able to regurgitate it. What counts is that the student has demonstrated his/her capacity for subordination.

Many working class—as well as middle class parents—have bought into this kind of discipline. Parents, in general, are almost as involved in the college admissions process as their kids. In addition to finding money for preparation courses, test books, photocopying and other incidental expenses, many are pressed by their children—and by guilt—into the grind. For those of us who have social and literary knowledge, research skills or who remember enough math and science, many evenings are taken up with homework. As a parent who has been recruited into the homework morass and can afford the mounting bills associated with middle class schooling, I now understand fully what it takes in this massively punitive and competitive culture to scratch your way to the top or the high middle of the candidate pool. Without backup, it's almost impossible for a student to overcome the myriad hurdles that the system erects to keep children of the working class in their place.

It's important to underscore, though, that the testing regime of the last decade has also trashed the counter-cultural traditions of middle class youth. Even the elite secondary school is no longer understood to provide a space/time for exploration, creativity or dissent. In fact there are practically no places for kids to cultivate creative marginality or healthy adolescent rebelliousness. Many middle class kids have precious little time to play, even on weekends. There are no supervised recreation programs, no regular dances, no theatre groups, nothing. So the emotional intensities are achieved through kids' fleeting interactions in packs and occasional sexual encounters (though, as always, privacy is at a premium). Those who choose to act young and keep playing—instead of keeping their heads down—are coded as fuck-ups. The very idea of youth has become suspect.

Other cultures acknowledge that adolescence is a special moment—dreamtime (as the aboriginals call it). And up until recently, when "It's the economy, stupid" began to rule our collective imagination, Americans looked with approbation upon rites of passage that allowed individuals to take their time about growing up. In the past, there was nothing particularly dramatic about stepping off from school in the 10th or 12th grade. Or deciding after high school to postpone entering college for a year or two in favor of getting a job and your own digs.

I'm not endorsing deschooling or anti-intellectualism in American life. The modern dream-work that makes for a rich adolescence is all about exploring new ideas. But few schools at any level inspire students. The brute fact is that most of our country'seducational institutions are not about encouraging creative thought or imaginative living, least of all when they focus many months on standardized tests.

The University as Sweatshop

Kate Millett

I have chosen my title with deliberate provocation but entire justification. If it strikes you as inappropriate—or unfathomable—give the respect which the university commands and its high social mission, consider this: over half of college and university instruction in the United States today is provided by adjunct faculty who are paid less than a living wage.

Adjuncts generally earn $1,200 to $3,000 a course. They are usually limited to two courses at one school—and must often work at two or three institutions to piece together a yearly income. They must struggle to earn $15,000 (or less) a year. This is below the poverty level—below the level needed to pay rent and eat and survive. No one attending their classes intends to earn this little. Are they crazy? Saints? Scholars?

Probably all three—but they also work for taskmasters who are getting by with this because the ongoing exploitation is a big secret outside the Academy. Inside as well. Students are unaware of their teachers' humiliation and poverty. And most adjuncts are too embarrassed by their circumstances to divulge them. Adjuncts fear they might lose their students' respect. They are victims of a curious class dilemma: to be learned is (supposedly) to be middle class/professional. They have spent years (and tens of thousands of dollars) acquiring the degrees that allow them to teach: who could admit (without shame) to such a negative investment in human capital?

A further irony: students are now paying the highest tuition in history to study under frantically overworked wage slaves who have no office; no telephone; no place to sit outside the classroom; no role in governance of the institution where they teach; no benefits for health or retirement; and absolutely no job security. Adjuncts are marginal labor who can be dismissed without reason. Should they complain or resist, they can be replaced in a moment. They are cowed. Afraid to speak up. Afraid to admit their plight even to themselves. Afraid to organize. They are nobodies, spare hands, part-timers, temps.

But any temp does better than this—I have poet friends who are temps. They earn more than adjuncts, have more job security and far more control over their lives. Adjuncts must often move to keep themselves viable, buy a car or spend an enormous number of hours commuting. Remember we're talking about jobs that pay far below a living wage—there are no allowances for transportation needs. And if you lose one of these jobs you don't just try another place a block away … because your record goes with you. If you have upset your bosses, you may be blackballed. After spending six to ten years in preparation for an academic career (and more years in service)—you may easily end up excluded from your chosen profession. Unemployable for life. And unable to anything else. (Except tend bar or flip hamburgers.)

You were trained to teach—you are a scholar. You were not trained to write advertising copy or be a flack. You could've done that with a B.A. so if you're reduced to such work your years of preparation and study are a joke on you. Yet the University was ready to sell you a degree (and create a pool of cheap labor). It commodified learning—happily selling you the certificate of competence—knowing there would be little chance of employment. It began doing this to women students. For decades now, women have been earning higher degrees from institutions that are unwilling to permit them to use their learning to teach or climb the academic ladder.

Thirty years ago, when those of us at Columbia Women's Liberation obtained and published the figures on female employment there, we believed we were on the way to exposing—and transforming—the sexist nature of the Academy. But, with the quiet death of equal opportunity, the situation of women faculty has actually worsened since the '80s. MIT has recently been forced to admit—as a result of a suit by a diligent and fearless woman scientist—that it has systematically failed to hire and promote women scholars. MIT is no worse than most universities on this score but other institutions haven't been forced to admit—or make amends for—their dishonest practices. The adjunct system tends to reinforce the bias against women scholars, extending it to a whole new generation of Ph.D.s.

A cruel joke: you can be sold a degree but you cannot use it to obtain a living wage. Is this merely the inevitable consequence of an overcrowded labor market? Not quite—the buyers of labor in this instance have conspired to exploit a part of their work-force—the adjuncts—while counting on the complicity of tenured faculty (now a minority of academics). The tenured professoriat amount to a kind of labor aristocracy, but they have also lost clout. Their role in the governance of their universities has been diminished.

Are not the relevant parties in education only two—namely student and teacher? What is the purpose of the administration then? I went to the University of Oxford where there is not even an administration building. The fellows—dons/professors—own the thirty-seven colleges that comprise the university. At St. Hilda's College we had a president and bursar and a secretary. And they managed splendidly.

How did American universities turn into businesses managed by a ruling class of administrators—an elite with salaries and expectations of CEOs? And how did this elite turn knowledge into a commodity, selling access to the rungs of an illusory ladder. The Ph.D. candidates keep coming as if that ladder were actually there. It isn't. Ninety percent of them will never have an appointment—a real job. They are condemned to joining an army of peons.

What does that do to a society? To a culture? The personal tragedies of adjuncts have a wider resonance. It's not healthy for a society to equate learning with poverty or treat the bulk of its younger intellectuals as suckers.

One is constantly told there simply isn't enough money to pay adjuncts a living wage. Let's simplify the economics here. Take a class with 10 students. Each one pays, say, two thousand dollars and the University makes $20,000. The teacher is paid, say $3,000—or (more likely) $2,000—so that the institution is left with $17,000 or $18,000. Figure in the expense for the use of a room at night for 3 hours a week. (A room used all day.) Add overhead, which can't amount to a hell of a lot. Profit? Aren't we looking at a serious return on an investment of a few grand? So where does the money go?

One wonders. There are no shareholders. Those who perform essential salaries receive only pathetic salaries. But there are (somehow) vast administrative costs and a great deal of what economists call consuming on the job. No taxes, though. The University is a privileged institution. Tax-exempt because it (supposedly) provides a public service—a good education at the lowest possible cost to the citizen and taxpayer. I remember when this wasn't a farce.

I attended the University of Minnesota—a land-grant state college—for $180 a year. The California system was once free from Kindergarten to the conclusion of a Ph.D. Hunter College cost $24 a semester when I taught there. The City College—and then later, City University—offered affordable educations once as a citizen's right. Private colleges and universities are still privileged and untaxed, still trading on old assumptions about their beneficent role in the society.

For most of this century, higher education in America moved steadily toward democratization. In the '60s, minority groups and the white working class seemed on the verge of achieving universal access through open enrollment. But in the following decade, higher education became an increasingly—and then prohibitively—expensive commodity. The middle class could barely afford the new tuition. And less privileged students could ante up only if they were up for a lifetime of indebtedness. Such students must now scrimp for years to pay off loans and/or deal for decades with collection agencies that dog them on and off the job.

So what happened? Why do my memories of Minnesota or Hunter seem so out of time? Well, it's not a mystery. What happened was 1968, the protests against the war in Vietnam … the national student strike against the bombing of Cambodia. I was at Columbia the night the tactical police force came in with helmets and clubs. That was a turning point. So were the killings at Kent State and Jackson State.

Politicians and business elites realized that democratizing higher education would be dangerous to (what was once called) the power structure.

The Academy "had to be brought under control." And it was. The student loan has been effective on this front. It's a tool that allows universities to promote a narrow corporate ethos rather than cultivating the older ideal of higher education as a common good. The new Academy no longer fosters community (or truth or beauty). It sells degrees that grant access to the job market. But the Academy isn't only a farm team for big business; it's in the service of government (in the larger—and meaner—sense). As a mechanism of social and political control, the Academy locks students into a pacified, slot culture.

Management rules. The faculty—the traditional governors of the university—have been demoted to adjunct peon status or tenured complicity. Administrations keep the pressure on the professoriat by pursuing "distance learning" options and computer programs copyrighted to institutions, not individual instructors. Academic officials act like CEOs. They are more committed to amassing endowments than adding to the store of knowledge. NYU has two billion dollars. Harvard has ten billion. Given the current stock market, these endowments are likely to increase 30 percent annually. Which means six hundred million dollars for NYU and another three billion bucks for Harvard. More than the gross national product of many small nations. Major universities have further enriched themselves through the acquisition of massive amounts of property. NYU and Columbia are the largest owners of real estate in New York City. Their holdings are fantastic and their income from rentals is enormous. Far from being unable to pay a fair wage to adjunct faculty, such institutions could afford to offer free tuition. One could almost say the Academy has become a kind of front for property-owners.

The adjunct system is crucial to the whole scam. The existence of a vastly underpaid labor force allows the Academy to keep pressing a profit-driven, conformist agenda. The adjunct system is the foundational rip-off. If the students discover this, they're likely to become incensed. And their parents—who sacrifice so much—should be even more enraged.

I love the idea of the university. I detest what it has become. I look forward to the day when the Academy once again acts in the public interest. But that won't happen without agitation. Like all labor forces, adjuncts need to organize and protect themselves. Graduate students at NYU have already organized under the UAW (AFL-CIO). Adjuncts everywhere must come together to force management to pay a living wage. The first step, though, is exposing the exploitation and shaming the administrators. American universities were built to be places of higher learning, not sweatshops.

No Sell-Out

Richard Hoggart

Hoggart gave the following talk at the 50th Anniversary celebration of the University of Glasgow's Department of Adult and Continuing Education in 2001.

It is an honour for me to be asked to speak at your 50th celebrations, especially since I know that Glasgow's Department is one of those which are keeping the flag flying in adult education, of the sort I first knew. I feel a little superior today because it is 55 years this month since I had my first appointment in adult education so I can beat you on that.

I want to recall, first, what it was like to start in adult education just after the war. Remember that famous line of Wordsworth, that bliss was it in that dawn to be alive. It wasn't quite like that, but it was a very good period for those of us who came out of military service at that time. Quite a number of us decided to go for this kind of work; I need mention only two famous figures—Edward Thompson and Raymond Williams. It's interesting that the fine early books they each wrote both came out of adult education teaching: *The Making of the English Working Class* and *Culture and Society.*

It was a curious period, there was the Attlee government, which was encouraging to us. There was the start of the National Health Service. From the Butler Act we had great hopes. More: the country was recognising adult education in a way it hadn't done before, especially university adult education. There was a spat between Churchill and Florence Horseburgh, who was Minister of Education in the next Conservative government and tried to cut adult education. Churchill was approached, and produced a wonderful sentence on the lines: "never in the history of this island has there been a more worthwhile cause." In short, he said "Stop it Horseburgh, give them the money." So, that was a great moment for us.

We remember then what we call the "Great Tradition" in adult education and the dominant figures in that were Archbishop Temple, and the famous conference at Oxford, Tawney, (I may be the only person in this room to have seen Tawney in the flesh). He was a wonderful man. He headed the WEA for many years. Then Albert Mansbridge who founded the WEA. There are others, naturally; and the baton went later to Titmuss, the great writer on the Social Services.

We admired those people, almost this side idolatry. We felt we were part of a sort of crusade, centred on the correct conviction that many people, far too many people in this country, in Britain, lacked the kind of education they could benefit from, and wanted it for the best reasons. They would be the focus and centre of our work. We were fond of phrases such as "the intelligent lay man" and one invented by Arthur Koestler, who spoke of "the anxious corporals," who could be recognised because their battle dress always bulged at the back of their trousers, because they had a Pelican paperback stuffed in it.

What we did not think about—in fact we tended to think ill of it—was adult education for vocational purposes; almost anathema to us was the idea of certification within liberal adult education. You did it for the love of God or the relief of man's estate. We went into the work with very great hopes but often found that what people thought we were going to do was give them socialist literature—George Bernard Shaw, H. G. Wells, *The Ragged Trousered Philanthropists*—but though we might be of the Left politically, we did not intend to introduce books labelled of the Left. In so far as we were Literature tutors we thought that nothing but the best was good enough for our students, we gave them Shakespeare and great authors. One test of the way we were, I discovered, was that if they became interested in Shakespeare—not talked down to about but personally *interested* in Shakespeare at its height—then the classes went shorter distances each week so that it gradually took about one term to reach Act 3 of *King Lear*. That was a sort of success because you were introducing them to Literature and what it could mean. I remember a little phrase which was that "the point of adult education is to get across without selling out," I would still stand by that....

Very briefly, the above was the sort of world we lived in. We went out 4 or 5 nights a week and then, if we were well thought of, did many Weekend Schools. In fact, after about 10 years of doing this our wives might say: "The children don't see enough of you. Why not try a job which doesn't take you away so much?"

How does our society look today, 50 years on? Obviously, we are much more prosperous, and in many other ways things have improved: housing is better; food can be better if we make it so. Education and the National Health Service have had a lot more spent on them. Those gains have to be qualified even though the facts and figures are remarkable. How do we qualify then? We must recognise more than we are doing at present that there is an underclass of about 10-15 percent who really are in a poorer way than we were in the Leeds working class before the war.

The body of working class people were not then a uniform group, they were mixed—they hadn't been filtered out. There were some very bright ones, some that should have gone out and upwards socially but didn't, some not so bright, some in work, some out of work, there were some talented in other ways. Those districts could rightly be called communities or cultures of their own.

Nowadays the underclass have been filtered out, partly by education but also by other opportunities as industry and commerce have changed. Good? Yes, to some extent. But those left in the poorest areas—it is not adequate to call them working-class now—they should be called, even though people hate the word, the "underclass." My own district in Leeds had about 30,000 inhabitants. One grammar school took about thirty aspirants a year, that was filtering if you like, of the racehorses. That place, when I last saw it a few years ago, has 15,000 living there. Forty percent are on relief, forty percent are one-parent families, mainly women. Some people there or in other areas are doing their best to improve matters. But it is not too harsh to call them "sinks." Most of those who have, as we used to say, "something about them" have got out; the others for various reasons couldn't get out. This is a deeply depressing because it is then easy to move into a cycle of deprivation, with drugs and the rest of it. Perhaps I have rather overstressed that but we should feel more strongly about it; more directly about the underclass than we do.

What about the National Health Service? It is in many ways a disgrace; and in many ways it is magnificent. I have greatly benefited from it as have millions of others. But the disgrace about it—which nobody in this government has firmly addressed—is that it is two-tier, that you get what you pay for. When people tell you that they "went private" and did this with a good conscience because it took the pressure off the waiting list, that is an illogicality. It doesn't take the pressure off the waiting list—it delays opportunities for those who can't pay. The two-tier National Health Service is something we must address.

Education is at least two-tier also and becoming more so in certain respects, certainly in England, so much so that now in a district such as Richmond-on-Thames there's a new breed of freelance tutors teaching middle-class children so that they may get into those selective grammar schools which still survive or those state schools which use some of the grammar schools' methods. So, in-fact, we are bypassing the problems of Comprehensives, making it harder for them to succeed because the system is once again becoming (or remaining) two-tier. What we are ensuring is a more divided society. To be divided does not mean to be varied, or diverse; those may be interesting conditions. To be divided, split, means that some have many opportunities and others few.

Behind all this is a major shift; to do with the sense of social place. We are told constantly—George Orwell was told almost 70 years ago that he complained too much about class in Britain—that we're becoming class-less. That was apropos *The Road to Wigan Pier*. I was told it with *The Uses of Literacy* 40 years ago. People of that type will tell you that they are the best of friends with their char women, except that they call them "cleaning" ladies these days. The best way I can think of approaching today's changes is to suggest that we are losing some of our old sense of class but its place is being taken by a sense of status, stratification and division chiefly by occupation. The meritocracy is at the top, the underclass at the bottom and the great body of people in between. So that, again, we are divisive. If you think of status in this sense, as a mat-ter of profession and other forms of stratification you would have about 10-15 percent percent who are the meritocrats, the successful lucky ones, about 10-15 percent in the underclass and the great body in the middle who make up "the mass audiences," the ones at whom the advertisers primarily direct themselves and the PR people and ITV.

What this of course is predicated on is the knowledge that this is now a secular society, but one of consumers, dedicated to commodities; whether we are consuming goods or ideas—well, not ideas so much as opinions; ideas are more intractable than opinions; opinions are easier and cheaper. What comes about then, in a society like this which is also prosperous—there are many more people worth the wooing—is a populist society; and that becomes a relativist society, in that it will not accept judgements between things or opinions, because that divides the customers—the consumers. You have a levelling society; you have a head-counting society. I wrote to the DG of the BBC, saying: "Your advertising men made a disgraceful set of adverts about *Lady Chatterley's Lover*. They made it appear to be nudge-nudge, joke-joke book with lots of bonking. But the book is better than that and you shouldn't distort it." He replied: "I do understand, but 'x' million people watched it." So where are we? This is just a non-argument. Numbers justify against all other considerations.

It is a society in which we are all assumed to be equal before the cash registers, in which there is no need to worry about individual or personal convictions. So, it is a society which has profound implications for adult education. Look if you will at just two items which I have already mentioned but now in a little more detail—Education and Broadcasting.

About 15 percent of this country are functionally illiterate—that is about 1 in 7. What does functionally illiterate mean? It means, in fact, that they cannot really decipher a bus timetable. Bus timetables can be sometimes rather difficult to read, but we should be able to expect that capacity in virtually everyone. The point is though that that 15 percent and some of the others who just get by are not literate enough for a democracy's needs. They are only literate enough to be conned by people who want to sell them everything from cereals to notions. They're the victims of what we might call the "stay as sweet as you are society" where you are implicitly asked: "Don't for heaven's sake have aspirations and don't break out of the gang because we've got to sell you things."

We are seeing some extraordinary effects. Two years ago, in a GCSE board of people considering what to put in the English Literature paper, it was heavily argued that there was no place for Shakespeare on the curriculum because—you know what the fashionable word is, don't you?—Shakespeare was not *relevant*. If ever there was a misuse of the word, that is one. It was argued that no books earlier than 1900 should be on the lists. One remembers Othello, and the base Indian throwing a pearl away.

The BBC again. If you tell them they are "dumbing down," they react with horror. They never meant to do that. And they say: "We have Attenborough after all, swimming away there. Or Simon Schama or … and we do many such good things." Of course they do all that, and feel we will thereby be diverted from criticising such programmes as *The Weakest Link*. A friend of mine who was a refugee from Nazi Germany ended his career as one of the top executives in the BBC. He rang me in shock after watching *The Weakest Link* and said: "This is the first truly fascist programme I have seen on the BBC. So much for Public Service broadcasting."

This is the division again: put in any sort of nonsense you like for the bulk of people and buy off the meritocrats by putting on one of those "quality" programmes I mentioned above. Whatever happens don't, for heaven's sake, criticise. One then remembers Maupassant's story *Boule de Suif*, with the elegant ladies in the coach which was stopped by the German troops during the 1870 war—worried about whether they would be robbed and raped. Luckily there was a prostitute in the carriage whom they had scorned. But now they said to her: "You go and give them your favours, and that will let us off." She does, and they revert to ignoring her.

Now, what should be the response of "adult education" to these current pressures towards populist relativism? We should remember first the old historical sense: that it is for the love of God and the relief of man's estate. And no certificates. Vocational education has a different role. I do not think that we will have much help from the government. Mr. Blair talks about the rise of the meritocrats as though this is a new insight. Has he realised that Michael Young's book *The Rise of the Meritocracy* is a satire against meritocracy?

The concentration on vocational, certificated education is now dominant not only in extramural thinking but in the universities as a whole. I know of weighty critics of this in Britain. The best such critic I know—he died not long ago—was Irving Howe in America; he wrote a very fine study of the state of American universities and said that the universities will stand for nothing if they do not "bear witness" about conditions of all kinds outside their walls. What he meant was that universities are more than technological or scientific institutions; they are places in which in almost Matthew Arnoldian sense they consider the true, the good, and the beautiful and try to make judgements about the nature of our lives, our relationships and society in general, especially in a democracy.

When there was a body called the Advisory Council for Adult and Continuing Education —which the last Tory Government let die as quickly as it could—it made, at what proved to be the end of its life, a large survey of the demand for adult education in Britain and, in particular, for the reasons why it was wanted. The results were astonishing. Very many people wanted adult education; even more surprising was the fact that the majority, when they were asked why, said they wanted that kind of education for all sorts of lovely old-fashioned reasons such as: "I would like to understand life better" and "I would like to understand society better" and "I would like to understand myself better." They had no certification or vocational impulse. They had something of the old Tawney, Mansbridge, Temple, Titmuss, Thompson, Williams aims.

So what we need, even the 75 percent of us who are officially literate but within whom the majority are only just literate—literate at a level at which they can be deceived—we have to go a stage further—is to demand critical literacy. Because in some ways it is harder to live in a democracy than in a totalitarian state because although apparently there is nothing demanded of you, much is all the time pushed towards you by the ubiquitous persuaders. So, if you do not learn how to say "come off it" or "stuff that for a lark." Or "bugger off" or something like that you will be conned, deceived. There is plenty of evidence of this. Have you any idea—most of you—how loansharks operate to get money out of people who are poor anyway? It is a dreadful story and is increasing.

But then in some ways we are a glib society and cheating society in many respects. That is one of the results of insufficiently corralled capitalism; feeding on almost universal instincts.

What we all need more than anything else is not simple literacy but critical literacy and that should start in schools. How to blow the gaff. Then there is an even further aim, which is much more difficult. We need to encourage imaginative literacy. Which is a society in which we know that *King Lear* matters more than the works of Jeffrey Archer. That is easy to say but hard to arrive at; remember the sales of Mr. Archer? So, greater Critical and greater Imaginative Literacy; those are the models before us and these the main targets of adult education—non-certificated, non-vocational, love of God education. Critical literacy, improved on by imaginative literacy. Great literature figures largely here, but you can introduce almost anything imaginatively, except perhaps Accountancy. Though, come to think of it … even that would be worth trying. I had a problem with a surveyor when we moved house; there was an extraordinary exchange of letters because we did not speak the same language. He was used to a world of protective, big-bow, semi-technical jargon. At first, that was a dialogue of the deaf but we broke through into daylight after about five exchanges.

For whom and to whom, then, should we try to speak? There is, of course, a special case for directly trying to help the worse-off, that needs many more special teams. Yet the most important truth about adult education in the 21st century is that now, if it means anything at all, it should apply to all parts of society, not only to the "anxious Corporals," and "intelligent lay people." We must do everything we can to serve them when they come to us. But virtually the whole of society is being incessantly offered trivial values, or the rejection of any value-judgements. The job of adult education is now both wider and deeper even than it was in the 1950s because we do not know now what we are missing and how comprehensively we are being deceived. What can you say of a democratic society which, in the last decade in the 19th century was able to declare that it was the first nation on earth to be fully literate, what can you say when that society, at the turn into the 21st century, has as its best selling newspapers such as the *Sun* and the *News of the World*. They will tell you that that's what people want. But how can they know what they could want if they are only given such limited perspectives?

Last night it was reported that the heads of ITV are going to put some very firm conditions into ITV now: "We are not going to have all this heavy stuff, we are going to have it lighter—it's what people want." It is, again, more the duty of broadcasters in the public service to give people what they *don't* know they want and what they need for society to mature itself, not to be mired in low-level tastes. That means that you should not start the news by saying that a famous football manager has had a heart attack. We may be very sorry to hear that, but not as the first item of national, even international, news. The BBC has by now much the same bad habit. The ITV executives above were implying that what is "the news" should be largely decided by what people already think and believe and know; whereas the essence of a civil education is that it shows that you do not know what you can like and what you can enjoy and judge well, until you have been introduced to it. As E. M. Forster reminded us: "How do I know what I like until I see what it is possible to have?"

The beauty of British Broadcasting when it has followed its Public Service remit is that it has tempted people beyond the boundaries they knew, until they discovered that they liked what they saw. That is not high-brow-ism; you can have high quality in popular work as much as in "high-brow" work. You can have second rate but pretentious low-level work, as you can have pretentious high-level work. This is not to say they are all equal. It is not to say that Monty Python is as imaginatively impressive as *A Midsummer Night's Dream*. Or the Beatles are as good as Mozart. Both in each pair have their proper place and worth. But that should not lead to a value-free levelling, where some say "We're Catholic and hospitable; we make no distinctions." There is a point where that attitude becomes porous, since you are simply saying that everything is equally worthwhile. The best of broadcasting in Britain—which has been a great success, but is now declining—has given its audiences new levels of wit and perception, as in Monty Python and many another, which you do not find anywhere else. An interesting point about these is that a class survey of the audiences showed that they were by social class pretty evenly distributed; as many "working men" as dukes were watching and enjoying the show.

So, in all this, I'm saying that adult education's job today in and from the universities is not only bigger but deeper. That is required by the kind of society towards which we are rapidly moving.

There are two mottos which I often quote because they are still immensely worthwhile. One of them is from the German Philosopher, Lessing; he said: "We must not accept the wantlessness of the poor." What he meant, I think, was that we must not accept that people in poverty should remain there, hopelessly. But the statement can be broadened to mean that we must not accept the imaginative wantlessness, the intellectual wantlessness, which can beset the poor; and so can apply to those in the underclass today.

The other sentence is at least as important as Lessing's. Bishop Wilson uttered it in the early 19th century. It seems to me to apply exactly to our society: "The number of those who need to be awakened is far greater than that of those who need comfort." In the '50s, when my generation started in adult education, the people who came to us were often those who, in Bishop Wilson's words, needed comfort; they knew something was wrong, they wanted to improve things. But they were a small body. As Bishop Wilson pointed out, the number of those who needed to be awakened was much greater than that of those who knew their condition. It still is. I would like to offer the Adult Education Department those two mottos, but especially the second one, for our move into the 21st century.

Part VIII

New Criterion

First's crew shares Hoggart's antipathy for "relativist" societies that will "not accept judgments between things or opinions, because that divides the customers—the consumers." But that's all relative too. Certain kinds of grading feed taste cultures in America's consumer society. *Entertainment Weekly* spoke from inside one of the culturebox's rec rooms when it invoked "the kind of book or movie or band the smart kids liked in high school." *Smart* became the praise word of choice among those who provide consumer guidance to college students and pop lifers in the '90s. And it still rules. Take the new journal *N+1*, which claims to enhance "the intellectual situation" yet happily cites those who praise it for putting "the smart back in smart-assed." Our crew has had a different rationale (and a more streetwise approach). But, back in the day, we never settled on a value word to sum up our resistance to the hegemania of those-who-would-seem-knowing. I've tried to float *soul* as *First*'s word, though it's really not for me to say. And I'm aware "soul" isn't all good. Fascists talk it up. Other less dangerous forms of piety lurk there too. But why don't we let Oscar Wilde handle them for a hot second: "Those who see any difference between soul and body have neither." *First* has done some schooling of its own on that score as this next section underscores. Forgive me for being so proactive but I'm going to submit that the material here upholds a *First* standard of soul that's better than clever and beats dim dualisms. I hope you can pick up on the value of the intensely realized feelings in this mix of fiction, poetry, personal witnessing, and (music, film and literary) criticism. The subjects are universal and racial, sexual and spiritual. The range of authors is catholic too. There's even a report by a Catholic doctor-priest who puts the heart back into a heartless world in Haiti as well as a consideration of texts by his co-religionist, William F. Buckley, who is definitely *not* our good Father's soul brother.

That reading of Buckley is embedded in the opening piece here by Michael Lydon on the realist tradition in literature. Since *First* has printed much more music writing than literary criticism it seems fitting that our exemplary piece of litcrit is by a longtime music journalist best-known for his biography, *Ray Charles: Man and Music*. Lydon is a pretty straight writer but he lets his I get into the act when he's making a case for his favorite 19th-century novelists. His moments of self-exposure—"I have snatched money up from the ground with a look over my shoulder to see if I could get away with calling it mine"—link him with other revelators in this section.

Someone once prophesized "the future literature of the West would be confessional in nature." Beats (like Amiri Baraka) ran with that projection. But the confessional impulse has often been traduced in our talk-show-your-ass Age. Privacy may seem like the key to authenticity now. Yet *First*'s version of soul is still outer-directed. Solidarity is the End. It's the true human way out of Hoggart's "glib" and "cheating" meritocracy (which has everything—and nothing—in common with that old desert of dollars and smartness).

Real Writing

Michael Lydon

Michael Lydon was one of the original '60s rock writers. In the '70s he became a professional musician. In more recent years, he's authored the biography, Ray Charles: Man and Music *and an instructional text,* How to Play Classic Jazz Guitar. *He's also produced a half-dozen self-published works on writing and life. What follows are excerpts from that material. The opening passages come from his pamphlet,* Bad Writing.

I's crop up inevitably in any first person narrative but William F. Buckley often pushes his "I" to the fore one, two, and three times a line:

> So I assembled most of the crew. This time I would take her to Mexico. During that trip I decided on its completion. I would experiment with a crewless boat. I would cut expenses....

After a run of "I"'s like that, a good writer might find a way to put it second in an upcoming sentence, for instance:
  "Reggie and I talked about it during the Mexican trip."
Not Buckley! His "I" must lead, must dictate:
  "I talked to Reggie about it during the Mexican trip."

and his crew had better enjoy being dictated to:

> "At what time do we meet at my suite, Tony? Very good, Tony, 7 pm is not 7:30 pm, is it Reggie?" Of course, when you say things in that tone of voice, it pays to make the schoolmasterliness hyperbolic, in which case it is accepted in good humor by the kind of people I sail with, who are all splendid, having in common their recognition of my unique qualities.

Page after page this "I" marches by the reader in pompous parade. Buckley's "I" makes sure we know he is no ordinary fellow. He was born to a wealthy family, had a pampered childhood, and he is wealthy today, though he proudly relates his penny pinching:

> ...I had undertaken to provision the wine cellar of the *Sealestial*. This is a very serious business. On the one-hand, money is very definitely a consideration. Anyone can provision a wine cellar successfully by averaging ten or fifteen dollars per bottle. My aim is to average $3.50 per bottle, and I can report that superb wines were drunk for twenty-nine days....

"I" has intimate dinners with famous people like Charles Chaplin. Besides his yacht and his houses in Connecticut and New York, he has a house in Switzerland, "(which is where I write my books)"—the parentheses stand like castle walls to exclude the reader from "I's" privileged precincts. Even when "I" writes about religion, he still insists on center stage:

> It was over ten years ago that I was asked to write a book whose title would be "Why I Am Still a Catholic." I demurred, using as an excuse that I had books charted for two book-writing seasons ahead. But after a month or so, I thought to accept....

> [I]n midsummer 1992 I came disconsolately to a decision to abandon the project I had begun in January, despairing over the reading and studying I wished to do and had no time to reschedule. I returned the publisher his advance payment, put away the copious notes I had taken, filed away the only chapter I had actually written (it survives, slightly altered, the opening chapter of this book), and then proceeded to feel lousy about my capitulation. The reason for this you can probably guess: I felt I owed something to God.

"You can probably guess?" Speaking as one reader "you," no, I hadn't guessed why Buckley felt lousy—the "I" parade had already so bored me that I didn't care enough to guess!

Buckley bores the reader because he loves himself more than his readers. He doesn't write; he preens; instead of holding up a mirror to nature, he holds up a mirror to himself. Under all his prose, whatever its apparent subject or argument, runs a monotonous subtext: "Look at me, aren't I wonderful?" This self-centered prose may charm some readers for a time. Like Buckley's crew, they may find it good politics to laugh at the wealthy captain's jokes. Yet time does not favor the fatuous ass, and soon enough Buckley's writing will smirk its final smirk and rest in peace forever.

Lydon realizes that "human character publishes itself" (pace Emerson). And that enables him to read right through the sort of conventional wisdom that conflates the ideology of a William Buckley with the sensibility of an Alexander Solzhenitsyn (who's one of Lydon's Gods).

Lydon knows Buckley isn't alone in trashing moral traditions he, Buckley, claims to uphold.

Despite the Bible's ringing endorsement of human equality, many who believe that they believe in the Bible find equality a hard truth to hold to. George Bernard Shaw opens *Candida*, with the Reverend James Morell in his London study, going over his calendar with his secretary, Miss Proserpine Garnett, who, Shaw notes, is "of the lower middle class." Proserpine sniffs that Morell needn't go to one meeting because, "They're only a half a dozen ignorant and conceited costermongers without five shillings between them." Amused to see that Proserpine has found someone to look down on, Morell comments, "Ah, but you see they're near relatives of mine."

Proserpine (staring at him) Relatives of yours!
Morell Yes: we have the same father—in Heaven.
Proserpine (relieved) Oh, is that all?
Morell (with a sadness) Ah, you don't believe it. Everybody says it, nobody believes it, nobody.

Shakespeare is a grand exception to that rule (according to Lydon):

...to every wandering bark,
Whose worth's unknown, though his height be taken

"Whose worth's unknown though his height be taken." What does Shakespeare mean by that?

Let's look at the second half of the line. To take someone's height means to evaluate a person by various rules-of-thumb that reveal his or her strengths, weaknesses, and overall usefulness in any given situation. When we take someone's height, and we all do, we have no hesitation in judging one person better than another.... Shakespeare knew all about height-taking from his own daily life, certainly from auditioning actors for his plays, and his line's second half allows that such inequality is part of making our way in the world.

Before making that allowance, however, Shakespeare has reminded us in the first half-line that we don't know the true worth of people whose height we take so casually. The neighbor we just judged to be lower than us, a beggar we stepped past in the street, perhaps, or a braying ass of a brother-in-law: who is that neighbor, what is he or she worth in the great welter of life? We do not know....

Since our worth is unknown, we may of course be worthless. Yet every syllable of the sonnet, every syllable of the *Complete Works*, tells me that Shakespeare believes, as I believe, that every human being, whether beggar or braying ass, has a soul of inestimable worth, and that souls are enough alike to be married in mutual love and understanding. Differences in wealth, talent, family or fame—that's height-taking, useful but superficial. Human worth comes not from rank, but from doing our best to live as decent human beings.... "Whose worth's unknown, though his height be taken"—true, we don't know anybody's worth for sure, but for that reason if no other, let's give other wandering barks the benefit of the doubt.

> **Faith that all humans are equal is foundational for Lydon. Beyond the surface noise of class and "difference," he hears a universal clock ticking for us all—"Neither you in your now or I in mine know what is going to happen next. We are equal." (Lydon spells out his common-sense existentialism in his pamphlet, *Now What?*) He searches for evidence of human equality "in great writing no matter where and how it may be hidden" in his recent essay, *Writing and Equality*. His approach to Jane Austin is exemplary.**

She may bow more to class than later writers raised on "All men are created equal" as their mother's milk, yet no writer before or since leaps more quickly than Austen to attack self-proclaimed superiority.... Has the absurdity of believing oneself superior ever been more wittily demonstrated than by Austen's portrayal of the vain Sir Walter Eliot:

> Vanity was the beginning and the end of Sir Walter's character; vanity of person and of situation. He had been remarkably handsome in his youth, and, at fifty-four, was still a fine man. Few women could think more of their personal appearance than he did; nor could the valet of any new-made lord be more delighted with the place he held in society. He considered the blessing of beauty as inferior only to the blessing of a baronetcy; and the Sir Walter Elliot who united these gifts, was the constant object of his warmest respect and devotion.

Austen's witty insights—Sir Walter thinks like a valet!—convey equality as if by lightning flash.

> *Writing and Equality* extends (and sometimes qualifies) arguments made by Lydon in *Real Writing*—his study of Balzac, Trollope, Eliot, Dreiser, James Jones and Solzhenitsyn. *Real Writing* is a real book, weighing in at over 250 pages. Along with *Writing and Equality*, it amounts to a kind of concentrated, American complement to Erick Auerbach's *Mimesis: The Representation of Reality in Western Literature*. Lydon's stuff won't transform the Canon or conceptions of the Novel. He's not

our Auerbach (or our Bahktin). Lydon doesn't have a scholastic bone in his body. But the colloquial ease with which he makes his case for literary realism not only adds to *Real Writing*'s charm, it's entirely on point.

In the wide shelves of Balzac, Trollope, Eliot, Dreiser, Jones, and Solzhenitsyn, we've found a body of truth which, though mundane, has the inestimable value of being known for certain. Do protons and electrons, misons and neutrinos spin in and about the nuclei of atoms? Does energy equal mass multiplied by the speed of light squared? Quite possibly, but I do not know the answers to these questions from my own experience. On the other hand, do flies buzz around cow shit? Does a person who sees money lying unattended consider grabbing it up and running away? *Yes*! I answer without the slightest doubt. I have seen flies buzzing over cow patties countless times. I have snatched money up from the ground with a look over my shoulder to see if I could get away with calling it mine. These are truths I can swear to body and soul. Put a gun to my head and I may deny them to save my life, but inside I would still know them to be true.

> Lydon's feeling for the inside truths of desire and dailiness shows forth in his reading of *The Human Comedy*. (He's particularly illuminating on *Lost Illusions*, capturing the, self-aware, prophetic quality of Balzac's "word-y" text about "the birth of writing in the age of industry.") *Real Writing*'s opening chapters on Balzac, Trollope and Eliot gather momentum as Lydon reads each through the other(s).

Balzac novels grow along straight lines of concentrated desire; Trollope novels meander with characters who hesitate, vacillate and procrastinate—who don't know what they want. When they do charge off to accomplish something grand, they soon fall back in baffled retreat. Human weakness, not desire drives Trollope's world, and three to six hundred pages of its perpetual motion make a Trollope novel....

In the first paragraphs of *Rachel Ray*, Trollope develops a metaphor from nature to describe Rachel's widowed mother. "There are women who cannot grow alone as standard trees," he begins:

> For whom the warmth and support of some wall, some paling, some post, is absolutely necessary—who in their growth, will blend and incline themselves toward some prop for their life, creeping with tendrils along the ground until they reach it.

In Mrs. Ray we can see all of Trollope's characters. None of them stand straight alone; they all tilt. Struggling to keep their balance, reaching for support, they collide with their fellow tilters, each collision setting off chain reactions that ripple out through the book's entire population.

Such meandering story lines pose a danger of formlessness.... Trollope shapes his novels on courtship. Two lovers, often four, are central to each novel; how long they take to muddle through to marriage determines it span. A welter of activity goes on about the lovers, much of it chronicled in detail, but when they say "I do," Trollope writes, "The End." Balzac in contrast, uses courtship as one of many story forms and often excludes major characters from romantic love—vengeful Cousin Bette is one striking example. Trollope is far more sentimental; if anything (besides a fondness for comic names like Lord Dumbello and Chef Millepois) tugs Trollope away from hard-and-fast realism, it is romance, the yearning for what he called "the orange blossom ending"....

A "craving for love" had been among his most powerful emotions since childhood Trollope admitted n his *Autobiography*, and he knew that many readers yearned for romance as he did. In *The Small House at Allington*, Lily Dale puts down a novel glad that it ended well for the heroine. Her sister Bell comments that she doesn't like novels, "they are too sweet:"

> "That's why I do like them, because they are so sweet [Lily replied]. A sermon is not to tell you what you are but what you ought to be, and a novel should not tell you what you are to get, but what you'd like to get."

Ironically, Lilly Dale is Trollope's only woman character who spurns the earnest love of a good man whom she knows, her family knows, and we readers know she should marry. Trollope tells Lily's tale over two novels.... By denying us the "orange blossom ending," Trollope proves the primal power of romance even more memorably than when he lets love lead to wedded bliss.

> **Lydon recognizes George Eliot has more in common with Trollope than with Balzac: "The 'trivial falsities for which we hardly know the reason ... [the] clumsy improvised insinuations' by which Eliot declares people make their way are the same weaknesses that motivate Trollope's stories." He points out the two writers "respected each other as craftsmen:" Trollope finding Eliot "always, like an egg, full of meat," and Eliot acknowledging that but for Trollope, "I should never have planned my studies on so extensive a scale for *Middlemarch*."**
>
> **But Lydon is alive to the differences that divide them as well....**

Though Eliot and Trollope use similar techniques, the *quality* of sympathy that each conveys—its tone of voice, sense of humor and pathos—is as distinct on paper as the two writers must have been as people. Trollope's sympathy is that of a well-meaning man of the world—hearty but bluff. He can say goodbye to a major character in a single sentence—"And now George Vavasour vanishes from our pages, and will be heard from no more." His asides often remind us tartly that human sympathy has limits. "Distances in time and place ... will diminish friendship" he writes in

Phineas Redux. "It is a rule of our nature that it should be so." Selfishness is a fact—"Each man is to himself the centre of the whole world"—and so is materialism "The Archdeacon was worldly who among us is not so?" Trollope's acceptance of these limits gives his sympathy a rough strength, but also keeps it within bounds the world readily recognizes.

Eliot's sympathy knows no bounds....

Lydon makes Eliot's "great theme" of sympathy his own as he tries to write up to her example:

[Eliot's heroines], Dinah, Maggie, Dorothea and Romola all have the same quick response to life, the same restless desire to understand its very heart. Their eager hope to love and be loved is a constant vital impulse, the main spring of their motivation. Had Eliot, like Balzac and Trollope, allowed the characters of her various novels to meet, these four searchers after sympathy would have recognized each other joyfully as sisters under the skin.

Eliot catches her heroine's common spirit in every mood, including its inconsistencies: nine-year-old Maggie grinds her favorite doll's head against the chimney bricks so she can nurse the poor thing back to health: nineteen-year-old Dorothea tries to tell herself that her delight in wearing her mother's jewels is really "mystic religious joy." Despite such frailties, other characters come to love her heroines as Eliot does. Dinah's sweet nature touches everyone in *Adam Bede.* "I know you have the key to unlock hearts," one elderly gentleman tells her and only Dinah can sooth Adam's crotchety widowed mother:

> "Eh, there's not comfort for us i' this anymore, wi'out thee couldst get Dinah Morris to come to us, as she did when my old man died. I'd like her to come in and take me by the hand again, an' talk to me. She'd tell me the rights on't, belike-she'd happen know some good i' all this trouble an' heartbreak...."

Above all, Eliot shows how the spirit's simple strength, like a flickering but unquenchable candle, can transform darkness to light. In one immortal scene of *Adam Bede,* Dinah visits Hetty Sorrel, imprisoned for the murder of her own child, in her gloomy cell:

> The two pale faces were looking at each other: one with a wild hard despair in it, the other full of sad yearning love. Dinah unconsciously opened her arms and stretched them out.

> "Don't you know me? Don't you remember Dinah? Did you think I wouldn't come to you in trouble?"

Hetty kept her eyes fixed on Dinah's face—at first like an animal that gazes, and gazes, and keeps aloof.

"I'm come to be with you, Hetty—not to leave you—to stay with you—to be your sister to the last."
Slowly, while Dinah was speaking, Hetty rose, took a step forward, and was clasped in Dinah's arms.

They stood so a long while, for neither of them felt the impulse to move apart again.

Eliot, of course, is the source of the common spirit that animates her heroines—together the four make one self-portrait, an extraordinary example of how subtly the self can present itself in art....

This brings us to the final difference between Eliot's realism and that of Balzac and Trollope: the latter delight in writing's power to construct, Eliot delights in writing's power to communicate. Balzac and Trollope write to make the reader believe that the characters truly exist in their word-made worlds. They invite us to slip unseen through real streets alive with real people as if we too walked among the jostling crowd. So does Eliot, and no less successfully, but for her the make-believe is but a means to close communion.... She writes to achieve wordless understanding with her readers. She grounds her fictions on timeless daily life so that readers generations hence will recognize their truth. She creates Dinah, who can unlock hearts, to unlock our hearts. As Dinah reaches out through the darkness of the prison cell to hug Hetty, Eliot reaches out through black ink to hug you and me.

The Saving Right to Reprove

Benjamin DeMott

From darkness a face appears—a scared-looking, black male adolescent. A grownup is talking threateningly offscreen.

You let anyone jump on your brother again, Boy, and you just stand there and watch, I'll beat you to death.

The last words come in a stammering jumbled rush; the stammerer has to start over:

I don't care who started what, if he was winning or losing, you get a stick or-or-or-or a goddamn brick and you knock the kid down whoever is fighting and if the son of a bitch is too big for you, you come get me. This off the wall bullshit about Henry started it—

The speaker breaks off again, this time in a coughing fit, and as the shot widens we see a heavyset man—the father—doubled over with coughing ... a pregnant woman, the boy's mother.... The boy's younger brother presses his face into his mother's apron and skirt.

The father resumes, in a stagey tone—a voice of paternal reasonableness and persuasion.

> If anything was to happen to me or your mother, you ain't got nobody but your brother, and that goes for your brother and he knows it. You are not a child. Son, you'll be a goddamn man soon. Start learning what life is about.

Abruptly as he pauses the boy's mother flings forth an arm—strikes her son across the face.

Thus begins Charles Burnett's *Killer of Sheep* (1977), a film set in the environs of the Watts section of Los Angeles. It's a movie about teaching right conduct to the young—or, rather, about trying and failing at that effort, trying again, ultimately giving up. The theme is the loss of that which practically defines the human essence, namely the saving right to reprove.

The father in Burnett's opening scene means to call up a world wherein choices count and elders give helpful guidance. Stand by each other. Respect experience. Life is hard. But there's static in the message. Mature reasonableness a la Judge Hardy ("You are not a child, son") clashes in the scene with bravado ("you come get me"), overdone profanity, and threats. The man chokes, seemingly, on the claim that he knows something worth knowing; his stammer and cough and fulminating—like the blow that the mother strikes—suggest bodily revulsion at the claim.

The movie digs deeper as it goes, probing comparable moments of frustration—comparable failures to speak up effectively for felt understandings of right and wrong. The filmmaker lives into his elders' doubt that lessons can be taught or paths chosen. His characters strike out blindly at each other; they regularly engage in defensive, mocking commentary on the delusion that, in the bottom-caste world, better and worse, right and wrong, exist. (The mockery is carried in variations on a single dominant refrain: "Shit on you, nigger. Nothing you do matters a good goddamn.")

The film's focus is the work and family life, in a black neighborhood, of the youngster who's chastised in the opening scene: Stan, now grown up—a husband and father in his thirties. Like every black adult he's ever known, Stan inhabits a world where the only jobs are befouling and the only living space is jammed, where nothing works—cars, appliances, whatever—for longer than a few days at a time, and where investments of aspiration seem programmed to prove senseless.

Stan's job is in a meat-processing plan (he slaughters and guts sheep); the pipes leak in his tiny cube of a house. When opportunity knocks, it's an invitation to disaster—a chance to earn money by serving as lookout for acquaintances bent on murder. When he attempts to speak of general life–forebodings to a friend, the friend asks matter of factly why he doesn't kill himself.

In "problem plays" mounded-up detail in this vein seems over-indicative; it leaves the impression that ideology, not observed life circumstance, is driving the dehumanization. In *Killer of Sheep* the impression left is that fantasts alone could avoid the truth that, hereabouts, bad news is the only news.

Pursuing his probe of lesson-giving and nurture, Burnett shows us that in these quarters indulgence of a child's truancy or other misconduct ("parental irresponsibility") functions as self-charity for grownups. It's their only affordable gesture of affection. Aberrant sexual behavior ("child molestation") arises from a cluster of closely related factors none of which is easily criminated. The factors include tight living space that incites sexual precocity in the young, the reasoned doubt that the young have a future, which undermines rationales for adult self-denial. People time and again imagine upholding the good as they conceive the good, and time and again, as in the opening scene, are balked.

Stan's daughter, a first-grader regularly exposed (in her family's tiny house) to her parents' sexplay, steps between her father's knees, caressing him; the child's mother, Stan's wife, watches her husband and daughter slip into a barely perceptible, quasi-sexual rocking movement; the parents' eyes meet, and inside the mother—in the involuntary movement of her jaw muscles—we feel an impulse of protest. But complicity shadows the moment, checks the response. What's the child doing but mimicking her elders? The grownup who wants to reprimand child or father would have to possess moral dignity and moral distance. Who can claim either?

Nobody speaks.

Stan's young teenaged son cruelly teases his sister, leers knowingly at his mother, calling her "my dear"—ducks and runs insolently from Stan's blows. Discipline is what's wanted, but reality tells the elders that discipline is unavailing; the misconduct needing correction lies vastly beyond anyone's reckoning. And as it goes in this house so it goes in the next. Grownups trying to act in accord with an obscurely intimated obligation to state rules or bear true witness lose momentum in mid-course—shed the obligation as though exhausted. A black adult bystander sees young black thieves stealing a TV from his neighbor and dares, briefly, to stare warningly at them. They stop in their tracks: "What you looking at, punk? I'll kick your heart out." The bystander turns away.

Once in the movie, once only, a voice of confident probity is heard—someone speaking as though it were conceivable for a black human being to point the better way efficaciously to another. It's a child's voice, naturally, one first grader scolding another: "How come you not in school any more? You gawn fall behind." The sound, which seems to come from a remote planet, defines the freakish direction of the ripening process in the castelike world: youngsters grow not into the authority of preceptorship but out of it—into the realization, as they "mature," that only frauds imagine they can teach.

Stan's wife tries to interfere when the would-be murderers come to enlist her husband as an accomplice, but they tell her her man is lucky to be offered a job. ("Nigger worked all his life and ain't got a decent pair of pants.") In the movie's most unbearable scene, Stan watches as a cripple lying helpless is kicked without reason—and he manages to cry out against what's happening. "I don't give a good goddamn about him," says a voice in response; others near at hand tell Stan to forget it, and their shared inertia fixes the horror.

Shit on you, nigger.

Charles Burnett, a son of Watts who's been a MacArthur Fellow, doesn't deal in gang warfare, drive-by shootings or black-white buddy sentiment. He seeks simply to do justice to the ordinary events that suck the most marginalized of his people into will-lessness and contempt for the fairy tale of "personal identity." In *Killer of Sheep* he quickens his themes through workplace images of faceless meat processors repeating the physical actions of herding, killing and gutting undifferentiated, unchoosing animal life.

Here, says his movie's manner, here is one basic level of black American life; consider the physical facts and the facts of feeling. Where there's work, it's miserably paid and ugly. Space allotments in the home and workplace cramp body and mind. Positive expectation withers in infancy. Minds fall into mockery of aspiration as though at the bidding of physical law. Obstacles at every hand prevent mates and children from loving and being loved in decent ways, prevent children from believing their parents can know what's what, prevent parents from believing they themselves know anything worth knowing. The only feasible acts of kindness the old perform for the young seem as likely to harm as to help them; men and women standing up for what is proper and good appear to themselves and others to be stupidly oblivious of their own impotence; one's only true self is the figure huddled under a sink in the cruddy damp (shit on you, nigger), swearing as a wrench slips again, wrecking the seal.

"Affliction," writes Simone Weil, "stamps the soul to its very depths with the scorn, the disgust and even the self-hatred and sense of guilt that crime logically should produce but actually does not." *Killer of Sheep* offers access to the terrible daily weight of such self-scorn. Burnett's art releases audiences from the abstraction that curses the standard language of compassion ("black despair," "absence of values," and the like); it offers direct access to experience in its wholeness and complication.

Our Man in Hollywood

Armond White

In Michael Bay and Jerry Bruckheimer's *Pearl Harbor* (as opposed to the rest of ours), Cuba Gooding holds down the ethnic market. He's cast as Dorrie Miller, the first African-American to receive the Navy Cross. (To date Gooding's only other real life portrayal has been naval officer Carl Brashears in *Men of Honor*. Denzel Washington's already done three impersonations—all pompous.) Not exactly a biographical performance, Gooding's Dorrie Miller turns out to be sort-of autobiographical. Gooding gives Miller his usual humble, boyish charm. His first scene is a boxing match with a physically larger white sailor. Evoking Montgomery Clift's Prewitt in *From Here to Eternity*, Gooding plays a sensitive, two-fisted nice guy before heading back to the mess where the other black sailors peel potatoes. He emerges later—during the Japanese attack—to man an unused machine gun, justifying the esteem that a white officer had earlier conferred upon his sportsmanship ("Yes Cap'n" is the believe-it-or-not response).

Why would Gooding, an established, Academy Award-winning actor agree to such a part that amounts to no more than six minutes of *Pear Harbor*'s three-hour running time? Probably because Dorrie Miller's isolated heroism conveys Gooding's sense of his own singular position. Asked after the boxing match, "What do you get if you win?" Gooding's answer—"Respect"—is the only thing a conscientious black actor can contribute to modern film culture. This *Pearl Harbor* cameo appearance is preferable to Will Smith's lead role in *Independence Day* because Gooding offers more than a liberal's exemplary cipher and more than the patriotic token for "The Greatest Generation" that Bruckheimer-Bay intend. Each of Gooding's roles has dramatized the black actor's ideological struggle in the Hollywood wars.

The principled quest that Robert Townsend has forgotten since making *Hollywood Shuffle*, that isn't even considered by most rap artists who go from record-to-screen (whether LL Cool J or Mos Def) defines every role Cuba Gooding has essayed. Despite his smiling radiance, it even shined out of his bare behind in *Jerry Maguire* where he played the bartered NFL object who carries family responsibility as well as self-esteem onto the field. "Show me the money!" might have been Cameron Crowe and Tom Cruise's mantra but it was clear what money meant to Rod Tidwell/Cuba Gooding: Respect. Hollywood rewarded him for making a bottom-line egotist so likable and full of life because that's the kind of professional the industry understands.

Gooding understands more deeply. At least his roles suggest he does; his presence creates a cultural dialectic in otherwise banal films that are a young black Hollywood actor's only recourse. In *Pearl Harbor* the glamorously photographed young white soldiers have a partly nostalgic, newly erotic innocence—the *Top Gun* style of hegemonic pop that makes viewers swoon while unconsciously ingesting political inanity. In a rare moment of doubt these glory boys with names like Rafe and Danny wonder, "Why did they choose us, because we're young and dumb?" But they find the answer in their own blue-eyed, All-American reflection: "We're the tip of the sword." White screen idols have been the idealized representations of group self-esteem for generations. There have been no young black men of comparable visual stature until Gooding's generation. Hollywood seems not to mind that this kind of segregation insults and belittles part of the audience. But Gooding, for his part, unzips the tip of a different sword.

1

Gooding ended the 1999 movie *Instinct* with the damnedest speech ever assigned to an African American movie star. The actor and the role meshed. He played Theo Caulder, a young doctor in the Psychology Department at the University of Miami. A long way from *Boyz N the Hood*, he's closer to Sidney Poitier's young shrink in *Pressure Point*. "I want to learn" he says eagerly when assigned to pysch out Ethan Powell (Anthony Hopkins), a white anthropologist and primatologist who went too native in Rwanda and killed a troupe of gamesmen who hunted down apes he was studying. Gooding's Caulder doesn't seem up to handling the international incident; earlier another patient warned him, "You don't know anything about politics do you? You're just a psychologist, you're not versed in this." So close to the estimation most people have of Gooding, that statement begs to be refuted and Gooding strikes a blow in *Instinct* that shakes all presumptions about blacks, actors, Hollywood, America.

Unexpectedly, *Instinct* exposes the get-ahead tragedy that swallows up most of the black performers seeking mainstream approval since the hip-hop era began. The contest-of-wits between Caulder and Powell can be seen to symbolize Hollywood competitiveness but, situated in a federal prison, it also evokes America's final solution—the place where those who fail to successfully compete are banished. Director Jon Turteltaub, who directed *Cool Runnings*, the genial real-life tale of the Jamaican bobsledding Olympic team, here does a compassionate analysis of social Darwinism. Knowing how competition drives people mad, he shows Caulder and Powell in a *Cuckoo's Nest* microcosm and more: the prison's warden recalls '60s Southern stereotypes and the African flashbacks (juxtaposed to academic and professional politics) beckon as a lost, ruined ideal. Wild-eyed, wild-haired Powell confesses his desire to retreat from Western civilization to jowly yet cherubic Caulder. If Willie Loman had a conscience, Powell—a weary, chastened Alpha male—would be it. ("You find peace, friendship, harmony, safety [in the jungle]. More peace there than any city in the world.") Fascinated by his patient's reminiscence of the jungle ("You want to follow?" Powell asks), Caulder draws closer to his African humanist roots.

It's aggravating that Walt Disney and Touchstone Pictures won't acknowledge the on-going Rwandan civil war; even the film's liberal allegory for slave- and animal-trade seems off when mixed with yuppie paranoia ("By now he thinks freedom is something he dreamed," Powell says, pitying a captive, emasculated baboon.) Yet the caged zoo-animal motifs are fecund. Powell tells Caulder, "I'll call you Tabiba Juba" a Swahili term that sounds suspiciously like "bourgeois." He sees past Caulder-Gooding's wide-eyed and mirthful look of interest to the buppie underneath. "You're curious, searching, unsatisfied, slightly pissed-off." Reversing the usual Hollywood bromide of the black as the white man's savior, he treats Caulder like the primates, instructing him how to maneuver in a white dominated world. "I want you to share it with the people you're close to. Are there any?"

That question resonates since Gooding doesn't represent the black male stereotype thought to be legion; his straight-arrow manners suggest some distance from the homeboy's mien. But for all his correct posture, no one ever thinks of Cuba Gooding as an Uncle Tom (he may have inherited some soulful good will from his father, Cuba Gooding, Sr. of The Main Ingredient, who sang "Everybody Plays the Fool"—a hit that could be Jr.'s theme song).

Gooding's nature is so ingenuous that Caulder instinctively chuckles when exasperated. But the marvel of this characterization is that Gooding's nervousness gets scarily deeper. And Caulder articulates it to Powell:

> You asked me a question once. What has you all tied up in knots when you wake up sweating in the middle of the night? You still want to know? I've been thinking about it. Been thinking about it a lot. It's not the work, I love the work. It's the game. The game, Ethan, and I was so good at it. I made sure the right people liked me. At night I'd do the checklist in my mind. Am I cool with Ben Hilliard? Am I cool with Dr. Josephson? Am I cool with all the people who can help? Am I cool with all the people who can hurt me? Nobody thought I was weak or a loser. There was nobody I was offending, nobody I loved. That game, Ethan. But guess what? You taught me how to live outside the game. You taught me how to live. And you know what scares me even more? That I'm going back in. [GOODING JUMPS UP AND WALKS CLOSER TO HOPKINS] Forgive me Ben, put me back in the game! I'll make you like me again! I'll do all the work, just put me back in the game! And do you wanna know the psychology behind this? Now, pay attention, because I'm good at this. [HE PAUSES HEAVILY] I'm trying not to say goodbye. I'm trying not to say I'll miss you. I'm trying to forget you. Ethan Powell, case closed. Ethan Powell, case closed. Look at me! [TEARS SLIP DOWN GOODING'S CHEEK]

Until August Wilson writes an original screenplay, no black actor is likely to have a more revealing moment than that farewell monologue. It throws you back to the uncontainable happiness of Gooding's Oscar night so that you realize his triumph over the anxiety every black actor, every actor, every New World Order competitor experiences. *Instinct*'s screenwriter Gerald DiPego (adapting the novel *Ishmael* by Donal Quinn) wrote out the modern distress but Gooding comprehended and conveyed it as sweetly, achingly as his father sang R&B.

Gooding wiped the smile off of buppie ambition. Caulder's embattled need seem to leap off the screen—a personal confession indicting Hollywood professionalism. It syncs with Rito Moreno explaining her sense of mission when she became the first Latina to win an Academy Award (for *West Side Story* in 1962): "After working in Hollywood since I was 16, it certainly put me in touch with reality because I didn't do another movie for seven years. I was only offered gang-related things. So I showed them." What Gooding showed, through Caulder, was the personal price of aspiration, the inadequate rewards of "success." Spike Lee's effort to dramatize the complexities inherent in recently afforded opportunities, *Bamboozled*, tripped up over the same complex by sensationalizing showbiz success and sentimentalizing media-workers' turmoil. Gooding caught a more useful, everyday essence—as when Caulder discovered the ethical nuances of a supervisor who "doesn't have the right [but] has the power" to fire him.

In an earlier confrontation, Powell flips power position on Caulder, binds his mouth with masking tape and demands, "Write what I have taken from you! What have you lost?" After scribbling "Control," then "Freedom," Caulder finally gets it right: "My Illusions." Denzel Washington's never had such a genuine moment on screen. Powell's solace to Caulder (from veteran actor to young Gooding) is also genuine and stinging: "You've lost nothing but your illusions and a little bit of skin." In this moment Gooding gets to the meat of Hollywood representation. Is skin identity? Blackness? Ethnicity? Professional status?

Millions of people who see *Pearl Harbor* will have to figure out how racism and segregation, though glossed over, are still practiced in the film's biased narrative and elisions. Half the Dorrie Miller scenes have a requiem mass playing on the soundtrack so that blacks figure sentimentally if not prominently in the filmmakers' concept. When blacks donate blood, it's transfused through a Coke bottle—an absurdly perfect metaphor for commercialized miscegenation, one-love product placement, commodified brotherhood.

Cuba Gooding's self-exposing integrity makes it possible to explode *Pearl Harbor*'s platitudes. His definitive movie moment in *Instinct* is not widely known but it should be. Pop as *Jerry Maguire*'s Rod Tidwell was, Caulder's apprehension—and Gooding's haunting realness—will outlast it.

The Soul of a Simulacrum

Jay Cantor

In *The Soul of a Man*, Wim Wender's contribution to the [2004] PBS *Blues* series, Laurence Fishburne as Blind Willie Johnson intones—and I do mean intones—words written by Wim Wenders as we watch a satellite probe its way into outer space. He—that is Blind Willie Johnson—says that NASA, which apparently gives out the Nobel Price in

Representing Humanity, put one of his recordings on *Explorer* to teach aliens what our civilization is like. I hadn't known that Johnson's work, his gravelly, authoritative, voice-of-a-prophet singing, required this kind of certification, but the tone and dialogue imply that it certainly made Johnson's after-life. "*My voice*," Fishburne says proudly, in a voice that is not Johnson's voice, *so whose voice is he talking about*—a question that will, unintentionally hang over this whole enterprise.

After our thankfully brief time in outer space, Wenders returns to a mock up of Mississippi in the thirties, with an actor playing Blind Willie Johnson, Fishburne/Johnson narrates, and we hear Johnson himself sing from a beautifully re-mastered audio track. Wenders has had the film stock processed to look weathered, and he sometimes even interrupts the images with dialogue cards—as if we were watching a fragment of a pre-sound newsreel, one not just *of*, but filmed in 1930s Mississippi. I cannot imagine what this could signify except "documentary," or "like documentary" (as Velveeta is like cheese) when in fact, it isn't documentary (or cheese).

I don't think Wender's game here is to make us question the nature of documentary, though it comes to have that effect. It's just, that he couldn't find a way to occupy a place where (I imagine) he would desperately, utterly, lovingly, like to be; he lacked a way to imagine himself into the people portrayed; so he used these technological means to fake past technologies, as if *that* could bring him closer, allow him to break into that past.

After this, Marc Ribot—the first of a number of musicians who perform snippets of Blind Willie Johnson's or Skip James's or J.B. Lenoir's songs—plays. With few exceptions, the performances here are grand or minor failures that ended up making me think about how the songs of Blind Willie Johnson, or the other major subject of this documentary, Skip James, are maybe, like few other things in music, *of this performer*, and that another performer can no more sing them than Pierre Maynard could write *Don Quixote* again—or Wim Wenders make a documentary of scenes in 1930s Mississippi that had never been photographed. What interested me is why one who loved the blues would even try, and why when he tried he'd end up doing such a desperate and silly thing as Wenders does, or, like most of these performers, why they'd find himself screaming, crying, shouting these songs, like a person having a tantrum or passing a hard stool—as if they, too, couldn't break in on this song, into its past or its present.

I think these songs by James or Johnson (Lenoir is another matter) just aren't made for different performers to interpret in the way a Gershwin tune is, or a Mozart concerto. This is not to their detriment nor does it make them better than Mozart, and this isn't true, of course, of every blues song. Ellington, for example, wrote marvelous blues for others to sing, and like Mozart's works, they will have many interpretations, none of which will be exhaustive. In a later episode of this sad series Ali Farke Toure says—a little snottily, I think—that American blues are flawed because they were made to get the singer a glass of whiskey. That is, they are commodities. This seems to me very partial. They *aren't* flawed by that—though the market may put pressure on these singers that prevented Toure's sometimes endless noodling. Toure's statement misses, too, what very odd commodities these songs are. If a person really wants whiskey, then like Gershwin, or Neil Diamond, he should write a song that others might sing, then, if he lives where there's enforceable copyright law, he'd get lots more whisky than Skip James ever managed to cadge.

Maybe James just didn't know how to do that because he lacked the lawyers, the context, the Brill Building, and enough exposure to the radio to hear what others had been doing and how. Maybe that's also a way of saying he suffered from a very peculiar—as in "the peculiar institution"—form of isolation, and that formed him and his music. I know Delta musicians shared verses and riffs and tunes, yet the best blues sound like the musician had been thrown back on himself, forced to confront who he is, where he is, trapped inside this particular body on this long empty Delta. Which makes me want to turn to the last refuge of the essay writing scoundrel, a thought from Rilke (feel free to skip the next few sentences) who said "art is the marks the dancer's fingertips make on the walls of her cell." All art? Well, not all, maybe, but some art, sometimes, surely, and I think that describes these blues in particular. Prison, I hear, is a place of isolation and of suffering—which makes it also a place where one con, or embodied sentient being, is very much like another. But it's also, strangely, where solitude and desperation, sickness and death, make the particularity of our one and only self sickeningly, ineluctably present—even while those forces wear away at us at the same time. You would think prison would make a person desperate. Not every one who goes to prison is a great artist, but the miracle in James's case is this; the markings his hands left aren't frantic or uncontrolled, but meditated, poised, ferocious and exact. It's his interpreters who sound hysterical.

The blues was (yes, okay, I know) played at dances, the blues was (yes, okay, I know that, too) a communal form. But I think the best blues are songs for others, and yet the performer sounds as alone as a man in hell, or a Parchman sweat box. Anyway, Skip James certainly doesn't sound like he's trying to raise his Q so you'll buy his song—as if he was stupid enough to think that with enough muzuma he could bribe his way out of his jail, his body in this Mississippi. James, or Charlie Patton, or Robert Johnson played the blues at parties—and to share something that intense, like the recognition that we're all in prison, might make us cling to one another and sway slowly together—but their works remain (*and at the same time*) amazingly inward, musing and angry, accessible and yet unsentimental, as if the audience didn't hear the songs, but overheard them. Towards the end of Wender's film, Dick Waterman, who managed older blues musicians during the Sixties and Seventies and did as much as anyone to keep their music before our ears says this more exactly than I can: "A lot of bluesmen played to the faces, played to the first row. Skip James dealt in the abstract. He played out over your head and into the great beyond."

Each of us in his or her particular historical moment may be trapped inside a dying body—we have that much in common with Skip James—but each of is *not* necessarily behind walls so think we can't blithely ignore them while we watch *The Bachelor*. And at this point, race having been mentioned a few times, I have to turn on myself with resentful suspicions, for in the American dream the role of the black musician has always been to be the authentic, the "soulful," the irreplaceable, artist. Those words are mostly hateful, but if you recognize the phenomenon isn't a matter of racial phenotype but an artifact of how race is Made in the U.S.A., it seems to me to point in the right direction, point to what makes for the continuing *difference* of the work of the great blues singers. And it's that that I think drives the people who love this music crazy. They want to make these songs their own; more, they're so filled with admiration that they want to be like the singer, share his knowledge and his grace, they want to be there with him, inside his prison. Oh, they want to be him. And they can't.

Of course I know that's usually an aggrandizing desire: like, *if only I had all that delicious suffering along with my fabulous prosperity, wouldn't that make for a nice life and some great art!* But sometimes it's a sweet impulse, as if the music so called to you that you want to provide the artist some company in his cell.

Collectors, to take another example, try to be *there* by buying the absolutely closest to the original pressing of the song that they can find. They take the totem home, and, out of respect, rarely even play the records—so they won't wear them out. Maybe it's not just respect, though; after all, their concern ends up redoubling the artist's isolation; so maybe it's *also* their unconscious revenge on this frustrating thing they love but can't quite ever get close to.

Dick Waterman, for example, shows the pictures he took of the *exact moment* that Skip James, who had been rediscovered in a Mississippi hospital some thirty years after his first recordings, played his "precise first note," at Newport, as if that might bring Waterman closer to James, still photos being often the democratic way to try to hammer yourself into the past.

So look, just as you now suspect, I *am* naively saying the Skip James's own performances of Skip James have an aura, but one, at least, of a new sort. In the age of mechanical reproduction the performance (thank God) *can* be repeated; you can still hear James's hands scrabbling on his guitar, but his work just *is*, like the poem described in that annoying poem of Archibald McLeish. James's song when sung by him at different times, in slightly different ways, as we have them on this record, or when it's not a Velveeta documentary, in this film, may be all we will ever have of James's song; he didn't exhaust the song so much as embody it fully—or it embodied him, in a dancer from the dance kind of way.

I don't think you can get into the cell by singing a Skip James or Blind Willie Johnson song. Bonnie Rait, whose involvement with this music and these musicians borders on the infinite, does have one idea, though. She says, "All right Skip, wherever you are this is for you," as if she's just singing his song back to him in his prison, or to help him pass the endless hours in heaven. And some of the performers give poised and nuanced performances. But most of the musicians flail away at the cell door from the outside; like Beck, or Steve Winwood, Nick Cave, or Jon Stewart. They shout and thrash and strut, like they were trying to break down the prison walls—though they do it so theatrically that I don't believe they think they can, or even really want to. I prefer the female performers who sound like they might entice their way past the guards, and join themselves with James that way, though I don't think that will work either.

These performances, then, mostly end up reversing what I would guess was Wenders's intention for them; they don't make me feel that Skip James's songs continue in new performances. The songs remained locked into his solitude, unassimiliably *his*—and if they continue it's because we can play the recordings of them, wonder at them, feel the bars of our own isolation, the gravity and commonness of our arterial blood. Blues goes on and changes—but not *this* blues and if James's songs continue that would be in their inspiring someone else to sing a new song so suited to the grain of her voice, the grain of her life, so aware of the cell that separates her and makes her like the rest of us, that no one else could sing *that* song either.

Meanwhile, Wim Winders himself flails in his filmmaker ways, trying to be *there* with Skip James or Blind Willie Johnson. Or, in his case, particularly with J.B. Lenoir, who is, we are told, his "all time favorite" blues musician. He has better (and worse) luck with Lenoir than with Johnson or James. First of all, there's footage of Lenoir so he doesn't have to mock up an animatronic Lenoir. And Lenoir is—to my ears, anyway—an altogether more minor artist than Skip James or Blind Willie Johnson, and in part, I think that's because he is so much more ingratiating, so much more easily accessible to our usual ways of relating to, or appropriating, the past. You *can* re-do Lenoir's songs.

Two very appealing Swedish admirers of Lenoir show some movies they made of Lenoir in the '60s—though it could be of course that Wenders did, after all, make up this charmingly geeky Swedish couple, and then faked up these amateurish films. I don't think such suspicions are his intention, but that you come to think such things is perhaps *his* unconscious revenge on the completeness, the unassimiliably of what he loves, that it doesn't need him and won't (in the way he desires) let him in. Wenders can't be there with Skip James, so through his faked up photos he makes it impossible to know if anyone *ever* was, if anyone was with anyone ever.

The Swedes talk about how Lenoir looked like Martin Luther King, and both were—of all things—family men, and both had tragic deaths. These two sweet Swedes, from admiration for Lenoir want to make the history Lenoir sang about have the same density in his distant and usually predictable lyrics, that King, by the manner in which he lived his life, managed to give to what might have been religious abstractions in his. The pseudo-Blind Willie Johnson then tells us that Skip James sung about his own experience, his own life, while "J.B. Lenoir wasn't *just* singing about him and his life. He needed to sing about the bigger picture." Say what? Wasn't *just* singing about his life? As if you were to say, "Chehkov just wrote about his life, but Dreiser saw the big picture." Whose picture? Whose life? The big world was, whether he liked it or not, Skip James's prison, and so it was the substance of what he made his songs on or against. The big world was *always* with him, late and soon.

Cassandra Wilson then sings something by Lenoir about Vietnam, and in case you don't get it, there are pictures of Vietnam. Or maybe outtakes from *Apocalypse Now*. Most devastatingly, Lenoir's songs need the pictures or they wouldn't have bite; that is: they're not the equal of the pictures. Skip James, singing about the killing floor, would have been. He already knew about the murderous self-righteous racist rage that would make Vietnam. It was part of the walls of his cell.

Then it's back to outer space for this film, and some clichéd shots of the *really* big picture, along with more marmalade about the blues "exploring the lowest depths and lifting us up to the highest heavens." The face of Blind Willie Johnson or the actor playing him is superimposed on the heavens—or some version of the stars done by computer graphics for all I know—while we hear Johnson's real voice. Then Wenders reverbs that amazing voice, as if he couldn't hear that the wonder and terror of this vital death were already nicely mixed in Johnson's voice in a way that no other singer has ever matched. Wenders then adds yet more *Twilight Zone*-sounding woo-woo to the soundtrack. And then Lou Reed plays over the credits.

So Skip James and Blind Willie Johnson, this is for you: *everybody, please, stop watching Wenders and stop reading this, and just go play their records, Thanks.*

Lost and Looking

Stephan Talty

Thirty-five years ago last December, Sam Cooke, the legal father of Soul, was shot to death by an L.A. hotel manager. In a time when pop stars died clean martyr deaths in plane or car crashes, the circumstances were sordid: the married Cooke, near-naked when he died, had been at the motel with a Eurasian prostitute, who later claimed he tried to rape her. The shock was palpable—for those who cared. *The New York Times* didn't care, and carried the news in a small item on page 34. But the black newspapers, the black nation and Cooke's deepest white fans reacted with honest grief. How could that beautiful man with that beautiful voice have died this way?

Cooke was the first famous black figure to become a kind of national martyr in the '60s before Malcolm and Martin Luther King. His funerals (there were two of them) drew 80,000; King's just 50,000. Private eyes were hired, there were protests, outrage, and a four-part series in Cooke's hometown black newspaper. The investigations aimed at larger questions than whether the shooting was legally justified. Sam Cooke was Mr. Elegance, his miraculous voice communicated a world full of new ease available to everyone. He was the first black singer to own his own record company (paving the way for later moguls like Berry Gordy and Puff Daddy). He had come up through gospel music and had risked everything by going pop, but had made his betrayal into a triumph, clearing territory for others (from Otis Redding to Michael Jackson) to settle.

So which man—the smooth idol or the naked, raging bull—was the real Sam Cooke?

Cooke's death tore his image in two. But in life he had always been a split personality, his bichambered soul pumping out hits whose innocent pleasures were in fact pivotal moments in American cultural history. Cooke was the black Elvis, the first major black figure to cross from deepest black music (gospel) to the purest white pop. Elvis is now everywhere in America. But Cooke, his partner in revolution, has been forgotten, or worse.

Talk to members of the hip-hop generation and Curtis Mayfield, James Brown and Al Green are cited as forefathers and influences. But Cooke is strictly an oldie-stations phenomenon these days, getting less relevant with every spin of "Cupid" and "Wonderful World" on 101.1FM. In the mind of America, he is an overpolite black man in a cardigan sweater—a fake white man. But it is impossible to truly understand the '50s—the decade that served as prelude to the new America—without understanding Sam Cooke.

He was born in Chicago in 1931, the son of a Mississippi-born preacher. A clean-cut prodigy, he led various teen gospel quartets before receiving, in 1951, the proverbial divine tapping on the shoulder. At only 19, Cooke was chosen to take over the lead of the legendary Soul Stirrers, the greatest and most famous gospel group of its time.

His voice was already a hypnotically clean and thrilling instrument, endlessly changeable but exquisitely controlled, its tone grounded in Mississippi soul but made urbane, self-regarding, swinging, cool. Along with Brian Wilson's and Smokey Robinson's, Cooke's voice is one of the miracles of the pop age.

But even then there was something new and disturbing in Cooke's voice. In the singing of almost every other gospel singer, you can hear their relationship with their God. Sometimes it is so reverential it is as if the singer can never really address God directly; it is half-turned away, like a glance away from direct sunlight (R.H. Harris, Cooke's predecessor in the Soul Stirrers).

Sometimes it is jazz theater masquerading as gospel (The Golden Gate Quartet) or a vessel almost breaking as God's power flows through it (Mahalia Jackson).

With Cooke, you heard something else. He was playful, brash, curiously secular. His voice soared and dived, played with the words, impudently stretching and remaking them in his own mouth. There is great joy in Cooke's singing, but little or no reverence. It is pop music disguised as gospel.

When he trades off the lead with Harris in the Soul Stirrers classic "Come, Let Us Go Back to the God," the difference is clear. Harris's rich but guarded, grimly experienced singing is in the tradition of the slave hymns. His voice is full of black history and it means to be. When Cooke takes over, he's swinging, vamping up and down the notes like a child released. He never beseeches God; on record, at least, he sings as though free from all of Harris's dread.

This completely new attitude carried over to Cooke's original gospel songs. In "That's Heaven to Me," Cooke wrote:

> A little flower that blooms in May
> A lovely sunset at the end of the day...
> The leaves growing out, growing out, growing out on the tree
> That's heaven to me

This is a gospel song without God—just kids and birds and tangible happiness. Cooke's music was not poised between Jesus and the devil, as was gospel and R&B, he was far more modern.

As Daniel Wolff points out in his Cooke biography, *You Send Me*, the gap was at least partly generational. If Harris is praying to God, he's also praying for protection from the realities of Eisenhower's America. Cooke was an optimistic post-war kid, he wasn't going to beseech anyone. In his voice you can hear not only joy but defiance.

There is a remarkable parallel here to another young black man who was growing up at the same time with much the same attitude. Muhammad Ali and Cooke would become fast friends as they both rose in the world. After winning his epochal first fight against Sonny Liston, Ali embraced Cooke, grabbed an interviewer's microphone and introduced Cooke as "the world's greatest rock and roll singer." (Fuck Elvis.) Cooke returned the compliment, calling Ali "a great example for our youth." This was just after Ali had shocked America to its Christian core by proclaiming himself a Black Muslim. (Fuck the Establishment, Cooke was saying, white and black.)

Ali and Cooke publicly departed from the old ways of being black in his country, and startled whites into new ways of looking at black men. Ali's most clear-eyed observer boxing doctor Ferdie Pacheco, believed that the boxer was a "divine" man, literally molded by God. "He was the most perfect physical specimen I had every seen, from an artistic and an anatomical standpoint, even healthwise," Pacheco said. It was a theme that ran through much of the writing on Ali.

Cooke's touched-by-God reputation was widespread among musicians; he could churn out 20 to 30 songs in one session, an astonishing rate for a jingle writer but almost incomprehensible for a first-class songwriter. He was a pop arranger of genius. And voice-wise, Atlantic exec and master-producer Jerry Wexler, who gave "rhythm and blues" its name, called Cooke "a perfect case." "He was the best singer who ever lived, no contest," Wexler said. "When I listen to him, I still can't believe the things he did. It's always fresh and amazing to me, he has control, he could play with his voice like an instrument, his melisma, which was his personal brand—I mean, nobody else could do it—everything about him was perfection."

The claims—the suspicion of divine touch—stand the test of time. There was something unearthly in the gifts both men possessed, and in the way they used them. But if both possess the air of black gods, Ali and Cooke went further, publicly leaving the God that blacks were almost obligated to worship. Ali's rejection of the white Jesus in favor of Islam and Elijah was a huge event, a satchel charge tossed into the placid cultural camp of early '60s American life.

But Cooke made a far more dangerous and lonely switch. He left Jesus's gospel for money and the idea of complete freedom. "This is my new God!" Cooke is said to have told the gospel group the Womack Brothers after he went pop, holding in his hand a fat wad of cash.

He wasn't kidding. The singer was obsessed with material goods and all they represented in American life; he gave away furs and automobiles like candy, and toured relentlessly to earn more cash. He reveled in the high suburban lifestyle, and took Hugh Hefner's deluxe swinger credo as his own. Cooke's (little) candy red Ferrari was the equivalent of Ali's prayer book.

When Cooke went pop in 1957, it was said he was selling out. Certainly, Jerry Wexler thought so—he refuses to this day to even listen to Cooke's pop records. Art Rupe, the white owner of Specialty Records—the Soul Stirrers' label—agreed. Rupe loved gospel and roots music, but when Cooke came to him, wanting to go pop, Rupe reacted with disgust. He couldn't believe that Cooke would trade the Soul Stirrers' ecstatic, deeply meaningful harmonies for white back-up singers, strings and pop "crap" like "You Send Me."

Here is a critical moment in American racial/cultural history, as important in its way as Elvis bursting into "That's All Right Mama" three years earlier at Sun Studios. Cooke was demanding to sound light, carefree, even empty—emotional terrain that was reserved for whites. Rupe instinctively revolted against the switch—black music was soulful, deep, ancient, possessed. Cooke stormed out of the session, crying "If that's how you see me, I quit," and took the song to another label.

"You Send Me" is an almost bizarre departure in the history of American music. If the fierce "That's All Right, Mama" was a midnight raid across the color line to steal some deep blues feeling and emotional freedom, "Send Me" is a counterattack on the storehouse of white American style—sung, crucially, in a voice that was clearly, deeply black. It is a masterpiece of nothingness, so airy it's barely even a song. There were no verses, no story, no content. For much of the song's two minutes, Cooke just repeats "You send me" over and over (and he had to be convinced to change that to "You thrill me" for the second verse). It was a trick he would repeat again and again—in "Just for You," "Soothe Me," "That's Where It's At" and others. He wanted to showcase his voice's modulations, his mastery of vocal ornamentation and the purity of his gift.

But, in doing so, he also created a universe apart from the deep-feeling blues and gospel that defined black music and black life. Cook was not abandoning feeling, but he wanted to unchain black musicians from their sense of racial obligation and fatalism, to allow them to fantasize. The fanatical perfection of the song influenced everyone from Otis Redding to Rod Stewart, but it anticipates nothing more the Carpenters, the true poets of masked white emotion. It was as if he was stealing back the right of black Americans to feel innocence.

"You Send Me" was a phenomenon, going #1 pop and R&B. Cooke had conquered new territory, but had brought his black fans with him. His incredible string of hits throughout the late '50s—"Only Sixteen," "Wonderful World" and many others—were pop fantasies in the same mode. But Cooke's ultimate reversal of what was expected of a black singer (even by blacks themselves) was epitomized in his 1960 smash, "Chain Gang."

The song was written after an experience Cook and some bandmates had while touring the South. Driving through deepest Georgia, they saw a strange vision ahead of them. "There against the endless red-dust field," Wolff writes in You Send Me, "They'd seen a dozen coal-black men dressed in eye-stunning pure white uniforms." It was a gorgeous picture, until they pulled closer and saw the chains around the convicts' ankles—and the shotguns in the hands of the white guards.

Who else but Cooke could see this tableau, the prisoners chanting in a call-and-response pattern as old as slavery itself, and think "Top 40 hit"? Another black artist might have turned his dread into money through a single, but the race-based shock of recognition wouldn't have been lost in the music. Imagine Ray Charles or James Brown doing "Chain Gang"—there would have been some gesture toward the scene before them, a note to say, "there but for the grace of RCA go I." But not Cooke.

The song starts with an echoing, grooving bass line and the chant of the chain gang: "Huuh," "Ha." The rhythm and moaning go on for almost a full minute—an eternity in a 60s pop song—before Cooke cuts in with the first verse. Clearly this is what attracted him to the idea of the chain gang—the sound. Not the scene, not the pity—the sound.

Cooke's voice floats in: "I hear something saying…." Cooke's toughness is amazing—he hears "something" not even "someone." A basso profundo voice has to intervene and inform him: "Don't you know/that's the sound of the men/working on the chain gang." Cooke places himself in the role of startled onlooker; he has to be told what this awful, beautiful noise disturbing his peace is, as if he were society matron out for a Sunday afternoon drive.

Cooke's lyrics are typically light; he imagines the convicts dreaming of the day they'll return home and see their women—but until then "they've got to work right here." He's matter-of-fact about it, clearly Cooke doesn't see himself in that chain gang. He feels the emotion a good reporter might—in fact he credited his songwriting abilities to "observation," an unusually cool term for a soul singer.

And yet that is not to say the song is cold and unfeeling. It swings hard, and like all Cooke's songs, it is supremely in the moment—not a convict's moment in the hot sun but Cooke's transformation of it into a pop artifact. Listening to "Chain Gang" is like watching a Rodgers and Hammerstein musical about convicts; it's not quite real, but it's intoxicatingly artful.

Could it be perhaps that his coolness is one thing his black—and even his white—audience loved about Cooke? In the brief integrationist moment of the late '50s, Cooke represented, or at least he sounded like he represented, a release from all the drama, toil, horror and depth of black American history. He sang as if soulful elegance could transform not only his own troubles but the past itself. If Elvis channeled gospel depths (and thus black history) through the voice of a Southern white boy, Cooke claimed the other half of the bargain.

Other black singers had crossed over with light pop of course, going back to Nat King Cole. But there were essential differences: Cole's singing style was not identifiably black; it was beautiful but dry-cleaned. Cooke carried with him his gospel inflections into white pop; you could never mistake him for a white singer. Chuck Berry sang countrified rock masterpieces about white teens, as cleanly phrased as John Cheever's short stories. But Berry's voice and pop persona didn't resonate with black folks as deeply as Cooke's. Ray Charles's voice was that of a sufferer who was so sure of doom he almost embraced it. (Characteristically, when he decided to take on a white music, he chose country and western, the most fatalistic genre of American pop.) Cooke, on the other hand, was almost ridiculously hopeful.

The singer did not cross over without costs. There was the emasculating disaster at the *Copa* lounge in New York, where he was taught some "elegant" dance moves, dressed up like a butler and sang some syrupy drivel to a bored audience. There was the story (still disputed) that when he tried to return to the black gospel circuit, and was shouted down with cries of "Get that blues singer off the stage!" Cooke, barred from going home again, left in tears.

But Cooke crossed the color line mostly on his terms, and that took a special, and perhaps cursed kind of man. In Wolff's biography, Cooke comes across as strong-willed, nobody's fool, full of deep surface charm. He had the looks and cockiness of a high-school quarterback who never loses, but is always searching for something beyond the admiration and applause. Sam Cooke was, one senses, emotionally adrift for most of his life. At one point, near his death, he was drinking a bottle of Chivas Regal a day. Less important than the alcoholism is the fact that no one, not his close friends or his biographer, can give a definitive reason why he was suddenly hitting the bottle. Cooke was not mysterious; it's just that he had the super-controlled inner toughness of the suburban '50s businessmen in *The Man in the Gray Flannel Suit*. He slips through his own biography like a ghost, with his swellegant patter and his bursts of rage, so that we never get a real sense of him. Nobody did. One could see in the singer a figure not from Toni Morrison but from William Inge or Arthur Miller.

One indication of his true self was his bleak romantic life. Cooke had the pick of black American girls in the late '50s, from debutantes to starlets, but he chose women one could only describe as "hardened"—marrying twice, both times unhappily. He cheated ferociously on his first wife, sired a handful of illegitimate children, and tolerated his second wife's open affairs. "I often said Sam would walk past a good girl to get to a whore," said his manager Bumps Blackwell after the singer's death. His widow showed up at the funeral with Sam's replacement, Bobby Womack, on her arm—dressed in his clothes. A supremely cold gesture, but appropriate to Cooke's whole romantic life.

It was like some kind of Biblical parable: the greatest soul singer of all time seemed to be as inwardly bereft as a game show host. Perhaps that is why he could inhabit his pop fantasies so brilliantly and sell millions to suburban whites; he possessed some of their searching blankness. Those songs not only made him rich (as his critics point out), they satisfied the part of his soul not appeased by gospel.

Cooke's life is now told as an American morality tale: the brilliant young black singer who rose to the top of gospel world, forsook his God and his people for white money, began to despair, attempted to return to the fold but was killed before he could truly return to his roots. Even soul's Boswell, Peter Guralnick, now accuses Cooke of passing most of his musical life. In his liner notes for Cooke's 1963 album, *Live at the Harlem Square Club*, Guralnick writes: "This is not the same Sam Cooke who appeared on the Tonight Show, who presented himself as a kind of urbane 'swinger' The Sam Cooke who sang to this club audience made up of working men and women is a harder, grittier version of the Sam Cooke that we have known from his records, a singer closer to the ecstatic gospel music with which he started out.... He is home free."

In other words, this is the black Sam Cooke. (The "black" is there, in the euphemism "working men and women.") The album was recorded on the Chitlin' Circuit, where Cooke spent large swaths of his life earning his living and wearing his voice to an exquisite edge. In trying to bring Cooke home and restore his blackness, Guralnick ignores one thing: *Live at the Harlem Square Club* is not Cooke's most authentic album—it is by far his worst record, his phoniest, his most self-hating, his biggest sham.

Here Cooke misuses his gifts, vulgarizes his art instead of authenticating it. Every note is forced and roughened: "You Send Me" is made raw, a horrible mistake—the song's perfection lies in it unearthliness, not its earthiness. The performance might have been the gutbucket version that the crowd wanted, but delivering it Cooke seems uncomfortable and robotic, a puppet as surely as he was at the *Copa*.

But near the end, Cooke did finally bring his two impulses together.

In the early '60s, his music got moodier, funkier, with songs like "Sad Mood," "That's Where It's At," even "Another Saturday Night." Whether Cooke was following his own mood or only the pop market (which was drifting away from '50s ethereal pop) is hard to say, but his music changed. "Bring It on Home to Me," his raucously felt single from 1962 (recorded late one night after Cooke had been drinking) is the signal song in this final act, and perhaps the high point of his entire career.

With Lou Rawls shouting behind him, Cooke cries after a departed lover and here, for once, his coolness is shattered. He begins in a convincingly self-centered way:

> I know I laughed when you left,
> but now I know I only hurt myself

That sounds like an authentic moment from Cooke's romantic life. And he follows it up with some playboy bullshit, now made urgent and almost pathetic by how Cooke is screaming the word:

> I'll give you jewelry—and money too
> That's not all, all I'll do for you. Whooaaa.

He is singing like he has never sung before on his pop records—his immediacy tearing the face off the patented Cooke elegance. In the next verse, his lyrics match the desperation in his voice:

> You know that I'll always be your slave,
> Till I'm buried, buried in my grave
> Oh bring it to me.

For a black man to call himself a slave, for Sam Cooke to call himself a slave on a pop record, when his whole career has been a rejection of the necessity to hit the slave note, is a devastating moment. Cooke reaches back to a haunted past the only way he can understand—through his own personal desolation. Life has ground into him an understanding of the gospel pleas he sang so blithely 15 years before. He still hasn't found God—he's calling after a woman, and probably not a good woman either—but he has found himself truly calling for redemption at last.

Cooke completed his spectacular exit from this world by leaving us one final tableau to consider. As his body was carried off to the morgue (where it would lay, unclaimed for many hours), police found the singer's beloved red Ferrari in the motel parking lot, bizarrely out of place in the low-life surroundings. On the seat lay an open whiskey bottle and a book: *Muhammad Speaks*, the handbook of the Black Muslims.

The Ferrari, the bottle of liquor and the prayer book—it captures Cooke's dilemma with a bluntness he might have laughed at. Certainly, he would never have been so crass in summing up himself—or America. Cooke's synthesis of the tectonic forces that were reshaping the nation and the national character—the racial revolution—was as pure and shimmering as light off a lake. Perhaps only a ghost could have pulled it off.

The Wright Stuff

Richard Torres

A great man has died without the usual pomp and circumstance that normally surrounds the death of an eminence. At the age of 86, a decade after he'd retired from a twenty-five year tour on the NYC civil and criminal benches, Judge Bruce Wright passed away at his home in Old Saybrook, Connecticut. By all written accounts, with the exception of repeated heart trouble, his retirement was a sedate one. It was a far cry from the maelstrom he caused in Manhattan's criminal courts during the '70s when he refused to set high bail amounts because he considered it a calculated form of preventive detention designed to oppress minorities and the impoverished. This philosophy had not only earned him the enmity of the NYPD, the DA's office and the editorial pages of tabloid newspapers but also the derisive nickname, "Turn 'Em Loose Bruce." Facing considerable political pressure, Wright switched after nine years to civil court in 1979. Three years later, he was elected to the state Supreme Court

When I encountered him in 1987, Wright was still a polarizing, controversial figure. I was starting out as a writer/journalist and was looking for work. I'd just read a galley of his then-upcoming book *Black Robes, White Justice* and was impressed by Wright's insight and candor. I called a friend of mine who was an editor for a national black magazine and pitched an interview with the judge. To my delight, my friend agreed to do it. In fact, I was informed that a Wright piece should and would be the lead story in their book review section. Details—length of story, deadline, etc.—were quickly hashed out. I called Wright's publishing house and secured an audience with him in his chambers that very week. I remember thinking the planets must be perfectly aligned.

Wrong-o. Next day, my friend informed me that certain senior editors were "highly concerned" about any inflammatory statements that Judge

Wright might make. So rather than court—pun intended—controversy, they insisted upon seeing all my questions in advance. Advance, in this case, meant immediately. I grabbed my reporter's notebook and dictated to my friend all the questions I'd prepared so far. When finished, my friend rushed off the phone for an editorial meeting with his "superiors." Two hours later, my phone rang. I picked up and was told my "options." For every "politically-charged" inquiry, I had to agree to ask a "friendlier" question. So for every "how does a minority fight the legal system?" I'd have to ask "so what's your favorite food?" In addition, I'd have to furnish a copy of the taped interview so the magazine heads would be certain I didn't sabotage their prepared questions. And, I'd have to promise that I wouldn't alert Judge Wright to this policy. Now my friend and I agreed this was a ridiculous situation. I mean, who'd believe that a major black magazine would be terrified of the political statements of a major black judicial figure? I was about chuck it all when my friend made a good point. It was far more important to get Wright and at least part of his message into the magazine than to pout and refuse to do the story. "You'd be helping the readership," I recall my friend told me, "they can always buy the book to get the whole story."

A few days, later, I was seated at a desk in Judge Wright's chambers with a tape recorder to my left, a legal pad full of questions to my right and the man himself in front of me. He was dapper. Perfectly pressed, he had on a dark pinstriped suit, powder-blue shirt and an almost irides-cent bow tie. He was an imposing figure with an angular face framed by close-cropped white hair. Behind his eyeglasses, his big, brown eyes rarely blinked. Those eyes seemed like they'd seen everything. He had the most intimidating stare I'd ever seen. I could feel the heat from those eyes in the back of my head. I gulped, turned on the tape recorder and began reading from my legal pad.

Looking back, my editorially compromised style of questioning must've made me seem schizophrenic to Wright. Every time we got a conversational flow going about serious issues, I'd have to pause, return to my pre-agreed script and then ask about, say, celebrity defendants he might have come in contact with—in response, a mordantly humorous Wright told me about representing Billie Holiday in the mid-'50s and how her face was so luminous "it made me think narcotics must be good for the skin"—or what he thought about women. (Unsurprisingly, the six-times wed Wright declared himself pro-female.)

Three tales Wright related stay with me to this day. We were talking about the presence of the NYPD when suddenly—and for the only time that afternoon—Wright raised his voice. "Of course, they are important," said Wright with his fist clenched. "Never forget that they are the occupying force meant to keep us in our community."

When we spoke later about the importance of physical fitness, Wright informed me that he was a dedicated walker and cyclist—he paused and then told me this story. One day while in his chambers he suddenly felt sick. After nearly collapsing, he was rushed by ambulance to the nearest hospital. On a gurney, he was wheeled into the ER and left in a corner next to a white homeless man. As he lay there, he heard an EMT call out for a doctor. A physician ran to the EMT who then informed him that they had a sick judge in the corner. The doctor ran over to the two carts, passed Wright by and asked the white homeless man: "Are you okay, Your Honor?" "It was the most miraculous cure," Wright told me. "I bolted up, jumped off the gurney, walked out of the hospital and went back to my chambers."

Finally, as I was leaving—and in the midst of thanking Wright for his time—another question came to mind. (One not on the pre-arranged sheet, but since I'd already packed my tape recorder away, I figured no harm, no foul.) With trepidation, I asked him if it was true that the vast majority of his judicial colleagues hadn't spoken or acknowledged him for many, many years. Wright unveiled his warmest smile as he clasped his hands onto my shoulders and gently led me to his door. "Son," he said with a nod, "they honor me with their silence." And with that the interview was over.

That night I transcribed the tape and wrote the piece. Of course, it was still "too political" for the magazine so various editorial hands whittled away until it finally saw print in a much-bowdlerized form. A once-meaty piece had been turned into pablum by the very folk I'd assumed would serve Wright's message uncut. A lesson learned and, yes, yet another cynical writer born. But that isn't what matters here. What does, what must be celebrated is the legal legacy that this brave, opinionated, erudite, complicated man left behind. Think about it. Think about his refusal to allow poor people of color to be callously imprisoned because they couldn't afford high bail. Think about his principled enforcement of the fundamental tenet that all defendants are innocent until proven guilty. Think about his exposure of the rampant racism in our legal system. And then wonder where is such bravery today. In this bling-bling age of partisan politics, journalistic indifference, internet smear campaigns, public disenchantment and dormant activism, Judge Wright's resolute and often solitary stance against a tsunami of detractors looms even larger. It's in tribute to his intelligence and indomitable spirit that after 15 years

I choose to honor him by shedding my silence and telling these truths. Long may his courage resonate in our hearts and minds.

A Winter's Tale

R.D. Pohl

One wintry night in February of 1982, a friend and I accompanied Leslie Fielder to a reading and discussion he had agreed to do for inmates in a writing workshop at Attica Correctional Facility. The friend, Anne Pilger, was one of Leslie's PhD students at the time and taught a creative writing workshop in what was then called Consortium College—a degree-conferring program that operated within the walls of Attica.

I was a little skeptical about the idea at the time, but I had a car with snow tires. Annie knew and trusted her students. And Leslie, as always, proved more than up to the task. He read a short story from his collection *Nude Croquet and Other Stories*—it had a kind of science-fiction theme, a little H.G. Wells, a lot of Edgar Allen Poe. The inmates were enraptured.

Leslie finished the story in about a half an hour and then asked the class for questions about the story or about writing in general. This was the unscripted portion of the evening. We didn't know what to expect. One inmate stood up and asked a rambling question that began with something like "How do you do it man? How do you get all those thoughts on paper like that?"

Leslie stepped out from behind the podium. He was not a big man physically, but there was nothing slight about him. He had a certain gravitas, as educated people are wont to say, and on this evening he looked positively burly. In interviews later in life, Leslie would sometimes refer to himself as a "rude scholar," by which he meant a freethinker unmoved by conventional wisdom, political correctness, or considerations of literary reputation and social class.

As he began talking and gesturing, and moving about the classroom, Leslie answered not only the inmate's question, but also what was behind the question. Good writing, he said (and I am paraphrasing here, because I was too dumbfounded to take notes) is about reaching inside to pull out your deepest desire or fear. Good writing is about reconnecting with your anger, your grief, your guilt, your shame. The greatest writers—even the saints—throughout the ages have had violence, greed, lust—all the sins you can name and then some—in their hearts. Becoming a writer is learning to bring all the ugliness inside you out into the light, into words for the world to see that it's not ugly at all. It's human. We are mortals: all flawed, all scarred. We walk this earth for a short time. Then we return to it. Writing and literature are what connect us through the ages.

We all sat stunned. There was silence in the room for at least a half minute. I looked at my watch. It was a quarter to eight. In less than 15 minutes, Leslie had covered more ground than I had traversed in my entire career. Another inmate asked him a question, something more predictable about getting his work published.

As Leslie launched into another response, I recall how completely at ease he seemed in that setting. This wasn't, heaven forbid, the Iowa Writers' Workshop. It was a classroom full of convicted felons in a maximum-security prison on a cold February night. Still, I'm not so sure Leslie wouldn't have told the Iowa Writers' Workshop the exact same thing.

Watching him move about the room, making eye contact with all the inmates and shaking each of their hands when the talk was over, I remember thinking how much of a throwback Fiedler was to the days when great writers and thinkers lived (and sometimes died) by their wits. He would have been at home with Ben Jonson and Christopher Marlowe in the taverns of London, soldiering with Lord Byron in Greece, mixing it up with Hemingway in Paris.

In the years that followed, I had many more opportunities to visit him again. Even after his retirement from active teaching at UB a decade ago and the early onset of his battles with Parkinson's disease and prostate cancer, he continued writing and publishing, granting interviews, giving readings and even attending readings by other writers about town. I spoke with him last about a year ago. I'm told he continued working—dictating new material to Joyce Troy, his secretary of many years—right up to the day of his death.

Now he is gone, but like every great teacher he lives on.

Time Will Take You Out

W.T. Lhamon, Jr.

A response to First*'s call for reflections on James Brown's passing.*

James Brown died? Quick as a wink, the late riser at my house wondered, "Overdose?" James Brown excessively lived the legends of our time, their blooming for tabloid fascination. Beginning by dancing for pennies, just the way Black Guinea did in Herman Melville's nineteenth-century novel, *The Confidence Man,* James Brown went on to White House invitations, to tv, to pop film. In words, he was incommunicado— just listen to Terry Gross's embarrassment asking him on NPR to explain any aspect of his work. In song, however, his grunts made novels about living in America. Like no one else leading early boomers through their paces, James Brown embodied the momentum of our time.

Brown bore that momentum in his body and carried its thickening weight wherever he went. It kept him company through prison terms, through his several troubled marriages, while he learned to code that momentum as punctuated sound. For all their compulsion, it's not news that his earliest songs were slight, even derivative. From Little Richard he learned screams, sentiment, and spectacle. From Louis Jordan he learned joy and the jump beat. Through all that development, you can hear his originality grow. He gave us more than one new style of rhythm 'n' blues, but he also shows how originality can realize and amplify what's essential in extant moods and ongoing modes. So, I'll let others laud his middle career when he passed beyond Doo Wop to speak up for rhythm, black pride, staying in school, and the hard work of black capitalism. I want to recall, instead, the late performance of, "How Do You Stop?" That's where he tamped his experience into song that found its own meaning without heeding any chamber of commerce.

In 1986, we were all more than three decades into James Brown's stream of hits. His lyricist and producer for the song was Dan Hartman, but the two most important phrases in the song are not Hartman's. They are the two that Brown mumbles at the beginning and end: "relaxin'" (or, maybe, "relax it") and "no lies." He's giving himself directives parallel to his famous hand signals that fined his musicians' missed beats or wrong notes. Brown's music always finely sliced discipline, but here his topic becomes the penalty of excess, both too much control and too much laxity. It's the threshold from one to the other that the brilliant beat constantly reiterates and crashes. The rhythm of this song enacts the "runaway train" that drives past the one to the other. And the continually stuttered triplets before the downbeat are the threshold he cannot hold. You think love will wait and you don't hold on, and then it's gone. Anh Hanh! It's not in Hartman's words that this performance communicates, but in the grunted vowels that remark the threshold's going. Then it's gawWwn.

"How Do You Stop?" anthemizes the brave dignity of carrying one's compounded meanings well past their decades. Tony Bennett, Bob Dylan, Art Buchwald, Eartha Kitt, James Brown: they all learned to make their whole maturing selves convey their message. The endgame for boomers, it turns out, requires pop guidance as much as the rocky beginning. I cannot find a video of Brown doing "How Do You Stop?" on You Tube, but there are lots of him doing "Living in America" from the same time. His thickened fire-hydrant body with its chunky belly and stubbed face are broad, marked like the boxers his performance precedes in *Rocky IV*. He is in calculated contrast to Stallone's demure cuteness—he who is not marked by pain. The paradox is that Brown needed disco's spectacle to salt his complexity and nestle his roughness. And disco needs him as a reality check. In that context he doesn't lecture me but growls articulate vowels. I miss him already. No lie.

Back in the Day

When we were boys
We called each other "Man"
With a long *n*
Pronounced as if a promise

We wore felt hats
That took a month to buy
In small installments
Shiny Florsheim or Stacy Adams shoes
Carried our dancing gait
And flashed our challenge

Breathing our aspirations into words
We harmonized our yearnings to the night
And when old folks on porches dared complain
We cussed them out
          under our breaths
And walked away
          and once a block away
Held learned speculations
About the character of their relations
With their mothers

It's true
That every now and then
We killed each other
Borrowed a stranger's car
Burned down a house

But most boys went to jail
For knocking up a girl
He really   truly   deeply   loved
          really   truly   deeply
But was too young

Too stupid, poor, or scared
To marry
Since then I've learned
Some things don't never change:
The breakfast chatter of the newly met
Our disappointment
With the world as given

      Today,
News and amusements
Filled with automatic fire
Misspelled alarms
Sullen posturings and bellowed anthems
Our scholars say
Young people doubt tomorrow
This afternoon I watched
A group of young men
Or tall boys
Handsome and shining with the strength of futures
Africa's stubborn present
To a declining white man's land
Lamenting
As boys always did and do
Time be moving on
Some things don't never change
And how
      back in the day
Well
      things were somehow better

They laughed and jived
Slapped hands
And called each other "Dog"

—Lorenzo Thomas

Nursing Ganesha

Your purr is the one
essential thing.

Pills in liver, mackerel,
whipped cream, ice
cream, crab.
Days a blur of bowls washed,
buying catnip, catgrass,
velvet wind-up mice.

Death is my final gift to you.
I hold it for exactly the right time,
the way my husband kept a
diamond ring inside his bathing
suit until we snorkeled near
dolphins and sting-rays.

He tries to hide his
disappointment when
my blood begins each month
the way I hide my crying while
your bony body snuggles in
my lap. I gaze into your
still-bright eyes,

memorize the pattern of your fur
and kiss you paws.
I am a mother.

— Alison Stone

Puce

Hans Koning

Excerpted from the author's unpublished novel, Rescue.

At a bar, evening, staring at a full glass of beer. I've had one and didn't want another but ordered it because the barman made me. I can't go back yet to the boarding house to lie through another unresolved night. I sit here feeling bitterly sorry for myself.

"Monsieur, monsieur," from someone beside me.

I turn with some difficulty, as I was sitting with my legs crossed, hemmed in against the bar. A man is looking at me from two stools away, short, with a mustache, and a cap on his head.

"Yes?"

"You are lonely, monsieur?"

I frown at him and take a sip of my horrible, lukewarm, beer.

"I take you to a bordel. Ten dollars. Okay?"

So they have one of those too. Complete my preparedness. Or have I heard wrong? "To where?"

"House of women. I have taxi. Outside."

"Okay."

He does not move. I fish a ten-dollar bill out of my wallet and hand it to him. Now he jumps off his stool, waits to let me go ahead, and opens the door of a cab parked at the curb.

"Tip also," he says as he starts the engine.

"No. You said ten dollars. Ten dollars is ten dollars."

He shrugs and just sits there. I dig up another dollar and hold it over the partition. He pockets it and we are off.

Soon we are driving through sad and shabby streets, the cab jumping and banging as its driver doesn't make any effort to avoid the potholes. We stop in front of a low building with wooden shutters on the windows and not a glimpse of light coming through.

"Bordel," the driver says with a certain pride in his voice.

I had expected a discrete townhouse with a doorman. This place looks like an empty warehouse, with maybe a mugger waiting inside to hit the gringos over the head. I do not move.

"House of women," the driver says and opens my door with his arm through the window, without leaving his seat.

"I'm not buying this. I want my money back."

"Money back." His voice is incredulous. He sighs, gets out, and beckons me with his head to follow him. He rings a bell and the door opens, on a chain. Someone is standing there in a dim hallway. They exchange some words and the chain is taken off. "Okay," the driver states.

I go in. I see that the doorman is a young woman, walking away from me with a lumbering gait to open another door. Only when she turns to me, do I see her face. She is indeed very young and she is retarded, she has the broad face of a Down's syndrome victim.

The second door leads me into a taproom with some tables and chairs and old couches. First it seems there is no one there, then I see in the darkest corner a group of girls or women around a table. The only light comes from a crown of red electric candles with red imitation wax drops, dangling from the ceiling.

A youngish man appears, I didn't see from where. He is in a sleazy kind of barman's outfit, a shirt with braces, and he near-cries, "There you are, gentleman! Sit down! Girls, this gentleman is offering a round of refreshments, be nice to him!," and he vanishes through a red curtain. Everything is red in here, the light, the rug, and the window curtains which only go halfway up the glass. Above them I see the rough wooden shutters.

What a dump—but suddenly I get hit by its eroticism, the eroticism of sin in this nineteenth century Lower Depths atmosphere, which is more real and more fitting to my low purposes than the major-credit-cards-accepted décor of such places in New York. In the uncertain red light one of the women, in a short low-cut, residue of a black evening dress, stands up.

"What's your name?" I ask, hating myself for the false cheerfulness in my voice.

"Mimi. You go upstairs with me?"

I nod and follow her to the narrow staircase covered with a red runner. She waits at the foot of the stairs.

The man in braces reappears with a tray of glasses and a bottle. He looks at Mimi and then nods at me, approvingly. He puts the tray on the table.

"She is Mimi," he tells me. "I am Germain. Mimi is very nice. You will pay now?" It is a rhetorical question.

I produce my wallet.

"It is twenty-five dollars for the champagne. And thirty for Mimi's company."

"Eh—" I open my wallet and inspect its contents although I know well enough how much is left in there. "I haven't got that much. I have thirty-six dollars."

Mimi has gone up a few flights. Her legs under the short dress put a lump in my throat. Writing this down, I realize I sound a fool, and a nasty one. I was just that. Am just that.

Germain's smile has gone. "But, gentleman—you do not enter my establishment with insufficient funds. We are not the Welfare Office."

"But I didn't order any champagne. I don't want it," I answer angrily.

He is not impressed. "It is the custom."

I take the bottle, which has already been opened, from the table. The label says, "Vin Mousseux do Shangri-La" and shows a badly drawn castle besides a waterfall. "That's not champagne," I tell him.

He pours some into a glass and hands it to Mimi who is still standing on the staircase, leaning against the banister. She takes a sip and announces, though in a toneless voice. "Champagne." He then fills the other glasses and hands me one. I put it down and count out twenty-five dollars on his tray. It leaves eleven which I give to Mimi, who gives them to Germain. It makes the other women laugh.

Germain counts the money. "Eleven dollars," he tells the women but they don't react any further and concentrate on the Shangri-Las. "For eleven dollars," he says, "you can only have Puce."

"Okay." I want to get it over with and he is certainly not going to give me any money back.

He opens the outside door and calls, "Puce!" and to my horror the retarded girl comes in.

"Are you mad?" I shout at him. "That poor girl. You can't do this."

Germain shakes his head. "Never mind, gentleman. She has the habit. She likes it. Don't worry. You will see."

I want to remove her, and myself, from this scene; I take the hand Puce holds out to me and follow her upstairs. I pass Mimi without looking at her.

We enter a little room with a bed and a table; on the table a basin and a jug of water. She takes off her dress and lies down. She was naked underneath.

I must take this girl away from this place, take her to some institution … this is Canada, not Sao Paulo or Bangkok…. But what I do is to take off my jacket and shoes and then my trousers, and to lie down next to her. I mustn't hurt her feelings, I tell myself. But when I furtively touch her firm body, a mindless desire overwhelms me and I kneel between her legs. As I enter her, very slowly not to hurt her, she turns her head sideways toward the wall and utters a little cry.

It is a sound I cannot place. It has no echo in any past experience. It could be an acted-out sound of pleasure, I guess, taught her by Germain of which she got the timing wrong. It could be a cry of pain although I had only entered her with the tip of my penis. Wondering about this hardly takes longer than Puce's cry did. But immediately after, the truth shows itself to me. Within her private world the little cry is neither pain nor imitation pleasure. It is a vocalization of her innermost being. Of a total and merciless solitude.

I withdraw with terror. I hastily struggle back into my clothes but looking at her, I see her greatly upset. Do they punish her when a customer is not satisfied? I sit on the edge of the bed; I must stay here long enough to avoid that.

I smile at her. I bend over and touch her hair for an instant. When I stand up I feel Bertrand's compass in my pocket. I put it in her hand; I've nothing else to give her. I close her fingers over it and hold one finger against my lips to indicate secrecy.

Two tears roll down her face.

I escape from that room; outside, in the shabby corridor, I force myself to slow down. I come back into the barroom with a kind of leer and find Germain standing near the door, looking at me, expecting—what,

I cannot guess. I force myself to nod at him. Then I am outside, alone, and I start running as if the devil is after me; he was. He is.

Man on the Run

Benj DeMott

Hans Koning, who died on April 13 [2007], was a writer's writer who never believed in art for art's sake. Or, to turn it around (as per the French newspaper, *Liberation*), Koning's works were "treasures of revolutionary writing and writing plain." He became a regular contribution to *First of the Month*—and a close friend to our crew—after we published his fiction in our first issue. He had a much longer history with mainline publications such as *The International Herald Tribune* and *The New Yorker* where he worked as a foreign correspondent ("in the grand tradition") for many years. Koning was best known for his novels (four of them were made into movies, though none did justice to his work) and for his devastating critique of Eurocentric accounts of the discovery of America, *Columbus: His Enterprise* (which moved Kurt Vonnegut to write, "I think your book on Columbus is important. I'm more grateful for that book than any other I have read in a couple years").

Koning was a leftist citizen of the world who loved the *Internationale*—a Dutchman who made his home in America and yearned for France. Writing novels began to seem like an "indulgence" to him at the height of protests against the Vietnam war in the late '60s, but, after a hiatus of a few years, he returned to what he called "committed" fiction. He defined his own (less than fashionable) political aesthetic in a *New York Times* piece:

> I keep aiming toward that novel that is just that, a true novel, but a novel for our time, dealing with an essential theme and an essential message in a subterranean, carefully hidden way, a message like a snake in the grass.

Koning credited that snake to Trollope (whose novels, at the end, weren't far from his bed) but one in his favorite Poussin painting, *Landscape with a Man Killed by a Snake*, probably raised its head in the back of his mind as his simile dawned on him. During the last hard weeks of his life, a print of that Poussin became his horizon when he wasn't gazing on the faces of his wife, daughters and son. The radical art historian T.J. Clark has just published a book, *The Sight of Death*, that places *Landscape with a Man Killed by a Snake* (and another Poussin, *Landscape with a Calm*) in opposition to the current "regime of the image."

Clark's account of returning over and over to look at these two paintings (while they hung for a year in L.A.'s Getty Museum) helped me connect Poussin's representations of the human condition with Koning's. The novelist had his own resistant vision of Man's fate that animated his stoical yet inspirational stories of love and death and men on the run. Reading *The Sight of Death* made me wish that somebody would return to Koning's classic, counter-cultural prose and give his art its due.

Perhaps because I was outside when the heavens opened up the Sunday after Koning died—spring freshets filling the man-made ponds in Central Park and flooding the steps of the Metropolitan Museum—my own re-reading of Koning began with a scene in *Pursuit of a Woman on the Hinge of History* where a character recounts how Byron's exiled father once found shelter from a storm with a French girl. Koning returned to their rainy day together near the end of his *Little Book of Comforts and Gripes* and he cut to its essence there:

> Byron's father was a n'er-do-well who was sent to France by his family to live in an empty house his sister owned in Valenciennes up north; in his letters he constantly complained about the cold and everlasting rain from the grey clouds. He also told her about his "amours," one particular girl "at the Aigle Rouge, an Inn here—I happened there one day when it rained so hard—She is very handsome and very tall and I am not yet tired." He died not long afterward, a suicide it was believed.

> I did not feel sorry for him, on the contrary, I thought that if life in the end had given him those few moments of making love in an attic of an old inn, whispering, an oil lamp maybe, the rain hammering on the roof, it was enough—as he had known perhaps when he killed himself.

> Maybe we have no right to ask more of life than our rainy hour in the Inn of the Red Eagle, maybe that is the justification for the vast structure of life on earth.

Those maybes lead on to the final passage in Koning's *Little Book*. Adapted from his '70s memoir, *The Almost World*, it's a perfect envoi:

> Most of our novels, our music, our films, our theater, is about love, love triumphant or love defeated. In modern life the mechanics are so much simpler: think how many novels and plays would be torpedoed by such inventions as contraception and free abortion. But the basic drama of love remains. It remains our utmost experience, the only breach in the wall of solitude surrounding each one of us.

> And there is something so much more to it than sexuality, passions, jealousies, suspicions. Whatever its psychic or bodily origin, theirs is something here of great happiness, deadly sadness, tenderness, nostalgia, regret. Our love of love is perhaps a longing we are born with, or a longing back to our very beginnings,

image-memories of being put to bed on summer days when the sun was still high, the swish of a curtain drawn by your mother, her soft voice in the hallway outside your door.

Who Killed Our Little Shani

Amiri Baraka

Who Killed Amina & Amiri Baraka
Who Killed Our Little Shani?

Who Killed Amina & Amiri Baraka's little Shani
Who killed our youngest child, our baby?
Our little Shani.

Everyday of her thirty-two years when ever I saw Shani I'd say "Shani little!" Playing ball in the backyard, coming home from school, eating a sandwich in the kitchen or dressed up and ready to go out with her parents. Same thing, "Shani little!" And she was very little. But that never stopped nothing. Not with Shani!

But don't get off the subject. Who killed our little Shani? Like that poem the terrorists in the Caucasian crib don't like, WHO? I ask it again in the most humble way. I ask it for her mother, my wife, Amina, for her brothers and sisters, her aunts and uncles, her nieces and nephews, for all the people who loved her, all the people who loved our little Shani. For her gay friends and her straight ones. All us wanna know who killed our little Shani. But even more important is Why? did something kill our little Shani? As little as she was we know you didn't have to kill her. Not if some big our bad macho man. Like one killed her aunt my sister, Kimako, back in 1983. Is this some twenty-year cycle of horror for our family? For everybody, that every twenty years some wonderful and surprising woman gets murdered by some insecure ignorant homophobic Negro Punk (and not the heavy metal kind!). Perhaps because we get women pregnant, and when the baby comes, will not marry them. Maybe because we have left unknown numbers of fatherless children scattered across the planet. Maybe we have married but betray our wives with Adultery.

So maybe we have more than a clue to Who killed our little Shani! Why do we think that? Because it was just such a Negro who couldn't stand non-passive self-consciously Independent Black women. Our little Shani was just such. So was her special friend and companion, Ray Ray Holmes. When you saw one you usually saw the other. That's why they were found side by side when this Negro Frankenstein murdered them.

You know they didn't want to die, but even so, from the way it was described, you know Shani probably told that Negro something he didn't want to hear. So he shot her straight in the heart! I guess he wanted her to be like him and have a hole where his heart should'a been!

And that's why Ray Ray had two bullets in her, because when he shot Shani, Ray Ray enraged, must have tried to rip the eyes out of his head, so he shot her two times. NO, Shani and Ray Ray loved life. All yall know that. They didn't want to die, but if they had to die, that's the way they wd have preferred it, side by side. Like they were in real life!

That's the Who and the How, except about that Who, there's some deeper Smack than that!

This particular Homophobic Ignorant Negro, who from this point will be called HIN, was so backward he did not understand separation and divorce. He was so backward his view was that women had no right to divorce, unless the man initiated it. So he was actually an 18th-century HIN. He also believed that women had to do only what men dictated and nothing else. HIN hates most, aggressive intelligent black women who have some ideas of their own and openly express them, even in contradiction to HIN.

So that when Shani's sister Wanda wanted a divorce from this HIN, he refused to believe it really mattered. What does a black woman know? She should have no say in the matter. So HIN refused to leave even when he was made to.

But he would not. He returned by dirty threatening phone calls. A great many women have that experience. Sick men harassing them. Wanda called the police. HIN returned this time to burn Wanda's car. She reported him again. He would come back to climb on her roof. Shoot holes in her pool. And in the most dangerous act prior to Shani and Ray Ray's murder, he put a gun to Wanda's head and told her he would kill her so he could become famous.

Wanda then filed 12 reports with the Piscataway police about this black woman-hating man. Twelve reports. She called them again and again. But it was only some nigger women. What do they know? We know there is a struggle for women's rights across the U.S., but we should also know that black women are triply oppressed by nationality (race), class and gender. One of the ugliest examples of this, and this is something Fidel Castro read to us from a United Nations Report, is that in the history of the United States, there has never been a single White man convicted of Raping a Black woman! In the U.S. there are many Negroes whose minds fit the perpetrator's description!

Our hope is that our new Police Director in Newark is working to correct this hideous aberration. Imagine the Police and the Murderer have the same Philosophy. We know because the 12 reports to the police were mainly ignored. Even when the HIN put a gun to Wanda's head, the Piscataway police ho hummed and did nothinged my daughter and Ray Ray into their graves.

The gob of spit that murdered our little Shani and Ray Ray killed them because they were Black, because they were women, because they were workers, because they did not live off stocks and bonds and other people's misery. But he also killed them because he thought they loved each other and this fake human felt it was wrong for these two women to love each other, to want to be together rather than with him or with other men, black or white, like him. So this homophobic male chauvinist Negro hated them even more for that. For what he saw as a crime of being Gay, and rejecting his sorry Ignorant and very dangerous homophobic male chauvinist self. I imagine, particularly when he burst into the house where the two sisters, Wanda and our little Shani lived. And anybody who really knew Shani know exactly what Shani would have told him. Straight up. Right in his face. Like she did to her brothers all those years she played round ball in our back yard and perfected her game.

Who killed our little Shani, a dangerous psychotic Negro murderer who was anti-woman anti anti-black women, that's what we mean by Male Chauvinist. Not just the word, but the most dangerous example of it, its not quite human personification. What killed our little Shani? What killed Newark Public Schools' little Shani. What killed the little Shani who was all city point guard at University High School, the little Shani at Johnson C. Smith University who was the Most Valuable Player and best Point Guard in the CIAA, the little Shani who was an honorable mention member of the Eastman Kodak All American Team, 1993 Co-Player of the Year, who still graduated Magna Cum Laude. Both the Who and the What that killed our little Shani, are deadly chauvinist homophobic murderers. As persons or philosophies. And little Shani and Ray Ray's murders confirm this.

The God of Rough Places

Fr. Rick Frechette

Fr. Frechette, a doctor and Catholic priest, has worked in Haiti for a generation.

February 24 (2004), Eve of Ash Wednesday

I cannot tell many people such stories but I also cannot keep them inside.

We were called to come right away to Wharf Jeremy this morning, the terrible slum area where we work Wednesdays (in fact we go tomorrow—we have started a school for 100 children there and a small program for disabled children, in addition to our medical clinic). We were called today because during the night a man offered 18 people—men, women and children—places in a boat to the USA. Many Haitians, running away from the violence, set out from the small wharf for Jamaica or USA, leaving at night so they are not seen by American boats that are out in the sea to turn them back.

After the 18 people had paid all the money they had to the man, and they got in the boat, he shot them all in the head.

So this morning I was called to pray over the dead. Some were on the beach in the hot sun, some were still floating in the water and a small canoe was trying to fish them out and drag them to shore. It was pathetic, horrible and sad. Sadder still to see children, with frozen faces, looking at the bodies.

Anyway after praying I wanted to put them in body bags and bring them to the morgue, but the people told me the police would not allow me to do that. They said "you will see, when you come tomorrow the pigs will be eating these bodies"….

March 6 (2004), Second Sunday of Lent,
the Transfiguration of Jesus

As Ash Wednesday approached last week, I wrote about being called to bless the bodies of a number of poor people who were savagely killed after giving their life-savings to get a place on a boat heading for Miami. It was a poor, rickety boat that, for them, meant hope and deliverance. They were deceived, betrayed and murdered, and their rotting bodies were washed up on the shore of a fetid slum. It was a very dark moment. My only thought, as I stood aghast, was how to bring some dignity to this nightmare. Focusing the attention of all present on a prayer for the dead, and for a better future, was all I could do. I carefully blessed each one with holy water. And then, as I was leaving, I was approached by a fierce-looking stranger whose manner put me on my guard, and then to my great surprise, he thanked me for coming to pray and said how important it is that goodness not perish. Suddenly, in that darkness, there was an amazing light, just like in the Transfiguration of Jesus. "Lord, it is good for us to be here." Yes, it was absolutely good to be there, and to see this man's faith and hope shine brightly.

Let me get the worse things over with. I also mentioned in that reflection I was told that when I came back, I would see the pigs eating those bodies. I did go back to Wharf Jeremy, as I always do on Wednesdays. But I had no intention of going to the shoreline where the bodies were. I had already offered, several times, to bury them—but it is interference with the State to do so. However, even without intending to go near the shoreline, fate had another plan. There, on the very road to the wharf, I had to stop the truck because of a bunch of pigs blocking our way. As I approached, I was horrified at what I saw, with my own eyes. We jumped out of the truck and chased the pigs away with stones. This was a different body—and there were many of them scattered in the area—bodies of people who had been killed while looting the nearby port. We tried once again to bring dignity to what can only be described as a scene right out of hell. Alfonso, Sister Lorraine, Malherbe and I rolled what was left of the body into a white body bag, chased the pigs off again, and once more offered prayers for the dead, and for a better future. I have heard Haiti referred to as a failed state. In the face of things like this, that is the understatement of the year.

To complicate the darkness even more, I soon learned that the man whose remains we tried to honor, was one of the three men who betrayed and killed the people in the boat. I could feel welling up within me the urge to rejoice in such a bad ending for him. But this is also NOT God's way, nor is it the way of light. I could only shake my head, so rattled by the strength of the culture of death, at the ferociousness of evil and how it devours those who enter into it. I remember in Dante's *Inferno*, every punishment fit the sin precisely, and they were pretty frightening images. This man's ending and his sin were well matched, but this is so not because of the nature of God, but rather because of the nature of evil. I thought of God's warning to Cain: the power of evil crouches at the door like a lion, eager to destroy and devour those who enter into sin.

The vast slums of Port-au-Prince are pretty rough places. Yet they are home for hundreds of thousands of people. Most of these are children. If people are there, God is there. After we chased off the pigs and offered our prayer, I raised my head and saw three powerful things. I saw the wind blow the hat off or a woman, and a child run barefoot through the muck to get it for her. I saw a home-made kite, fashioned from twigs and old bags, and many pieces of old string joined together, soaring high above the filth. And I saw the children running to meet us, squealing in joy, as we approached them with our music, our food and our books. Yes, this darkness is filled with countless twinkling stars. They are called children. I think of our home for orphan children in the mountains of Kenscoff. How many people remark it is like an oasis! How we have seen children from places like this recapture their childhood there! But there *must* be a way to help these children cling to their childhood, even in the face of brutish realities and hellish images. The blessings we have at our orphanage ... security, beauty, peace, food, medicines, books ... surely must overflow and reach here. Why not? Here is some great advice from Sister Mary Alban, a Canadian Sister of St. Joseph who has been in Haiti for years. "If it's old and ugly, paint it a bright color. If it's barren, plant a flower. If it's broken, glue it together (or even make something new) with the pieces. If it's garbage, make compost. If they're fighting, sing a song. If they're sick, sit with them on the bed. If they are hungry, make soup."

Guess who is parading into Wharf Jeremy with paints, plants, glue, guitars, medicine, food, and books. We are. And we will do our best to give these children a childhood.

On our way to the poor areas this past week, every day we made an extensive drive around Port-au-Prince in order to look for the wounded. Guardian angels in the form of absolute strangers detoured us away from areas of shooting, parted chanting mobs to let us pass through (as Moses parted the Red Sea), and signaled to us different people in distress. I will tell you about one of them. A man was pushing what we thought was a dead woman in a wheelbarrow. We thought he was heading to the morgue of the general hospital, already overflowing with 200 rotting bodies. We stopped to talk with him, and saw that the woman was not dead. She had been shot in the head *yesterday,* in the shoot-outs in the capital, and he had been wheeling her all around the city *ever since,* looking in vain for help. She was nearly dead, and beyond saving. But we took her to a private hospital and paid all the bills for the best care they could give her. A visiting doctor chided me: she needs the home for the dying, not a hospital. I replied, "I am not putting her in the hospital for her, I am putting her in the hospital for her husband." To me it was very important that her husband see that someone did everything possible for his wife, against all odds. Why? Because for me, he was the brightest light in Port-au-Prince that day, giving us an incredible witness of fidelity and love.

The holy ancient writers tell us that the purpose of the Transfiguration, when Christ's face shone out as radiant as the sun, was to strengthen the apostles for the terrible darkness of Calvary, that would

come before the Resurrection. It didn't work. Most of Christ's followers, including the first Pope, ran off in terror, just as most of us would
have done. But that doesn't make the reality of the Transfiguration any
less true. Every word of the Bible is written for today, not yesterday.
Beneath the most ordinary, or the most difficult, or the most brutish
situations of life there is a light for us to see, and it bears a wondrous
message of God's love. It is always there, as a gift, when we pray for
the right eyes to see it.

The Hidden Face

Donna Gaines

A contribution to a First *forum on 9/11 ("Five Years On") published
in September, 2006.*

Five years later, two images from 9/11/2001 compete in my memory.
The first is the image of a friend, a musician named Johnny Bully. The
morning of 9/11 he kissed his wife and kid goodbye and rode into NYC
from Middle Village on his Harley. He had the day off, but he needed the
overtime. An hour later Johnny Bully aka Fire Fighter John Heffernan
was crushed as the second tower went down. Like so many people, I
wondered, where was God as the concrete and steel pummeled another
Rockaway hero.

But there's a second image from that day—of the American workforce
drifting up First Avenue from WTC in droves, ties flapping in the wind,
suits, high heels, blue collar, white collar, carrying briefcases, jackets,
water bottles, marching North towards the 59th Street Bridge homeward
bound. The American people, all races, sexes, classes, nationalities, religions and regions of the world. Everywhere, neighbors, shopkeepers offering water, prayers, sneakers, food, and loving-kindness. We assembled
on street corners, bound together in one moment. Up from Ground Zero,
one nation, one race, one wound, one scar, one fate. Slowed down, we
saw each other. One soul, one life, one love. That was God on 9/11.

Part IX

Where Were You...

First's editors, longtime New Yorkers, were fully alive to experiences of love and death on 9/11. We printed a set of responses to the attacks that implicitly contradicted those who assumed "anti-Americanism is a necessity" (without imposing a patriotic litmus test). Our post-9/11 issue featured red, white, and blue colors above the fold. Though that wasn't a simple flag-waving gesture. The exemplary Americans (and New Yorkers) invoked on our cover were Latinos and Afro-Americans: La Lupe, Eddie Palmieri, and Jay-Z.

This section is devoted to material from our 9/11 issue. I think it displays our commitment to candor and variousness. Most readers welcomed *First*'s openness. (Historian Christine Stansell spoke for them: "Your Sept 11 issue was the only thoughtful response I saw from the left.") But there would be drop-outs from *First*'s community of contrarians. Unwilling to stomach our readiness to give equal time to writers who supported a "just" War on Terror, Charles Keil quit writing for *First*. (See p. 382 in the "*First* Draft of History" section for his last word on *First*.)

That was a heavy loss for our tab. Keil's wonderfully fervent writing on musicking and participatory consciousness helped provide early *First*s with a cultural program that soundtracked our radical democratic politics and moved readers to step up ("Dance Early! Dance Daily! Dance Now!"). It was a heavy personal loss too: the "great" Charlie Keil (to quote a heroic epithet applied to him without irony by another original thinker/groover) is a great guy. A few days after 9/11, I found myself feeling a little panicky after a mad subway ride with ominous delays, smoke on the tracks, rumors of bias attacks on the platforms. I didn't want to worry my fam and I would've felt small if I'd called friends in the city because nothing, after all, had happened to me. So I telephoned Charlie Keil in Connecticut who heard me out and calmed me down like an unmacho mensch should.

Keil's first response to 9/11 ("Waging Peace") is placed beside Charles O'Brien's ("The War") here. The two Charlies would argue things out in a later issue of *First*. I wish to hell they were still fighting for clarity in our pages.

Skies Over America

Wendy Oxenhorn

Right now I am looking out my window, listening to planes—they sound a little louder than before—and I wonder if I am right to stay here and go to my work each day, to send my children to school each day. Every evening, I take my daughters out to a café—I see people in my neighborhood and we all stop to talk a little more than usual and laugh nervously and embrace those we hadn't seen since before all this changed. I am torn. I like this new solidarity, this new seizing of every moment. There is something beautiful in this strange fear-based appreciation that causes me to dance in the street with my child as a car goes by blasting salsa, to speak a bit more frankly to people without trying to find the "right words," to find a beautiful dress to wear even though I'm just going to the grocery store, to let go of my world, to stop right now as I'm writing to you and feel the wind coming into my room and the morning light that is touching me as I write, the sky is amazing. I have to stop writing and take a look at it.

There are enormous white clouds reflecting the most glorious gold light and they are remaining completely still, while smaller clouds below are being blown across them by strong winds. They look like hundreds of people running, yet those white clouds, those magnificent light-reflecting clouds just remain, in perfect peace. There is a sea gull flying alone, enjoying this moment of freedom, unaware of my thoughts, unaware of the people below who are in their homes, thinking what I am thinking now. He continues to fly, unaware that I am watching my sleeping child and wondering if we will be together when something else happens.

The sky just got gray and the sun is hidden, everything looks dark, there's another plane overhead and it's remarkable how much louder they sound now. A huge crow just perched himself outside my window, and he's screaming at me. I'm not sure if he's yelling at me to get the hell out of New York now, of if he came to wake me up from this dream I am having and remind me that this is all just part of the plan—how can I be wasting this glorious morning with such rambling thoughts, when there is a day to be lived.

All the noises have stopped. There is a strange quietness. No planes, no birds, no thoughts. Maybe I'll go back to sleep for just a little while longer.

Crisis of Meaning

Peter Lamborn Wilson

A few days after the event, *The New York Times* ran an interesting article on the advertising "industry" and its crisis. Not only zillions of dollars a day etc. etc., but a weird effect: suddenly it seems impossible to have advertising at all. It seems massively "inappropriate" to move product as per usual with shrieking & insinuating, mocking & sneering, prurience & peeping; with hate & envy masked as fashion, with greed thinly disguised as freedom of choice.

Death and tragedy occur every day, every minute, not only in the former Third World, even in New York, even in America. Why hasn't advertising ever seemed shameful to anyone ever before? The media—which cannot utter a sound without puking up a cliché—speaks now of the waking of a sleeping giant (meaning that we will no longer tolerate terrorism etc.)—but what was this sleep? And what does it mean to wake into a feeling of shame?

Last week, it seems we were willing to admit that our highest social values could be expressed in price codes (the "mark of the Beast" as the cranks say, the "prophets of doom"). This week, we feel shame. In a *Times* interview a fashion designer expressed doubt that her work had any significance and wondered if she could go on with it.

The fashion industry is also ashamed; Hollywood is ashamed; even the news media expressed some fleeting longing for decorum & dignity & decency.

Are we supposed to feel this shame over our triviality, our mean-spiritedness, our PoMo irony, our consumer frenzy, our hatred of the body and of all nature, our obsession with gadgetry & "information," our degraded pop culture, our vapid or morbid art & lit, & so on & so on?—or should we defend all this as "freedom" and our "way of life?"

Our leaders are telling us to return to normal routines (after a decent period of mourning) in the assurance that they will assign significance to the event, they will embody our hate & desire for revenge, they will mediate for us with the forces of "evil." But what exactly is this normal life to consist of? Why do we feel this shame?

Schoolchildren (again according to the *Times*) ask their teachers what it means that the terrorists were willing to die, to kill themselves; and their teachers evade the question, saying that "we don't understand." And the ad execs, they don't understand either—they're bewildered. Awake but confused by a crisis of meaning. Last week all meanings could be expressed in terms of money. Why should 5000 murders change the meaning of meaning?

A hyper-fashionable Italian clothing company uses death to sell its products. Photographs—even huge billboards—showing people dying of AIDS or waiting to be executed—designed to sell woolly jumpers. In this life as normal? Should we return to it?

For a few days no music was heard in the streets. No thumping bass speakers rattled the air, no chants of hate for women & queers, no "Madison Avenue Choirs" hymning the celestial delites of commodities or vacations in the midst of other peoples' misery.

For a few hours or days there appeared no official spin on the event, no slogan/logo in the media, no interpretation, no meaning. We watched the cloud drift around the city, first to the East over Brooklyn then up the west side of Manhattan, finally over the east side as well. With the smell and the poisonous haze around the moon came a nightmare abut the occult significance of the cloud:—angry bewildered ghosts in a vast white cloud. And we breathed that cloud into us. We'll never get it out of our lungs. What the cloud wanted was an explanation, a meaning.

But next day the spin was in, the media had found or been given its answer—"Attack On America," our freedom, our values, our way of life, carried out by "cowards" who were nevertheless not "physical cowards" (as some official explained in the *Times*). Perhaps they were moral cowards? He didn't say.

Why do they hate us? A few people have asked but received no coherent answer. Do "they" hate "us" because we use 75 percent of the world's resources even though we only constitute 20 percent of its population?, because we bomb Baghdad & Belgrade without risking even one American life?, because we export a vapid sneering mean-spirited culture to the world, video games about death, movies about death, TV shows about death, commodities that are dead, music that kills the spirit?, because we've made advertising copy our highest artform?, because we define "freedom" as our freedom to rule & be ruled by money?

The politicians have told that "they" envy us and our way of life and therefore wish to destroy it. Envy—yes, why not? The whole system of global capital is based on envy. It has to be. No envy, no desire. No desire, no reason to spend. No reason to spend, implosion of global capital, q.e.d. But then why should the ad execs & fashion designers & sports teams & entertainers feel this strange unaccountable shame?

And why should the terrorists have been willing to die just because they envy our wealth & our way of life & our freedom to buy, and spend, and waste? What does it mean?

After the Holocaust (or Hiroshima, or the Gulag) certain philosophers said that there could be no more art or poetry. But they were wrong apparently. We have poetry again. It may not mean the same thing it meant before. It may not mean anything. But we have it. And who could have dreamed at the gate of Buchenwald or Treblinka that one day we would have—Nike ads or sitcoms about lawyers?

Is any meaning going to emerge from the 9/11 event? Without meaning tragedy ends not in catharsis but simply depression, endless sorrow. Our leaders "seek closure"—perhaps by killing many Afghan children—perhaps by a new Crusade against the Saracens—and of course by a return to normal. We'll show "them"—by refusing meaning. We will sleep because it is our right not to awake to confusion & shame.

Our sleep will be troubled. We'll have to "sacrifice a few freedoms" to protect Freedom. We'll have to fear & hate. But within a few weeks or months we will have buried even the fear & hate, rather we will have transformed all that emotion to the Image, to the Evil Eye of the media, our externalized unconscious. We'll have sitcoms again and gangster rap and arguments about our right to download it all for free into our home computers. We'll get those airplanes flying, once again polluting "our" skies with noise & carcinogens. We'll overcome our shame. And that will constitute our revenge. That will be our meaning. Our morality.

Citizen Jay-Z

Armond White

Jay-Z is a "citizen" in that specialized sense that the movie *Starship Troopers*—a delirious cautionary fantasy on war and patriotism—distinguished from "civilian." ("What is the moral difference, if any, between a civilian and a citizen? A citizen accepts personal responsibility for the safety of the body politic, defending it with his life. A civilian does not.") This pop-satirical "citizen," willing to fight for his or her people, country, planet and species (an expansive universalism), defines hiphop's highest ideas of how an artist earns privilege and esteem.

Always projecting fraternity, Jigga (as Jay-Z immortalized himself on the 1999 track "Jigga My Nigga"), seeks artistic solidarity for his civilian self (nee Shawn Carter of East Trenton, N.J.). He does it through such identities as "Jigga Man" or his current parodistic-sanctimonious badge "Hova" (as in Jehovah), but especially through music. Biggie Small's death cleared the field but through terrific, under-appreciated craft, Jay-Z has ascended to the top of the rap pack. The ultimate test of Jay's citizenship took place when his new album *The Blueprint* dropped (music industry lingo for premiered) on September 11. Better than an old school "Prophet of Rage," Jay-Z proved he was, simply, ready. An exemplary American artist-citizen.

In the midst of the confusion most Americans feel post-Sept. 11, track 5, "Jigga That N***a," took on uncanny resonance. "If y'all got love for me/I got love for y'all/And if y'all go to war for me/I go to war wit' y'all," Jay-Z rapped. Coincidentally, members of socially conscious rap groups Black Star and The Roots have gone on record opposing black participation in military action after 9/11—received wisdom from the Vietnam/Civil Rights era (a time before most practicing rappers were even born). Without going political, Jay-Z remains practical. "What you're about to witness is just my thoughts. Right or wrong it's what I was feeling at the time," he says on the album's now timeless introduction. His artistry is defined by his capacity to evoke the felt quality of contemporary black street and home culture.

Increasingly prolific and popular, Jay-Z has turned back the reign of gangster rap by mellowing such rancid sentiments as "We don' love them hos." His all-star album *The Dynasty* featuring Snoop Dogg, R. Kelly, Beanie Siegel and others is full of songs that blend social hostility into harmony. A kinder, gentler thug, Jay-Z takes you back to the origins—forgotten by Black Star and The Roots—of loyalty and solidarity (nascent forms of patriotism).

Jay-Z's "I go to war wit' y'all" expresses the opposite of the disagreement and fractiousness usually heard in rap records. Instead of neo-black nationalism, Jay-Z promises to return the favor of protection and defense. It's an instinctive oath rather than an intellectualized, ideological response but the implied fidelity, learned from living a street life and interpreting it, is as good as any political commitment. That faith is kept in the phrase's sing-song rhythm and Jay-Z's virtually patriotic assertion, "He is I and I am him."

Personally redeeming the term "nigga" (a mountain to be scaled on some future expedition), "Jigga That N***a" is all about building one's self-esteem and defending one's life. "He is I and I am him" comes out of Jay-Z's sense of family—as does his knack for the popular which is evident in *The Blueprint*'s marvelous choice of samples. Reaching out towards brothers everywhere, Jay-Z complicates rap's typical bellicosity: "Sensitive thugs y'all all need hugs." Better than some politicians or the black intellectuals and careerists who ride hiphop's coattails, Jay-Z understands his pop moment is a cultural phase that he'd best make the most of and do his best with—an occasion for pride plus largesse: "I know you waitin' in the wings/But I'm doin' my thing."

I

Jay-Z's thing protects and defends the range of African American life. His influence was unmistakable on last year's "This Can't Be Life." when his guest-artist Scarface, of Houston's Geto Boys, got surprisingly churchy and testified: "I could have rapped my hard times in this song/But heaven knows I wouldn't been wrong/It would't been right/It wouldn't been love/It wouldn't been life." Each song on *The Blueprint*—poised between the Tough and Tender—comprehends habits and attitudes germane to Black American experience. Unconfused in the current upheaval over flagwaving vs. patriotism, *The Blueprint* lays out the essence of Black American life others have garbled. Jay-Z doesn't need to show stars and stripes (or green, black and red) because, his inherently recognizable drama is more than political, and, for open-minded listeners, it transcends borders. There's no part of the pop universe that is unavailable to Jay-Z for sampling and improving: The Doors on "The Takeover," (even turning David Bowie's "Fame" into "Lame"); The Jackson Five on "Izzo;" Al Green on the title track; Bobby "Blue" Bland on "Heart of the City." This is the world-conquering hiphop achievement first defined in Jay-Z's summer 2000 single, the irresistible "Big Pimpin"—one that Sean "Puffy" Combs has tried for but only partially pulled off on record. (Puffy's exploits on Wall Street and in the Hamptons are more resonant than his raps.) *The Blueprint* is a call-out to whoever imagines themselves in the hiphop Community—which would be all those who can find their way into these uniquely constructed, startlingly affecting tracks. Hearing one of the cuts on the street coming out of a car stereo or a radio, you get the redoubtable feel of American community.

Appreciating Jay-Z's art in the face of a conventional rap screed like DMX's "Who We Be" requires re-orienting oneself to the particular sensations associated with the making of a social identity. You have to feel Jay-Z's accounts of the struggle to sustain a self—his fight to hang on to

integrity within society and despite the music industry's constant challenges. DMX tries to do this through now-co-opted, formulaic anger; *The
Blueprint* clarifies this issue of authenticity in the course of articulating
Jay-Z's artistic crisis. The song that digs deepest into his psyche is "Girls,
Girls, Girls" (even moreso than "Takeover"—the amazing throwdown to
less talented rappers like Nas and Mobb Deep who should not leave the
house now that Jay-Z's whipped them). In this romance, Jay-Z enters male
hiphop's especial kingdom of the baller-mackdaddyhood. "Girls, Girls,
Girls" is not a self-regarding, heterosexual pronouncement (like Lou
Reed's fatuous "I Love Women" from 1982's *The Blue Mask*); Jay-Z raps
like his favorite women are inside him. (The album's closing, title track
"Blueprint: Momma Loves Me" is "Girls, Girls, Girls'"complement.)
He appreciates that they provide his cultural backbone (pace Chaka
Khan). Jay-Z's self-examination through the Other recalls nothing in
popular culture so much as Fellini's *8+*, especially Guido's harem sequence where assorted women from the artist-hero's history reappear
in his imagination, forcing him to rethink his past and his objectives. It
begins "Je t'adore Jay-Z"—like Prince's "Boys and Girls"—but goes
on to relay the international pleasures of hiphop experience (joy packed
into the way Jay-Z's ascending notes boast about being on tour as "on
tah!"). Having risen out of the ghetto, he expresses his pride in vernacular
dialect. The Spanish, French, Indian, Chinese, African, even the project
chick—so many girls across the globe, foreign yet specific—evoke Rick
Nelson's "Travelin' Man" as well as the Beach Boys' "California Girls."
A smorgasbord that reverberates like a recurring dream of affirmation
tied to cross-cultural achievement. If the song's Tom Brock quote ("This
world!") sounds androgynous, that only serves to hint at the range of
Jay-Z's cultural allegiances. The echoing (female) voice derives from the
same pop vocabulary Green Gartside employed in Scritti Politti's "The
Word 'Girl.'" It's a tune we all whistle, acknowledging pop's generic
romantic ideology, a predominantly male hierarchy.

Pop's ubiquitous courtliness communicates to men as well as women,
conveying a fluid gender appreciation. (A ploy used last year on "Parking Lot Pimping's" all-girl Jay-Z chorus, "You can catch me in the
parking lot/Hollerin' at bitches/Parking lot pimpin'/ Everyday we be
off the chains/Workin' with brains/Sittin' on things.") So the backing
vocals heard on "Girls, Girls, Girls" not only echo sexy enthusiasm,
they express a star's sweetest appreciation and -despite the gender-spe-
cific details—affirm a multivalent affection for his audience. The "Ahh,
Babys" that well-up after Jay-Z's grateful rap are also an encourage-

ment. Jay-Z's rapping could be praised for its Joycean quotidian (parse the orgiastic lines, "Hopefully they menage before I reach my garage") yet a more apt and laudatory comparison is to Biggie Small's ingenious wordplay. Jay-Z extends hiphop's tradition of uncommon creativity through common language. "Girls, Girls, Girls" is animated by Jay-Z's sense of beauty and by an r&b aesthetic which doesn't simply conform to hegemonic patterns of storytelling or pop songwriting. Men, women, gays and straights can hear how "Girls, Girls, Girls" catches an esprit de corps—and that's what makes Jay-Z a citizen.

II

Consider "Izzo." It's a new kind of sing-a-long—ineffably infectious like 1998's "Hard Knock Life," which borrowed from the Broadway musical *Annie* for the truest, subtlest expression of Black/Jewish solidarity; one in which common American experience of struggle, uplift and entitlement were explicated through established musical institutions (Broadway meeting Hiphop). The children's voices on "Hard Knock Life" underscored a cross-cultural truth—not every "Annie" is a red-haired white girl. Jay-Z's child's play countered injustice and was practically a civic virtue, justifying hiphop by linking it to another cultural tradition. That's also the charm of *The Blueprint*'s "Heart of the City" where Jay-Z's accounts of black pop history—"First the Fat Boys break up ... Biggie's death.... And then The Fugees go break up.... Then Richard Pryor go and burn up, and Ike and Tina Turner break up"—allude to parallel instances of social heartache and dolor. These tricky cultural references prove Jay-Z's got the moral goods to measure life by hiphop standards. He rebukes jealousy ("Respect the game/That should be it/What you eat don't make me shit") and reasserts his personal imperatives—"I got nephews to look after/I'm not lookin' at you I'm lookin' past you"). His pride isn't simply boastful ("I told you '96 I came to take this shit and I did/Jigga held you down six summers, damn!/Where's the love?") but magnanimously acknowledges the pressures of everyone's everyday life.

Bearing up under those pressures is what prepares one for patriotism, citizenship. *The Blueprint* is engaged with the difficulties of social life. The final track, "The Blueprint (Momma Loves Me)," is Jay-Z's shout-out number, but it's also his It-Takes-A-Village song. Familial love replaces the stridency of rap's cliche radicals and gangsters. Here, finally, is a true depiction of African American striving ("just make the transition from the streets to the fame") that most rap artists sell-out and falsify for commercial success. Jay-Z refuses to distort or abuse hiphop;

he doesn't romanticize this cultural form by treating it as an excuse for manifestos against racist oppression or turf wars. ("Song Cry" is the first composition by a hiphop artist that consciously uses music to express the inexpressible.) Jay-Z's interest in the particulars of enjoyment and struggle clarify what is worth fighting for in this life (and in this country). There's no way Jay-Z could have planned *The Blueprint* as a response to 9/11 but it stands up beautifully in the aftermath because he has found a way to make art out of America's complexity.

Waging Peace

Charles Keil

I'm all for enduring freedoms here and worldwide. I'm for finite human justice, "patient justice" (Bush) as a path toward peace, and Gaia's Infinite Justice too. I want terrorists, war criminals, mass murderers of all sorts turned over to a world court for trials and punishment. Sometimes I can think I'm on the same page with key slogans in a Bush speech and the shifts in overall administration rhetoric often seem to be seeking a better direction, a proper multilateral response, an alliance that will work. I would really like to feel unified with my fellow Americans and with world citizens who are seeking justice, freedom, freedom from fear, peace, democracy, all the good goals.

But it's called "America's New War" in the corporate sponsored media campaign. "War" of some kind is just assumed by our politicians to be the obvious response to this terrorism. It is not.

None of the possibly good reasons for airstrikes or sending in an army or police force—to stop genocide? to stop fascist aggression?—can be applied here. And, perhaps more important, none of the bad or greedy reasons for war apply either. This time we can NOT protect our oil supplies in the Middle East by going to war. This time we can NOT revive our economy and world capitalism by going to war. This time we can NOT win or control "the enemy," claim enemy turf or destroy the enemy's capacity for violence with conventional or unconventional warfare. They are not located in any one place. They are few and far between. Many small needles in many very big haystacks. What if we got super lucky and hit Sammy B. Laden and his entire gang with the very first bomb dropped somewhere? Instant Martyrs inspiring generations of terrorists. His tapes will be dubbed and distributed widely. Even if the very first miraculous mission by special forces brought a bunch of terrorists back alive in some helicopters for a fair trial? We still could not possibly win a war against terrorism.

The suicidal maniacs are spread around. Could be anywhere. Are everywhere. They don't need orders or a plan from a center anywhere. They need $3 box cutters. They don't need to know how to take off or land. They need $100 to bribe the guy who gives licenses to carry hazardous materials in a truck. Under present circumstances any terrorists caught or rounded up can easily be replaced. And with a war of any kind, many more terrorists are likely to be produced. And not only from a few dozen countries in the Muslim world. It only takes two (Tim M. and his friend), or a few pals, or even just one person home alone (Ted K.), a tiny splinter group from a Chinese cult or a Japanese clique, a few smart skinheads in Dresden or Budapest, an angry little cell or faction within any one of almost 200 nationalist states or within any of the over 1000 ethnic groups oppressed within those nationalist states? angry Kurds, angry Tutsi, angry East Timorese, angry Basques, angry any one person anywhere....

Once you put yourself to sleep counting angries jumping over security fences, then you can wake up and starting counting crazies. And when you have finished with angry man scenarios, and crazy man scenarios, think of the angry and crazy women who can bring down half the sky more easily than men—would a cute, blond farmgirl-looking pilot have any trouble renting a cropduster tomorrow?

War won't work any more at all and terrorism will work better and better with every passing day, because of one very simple fact: increasing complexity.

Let me repeat it a few times for emphasis, because it is a fact that doesn't seem to be registering quickly enough with the Overcentralized Intelligence Agency and our leaders.

War won't work any more at all, and terrorism will work better and better with every passing day, because of one very simple fact: increasing complexity.

War won't work any more at all, and terrorism will work better and better with every passing day, because of one very simple fact: increasing complexity.

The system has become too complex, too intertwined, too vulnerable in over a million ways. You, whoever you are reading this, have already imagined in your head at least 2 or 3 ways in which one person acting alone, or just a few people acting together, could produce a more horrible day for the USA than what happened on Sept. 11.

Once the global economy, global communications, global resource depletions, global invention of new chemicals, global productions of new bacteria, new viruses, new prions, new technologies for spreading everything to everyone (make that 2 simple facts, increasing complexity and lots more bio-engineered bad stuff) have gotten to the stage we reached on Sept. 11, all the big tech war machinery is worse than useless.

What can we do? We can declare peace anytime. Enact peace. Be peace. Each of us. Now. And as we transform ourselves we transform the military industrial oil-based economy into a peacetime sustainable economy. Some will do this out of idealism or religious obligation or from spiritual awakening. Others will do this out of pragmatism and realpolitik. Machiavellian motivation to seize whatever power remains might easily motivate peace work at this time. Honest patriotism and just wanting to do something could bring millions of Americans to a peace and justice plan of action.

War won't work against terrorism. Peace will. Waging peace will create jobs. Waging peace will bring European and Japanese investors back to America. Waging peace will make friends and trading partners for America throughout the globe. Waging peace will put capital to work in productive, life affirming, sustainable ways that solve the major problems of our times. Waging war in this new era does the opposite of all this. Loss of jobs. Loss of overseas investors. Loss of capital. Loss of trading possibilities. Rippling losses in all directions. We can do comprehensive peace work in place of a stupid war that can only be a loss-loss-loss-loss situation.

Waging peace will stop terrorism the only way it can be stopped, by giving everyone a minimum but absolutely necessary faith in the way things work: mass murderers will be brought to justice, the biggest thieves will be caught, justice will be witnessed in the light of public space and people will be able to "keep the faith" just enough to not want to commit suicide while taking a lot of people with them.

No guarantees here. But we can try to heal the angries, soothe the crazies, defuse fanaticism, pray that no serious accidents will happen as the already released pollutants combine in new ways, as the already released radiation speeds up mutation, as the already bio-engineered creatures make their way thru the environment and start shaping an evolutionary process that used to be Gaia's alone.

We need about $225-250 billion a year to give the world exactly what it wants (see below), to actually save the world, to end terrorism, to move into sustainable economics and a balanced ecology, to have the broad parameters for peace and justice in place.

Selling off half of GE's stock value ($500 billion) would pay for it the first year.

Coca Cola is capitalized at around 110 to 130 billion. Pepsi is worth 60 billion.

Cash in the sugar water kings to pay for the second year. Things could go much better.

Or we could ask each country with a big military budget to give the world a third of their military spending. They would still have 50 billion to waste on useless war machinery.

One way or another, I know we can find the money. And we have to find it all because waging peace MUST be comprehensive on all fronts. If we leave one world problem unsolved, that will cause serious terrorism eventually.

A few years ago the World Game Institute identified 18 fronts and proposed 18 detailed strategies, putting an annual price tag on each to achieve "What the World Wants." Here's their short list of problems along with very approximate costs to solve them as of 1997:

1	Eliminate Starvation and Malnourishment—19 billion per year for ten years
2a	Provide Health Care for All—15 billion per year for ten years
2b	Provide Special Child Health Care
2c	Iodine Deficiency Program
2d	AIDS Prevention and Control Program
3	Eliminate Inadequate Housing and Homelessness—21 billion per year for ten years
4	Provide Clean and Abundant Water—10 billion per year for ten years
5	Eliminate Illiteracy—5 billion a year for ten years
6	Increase Energy Efficiency—33 billion per year for ten years
7	Increase Renewable Energy—17 billion per year for ten years
8	Debt Management—30 billion per year for ten years
9	Stabilize Population—11 billion per year for ten years
10	Preserving Cropland—24 billion per year for ten years
11	Reversing Deforestation—7 billion per year for ten years
12	Reverse Ozone Depletion—5 billion per year for twenty years
13.	Stop Acid Rain—8 billion per year for ten years
14	Reverse Global Warming—8 billion per year for twenty years
15	Removal of Landmines—2 billion per year for ten years
16	Refugee Relief—5 billion per year for ten years
17	Eliminating Nuclear Weapons—7 billion a year for 10 years
18	Building Democracy—2 billion a year for ten years

Note: You could do 15 or 18 for less than it costs to build one B-2 bomber or for less than one half of what the US spends on perfume each year or for 0.025 percent of the world's annual military expenditures.

Go to World Game Institute's website, www.worldgame.org, for the more detailed strategies. Do the math. Write your congressperson.

Everything points toward comprehensive peace-making now, or maybe never.

The War

Charles O'Brien

On September 11, the question whether there would be war was, by 0900 hours, settled. But people didn't know what was needed right away; and so they hurried to give blood, and all the city's hospital beds were made ready for the wounded. Given the peculiarities of this first battle, however, the donors were turned away, and the beds went empty. And a little later, it turned out that not very many body bags could be used, since so many of the dead had been vaporized.

The Vichy Left knew immediately what was necessary. We all needed to have them explain the thing to us. Unfazed, hardly missing a beat, in this time of emergency, they stood prepared to serve up, again, the same mess, again, they had served up, again, only a day before. The standard pitch opened with a ringing—but quick—deploring of the event: ringing, because these gentlemen and ladies of a fancied left habitually talk in such tones (and because, allow them this, their hands really are spotless); and quick, because they had some serious self-congratulation on their minds. It is telling that before getting to the meat of their arguments, they didn't pause to note a thing that was clear to most people: that September 11 also witnessed a great deal of heroism, most obviously the hundreds who sacrificed their lives to save many thousands of others. There were to be no distractions from, in Edward Said's loathsome phrase, "this community of conscience and understanding," secure in the consciousness of its own virtue, snug and smug.

And then, God help us all, came the explanations, explanations to a fare-thee-well; after the fire, the flood. The collective wisdom of the Vichy Left has been a compost of told-you-so's and chickens come home to roost, root causes and deep breaths. Americans, we are assured, have neglected to ask why this happened. But of course, they have done no such thing. The many justifications (as they undeniably were, let the Vichyites deny as they will) offered up by the aspiring collaborationists amounted to no more than the truism that somebody wanted something.

And the justifications came. Poverty caused it, even though the perpetrators were all solidly bourgeois, and the Moslem ultra-right is funded by the largest reserves of unearned wealth in the world. Desperation caused it, even though the perpetrators imagine themselves to be on the cusp of victory. It was American hegemony, even though no one from the Western Hemisphere was involved. It was American political domination, though no one from a NATO or OAS or G8 country did it. It was a protest against American pre-eminence: political (with no Antilleans involved), military (with no Serbs), economic (with no Mexicans), cultural (with no Canadians). It was our checkered past: Wounded Knee (no Native Americans), Dresden (no Germans), Hiroshima (no Japanese), My Lai (no Vietnamese).

We have been asked to reflect on why they hate us—with the suggestion that they're probably right, and in any event, we'd better throw them a bone or two. Wrong answers, wrong questions. It does not appear that the Moslem ultras have visited anything upon us they would spare each other. An Arab state at peace looks like, say, Syria. An Arab state under stress is, say, Lebanon in the '70s, Iraq in the intifada, Algeria in the '90s, Sudan today. The World Trade massacre was conventional Middle Eastern politics, by somewhat unconventional means. It should be no surprise that most Americans would rather be dead, or dogs, than Arab subjects.

There is, of course, no Arab grievance with the United States. Nonetheless, we should pause to consider the imagined hurts of Araby. Noam Chomsky, who insists that the Khmer Rouge have been outrageously maligned and who has branded Vaclav Havel a front man for Central American death squads, has predictably weighed in. And he has outstripped his old hero Faurisson by revising history while the smoke that contained the dead was still overhead. Chomsky advises us that "we can do no better than to listen to the words of Robert Fisk, whose direct knowledge and insight into affairs of the region is unmatched after many years of distinguished reporting." Fisk, our very own Brasillach, a frantic coupling of sub-Hugh Sidey insider knowingness and Karnak the Magnificent ex-oriente-lux posturing, offers this knowledge-and-insight: we are to blame "the lies of T.E. Lawrence" and "our destruction of the Ottoman Empire."

It is alleged that the United States has perpetrated "atrocities" against the Arab world: clearly, fantastically untrue. It is alleged that the United

States has supported or at least done business with, undemocratic regimes. That is true, but who exactly is at fault? It is not as if American troops are keeping the Middle East from being Scandinavia. "Pro-American" and virulently anti-American regimes there are alike anti-democratic. When Edward Said claims, risibly, that the United States is unwilling to have dealings with "secular" regimes, we should recall that the United States is itself such a regime, that every member of NATO is such a regime, that Saddam added some pious scribble to the flag of Iraq precisely in order to combat America, that in Iran, acts of war against the United States and the consolidation of theocracy were a single cause. In sum, other peoples have freed themselves, and these have not.

There are three very specific "wrongs" urged against us: the presence of American troops in Saudi Arabia, the terms of the post-Gulf war cease-fire, and the question of Palestine. Before considering these individually, as they deserve, we should observe how the raising of these issues differs from the more nebulous anti-American tantrums. First, the suggestion is made that if only these issues could be resolved, the war against us would end. It would not. And second, we are assured that the resolution of these issues is something that should be done. The trouble here is that in the present time, after September 11, with ongoing biological warfare, with the certainty of future atrocities, very possibly including one or more nuclear devices, what is proposed is not morality but extortion.

American military personnel have been stationed in Saudi Arabia since the early 1940s. They have never been used, never contemplated to be used, to suppress the national democratic stirrings of the domestic population. Their numbers increased at the time of Desert Shield, and today there are a few thousand left. These troops were sent, initially to protect Saudi Arabia from Iraqi invasion, then as a base for the expulsion of Iraqi forces from Kuwait, and today as a safeguard against a more remote, but still real threat of military conquest by Iraq. The offense offered by the presence of America troops is one neither to the Saudi state, which it preserves against foreign invasion, nor to its disaffected subjects. The objection raised by the aggressors of September 11 has been not to the actions of American soldiers in Saudi Arabia, but their very presence in that putative "holy" land. The crime of the non-Moslem is to exist. It is not happenstance that September 11 was a predominantly Saudi operation. Saudi Arabia is the most viciously apartheid state in the world, and it is only natural that its politics projected militarily into the world is openly genocidal.

Then, too, we are assured that we have behaved deplorably in Iraq. True, but only in not taking Baghdad ten years ago and not executing justice on its rulers. The derisory bombing conducted there is in response to clear cease-fire violations and is, plainly, not enough. It is claimed that we have murdered a million (1,000,000) Iraqi children. The number, of course, corresponds to no reality, but it is true that there has been suffering. But sanctions do that. The very real suffering of the French people was a commonplace of Petainist propaganda; what was unreal was the placing blame on de Gaulle and the British and the Americans and the whitewashing of the Nazis and their native collaborators. Iraq is awash in money, freely spent on luxury items for those in power and for military expenditures. Hunger and shortages of medical supplies in Iraq are only weapons of war used by the Iraqi state against its subject population.

But the main justification offered for September 11—not by its perpetrators, to be sure, but by the extortionists nearer to hand who see the date as Christmas come early—has been the Israeli-Palestinian conflict. There is a real Palestinian grievance, but the Palestinian issue is fraudulent. The 20th century saw many millions dispossessed and slaughtered, made stateless and homeless. Maps of the world don't stay current long. In 1947, for instance, only a year before the nakba of the Palestinian Arabs, around one million people were killed in the course of the creation of a Moslem separatist state in Pakistan. The remark attributed to Hitler, "Who now remembers the Armenians?," has lost none of its force. The rest of humanity may be swept aside. Palestinian Arabs alone have enduring rights, and any atrocity, if claimed to further the redress of those rights, will be claimed to be justified. Palestinians are being "killed," we are constantly being told. But guns are being fired on both sides, and even in grossly unequal contests (e.g. the Warsaw ghetto in 1943, The Warsaw uprising in 1944, Budapest in 1956) that's called fighting. Only Palestinians can be killed because their humanity alone will be acknowledged. To be told that 79 percent of Egyptians—with no rights, no food, no health, no future—regard Palestine as their most pressing problem—Palestine!—is to understand that a decent respect for the opinions of mankind will have the good sense to disregard Egyptian "public opinion" entirely. We certainly did not—and would not—celebrate the massacres at Deir Yassin or Sabra or Shatila, three centerpieces of the permanent Palestinian atrocity exhibition (rendered a little secondary after September 11). They, along with their most ardent sympathizers, applauded our misfortune. By all means, we should acknowledge injustice, and hope for its righting, but more immediately, having seen what we have seen, we should cast a cold eye.

"Specific actions and specific alliances" have nothing to do with September 11. It is not what we did, but what they did. And what they did was initiate, unambiguously, war. September 11 was genocidal means to genocidal ends. There has been a perception, among the enemy, that such measures work, that one must be willing to accept some casualties oneself, but that we will give up once our dead begin to mount. Think of Algeria. The FLN, even with a great deal of foreign support, never came close to defeating France militarily, yet it prevailed. It did so by killing thousands of civilians, the overwhelming majority of them Moslems, and in victory, it drove out the non-Moslem population and expropriated their property, and it conducted a general massacre of the harkis (along with their families). Marines sent to Lebanon to secure the safety of the local Palestinians were killed by a truck bomb, and the American military were withdrawn. In Somalia, 29 Pakistanis and 18 Americans were killed by local allies of al Qa'eda, and the Americans withdrew. The World Trade Center was bombed in 1993, and not a single member of al Qa'eda answered for it with his life. The same is true of the 1998 embassy bombings and of bombings of military targets in Saudi Arabia and Yemen. But soft targets—civilians—are preferred. September 11 ("Hiroshima," as its perpetrators giddily call it) is linked so often with the Palestinian Arab cause because there is a commonality of means. Attacks on international civil aviation have been a Palestinian specialty for over thirty years, and it was entirely in character that when the Achille Lauro was hijacked, the one person selected to be shot, out of the hundreds aboard, was an old man in a wheelchair. And "the heroic struggle of the Palestinian people" today takes the form of suicide bombings of public spaces and random shootings on the roads.

What do our attackers want, and what do their multitudinous sympathizers want? It matters only that, understanding them, we may better frustrate their purposes. But finally, it doesn't matter at all. Political viruses have raged through that part of the world since the 1920s: pro-Hitlerism, Nasserite national socialism, anti-Zionism, the Palestinian cause, "anti-imperialism," Third-World-ism, Third International-ism, alliances with the USSR (in the 1980s!), Ba'thism, Shi'ite triumphalism, Sunni triumphalism, this latest thing. All begin in failure and end in failure. Mohammad Heikel, the pre-eminent Arab journalist of the second half of the 20th century is a representative figure. For many years, he served as Nasser's spokesman, then in the late '70s, he could be heard gushing over Ruhollah Khomeini, in the '80s he was publishing book-length eulogies of the Egyptian jihad. What intellectual integrity is to be found here, going from National Socialism to one fundamentalism to another? Forget what such a man believes, what does he even want? The answer is: September 11. And the wider context for September 11 is not policy changes that will work to everybody's benefit, but further atrocity: more bombings, more torture of captives, more human shields, more, and more effective, biological and chemical weapons, and as logistics allow, nuclear attacks here. A war of genocide has been proposed. It ends when one side dies.

What will that war be? As is usually the case, we don't now know. However much the Civil War was rooted in the question of chattel slavery, the United States did not begin to fight under the banner of emancipation, but the war's end was Lincoln being carried through the streets of Richmond on emancipated shoulders. The Paris Commune, which began with public demolition of the guillotine, ended up driven to shoot hostages. Between Sept 1, 1939 and V-E Day, both Italy and the USSR, initially Hitler's allies, ended up allied against him.

In the Second World War, the United States, reaching accommodations with Franco's Spain, nevertheless fought to the end a war against fascism. The land of Jim Crow and Nisei internment nevertheless fought a war against racism. The allies of Stalin nevertheless fought for democracy. The destroyers of Japan's and Germany's cities nevertheless fought a war against genocide. We live in contradiction, and to say so is neither an admission nor a recommendation of inaction. The "war on terrorism" will not end "terrorism," nor even define it successfully. We will be employing against our enemies assassination, "surgical" bombing, sabotage, seizures of bank assets, clandestine operations, and general eschewing of judicial process, ending states: in other words the repertoire of the 19th century's most militant working class practice. What an earlier time vapidly denounced as terrorism, we can now recognize as the purest democracy in action brought to bear on democracy's most fervent enemies.

This war will not achieve infinite justice nor, on its own, enduring freedom. And since not even Mr. Bush's favorite political philosopher ever promised to root out evil from the world, we should not presume to try. We must merely, in all our imperfection, overcome the nothingness offered by our enemies.

It is the duty of the left in this time not only to be a party of war, but to be the maximalist party of war. Hostilities must extend not only to

Iraq, Sudan, etc., but to the supposed friendlies, the darlings of many on the domestic right: Saudi Arabia, the UAE, and Pakistan. We can do no better, to use Chomsky's phrase, than, first, to disregard Chomsky utterly (along with such organs of disinformation as *Z* and *Counterpunch* as well as the more genteel *Harpers*, *LRB*, and *The Nation*). But more important, we can do no better than to emulate revolutionary France: which, with audacity, without indulgence, summoning up the people, carried the war, across whosever borders, to the enemies of the republic.

Part X

First **Draft of History**

The Iraq war is the subject of this section.

"So far everyone has been wrong about something," wrote British journalist David Aaronovitch soon after the fall of Baghdad. I'll come clean about one of my failings on this front since evidence of it isn't in this set of pieces and I wouldn't want readers to suspect a cover-up.

On the eve of the invasion of Iraq, citing a *Times* report about how the Saddam Fedayeen had just cut someone's tongue out as a gift for Qusay Hussein, I argued in *First* the choice now came down to "War or Torture." If only it had been a few bad apples at Abu Ghraib who turned that into a false opposition. But the shaming had just begun. It would get worse when I read Tony Lagouranis's *Fear Up Harsh: An Army Interrogator's Dark Journey Through Iraq*, which describes how U.S. army interrogators found it impossible keep luxuriant releases of rage in check once Defense Department officials gave them license to go wilding.

That was all supposed to be on the down-low but the Iraqi government went public with its derelictions of duty when they allowed Moqutar Sadr's militia to turn Saddam's execution into a sectarian hate-fest. It was a humiliating moment for most of us who had spoken up for the justice of removing Saddam from power. In the days following Saddam's hanging, Jalal Talabani—the famously gregarious tribune of the Kurds (and a man who had been in the struggle against Saddam for generations)—reportedly locked himself in a hotel room and refused to see anyone.

Talabani acts his way out of guilt. (He recently caused a crisis in the Iraq's governing coalition by refusing to sign death warrants for lower-level Baathists.) But the Iraq War has produced some suspect self-laceration. The narrative of George Packer's "definitive" book on the invasion and occupation, *The Assassins' Gate* (2005), slid around set-pieces of disillusionment that felt contrived. While it was easy to identify with Packer's disdain for the Bush administration's "criminal incompetence," there was something off about his aggrieved tone and the new journalistic animus he directed toward Kanan Makiya. Packer blamed Makiya (though he claimed to "love" him) for providing rationales that caused his own heart to rise as he contemplated the invasion of Iraq. Yet, "sweets and flowers" notwithstanding, Makiya was much more realistic about the prospects for democracy in Iraq than Packer lets on. At the end of chapter called "Exiles," Packer quoted lines from a pre-invasion email that Makiya wrote from Kurdistan, finding in them his friend's true voice—"the fearless voice of his books"—rather than the compromised sound of Makiya banging drums for war. But the email by Makiya that Packer cited was addressed not (as *The Assassins' Gate* suggests) "to a few friends" but to "every Iraqi democrat in the world." Makiya distributed it through various e-mail listservs and then published it in *The New Republic*. The email wasn't a sign the pure Makiya had momentarily re-surfaced; it was another political act. And a pretty prophetic one.

Makiya began by telling how a fellow member of the Iraqi opposition had threatened to "wipe him off the face of the earth" after fantasizing a slight. This was a genuine threat from a deeply disturbed man. But Makiya wasn't out to make himself appear heroically embattled. He invoked the threat because it came from someone who was an *ally*—a person "who had suffered as much as any human being at the hands of the Baath party … at one point he weighed 30 kilos." Makiya asked his readers to see this man feelingly—"try to imagine the worst and you will not come close to what this man has suffered in his life"—and then recognize—"this is the human raw material that you want to build democracy for…."

> Every day for the last five weeks, I have come across such damaged and wounded people, people who breathe nationalism, sectarianism, without knowing that they are doing so, and people who are deeply suspicious towards their fellow Iraqis. These are the facts of life for the next generation in this poor, unhappy, and ravaged land.

Makiya had developed the impression:

> Some of you think you can lift your noses and ride into Iraq on American tanks, above the stink of it all, without having to wade knee-high in the shit that the Baath party has made of your country. You cannot. That is a pipe dream.

Makiya elaborated on his warning and as he came to the end of his note he anticipated a future of disillusion.

> The United States … is bound to let you down if you think you can ask her for too much. Actually, if you think about it hard enough, it is not the U.S. that is letting you down, nor is it President Bush or even his CIA and his State Department … it is you, who by coming face to face with your own illusions, will end up letting yourselves down the most, and it is you and all those Iraqis who have put their faith in you, who will end up paying the biggest price of all.

Packer left this passage from Makiya's pre-war message out of *The Assasins' Gate*. The timing of Makiya's prediction about what lay ahead for his side (and himself!) didn't quite fit the arc of Packer's story. What counts now is not that Makiya was right on. (He wasn't done being wrong yet.) What matters is that he was thinking hard, offering Iraqis who had put their faith in him not certainties but a chance to join his search for moral precision.

Millions of Iraqis came along on that search on January 30, 2005. Makiya celebrated Iraq's first election with them:

> Millions of people actually made choices, and placed claims on those who will lead them in the future. To act upon one's own world like this, and on such a scale, is what politics in the purest sense is all about. It is why we all, once upon a time, became activists. And it is infectious. The taste of freedom is a hard memory to rub out.

That memory soon seemed like a lie to many Iraqis. (Though Makiya underscored there were no guarantees in his post-election analysis: "the nature of great historical turning points, and the source of the wonder and beauty they bring into the world, is that we can't predict their outcome.") The country's democratic momentum stalled as sectarian violence ruled. But there is still "no final word on Iraq." To borrow a phrase that jumped out at me at the end of a long piece last summer in *Der Spiegel* by two German reporters who allowed they'd been surprised to find evidence the Surge was working. Their report—and others like it—go against the narrative of the war preferred by WE WERE RIGHT leftists such as *The Nation*'s Katha Pollitt. Pollitt et al. should call it as they see it but *she* needs to get her own story straight. Responding to Michael Ignatieff's mea-culpa—"Getting Iraq Wrong: What the War Has Taught Me about Political Judgment"—Pollitt recently insisted "Bush's stated reason for war was not the liberation of the Iraqi people." But she's shading the truth there. A few weeks before the invasion, Pollitt pointed out in her own column that Makiya and Iraqi democrats had rejected a State Department blueprint for an authoritarian regime in post-war Iraq:

> In a remarkable cry of despair published in the February 16 London *Observer* Makiya rages that U.S. plans for post-invasion Iraq include the betrayal of the Kurds, the sidelining of the Iraqi National Congress and, beneath a top layer of U.S. military brass, the continued hegemony of the Baath party—Baathism without Saddam.

Yet later that February, Pollitt went missing when Bush publicly committed himself to establishing democracy in Iraq, reassured Kurds by speaking of a future "federation" and even State Department officials began talking up de-Baathification. Pollitt failed to alert her readers the administration seemed to have heard Makiya's No in Thunder (after it was amplified by the Turkish parliament's refusal to facilitate the U.S. Military's invasion plans). She left *Nation*ists with the impression Iraqi democrats had bought out of "Bush's War." And she's still dissembling. The next section includes a transcript of a pre-invasion speech by Barham Saleh, the former Prime Minister of Kurdistan (who has gone on to become a major figure in Iraq's governments since the handover of sovereignty) that calls attention to democratic political forces Pollitt was content to marginalize.

Take the following set of writings as a *First* draft of recent history—a sketch of public movements of mind on the left about the Iraq War. While I'm wary of associating our tiny writers' collective with world historical events, the uniqueness of *First*'s politics of culture was underscored during the run-up to the invasion of Iraq. I can't think of another American publication on the left that would have printed in the same issue (as *First* did) Makiya's pro-war, NYU talk (see p. 46) *and* Tim Shorrock's detailed critique of Paul Wolfowitz's reactionary diplomatic record in Asia, which leads off this section. Makiya's and Shorrock's voices and the others in this mix implicitly call each other out. As I hear them in my head now, I'm struck (again) by how *First* has tried to be a "device" that would let argument breathe.

Asian Fantasies

Tim Shorrock

Adapted from a piece available online at http://www.firstofthemonth. org/archives/2002/12/asian_fantasies.html.

On September 22 [2002], *The New York Times Magazine* ran a lengthy cover story about Paul Wolfowitz, the number two man in the Pentagon and the Bush administration's most ardent proponent of overthrowing Saddam Hussein. Under the title of "Stalking Saddam: How Paul Wolfowitz's agenda became the Bush agenda," the *Times*' Bill Keller used over 10 pages of the weekly to reshape Wolfowitz's hawkish image into that of a man of peace and optimism who has become, in Keller's view, a trusted confidante and key advisor to "our born-again and resolutely unintellectual president."

The makeover of "Wolfie," as Bush calls his Pentagon buddy, was badly needed—and probably eagerly sought—because Wolfowitz's name and reputation was seriously tarnished in the press during the confusing aftermath of 9-11. Most damaging was an anecdote that appeared in the Washington Post under the byline of veteran reporter (and self-appointed Bush historian) Bob Woodward. It portrayed Wolfowitz as so fanatical about Saddam that once, during a meeting at Camp David, he drew a silent but withering rebuke from Bush, and a reprimand from Chief of Staff Andrew Card, for interrupting Donald Rumsfeld to push his own arguments for invading Iraq. "The story has congealed into Washington wisdom, confirming the image of Wolfowitz as a man possessed," Keller wrote in his puff piece.

But according to Keller, the Washington "caricature" of Wolfowitz doesn't do justice to the man. His story, based largely on interviews with his subject, described Wolfowitz as a man who "relies on patient logic and respectful, soft-spoken engagement" to explain his image of a post-war Iraq that could "become a democratic cornerstone of an altogether new Middle East."

Opening the spread in the *Times*, readers were treated to a photo of Wolfowitz working intently at his desk with a bright red folder emblazoned with "Secret" strategically lying at his elbow; another shot designed to underscore Keller's theme showed him whispering in Bush's ear "at the Pentagon days after the terrorist attack" (unfortunately, Bush doesn't look very engaged). Wolfowitz's hard-line views, Keller argued, were shaped by long years of association with Dick Cheney at the Pentagon during the first Bush administration and as a low-level skeptic of détente with the Soviet Union during the 1970s. Moreover, claimed Keller, his sunny views about Iraq's potential as a stable democracy were developed during the Reagan administration, when Wolfowitz served as US ambassador to Indonesia and Washington's top diplomat for East Asia during the height of the Cold War.

Here is where Keller transforms his article from history into hagiography. In one paragraph, Keller—relying solely on his subject's own recollections—described Wolfowitz's record in Asia. The former ambassador, it seems, "prides himself" on a public speech he delivered once in Jakarta urging Suharto, Indonesia's dictator, to "introduce political openness," thus "infuriating" the general-turned-president. Wolfowitz's direct role in "the incubation of Asian democracies and the more recent currents of freedom of Indonesia," Keller wrote, are "reason for hope for something similar in the Islamic Mideast."

Keller's research is badly flawed. If he had bothered to look into Wolfowitz's role in Asia during the 1980s, he would have found that Wolfowitz's views on what democracy looks like are highly skewed. During his years as Reagan's point man on Asia, Wolfowitz's job was to portray some of the world's most notorious police states as worthy allies who simply needed a little patience from US policymakers and Congress. He was willing to overlook systematic human rights violations in the name of the greater good: US national security and economic interests....

During his tenure in the Reagan and Bush administrations, Wolfowitz played a key role in defining US policy toward South Korea and the Philippines at a time of intense repression and growing opposition to authoritarian rule. In a speech in 2000 to the right-wing Heritage Foundation, he castigated those who criticized Reagan for embracing Chun and Marcos, and defended Reagan's policies as the best hope for Asian democracy.

During a 1983 visit to South Korea, he recalled, the Korean government jailed many dissidents, requiring Wolfowitz to become a "poor hapless administration official sent out to brief the traveling press corps on what was going on and to explain what was our human rights policy." That policy, he insisted, was to quietly advise Chun, who was later held responsible for the murders of at least 200 people during the 1980 Kwangju rebellion, to "honor the South Korean constitution and to step down after one term as president." Chun's decision in 1986 not to run again, he argued, "has indeed been far more important in resolving human rights problems in Korea than any number of lists of political prisoners that the American president might have taken to him."

That is fantasy, and an insult to the hundreds of political prisoners jailed and tortured by Chun as Reagan and Wolfowitz whispered democratic shibbeloths in his ear. Even long-time diplomats who supported the basic thrust of US policy in Korea believe that Reagan's public embrace of Chun discouraged Korean dissidents and fueled the fierce anti-American sentiment that still burns today. But more to the point, it wasn't American pleading that forced Chun out. Rather, it was millions of students, workers, and ordinary citizens pouring into the streets day after day that forced Chun to back off and eventually slink away to his family home in the mountains before he was tried and convicted in 1996 on charges of murder and treason.

In his Heritage speech, Wolfowitz also took credit for the downfall of Marcos. The "private and public pressure on Marcos to reform," he asserted, "contributed in no small measure to emboldening the Philippine people to take their fate in their own hands and to produce what eventually became the first great democratic transformation in Asia in the 1980s." Once again, Wolfowitz was rewriting history, implying that the Filipino people, like the South Koreans, ignored two decades of massive US military and financial support for Marcos. In both countries, US policy toward these dictators (which in Korea would include Park Chung-hee, Chun's assassinated predecessor) only began to weaken when US officials decided that their continued hold on power would lead to further instability, thus threatening US "interests."

With anticommunism no longer the dominant theme in US foreign policy, US military support for people like Chun or Marcos will be harder to defend. But given the history of Wolfowitz's dealings with US allies, it seems reasonable to conclude that he and the Bush administration will conjure up other national security justifications to support unpopular leaders.

Imagine what would happen in Iraq, for example, if its US-backed opposition (which Wolfowitz strongly supports) somehow manages to overthrow Suddam Hussein, despite its lack of support inside Iraq. Overnight, the new leaders would become strategic US allies, they would be presented with new weapons systems, and their life stories would be embellished into legend. When authoritarian tendencies eventually emerged, the American people would be told that allies can't be perfect, but that we have Paul Wolfowitz working behind the scenes and in public to get our allies to straighten up.

If that sounds like hyperbole, consider Wolfowitz's recent public comments on Indonesia. As late as May 1997, he was telling Congress that "any balanced judgment of the situation in Indonesia today, including the very important and sensitive issue of human rights, needs to take account of the significant progress that Indonesia has already made and needs to acknowledge that much of this progress has to be credited to the strong and remarkable leadership of President Suharto."

Three years later, Suharto had been swept out of office and replaced by an uneasy coalition of reformists, led by President Abdurrahman Wahid (who would be replaced in 2001 by Megawati Sukarnoputri, the daughter of Sukarno, the independence leader Suharto overthrew in a bloody CIA-backed coup in 1965). Standing alongside Wahid was the Indonesian army, led by General Wiranto, who for years was a key ally of Suharto and who maintained extremely close relations with the U.S. military. But that coalition was deeply split when Wiranto's military supported the death squads that murdered hundreds of people and laid waste to much of the territory of East Timor in 1999. In February 2000, Wiranto was forced to step down after being accused by international observers and his own government of masterminding the rampage.

A few days later, Wolfowitz appeared on the *PBS Newshour with Jim Lehrer*. In the opening segment, reporter Gwen Ifill ran a clip of Richard Holbrooke, then the UN ambassador, calling the struggle in Indonesia one between "the forces of democracy and the forces that look backward." Asked to comment, Wolfowitz quickly agreed with Holbrooke's characterization, saying "the stakes [in Indonesia] are huge ... it's very, very important to the United States." Then Wolfowitz commented on the credentials of General Wiranto—a man he knows well.

"You asked is Wiranto a reformer or anti-reform," Wolfowitz said, "I think the truth is he is history, whichever he was.... Wiranto was the general who commanded the army during the first elections in Indonesian history ... where the army genuinely played a neutral role. He may have done bad things in East Timor or failed to stop bad things in East Timor, but that's what makes it so tricky is this president [Wahid] is a reformer. The old president [Suharto] without any question was fighting reform every step of the way.... Wiranto, we don't know. And I think he should be given a fair trial on these charges in East Timor."

The fact is, we did know about Wiranto; apparently Cold War habits die hard. Wolfowitz's efforts to whitewash the likes of Chun, Marcos, Suharto, and Wiranto illustrate the bankruptcy of US foreign policy from Reagan to Bush. Americans concerned about what is being done abroad in their names need to watch Wolfowitz's every move, from Korea to Iraq to Colombia.

The Ballot and the Bullet

Barham Saleh

Barham Saleh delivered the following speech to the Socialist International in Rome on January 20, 2003. Saleh was then prime minister of Iraqi Kurdistan. He is now Iraq's deputy prime minister.

Dear Comrades and Friends,

I come to you from Iraqi Kurdistan—bringing you greetings from the Kurdish leadership—and a message from our people who hope for your support and solidarity in the struggle for democracy and liberation.

It is profoundly symbolic that we are meeting here in Rome. As the world watches the gathering storm around Iraq, there is no better place to meet than in this city, so laden with history, to reflect on the imperative of freedom and liberation from fascism and dictatorship.

For it was on June 4, 1944, that this city was liberated by Allied troops. Two days later, on June 6, 1944, the liberation of France began.

The enemy then, as now, was an aggressive, racist ideology that brought the world nothing but suffering and pain. Back in 1944, socialists, democrats and other people of good conscience stood shoulder to shoulder against Fascism.

Some of those who opposed Fascism went on to become remarkable Socialist leaders in their own countries, to promote just societies. Let us recall with honor the names of Francesco De Martino, Willy Brandt, Pierre Mendès-France, Clement Attlee, Francois Mitterand and Andreas Papandreou.

For Iraqis, our D-Day is at hand. As we watch the military preparations and the game of cat and mouse which the dishonest dictatorship in Baghdad is playing with the UN inspectors, we sense, and we hope, that deliverance is near.

The anticipation and nervousness that must have been felt in Rome nearly 60 years ago is today palpable in Iraq, both in Iraqi Kurdistan, the Free Iraq that was liberated in 1991, and in the areas still under the control of the Ba'athist regime.

In my office in Suleimani, I meet almost every day some traveler who has come from Baghdad, and other parts of Iraq. Without exception they tell me of the continued suffering inflicted by the Iraqi regime, of the fearful hope secretly nurtured by so many enslaved Iraqis for a free life, for a country where they can think without fear and speak without retribution.

Today, I stand before you not only as a representative of the Kurdish people in Iraq, but also as a messenger for the oppressed peoples of Iraq.

My Iraqi compatriots, of all backgrounds and religions, Shi'a Arab, Sunni Arab, Turkomen or Assyrian, Muslims, Christians or Yezidis have been united by what they have endured at the hands of the Baath dictatorship.

The overthrow of a racist regime that used chemical weapons against the Kurds and that wasted a nation's natural resources on war rather than schools, the reform of colonialism's most disastrous legacy, the state of

Iraq—these are goals worthy of the support of every Social Democrat.

Equally, every person in this room can take pride in what has been achieved in Iraqi Kurdistan:

- In Free Iraq, we have rebuilt villages destroyed in the genocidal ethnic cleansing of the Anfal campaign in 1988;
- We have invested in education and health, brought infant mortality down to its lowest level ever in our country;
- We have used our share of oil revenues fairly, to invest not in swords but ploughshares, in clinics and not chemical weapons;
- We have a free and diverse media;
- We respect the rights of minorities. The ethnic differences with which all societies struggle are increasingly accepted as part of the landscape rather than seen as a cause of conflict.

These achievements should be celebrated and be a model for the rest of Iraq.

But, what we Iraqi democrats are hearing from many in Europe is that Iraqis should not ask for outside help to be liberated from tyranny; that the war is for oil; that war is always wrong; that the so-called Arab and Muslim "street" will rise up as one against those who liberate Iraq.

Friends, let me take this opportunity to tell you how misguided such sentiments could be. I know that many of those who believe such things mean well, that some of them are human rights activists who had noticed our plight long ago. I admire the passion of those who organize and demonstrate for their beliefs—it is a right that we have made great sacrifices for.

Sadly, persistence alone cannot rid us of the dictatorship in Baghdad. Instead, we have suffered for over 35 years of Ba'athist rule and over 80 years from the colonially created instability of Iraq.

In that way, we are rather like the Italians, the overwhelming majority of whom cared little for Fascism, but who had to wait over 20 years and for a foreign force to liberate them.

We have a free bridgehead in Iraqi Kurdistan, but we need international help to finish the job, to end the war that the Ba'ath dictatorship is waging on the people of Iraq.

Some of the people demonstrating on the streets said that this war is for oil. Iraqis know that their human rights have too often been ignored because Iraqi oil was more important to the world than Iraqi lives. It would be a good irony if at long last oil becomes a cause of our liberation—if this is the case, then so be it. The oil will be a blessing and not the curse that it has been for so long.

Many people out on the streets say "No to War." Of course, I agree because I do not want war and I do not want civilian casualties, nor do those who are coming to our assistance. But the war has already begun. The Baath dictatorship has been waging war for decades and he has inflicted hundreds of thousands of civilian casualties. We have, as we speak, an ongoing brutal campaign of ethnic cleansing in Kirkuk, Khanaqin and Sinjar—and other parts of Iraqi Kurdistan controlled by the dictatorship. At present the Iraqi regime has intensified the economic blockade of Iraqi Kurdistan, making our position even more precarious.

To those who are going to Baghdad to be human shields, I ask, why were you not you allowed to be human shields at Halabja in 1988 when 5,000 Kurds were gassed to death? In a way, the dictatorship killed all the human shields of Halabja displaying no regard whatsoever to human lives!

Why were you were not allowed to be human shields in Najaf and Karbala in 1991 when the Iraqi Shi'a Arabs were slaughtered and their holy shrines were desecrated?

Others says, "No War against Iraq, Justice for Palestine." Since when is justice for the Palestinians, and for the Israelis for that matter, to the exclusion of justice for Iraqis?

So to those who say "No War," I say, of course "yes," but we can only have "No War" if there is "No Dictatorship" and "No Genocide."

We hear much about Muslim solidarity and the so-called "Arab Street." I know the streets of Baghdad. I can assure you that they will be filled with jubilant Iraqis after the dictator has gone.

Let us remember the joy of liberation in Rome in June 1944, the scenes of cheering crowds in Kosovo in June 1999, the Afghans who danced in the streets in November 2001. Liberation did not create paradise in any of these places, but it created hope and opportunity.

Your experience here in Italy is especially important for us. The Iraqi regime will prove to be like Mussolini, a miscalculating brute whose dictatorship will not endure long in the face of determined international resolve backed by a credible threat of use of force. Many will escape from his clutches. Others will defect. A democracy, albeit messy at times, could emerge in a process more like your own.

For this to happen, for our future to be better, we need your support.

We need you to be with us after our liberation, to ensure that a post-war Iraq is federal and democratic, peaceful and stable. We need your passion to ensure that a free Iraq enfranchises all its peoples, that there is an Iraq in which the state is constrained by law and that works for its citizens.

Friends, there will be no war on Iraq. There will be, AND MUST BE, a liberation of Iraq.

You have a role to play in that liberation, for your values, the values of the Socialist movement, are utterly opposed to the values of dictatorship and racism. Let us join together in the spirit of solidarity that has always animated Socialists, to make Iraq and the Middle East a place of freedom and peace.

Rivers of Babylon

Kurt Vonnegut

Kurt Vonnegut gave this short speech on the night of September 11, 2002 at St. Marks Church-in-the-Bowery.

My text for tonight is from the Gospel of Matthew:

"Blessed are the peacemakers for they shall be called the children of God."

There has so far been only one nation crazy enough to detonate atomic weapons in the midst of civilian populations, turning unarmed men, women and children into radioactive soot and bonemeal.

Let us pray in this holy space: "Dear God, please don't ever let there be another nation like that." Amen.

The world will little note nor long remember what we say here. This is because we are powerless. Peace has no representatives in Washington DC. Why not? Peace is not entertaining. Restraint is not entertaining.

What is entertaining? Take it from this old hack writer. Revenge, like sex, is terrifically entertaining. "Closure. Gimme Closure." Grrrr.

George W. Bush, with his no-frills education, may believe that God or Moses, or some other sacred advisor, gave us this as a commandment: "An eye for an eye, a tooth for a tooth."

It was in fact the Babylonian king Hammurabi who said it first. And he wasn't urging his own people to be more ferocious, more bloodthirsty. He was trying to make them less so. He was saying, in effect, that if you must seek revenge, you are entitled to this much of it, and not one bit more. Otherwise, you will create more people entitled to closure, until everybody in Babylonia is going to be seeking closure, and our once great country will go down the toilet of history.

Which it did.

And I thank you for your attention.

Reality TV

(1)

In a nation run by schoolyard bullies
It's always recess—teacher never comes
or else the teacher's one of them—
school never closes—they have all the guns

& you know who you are—sissy—queer—
insignificant other—cripple—girl—
better keep quiet—give them yr lunch money—run
but run where?—schoolyard is the world.

Let them pick on someone else today
Drag someone else into the Nitemare zone
Beat up kids from the wrong side of the tracks
Or torture frogs & cats—leave me alone

here in my corner, paranoid but free
enjoying someone else's misery

(2)

The whole world in a sense becomes Vienna
entire culture based on schadenfreude
& other strange unspeakable forms of angst
Once known to Freud but now considered void:—a

gray malaise sensed only as the evening
falls upon forgotten sad foubourgs
for instance—passé fears—fetishes
of disgust—machinations of sinister orgs

with unknown technologies to steal yr dreams
or stir the last ashes of libido with hate:
a vast economy based on the Evil Eye
of chilling envy, ressentiment in spate

& always someone else to take the blame
or commit the crime—but never in my name

(3)

Two of the rivers of Paradise flow by you
Abode of Peace—& not since Hulagu

or Tammerlane or Lawrence-of-fucking-Arabia
has there been such a spectacle on view:

Capital of a thousand nights & a night
Haroun al-Raaschid & Aub Nuwas drink & repose
in yr gardens haunted by the nightingale—
Ahmad Ghazzali drunk on a single rose:

O Baghdad of the bombs, the cluster bombs
Baghdad of the Poets, Babylon of the Caliphs
lo the handwriting's on the wall (or rather screen)
thou shall be razed—as a kind of comic relief

from more serious matters. Death makes good TV
to take our minds off sad reality.

—Peter Lamborn Wilson

Welcome to the Reality of the Desert

Kyle Thibodo

The author, a hospital corpsman with the U.S. Navy stationed in Iraq, wrote the following email soon after Coalition forces invaded the country.

Greetings to all family, friends, associates etc., etc.

I can tell you that I'm in Umm Qasr. It's a port on the south border. A small boil on the @$$ of the world. Don't ask the temp cuz I don't know. I just know I hate waking up in a sweat and not having the matching fever to go with it.

First I need you guys to keep my friend's son in your prayers. His name is Mike and his kid's up in the Baghdad area with a forward element of the Marines. Apparently it was rough going for those guys, and I think we need to give all of them all the help we can physically and spiritually....

I'm not sure what to make of all the pandemonium in Baghdad. But after being here for some time, I have had a chance to do some real soul-searching about what we're supposed to be doing. I admit to mixed feeling about the excuse we used but having seen what things are like here I can say that something had to be done.

Whether this was the right thing is another story.... Some soldiers escorted an injured woman and her husband to us with SEVERE burn injuries from a tank round. She was 2nd/3rd degree burned on both arms from hand to shoulder, all of her face except eyes, neck and chest. The wounds were about 5 days old and the hospital at Basra essentially sent her home to die. The best we could do for her was give her pain meds, attempt some rehydration and fly her to a better facility. I have also met a few more folks that had injuries or ailments treated by local medical but still too far along or too bad for us. I have been told that under the old system essentially it was the higher the rank the better the care. Between that and how desperate folks are for food and water, it's amazing. These poor folks didn't just get like this when we entered the country.

I'd say the U.N. should be held in contempt for allowing this to go on for so long under the former regime. It's as bad here as it was in Rwanda or Uganda. I'd say that if the U.N. expects to have any teeth, they have to come up with a better game plan that doesn't require us to go in and clear crap out....

I was thinking out loud while lamenting to a friend a few nights ago about the living conditions here. Most of you know I did a few minutes in Honduras a couple times and I actually enjoyed the trip even though hanging in Honduras (Guyape region) was like going back to the 1800's. Well, Umm Qasr makes Honduras look like Vegas.

I'll get up on my soapbox again because I wonder what was on the U.N. menu for this area after Desert Storm since it looks like they missed a lot. Ironically enough, if you saw the U.N. compound that was attached to the port and then looked over the fence at the local village it's like a Lexus next to a wheelbarrow. The living conditions here for the "have-nots" are like a scene out of a time warp. The houses in many of the rural areas look like they belong to some sort of modern Stone Age family. Inside living areas you find a small appliance or gadget next to a rattan floor mat on top of some old Styrofoam padding. This is someone's bed?

Basically we're talking about a barter economy. I do a fair amount of wheeling and dealing here in the compound but I can't imagine the magnitude of what goes on outside. The locals steal everything that isn't bolted down and trust me, if it's not being used it's being traded. The Construction Battalion (CB) Corpsman was telling me about some of the stuff he has to deal with from the kids on the street and one CB carpenter painted a bleaker pic. Last week they went into the local town to build a new playground (among other things) and now it's trashed.

I know that weapons of mass destruction (WMD) were the big issue for a little while and certain countries were kinda irritated about what our motives were for coming here. Well, if Germany and France and the rest of the countries that were on that issue had taken a ride down here and seen how the U.N. was living compared to the neighbors, you can only hope someone would have said OMG and then chastised all of us for not intervening sooner. This could have been a war on neglect and poverty. (We need to have a realistic look at the same in the USA before we end up like this place!)

We may never find the actual WMD. So what? Look what we did find!!! A country with potentially more oil money than they can spend with a large population of its own native people living as if this was a chapter out of Jeremiah! You can easily be mad at the locals for destroying every new thing we give or build but given that they are used to having little or nothing and have almost no education, what can you expect? Our mistake in the humanitarian area has been a lack of preparation before the massive distribution of aid materials. This place might do well with old-fashioned grassroots village organization and education....

By the way, this is supposed to be all about the Iraqi "Arab" populace, but is anyone beside me interested in what happened to the large Jewish population that was here in the late '40s? A reference book of mine briefly touched on the issue and mentioned large numbers of Jews formerly living in Baghdad. I just read about it today and need to do some research on the subject when I escape from here....

If you promised to buy BBQ for me, you will hear from me as soon as I get outta this. Right now, current stops that are ranking high on my list are the Ameristar Buffet, Jazz Creole restaurant, almost any BBQ place, IHOP, one of those Mexican holes in the wall on Independence Ave., Worlds of Fun, Baskin Robbins, and did I mention BBQ?

Thanks for the love, care packages, letters and email. Peace.

An Avuncular "No!"

Howard Zinn

Zinn wrote the following letter in 2004 protesting against First's *pieces in support of the Iraq war.*

Dear Benj:

I enclose a small contribution for *First of the Month*. I've been meaning to respond to the provocative pieces in support of the war (of course, I'm easily provoked). But I've been so involved writing and speaking against the war that I could not find time. After all, the arguments in *First of the Month* are more sophisticated than the ones given by the Bush Administration even if they end up with the same conclusion. One reason for my not writing is that I assumed that unfolding events would themselves make my argument for me—that the endless deaths, the endless and brutal occupation, the outrageous imperial arrogance—would become clearer and clearer. We have always had liberal imperialists, people who found a moral cause on which to expend the blood of thousands—or millions, as in World War I, when some of the most impressive liberals, even Socialists, saw the evil of the Kaiser (read Saddam Hussein) as justifying the slaughter taking place on the Marne. The liberal supporters of the war in the Vietnam were many—though the bitter realities soon diminished their ranks.

The liberal imperial argument seems to come down to the war is worth it, because the tyrant Saddam Hussein, with all his cruelties, is gone. Against the value of the fall of Saddam must be set the 600 U.S. dead, the thousands of U.S. maimed (the blinded, the armless, the legless), the ten thousand or so Iraqi dead (I use a figure even less than that compiled by the Iraqi doctor in London, an enemy of Saddam, who has headed a grass-roots effort to count the dead in the hospitals of Iraq) and the countless Iraqi wounded. Set against the removal of Saddam, all of that mayhem, still going on, along with the detention, accompanied sometimes by torture, of thousands of Iraqis by the U.S. military, held on vague suspicions and no more. And throw into the moral equation the fact that there is hardly a chance that democracy will come to Iraq via the presence of the U.S. military. The history of military interventions by the U.S. gives virtually no hope of a good outcome. The fact that the Bush administration cares not a whit about democracy is another factor. Sure, good things can come from bad intentions, but only rarely.

My opposition to this war comes out of a generalized principle, which I am willing to reconsider if the facts of a specific case warrant it, but which I find in this Iraqi case painfully relevant. It's a matter of means and ends. The means of war are, with absolute certainty, horrible. The ends of war, however presented as beneficent, are always uncertain.

Just one more thing, I find some of the writers in your pages talking very confidently about "the Left"—and it's easy, given the diversity of the Left, to find all sorts—but so much of how they characterize "the Left" seems to show an ignorance of what much of the Left is saying.

That's the end of my rant.

Best Wishes, Howard Zinn

Snow White and the Seven Chumps

Sheldon Wolin

First a word about my title: Martha Stewart's conviction was recently thrown into jeopardy by the revelation that a witness for the prosecution had lied and misrepresented some facts. Regardless of the eventual outcome—or that she was accused of the kind of insider trading that is hardly a rarity on Wall Street; or that the chump money involved could not purchase a respectable home—what mattered was the object lesson. By convicting a wealthy celebrity justice may have peeked beneath her blindfold but at least she was not beholden to the rich and famous—well, at least not to the rich who happen to be engaged in selling pots and pans instead of defense contracts. Martha Stewart, the self-made Snow White and the designated sacrificial lamb was judged responsible because she had lied. As for the Seven Chumps of Abu Ghraib, the soldiers accused of injuring and degrading prisoners, even of homicidal acts, they, too, are promised a show trial, in fact a series of them where predictably the lowliest of soldiers will be sternly prosecuted for crimes that are being cast as aberrations. Meanwhile the country in which the crimes took place is being terrorized, reduced to rubble, its economy shattered, and its people demoralized. Like Martha Stewart only chumps are held responsible for their actions. In the recent, uncouth words of the vice president....

"I take responsibility."

These words echoed and re-echoed in Washington and in the media following the publicizing of the revelations of torture, homicide, and humiliation in Abu Ghraib and Afghanistan. First the chairman of the Joint Chiefs of Staff, then Rumsfeld, then the president himself allotted a moment to "responsibility." When followed was ... nothing. Except for the quick prosecution of a private whose subsequent sentencing seemed grossly disproportionate to the actions of which he was accused and a promise of a show trial to exhibit the salacious misdeeds of a female soldier—all of this in contrast to the utter lack of consequences for the leaders who proclaimed their responsibility. A chorus of generals, after an obligatory and fleeting admission of responsibility, followed the example of their political superiors. Somehow reports of abuse got stalled just short of their desks or near the top of the stack. So we get a topsy-turvy version of the Nuremberg principle: the little ones get caught while the big ones get away. Somehow the principles of honor taught at West Point have been melded with a CEO ethos that taught, "cover your butt" and shift the blame to the expendable underlings. In effect, downsizing responsibility. For those with the greatest power and authority responsibility is the art of avoiding any consequences. As Kenneth Lay explained, "I take full responsibility for what happened at Enron. But saying that, I know in my mind that I did nothing criminal."

Minimally, responsibility means being accountable for what is within one's power to do or prevent and paying the penalty. It is notoriously more difficult to affix accountability in large organizations in which there are layer upon layer of authority and degrees of responsibility. And that only relates to internal responsibility. A large organization's actions will typically affect the outside world. It is not uncommon, however, for corporations to be adjudged in violation of some statute or rule and to have a "settlement" resulting in a huge fine but "without admission of responsibility." That is what "paying the penalty" has come to mean in the age of unrivaled corporate political power. Apparently it is an option unavailable to drug dealers.

But as suggested by that example irresponsibility may be inherent in huge organizations. Responsibility is commonly described as "personal" yet such organizations are commonly depicted and experienced as "impersonal." That tension between organizational scale and personal responsibility takes on political significance at a time when the United States is increasingly perceived as a "hyperpower" and an "empire," terms that denote the emergence of a new scale of combined political, military, and economic power. Clearly the doctrine of preemptive war, invoked to justify the invasion of Iraq was a reflection of the expanded global interests that required a commensurate expansion of American power. The question raised by Abu Ghraib goes beyond the sordid and inhumane actions of American soldiers, beyond the evasions (at once pitiful and arrogant) of responsibility by our leaders, and beyond even the unjust and flagrantly misrepresented war in Iraq itself. The fundamental question is whether as citizens we want to remain tacitly complicit in a political system which, at home and abroad, consistently attempts to expand the reach of its powers while weakening or disavowing the traditional restraints at the heart of our constitutional notions of responsibility.

What is at stake, both in the Oval Office and in the cellblocks of Abu Ghraib is the same question of restraints, of established limits, of something that seems alien to the political culture permeating the White House. From the outset, the Bush administration made no secret that it would follow a policy of renouncing both external and internal restraints upon its actions. It would allow the Anti-Ballistic Missile treaty to lapse;

it would prevent its agents from being prosecuted for war crimes; it would reduce or evade environmental safeguards and relax public health standards, it would place its ideological agents on regulatory bodies and courts where they would dutifully make it easier for companies and government officials to evade control. Predictably, in a situation where governmental and military authorities operate in a pre-existing context of relaxed safeguards, of contempt for restraints, and of wielding "the world's greatest power," responsibility amounts to exactly how the Bush administration reacted to events at Abu Ghraib, denouncing a few bad apples at the bottom while defending Rumsfeld as "the finest Secretary of Defense in American history" (Cheney). In that show of utter contempt for the American public the regime of Hyperpower made clear that the meaning of responsibility had been turned upside-down, inverted, those at the top were practically absolved, those at the bottom took the rap. In the process, we, too, were absolved; the perpetrators were declared to be unrepresentative of "real" Americans who, while they solidly supported the invasion of Iraq and presumptively accepted the inevitable killing of the innocents and the destruction of a society's basic structures, would never condone sodomizing prisoners, especially not for cameras; kids, for whom violence and pornography are only a click away, should not be "exposed."

The Bush notion of responsibility is also deeply indebted to the context created by the administration's theological depiction of the "War on Terror." If the enemy is the incarnation of evil and capable of the most diabolical actions, we, who strive earnestly and sincerely for the most personal relationship with our god, are absolved. Justified not only in the methods of interrogation, but of visiting death and destruction upon an "evil" society. Harsh interrogation thus becomes the latter-day adaptation of the Holy Inquisition. Faith alone convinces us that Saddam Hussein aided terrorists and therefore bore some responsibility for the martyrdom of September 11—at least according to the administration's political theology.

But as the careers of Falwells and Robertsons remind us, evangelicals can be on friendly terms with corporate capital. If evangelicals have their "last days" of Armageddon, corporate capital has its moments of "creative destruction" where the inefficient (= unregenerate) will fall by the way, casualties in the collateral damage that inevitably accompanies the free market and its version of progress. No account of how responsibility is practiced by today's high governmental officials is comprehensive without first noting how widespread and influential is the CEO experience among the highest-ranking cabinet officers. Thanks to the established practice of "the revolving door," the top-level military and civilian officials have either acquired their managerial experience in working for corporate enterprises or expect to learn the skills for the time when they will leave government for private enterprise. In either case they learn to follow the adage of "take no prisoners." They also rarely appreciate the idea, much less the practice, of loyal opposition. Their advice to dissidents is, Get on board or get out of the way.

Perhaps Clausewitz needs amending: politics is not war carried on by other means. Rather war and politics are business carried on by many of the same means for similar ends of conquering rivals and/or profiting. The corporate ethos that now pervades government has dislodged the older notion of disinterested public service. Although that change did not begin with the Bush administration, there can be a little doubt that it has done nothing to temper it, much less reverse it.

The question of responsibility then takes on larger dimensions and involves more than the question of evasions at the top or misdeeds at the bottom. In principle ours is a system of responsibility, from the highest officials to the lowliest citizen. How did it work during the build-up to the Iraqi war and its aftermath? Were the pundits acting responsibly when they repressed the possible consequences of invasion in favor of recounting what no one doubted about the atrocities of Saddam? or justified the war by broad-brushing Islam as "totalitarian?" or simply labeling the preemptive war as a just war of defense? Or was the Democratic Party performing as the responsible opposition as it signed over to the administration one blank check after another?

Perhaps the principal bearers of responsibility were to be found elsewhere, withered under the sarcasm of pundits, ignored by the administration, grossly under-reported on tv, and buried in the very back pages of *The New York Times*. Those hundred or more city councils that passed resolutions opposing the war, those hundred of thousands, even millions in the U.S. and western Europe who took to the streets, braving the hostility of patriots, police and pundits, perhaps they were the truly and honorably responsible ones. And perhaps they were chumps. According to the dictionary's first entry a chump is a blockhead; according to the second it is the blunt end of anything. Of responsibility perhaps?

Into the Breach Again

Fredric Smoler

Omaha Beach, June 6, 2004

They'd woken the tour members at 2:30 a.m. and boarded them at 3:00, because the gossip and the leaks agreed that the security would be fierce. By the end of the ceremony a lot of people in their eighties had been without food for ten hours and had spent a fair amount of time baking in the sun; some of the media-savvy thought that the seats had been arranged to provide the best photos for Bush—a sea of rapt faces—rather than protection and comfort for the audience, a fair number of whom were survivors of the invasion. They'd put up with worse sixty years ago, but this was pretty grueling for some of them. An hour or so later one elderly man fell, suffered a stroke, fractured his skull and broke his shoulder.

We'd been given color-coded badges by the Defense Department, green for an ordinary guest, other colors for vets, their escorts, family members, press and VIPs. There was a lot of confusion and vets bereft of the passes they were due wandered uneasily, a bit lost, jostled by crowds of pushful youngsters. DoD had invited something like 14,000 people for some 8000 seats, and the resulting snafu produced a sea of seats in the mid-range held empty by the MPs, while some of the bewildered early-arrived vets were herded into the back rows. When order finally collapsed, the younger, late-arriving crowd surged forward, shoving past the survivors and grabbing the seats closer to the podium from which Bush and Chirac would recite their pieties. The *mana* in the space seemed to radiate from the place Bush would occupy—to be closer to that space was somehow to win something, to suck up some of the celebrity the American president incarnated, or which emanated from any media-attended decennial anniversary. Two middle-aged men behind me speculated enviously on the joys of keeping thousands waiting for many hours, forcing them through laborious and invasive layers of security, only to land by helicopter, descending like a god: "what an ego trip!" From where we sat, the flat-screen TVs were hard to see in the blinding sunlight, and Chirac's voice, over the loudspeakers, was a bit hard to hear: a torrent of *jamais*, but I couldn't tell what he was *jamais*-ing about: "we shall never forget," I think, but there were some other possibilities. Still, all the bustling vulgarity in the world couldn't make the occasion farcical, and it is impossible to strip the American cemetery at Omaha Beach of power and dignity. That chivvying, mindless competition for physical proximity to celebrity arguably came as close as one could, but no cigar. To a sufficiently cold and severe moral imagination, Verdun can be merely a monument to cruelty and error and folly—sacrifice alone does not gild slaughter—but Omaha Beach is not, and cannot be. The combination of necessary means and urgent ends defeats any effort to mute the significance of what happened there, and even fairly cranky Europeans seemed to know it. And the moments of real imaginative or physical proximity to what happened sixty years ago were eerily potent.

After the ceremony, the crowd ebbing back to the buses, we bumped into a lively, sturdy octogenarian accompanied by two gigantic and affable middle-aged sons, the older guy a veteran of the 16th Infantry, one of the two regiments that first landed on Omaha Beach. He was Ed Jeskey, a Polish-American retired autoworker with a sense of humor: "it's an Irish name." When queried, he announced that he'd been in F Co—which if my memory serves, took 91 percent casualties—and he'd hit the beach in the first wave: "nothing in front of me except a fish, pal!" Bumping into him and his sons a couple of days later, you learned a bit more. Within a very few minutes, Jeskey was the only survivor of his platoon. He was skeptical about films of men running up the beach to attack the German fortifications—he thought it had taken him ten hours to crawl ten yards—and proud of the fact that to the best of his knowledge, sick with swallowed seawater, amid omnipresent shelling and machinegun fire, he'd been the first American to take a shit in France. It was a cheerfully self-mocking and in part anti-heroic story, yet according to Jeskey's sons, when he saw current members of the First Infantry Division at the cemetery, he pumped his fist and shouted "Big Red One!" And they pumped their fists too, and shouted back: "Big Red One! Wahoo!" Maybe pumping your fist, grinning and shouting is mere theatricality. Or maybe that's the real part, and joking about how frightened you were is the theatre.

Jeskey seemed impervious to what the French commentariat had taken to calling the paradox of June 6th. It wasn't always entirely clear what they meant by this, but the paradox seemed to result from a collision of the lingering (sometimes grudging, sometimes palpably sincere) French enthusiasm for being liberated with the broad French loathing of the American and British attempt to extend what was described as a similar favor to the Iraqis. The French commentariat insisted that these efforts had nothing whatever in common, and that the two Americas—Bush's and Roosevelt's—had nothing in common, either. That same week, *Le Monde* ran a headline speculating on the date for the construction of an

American Gulag, and one striking proposal sought to deny Bush access to France on the 60th anniversary: Bush led an America that "does not chase out an occupier, but occupies, does not crush oppressors, but oppresses, does not chase out an invader, but invades, does not crush fascism, but nurtures its 'Islamist' form." To most Anglo-American eyes this list of antitheses, while disturbing, was imperfectly persuasive: the Americans and British had crushed one form of Iraqi fascism at the risk of abetting another, they had removed an Iraqi oppressor while at least a few of them had resorted to some shameful oppressive tactics themselves, etc. But these smaller paradoxes did not aggregate to a vast and paralyzing paradox of June 6th. The Anglo-American mind may be less supple than the Gallic journalistic mind tends to be—these paradoxes were troubling, rather than dispositive, and they were less airily entertaining to the reader than they'd probably been to the writer—but after fuller consideration, they did not seem irresolvable. Speculation about an imminent American gulag suggested an imperfect familiarity with Mogadan, Vorkuta and Kolyma.

And the paradox of June 6th lost some of its tension in the face of the trouble various European opponents of the Iraq war had in getting their story straight. Up the beach at Arromanches, Schroeder was insisting that Germany, too, had been liberated on D-Day. None of the vets on my tour remembered the Germans welcoming this liberation with any great enthusiasm: a number of them still carried scars, and a few shrapnel, which they thought testimony to the imperfect German appreciation for their efforts. In 1944 and '45, the Germans had resisted their liberation much more strenuously than the Iraqis had in 2003, and if thousands of Iraqis were trying to blow up their liberators a year on, and mutilate their corpses, this may have been because the liberators didn't have any French troops with them: back in '45, the French had replied to terror aimed at their occupation force with extremely effective mass reprisals. A darker thought intruded—maybe it was because the British and Americans had taken fewer pains to spare German civilian lives in the process of liberation, and those civilian deaths may have finally soured the Germans on war. When truly aroused, the Americans and British practiced terror wholesale: retail terror as a resistance tactic may not have seemed a very promising approach in 1945. In any case, Schroeder seemed to think that Germans could be liberated despite their striking lack of cooperation in the process, although he did not seem to have worked out that this was a dangerously suggestive argument, one capable of extension from the Rhine to the Euphrates.

And as it happened, not all the civilian dead had been German: many thousands of French civilians had died in the course of the Normandy invasion and the subsequent fighting. Perhaps this was some part of what the French meant by the paradox of June 6th. But while the reporters made a few attempts to imply that those civilian deaths dissolved any moral credit that might otherwise have attended the US and British destruction of a tyranny, this move did not seem to catch on. Most of the French seemed to understand that freeing France was worth civilian casualties. They were at least as confident that freeing Iraq from Saddam wasn't. Maybe that was because the French and Germans had grown more tender-hearted over sixty years (although the Algerians, the Tutsi and the Bosnian Muslims, *inter alia*, might have doubted this interpretation). Or maybe they just cared less about other people's liberty than they did about their own. A most ingenious paradox, that French paradox of June 6th, but it resisted easy unpacking.

The Afternoon of June 6th, a Parking Lot, Normandy

When the old man fell, suffered his stroke and fractured his skull, broke his teeth and damaged his eye and bled furiously, retired nurses and ex-army officers and one black man from the next tour bus—the nurses initially thought him a paramedic, and were relieved to have kept this to themselves, when he turned out to be a neurosurgeon—rushed to his aid. The French ambulance, caught in the congestion of the D-Day anniversary, took an hour to arrive, and for that period the tourist-rescuers were immensely impressive, cooperating spontaneously in the face of everything that had gone wrong. The Feds were searching the buses, and we'd been instructed to leave nothing at all on them, nor bring anything that might perturb the Secret Service. So with no medical records, no prescriptions, nothing to cut bandages or perform an emergency tracheotomy, they cooperated perfectly and kept him alive, meticulously policed the scene for bio-hazards, and somehow made the UK newspaper speculations about whether anyone alive today could do what those old guys had done on D-Day seem transparently silly. It took me a minute to work out why, and then I had it: if what I took to be Ed Jeskey's opinion, voiced thirty minutes before, was worth anything—and if his wasn't, whose was?—the young guys from the Big Red One just back from Iraq were his posterity. And the scratch trauma team, all but one of them vets, laboring with no tools at all, seemed part of his posterity, too. It occurs to me that these speculations never go out of fashion, and that the German military cemetery up the road is filled with men who derided the military capacity of commercial societies.

June 8th, Near Metz

The bus has a microphone, from which I give little lectures on the history of the war, and from which the vets reminisce. We've been driving for most of a day, and now two farmers take the mike in turns, pointing out the varieties of crops and cattle, working out aloud the slight discrepancies between American and French agricultural techniques. It has a sweetly retardataire feel: had this been a popular front movie back in the day, we'd now be solemnly reminded that we were all sons of the soil, that borders are only lines on a map, but the scene is curiously unmoving, probably because we're not all sons of the soil; *La France Profonde* is dead, and it is hard to sentimentalize Monsanto. Still, last night, in a Deauville hotel room, watching what looked like a letter-perfect German rip-off of *Saturday Night Live* on *Sat Eins*, one remembers that there is a case for it being one world, after all. The pretty blonde comic rolled through her lazily scornful introductory monologue about Bush and Chirac, while the camera panned across smug, aerobicized, early-middle-aged would-be-hipster faces in the studio audience, and then the comic essayed the same absolutely unconvincing show of enthusiasm when the guest rock band was announced. It feels like a backhanded but not unpersuasive tribute to Ed Jeskey and his friends, a democratic consumer society's mass culture being their gift to Europeans. It has its abundant faults, but it sure beats torch-lit Brownshirt rallies. Nowadays, the Europeans differ chiefly in their sturdy refusal to acknowledge what it took to stop Brownshirts, and what it may still take.

June 9th, 2004, the American Military Cemetery in Luxembourg

The US ambassador had served in the Reagan White House, and his remarks, prompted by Reagan's death, rather suggest a third string comic warming up for some strippers in Las Vegas. He switches tone, too late, to invoke the sacrifices of the Second World War, tries to steal some of the glory of the graves fanning out below, fails utterly to pull it off. Helen Patton, the general's granddaughter, now married to a German, announces that we mourn equally all who sacrifice themselves for a cause. The tourists are pleased to meet the granddaughter, but some of them seem to think that this is to some degree nonsense, that the men who lie twenty yards away are ennobled by the cause for which they died, no matter how mean their motives at the time, while the Germans lying a few miles away are to some degree disgraced by the cause they bled for.

June 10th, 2004, the Ardennes, Near Malmedy

Max had come ashore on Omaha Beach on D+ something or other, carrying a Browning Automatic Rifle. Wounded in the *bocage* country, he'd been evacuated to the UK, patched up, and sent back to the 30th Infantry Division, arriving in time for the Battle of the Bulge. He no longer carried the BAR, he'd become a telephone linesman, but when elements of the First SS Panzer Division tried to break thorough the 30th's very thin line, he'd been sent forward with an M1, along with every cook, laundryman and bottle-washer they could find. It wasn't too bad, he says—the snow was deep, they kept to the road, when you knocked out one tank the others had to stop, and that helped a lot. Then, looking out over a field, Max seems confused, and mildly querulous—there'd been more trees, and fewer houses, and everything looked very different; one got the sense that the difference was a bit disturbing. Then Max looked down the grassy slope again, and his memory kicked in, and his voice, with its very ripe Boston accent, became not smug, not even cocky, but a little colder and, briefly, much harder. He remembered that one American battalion had been deployed over there, with his own drawn up behind them. The panzers had broken through the first battalion, but here—he pointed a very few feet in front of his present stance—"that's where we stopped the 1st SS Panzer division." This is not a claim that many people can make, or ever could, and one suspects that Max knows it, but tactfully downplays it. Still, there is in his voice a faint echo of what Virgil ascribes to Turnus: "an awareness of his own high worth."

Later, Max remembers more. They took a prisoner, a 17-year-old boy, and a Dutch interrogator slapped the boy, and stuck a pistol in his eye, and barked out a question, and the boy spat in the Dutchman's face. They all froze, and then the Dutchman slapped the boy again, knocking him to the ground, and, thankfully, that was the end of it. But that kid had guts, Max observed, respectfully, but without agonies of self-reproach. The battle was only a few hundred yards from the field where the 1st SS Panzers murdered 70-odd American PoWs, one of eighteen massacres that division committed in the Ardennes during the Battle of the Bulge. Max seems to imply that slapping the boy around, even threatening his life, does not wholly annihilate the moral import of stopping the 1st SS Panzers in its tracks. Maybe Max, too, has some notions of a paradox of D-Day. If so, it seems possible that Max handles modest paradox more briskly than do some.

Radicle: The Root is Women-in-Nature

Charles Keil

Radicles	*Rootlets growing from the stem.*
Radiculose	*With radicles.*
Retuse	*Obtuse or slightly indented.*
Revolute	*Rolled backwards, as of the leaf margin.*

A *found poem from the* Manual of Hawaiian Mosses, *by Edwin B. Bartram, Bernice P. Bishop Museum, Honolulu, Hawaii (1933:267).*

> For it is not enough either to devise a morality that will allow the human race simply to survive. Survival is an evil when it entails existing in a state of wretchedness. Intrinsic to survival and continuation is felicity, pleasure. Pleasure has been much maligned, diminished by philosophers and conquerors as a value for the timid, the small-minded, the self-indulgent. "Virtue" involves the renunciation of pleasure in the name of some higher purpose, a purpose that involves power (for men) or sacrifice (for women). Pleasure is described as shallow and frivolous in a world of high-minded, serious purpose. But pleasure does not exclude serious pursuits or intentions, indeed it is found in them, and it is the only real reason for staying alive.
>
> *Beyond Power*, Marilyn French

I've stopped endorsing, writing for, participating in, sending money to *First of the Month* because events in Iraq and the USA have confirmed some basic understandings I've held to with varying degrees of tenacity since about the age of 16 (circa 1956) when I decided to register as a CO (Conscientious Objector): war is hell on humans and Nature, war is waste, war is the health of the state, war solves no significant problems, war creates new and worse problems, war oppresses men by training them to kill or be killed on command, and, in the era of proliferating kinds and quantities of nuclear, biological and chemical weapons of mass destruction *deliverable by a single person*, the reign or hegemony of patriarchal military-industrial-power is clearly over, finished, kaput, finito. The only question is whether we want what's left of western snivelization to go down in flames, a final ecocatastrophic, flare-out of Fascism & Imperialism, Inc., or do we want to work rationally for a diversity of species and cultures within a sustainable ecologic? Do we go along with some version of the corporate military stat=us quo, or do we not? The fact that *First of the Month*'s editors still want warmongers and peacelovers to have a dialogue in their pages seems like a serious waste or misdirection of precious time, energy, thought and feeling. Arguing with people who want to spin rationalizations for the insanity of war makes no sense to me.

I take *First*'s failure to evolve a supportive structure for the "radical imagination" (or "radicle" rooted in the moss manual) as symptomatic. The disease is "civilization" (a convenient cover term for excess literacy, alienation, division-of-labor, progress, his-story, triumphal capital on the brink of collapse, overdevelopment, etc.) and the symptoms of the disease at *First* might be described as: 1) not having read and understood Dwight Macdonald's 1940s wartime essays collected in *The Root is Man* (Cunningham Press 1953; and reprinted by Autonomedia 1995); inadequate grasp of feminism, ecology and "spiritual health" (I prefer "participatory consciousness" or "joyful science") as the three intellectual force fields that can help shape a sustainable or Earth-friendly political economy. Tall order, but basic. Otherwise we're goners.

Where there is no vision, the peoples do perish. MacDonald's text is crucial because he debunks the defunct "progressive" vision as concisely as I've seen it debunked. William Blake, Paul Goodman, Ivan Illich, the philosophical lit crit of K. Burke and O. Barfield, Bateson's great trilogy (*Steps to an Ecology of Mind*, *Mind and Nature*, *A Sacred Unity*) and Stanley Diamond's *In Search of the Primitive*, establish something like a masculinist "call" for the prophetic or visionary work we need to do. The feminist "response" to the decline and fall of alienating civilizations, the perishing of peoples and species, has been, quite sensibly to put Gaia, women and children first. Jane Ellen Harrison's *Themis* and *Prolegomena*, Marilyn French's *Beyond Power*, Dorothy Dinnerstein's *Mermaid and Minotaur*, Starhawk's *Spiral Dance*, Elisabet Sahtouris' *Earthdance: Living Systems in Evolution*. Edith Cobb's *The Ecology of Imagination in Childhood* are seven classic statements of how important it is to put the dance before the music, rites/rights/wrights before writes, myth and ideology, pleasure-with vs. power-over. Old Mother Nature/biological evolution before everything else. If we don't listen to these women's voices first, starting with Gaia's, there's really no hope for freedom, justice, democracy, or a sustainable rediversification of species and cultures.

I kept hoping *First* would make the turn toward feminism, ecology, spiritual growth/joyous science/participatory consciousness, and living simply that others may simply live. Didn't happen. And now I don't see a place to publish little pieces like this one. I'd like to be contributing regularly to a weekly, monthly, or quarterly newspaper aspiring toward broad circulation that is focused on the question of how we can create enough global or civil society (rule of law, international courts, regional and global police forces capable of stopping "administrative massacres" and apprehending terrorists) so that the states can gradually disarm and spend the funds on problem solving and co-evolving rather than war-making. The paper I'd like to write for will have ecologically minded feminist editors eager to see children dancing happily into the future. In passing and in closing, let me say that *First*'s concern with Africa, Haiti, respect for poetry as politics, keeping music and movies in the mix, editorial skill in juxtaposing positions and perspectives, has kept me interested for a few years by now. But history gets made day by day, and in times of war people like Dwight Macdonald are forced to dig deeper and think longer and harder about keeping the radical imagination alive. Macdonald did not see WWII as "the good war" or the "the just war" and I can't see the "war on terror" as anything more than an old-fashioned power grab for resources abroad that has the capacity to destroy the constitution and civil liberties at home. Thanks to the Patriot Act I can now be searched and seized as a Bush designated "bad guy," at any time. And sent to Guantanamo for "questioning." Fascism is here. And the ecocatastrophe is here too. A quarter to a third of amphibian species appear to be on their way to extinction worldwide. We need newspapers, radio stations, magazines, Path bands and sounding sangas that put frogs on the front page every day and speak clearly to the material conditions our condition is in.

In sum, I'd like to be writing for an outreach newspaper where women are in charge, where women's voices and concerns for the quality of children's lives to the 7th generation is the dominant theme, where interbeing and deepening our understanding of "the laws of Nature and of Nature's God" is the quest and where the radicle imagination is not about men's transcendent projects or the myth of progress but rooted in the forever-immanent pleasure centers.

The Perils of Political Maternalism

Jean Bethke Elshtain

Now that Cindy Sheehan has taken up attacking all who disagree with her, including Sen. Hillary Rodham Clinton (D.-N.Y.), Democratic commentators are singing a different tune. Where once Sheehan was a sympathetic mother rightly demanding a meeting with President Bush—presumably in order to call him a "spewer of filth" to his face—now she is guilty of making bad judgments and allowing herself to be manipulated by extremist groups who have turned her protest into a media circus.

But Sheehan hasn't changed at all—she's simply broadened her field of targets. At this point, one wonders whether *New York Times* columnist, Maureen Dowd, still believes her mind-boggling assertion that a mother, like Sheehan, who has lost a child, possesses "absolute moral authority." Dowd is no moral philosopher, of course, but any thoughtful person can take note of how mischievous such a proclamation is. Presumably, by implication, it means the grieving mother of an SS officer fighting for Nazi Germany possesses a similar "absolute moral authority." If not, why not? She, too, mourns her loss.

This observation points to but one of the dangers of politicized motherhood. If the grieving mother holds absolute moral authority, everyone else, by definition, has no moral ground to stand on at all. Or, better put, whatever moral authority anyone else claims is trumped by maternal authority. Unfortunately, maternal grief does not distinguish between deaths for a noble or an ignoble cause. When maternal loss is politicized in a highly partisan manner, as in Sheehan's case, it exercises a chilling effect on political speech. Criticism seems churlish and mean-spirited. One is being mean to a grieving mother.

As well, the woman without children is told she has "no idea of what it's like," so she had best demur. (Unless, of course, she agrees completely with Sheehan, in which case she has presumably triumphed over her childless condition and made a moral leap into complete identification with Sheehan's loss.) One wonders, as well, where fathers belong in all of this. Mr. Sheehan disagrees with his wife about the Iraq War. Is his grief not as authentic as hers? But a father's loss lacks the wrenching immediacy afforded by maternal imagery, so dads fade into the background.

A second troubling feature of Sheehan's world is that a 24-year-old adult son who served one tour of duty in an All Volunteer Force, then signed up for a second tour of duty, then volunteered for a dangerous mission during which he lost his life, is frozen in time as perpetual "child." For we hear the staccato refrain over-and-over again, "She lost her child in Iraq." This loses sight of certain salient facts. Casey Sheehan wasn't a reluctant conscript, hauled off to fight against his will. He was an adult. Does this not count for anything? Rather than respecting the adult son who made tough decisions and paid with his life, the "Lost Child" motif strips Casey Sheehan of his adult status. Young Mr. Sheehan made some choices, but that is lost sight of.

The sad truth is that grieving mothers are no more immune from political mischief and misjudgment than anyone else. Sheehan's claims must, therefore, be evaluated as the extreme political claims that they are, laced through and through with conspiracy theory, vulgarisms, cheap shots, and plain old-fashioned ignorance. Her colossal mistake lies in the fact that the power of maternal loss, if it is to be galvanized to political ends, must be represented with dignity and gravitas. I think here of the Mothers of the Plaza in Argentina and the central role they played in calling attention to murderous policies in their country in the late 1970s and early 1980s. Although the mothers eventually fragmented along partisan lines, at the height of their protest they were the conscience of an Argentine society ripped apart by state-sponsored terrorism, governed by a military junta.

The mothers pled for fundamental human dignity and human rights. They argued against tyranny. They had no publicists nor spinners. In effect, they proclaimed: who among us will openly defend the abduction, torture, and murder of young people? Who among us will step forward and openly denounce basic human rights? Witnessing Las Madres in their powerful vigil in the heart of Buenos Aires, I was struck by the power their imagery evoked. And it did so precisely because the moral message was clear and unambiguous: A decent society does not "disappear" people, does not criminalize dissent. When I interviewed Las Madres, they told me that their protest aimed to prevent massive and egregious human rights abuses of the sort suffered by their sons and daughters from ever occurring again in Argentina. Further, they didn't want their sons and daughters obliterated from cultural memory. Their vigil and protest constituted a living memorial to those lost to political criminality.

In Cindy Sheehan's world one pillories, one inflames, one doesn't worry if one has the facts on one's side. She has apparently voiced sympathy for conspiracy theorists who opine that it is the "Jews and Israel" who are responsible for the Iraq war in the first place. Saddest of all is the fact that Sheehan's traveling protest now revolves around her. Casey Sheehan has faded into the backdrop. Cindy Sheehan's brand of political maternalism narrows rather than broadens our sympathies and our understanding by claiming a unique moral authority and insight that is hers—and, by extension, that of all who agree with her. Mothers who dissent from Sheehan's extreme position, and who have also lost sons, are regarded as ninnies who have been gulled. Surely it is far better for our political process to operate on the assumption that all citizens qua citizens have standing and moral voice and no single person or group of persons' moral authority is, or can be, absolute.

The Way Old Friends Do

Charles O'Brien

"You can never have too many friends."
Miller's Crossing

Oh, yes you can. And one of the things that has hampered the debate on that weary topic, the-left-and-the-war, is that too many people seem to know too many other people.

The Hitchens-Galloway debate had some promise as an *Event*. Sponsored jointly by the International Socialist Organization and The Nation Institute (and with the big signs to prove it), with the old *Nation* regulars, Navasky and all, seated down front, and with Amy Goodman as moderator (Vince McMahon would have been so much better), the actual hall was a place to steer clear of. A transcript wouldn't suffice: Galloway would just lie, Hitchens would say what he'd said elsewhere, Galloway's insults would be unearned, and Hitchens' superfluous. The telecast would be perfect. C-SPAN, unfortunately, was too chaste for the job, which called for razzle-dazzle camerawork and *lots* of audience shots. Long before Hitchens complained of "zoo noises," the viewers should have been pelting the screen with peanuts.

What was most interesting, though, was Galloway's attack: he threw Hitchens' past in his face. "You did write like an angel," he said toward the end. Hitchens once defended the Algerian FLN, that corrupt, murderous bunch. He once defended the massacre at the Munich Olympics. He once wanted the Iraqi annexation of Kuwait left alone. He once debated the Gulf War with Charlton Heston. Heston claimed that Saddam was a danger to his neighbors—demonstrably true. Hitchens recalls,

> When I asked him what the neighboring countries were, he said "Bahrain," which is, of course, an island. And it was all good sport.

He also told Heston—as Galloway happily recalled—to keep his wig on.

There would seem to be some few things in his past Hitchens might want to run away from, or at least wish unsaid. He's often asked, these days, and professes to regret just about nothing. Let's look at the Heston speech again since Hitchens seemed to recall it fondly. We learn that that an elderly Hollywood actor can't manage the kind of "geography" trick that eager third-graders excel at, memorizing a map; and that he attempts to look younger than his years. On the substance, Heston was right, and Hitchens was wrong. Iraq *has* attacked its neighbors. And the fact that Bahrain is an island would not have protected it from the region's largest military. The "of course" in "which is, of course, an island," is nice. It flatters the audience, but more important certifies that Hitchens who *is* *smart* for a living will not be seen even for a moment as less than smart. And the wig?

- What did you do in the war, Daddy?

- I humbled a bald man.

After the war, what Hitchens did was change his mind. He never saw that George H.W. Bush had been right to go to war against Saddam. Challenged by Galloway to explain the shift, Hitchens invoked his Iraqi "friends." It's often been noted that Hitchens talks a lot about his *friends*. Let's take one friend as an example: Salman Rushdie. Hitchens attacked the fatwa against Rushdie, attacked it, often, loudly, and eloquently. What's not so good is that Hitchens has said that his opinion of Khomeini and his regime was the product of that fatwa. But the fatwa came after the clerical seizure of power, and consolidation of power, the hostage-taking in Tehran, the hostage-taking in Lebanon, the profligate spending of Iranian lives in the war with Iraq. Khomeini's very route to power was the sacrificing of thousands upon thousands of his followers so there would be no delay, no negotiations, and no rivals. There was nothing occult about this iman. To anyone paying attention, it should have been obvious that he should never have left France alive. His barbarity should not have escaped notice until it touched a friend.

Or go back to those friends inside Iraq after the Gulf War. They welcomed the American military presence. Hitchens became convinced. But how? They made him see the badness of Ba'th rule. But old George Bush, or James Baker, or Charlton Heston could have told him the same thing. And what about his own earlier understanding of that war? It was a war for oil, a war of imperial aggrandizement, a conversion of a foreign land mass into a land for testing new weapons systems. These claims, if true, would not be negated by the bad experiences of those shut inside Iraq. They would be negated if they came to be seen as flimsy ideological constructs. It would be more useful were Hitchens to show those constructs collapsing rather than summon up some new batch of friends. Better than *friends*, friends in high places or low, near or far, is the willingness to see through preconceptions—those old friends. Similarly, Hitchens is right to pay attention to the Kurds of Iraq. They have great opportunity and grave responsibility. What their future will bring or should bring is not clear at all. The Kurds of Iraq are *important* but not because some of them are Hitchens' friends.

In the '60s, it was possible for people on the left to look back on an earlier generation of the left and think, "Well, that'll never happen to me." It hasn't worked out: the '60s left haven't aged well. The crowd at the debate was more pro-Galloway than not. Even forgetting the charges of financial corruption that trail him (supported by everything from Iraqi files to U.N. reports), there are his actual positions, which go beyond a simple "anti-war" stance. He has embraced Saddam and Assad, and from a safe distance, al-Zarqawi. From Algeria to Iraq, he applauds the bomb detonated among crowds of civilians. Yet when booked into a hall in New York, the seats were filled with people to cheer him on. Amy Goodman (author of *Exception to the Rulers*[1]) smiled a lot, and for two hours, "Amy" and "Chris" went pinging around the room. But when her opportunity came to ask Hitchens a question, she used it to, in effect, call Hitchens a whore:

> You've got a lot of nerve to say you are my friend, if you won't crawl out my window.

"You did write like an angel," Galloway finally said "but you're now working for the Devil, and damn you and all your works." Damn you and all your works: was it not for Hitchens to throw that line at Galloway, at Goodman, at The Nation Institute and the International Socialist Organization, at the people who had come to jeer at him?

II

Given its ostensible subject matter, the Iraq war, Paul Berman's new *Power and the Idealists* (Soft Skull Press) looks like an obvious follow-up to 2003's *Terror and Liberalism*.[2] But given its actual business, following a number of '68ers (especially Joschka Fischer) through the opening years of the century, it is the necessary continuation of *A Tale of Two Utopias* (not the "freestanding sequel" he calls it). The earlier book was a narrative of promises pretty much redeemed—but wasn't it too soon to say? This book is an account of lives lived, with all that mess, with a greater sense of actors who are nevertheless in the hands of events. There's more here.

If there's a problem, it's that he's too close to the subject. He's a slightly better friend than he is an observer. Berman devotes a few pages, for instance, to a debate between Richard Perle and Daniel Cohn-Bendit. He cares more for Cohn-Bendit—and who wouldn't? But the point—at *this* moment—is that Perle had the better of the argument. That as attractive a figure as Cohn-Bendit could be wrong against the former Reagan functionary is instructive; but figuring out just what the lesson is is hard work yet to be done.

Berman recalls Edward Said in the late '60s. He was Said's student, and he describes Said as "already an accomplished intellectual, in the early stages of his career." Berman and Said would stroll around the Columbia campus—bliss! Said was a brilliant academic politician. He was elegant, clubbable. The stroll around the campus is Said in full flower. What became of all that?

> By 2002, Edward Said, was a titanic figure in the universities and on the intellectual left, all over the world—a Sartre, in his fashion....

Titanic! Poor universities. Poor "intellectual left." His leftism was that thing one sees often these days, fashion-statement leftism. As a democrat, he was a gentlemen. And that he was "a Sartre, in his fashion," our Sartre, is too true. Sartre had his appeal. He was unattached, and lived a life parallel with bohemianism. He was a literary artist. As a philosopher, he was a vulgar Husserl, the vulgarity neither a good or a bad thing in itself, but Husserl was the less likely to intrude on Sartre's celebrity. Awarded the Nobel Prize, he refused it. Now, Said: He was a creature of great institutions. He was a literary critic, or rather a theoretician. His early celebrity came in large part from his absorption and use of then current—and un-translated—French theory. Soon enough, French theory became freely available throughout American academia. Said—never derivative, let's grant—would lose the aura of being singular. Said never turned down a Nobel. But he was that emblematic figure of our day, the oppositional intellectual laden with official honors. "Better wrong with Sartre...," it used to be said. Has anyone ever said, "Better wrong with Said?" More inevitably wrong, yes, sooner tenured, yes, less likely to disturb in polite company, yes—but is "wrong" something we even care about? Berman says of the 2002 Said:

> In writing about [Kanan] Makiya in *Al-Ahram*, Said adapted Sartre's style of polemic too, in its least attractive version—the disdainful air, the dismissiveness, the vindic-

tive ferocity dealt out from on high with the irritated air of an aristocrat shoving a peasant down the stairs.

But that Said of 2002 was not new; and he had, in fact, abused Makiya years before. Said's style of polemic was consistent. And there's some fun to be had from his obtuseness. His response to critics: they just want to make a name for themselves. To former students: Oedipal rage. Ariel Sharon: obese. Ari Fleischer: an Israeli citizen. The lordly Said of 2002 was the lordly Said Berman once admired in the late '60s (was, for that matter, the lordly child of privilege of the '40s and '50s). Early and late, he disserved human liberty.

Bernard Kouchner—founder of Doctors Without Borders—is one of Berman's heroes, and properly so. His admiration, though, leads to one serious misstep:

> In 1968, Kouchner thought about Nigeria. A ghastly war had broken out in the Nigerian provinces of Biafra in 1967. The war was a local affair, without any meaning for other people around the world.... [It] was a violent event that could not be described as the Spanish Civil War.

For a very different view, see Renata Adler's "Letter from Biafra" (in *Canaries in the Mine Shaft*). The Biafran War was anything but local. It was, precisely the Spain to our current war. Nigeria was strongly backed by the Arab world, Biafra only by Israel. The war was provoked by Mohammadan massacres of the Ibo, and the Islamist violence and encroachment of Sharia that dominate the news from Nigeria today are the natural consequence of the extinguishing of Biafra's hope. To use Biafra as mere backdrop for Kouchner is, whatever Berman's intent, to diminish Kouchner. He noticed Biafra, and grasped its significance. He was not a quirky guy with a big heart, but a canny witness to his time.

Joschka Fischer is the dodgiest element in the book. The original essay, "The Passion of Joschka Fischer" traced Fischer's passage from the fringes of the Red Army Faction to the NATO operation in Kosovo. He had to come to terms with the past (and there was a lot of that) and with the inclinations of his present party, the Greens. It would have been much easier to fall back on quasi-pacifism and "anti-imperialism." That he came down where he did is man-bites-dog. The expanded version of "Passion" is the first chapter of this book. Fischer's story did not end with the fall of Milosevic. What happened later with Fischer was this: a dog bit a man. Fischer may be, as Berman insists, an interesting politician, but the easy assumptions of the Greens, of Germany, of the E.U. will only carry him so far.

Berman devotes several pages to Fisher's public confrontation with Donald Rumsfeld. When Rumsfeld went to Europe—"Old Europe"—to ask for support in the nearing invasion of Iraq, Foreign Minister Fischer refused that support. He did so to Rumsfeld's face, and in English. The line that made the headlines—in Germany, here, around the world—was, "Excuse me. I'm not convinced." Berman says this,

> His English words said, in effect, that he had listened to Rumsfeld very carefully, and had done so in Rumsfeld's language, without risking any of the misunderstandings that crept into translated remarks. Fischer's English sentences demonstrated that he had leant over backward to accept the American arguments…. Or perhaps Fischer switched into English because he was still speaking to Rumsfeld man to man, and he wanted to be absolutely positive that Rumsfeld understood. He wanted to give Rumsfeld one more chance to look at the world through someone else's skeptical eyes.

This is all pretty dubious. Rumsfeld's message was not likely to be lost in translation. Central Europe, "New Europe," where fluency in English could not be assumed, understood just fine, understood and sent troops. If linguistic nuance had mattered, Fischer's using English wouldn't help. What Fischer told Rumsfeld just before "Excuse me" was this:

> To make the case in a democracy you must convince by yourself.

"Convince by yourself" is not idiomatic. You think you know what he meant, and immediately think not. And as to Fischer's getting at the particularities of what Rumsfeld said, it is doubtful that a non-American, native speaker of English can catch the full flavor of Rummy's performances. Fischer "had leant over backwards." All evidence suggests the opposite. He was speaking to Rumsfeld "man to man." Rather he was creating, consciously so, a moment of theater. And giving Rumsfeld "one more chance;" Fischer's words don't say, Give me a little more, something to work with. Not in public, they don't. They say: I've heard you out; you've been heard out; time to go. After the last parliamentary elections in Germany, Fischer lost his job as foreign minister and has retired. The German papers summarized his tenure by printing his English words to Rumsfeld. Are these the capstones of a great legacy, I'm not convinced.

You're not where you were, and there's no going back there.

Notes

1.   The best line of the night was Hitchens' claim that he recognized his hecklers' "leftist revolutionary credentials and the scars you can demonstrate from your long underground twilight struggle against Dick Cheney." He could have been quoting Ms. Goodman's c.v.

2.   *The Nation*'s review of the book was, predictably, a hit piece. Berman was accused of splitting the left. A war against a '30s vintage fascist party, a war denounced by a wide array of figures on the right, a war labeled "Trotskyist" and "Bolshevik," might just be a cause of the left. But no, say the arbiters at *The Nation*, there is *a* left position, and it is theirs.

Reason and Revolution

Russell Jacoby

A contribution to a First *forum on 9/11 published in September, 2006 ("Five Years On").*

Once upon a time politics—even assassinations—required manifestos and statements. The Russian "People's Will," which assassinated Alexander II, peppered the world with demands: free speech, a free press, and universal suffrage. Now nineteen highly-organized Muslims snuff out thousands of lives and decapitate a city but are unable, or unwilling, to put together a single sentence as to why. We still can only guess. American bases in Saudi Arabia? Israeli occupation of Palestine? Pizza Hut in Cairo? A revived Muslim Caliphate? In one respect at least talk of Islamic fascism may be too generous. Mussolini enlisted a credible philosopher to write up the entry for Fascism in the Italian Encyclopedia. Even the Nazis had a party program.

A left flags when the status quo is better than the alternative. Today this is almost the case—not intellectually, but emotionally. Those who disembowel Dutch filmmakers, riot over Danish cartoons, behead American journalists, issue death sentences for English writers and slay Algerian novelists seek a future that makes the Inquisition look like a PTA meeting. We have nothing in common with them. Yet to defend a bad establishment against a movement that is worse is one thing. To forget it is bad is another. The captains of government that are unwilling to raise the meager minimal wage—now $5.15 an hour—without exempting $10 million estates from taxes deserve a fate they will probably escape. These same folk call special congressional sessions to intervene in the case of one brain-damaged woman and contentedly watch millions scramble for health care amid a collapsed system. And this only begins their sins. A critical path is still open. A left emerged out of the Enlightenment with its Voltairean denunciations of state and religion. We can do much worse than to return to it.

The Truman Show

Eric Lott

A contribution to a First *forum on 9/11 published in September, 2006 ("Five Years On").*

Five years on from 9/11, and especially since the 2003 start of the war in Iraq, what I resent most is that a surprising number of writers and thinkers have raised the Cold War analogy to the status of faith. Liberal hawk philosopher prince Paul Berman, for one, has in his books *Terror and Liberalism* (2003) and *Power and the Idealists* (2005) consolidated his unapologetic Cold War liberalism for a post-Cold War era. In Berman's words, "[t]he war between liberalism and Islamism mirrored perfectly, in [its war of ideas], the earlier wars between liberalism and other forms of totalitarianism." And: "Today the totalitarian danger has not yet lost its sting, and there is no wisdom in claiming otherwise. The literature and language of the mid-twentieth century speak to us about danger of that sort. That is the thesis of my book [*Terror and Liberalism*]." Given all this, it is interesting to note that man-of-the-left Berman warmly reviewed in the *New York Times* ex-neocon but still man-of-the-right Francis Fukuyama's *America at the Crossroads* (2006)—as did, for that matter, *America Right or Wrong* author Anatol Lieven (in *The National Interest*), who in 2004 polemicized against liberal hawks like Berman! Lieven writes that his new book (co-authored with the Heritage Foundation's John Hulsman), not unlike Fukuyama's, will try to steer a path between neoconservatism and liberal hawkishness in the interest of "returning to the best traditions of the Truman and Eisenhower administrations, advocat[ing] generous aid for the development of key allies—and not only development but equitable development." Who would have thought such a more-or-less synchronization of views possible even a few years ago? But there's more.

The occasion for Lieven's 2004 polemic was the publication of *New Yorker* writer George Packer's edited collection *The Fight Is for Democracy*, where again the language of liberal anti-totalitarianism is mobilized in several essays, including Packer's introduction and Berman's envoi. Lieven, in *The Nation*, deemed most of Packer's writers reminiscent of '70s Scoop Jackson Democrats, most of whom eventually became Republicans via the neoconservative movement; Lieven suggests the new breed ought "to take the same route to the Republican Party as their Scoop Jackson predecessors, but much more quickly.... For as long as they continue seriously to influence Democratic thinking, they will make it much more difficult for the Democrats to emerge as a clear foreign policy alternative to the Republicans, and much more difficult for a genuine national debate on foreign policy to take place in the United States—particularly when it comes to strategy in the Middle East and the war on terrorism." Packer, responding in a letter to *The Nation*, defended what "used to be the aims of American liberals" and charged Lieven (surprise!) with sectarianism: "Presumably, once the party is purified of anyone who challenges its least useful orthodoxies, victory will be within its grasp." And yet, minus the litmus test of the war (Lieven anti, Packer pro)—and even that has been a matter of wild vacillation in recent months (Packer, for example, now appears to have lost heart; see the comments he gave the *San Francisco Chronicle* in December 2005)—there seems very little indeed that separates the positions of Lieven and Packer or a host of other liberals. A memorable set piece in Packer's bestselling book *The Assassin's Gate* strikes the essential, common note: in passages of understated but unmistakable sympathy, Packer writes of an Iowa man whose son, a private in the army, is killed by roadside explosives in Baghdad in 2003 and who becomes, in essence, a Cold War liberal —an avid reader of Cold-War history, a believer in the present relevance of the Truman Doctrine, and a supporter of (then pro-war) Democrat John Edwards in the Iowa caucuses the following winter.

The siren song of the Truman Doctrine, in other words, plus or minus a few particulars, has in short order begun to constitute a new kind of political common sense, a psychic limit beyond which it apparently has become difficult for many U.S. intellectuals to think. It is not just the liberal left who live in this Cold War simulacrum: a recent article in Fukuyama's new journal, *The American Interest*, invokes the comparison of Bush and Rice to Truman and Acheson (so often made by the Bush team itself) mostly to defend the latter against the former. Even a recent study of neocon godfather Leo Strauss himself describes Strauss's position as "liberalism without illusions" and associates him with Cold War liberals such as Raymond Aron, Isaiah Berlin, Walter Lippman, and Lionel Trilling (Steven B. Smith, *Reading Leo Strauss: Politics, Philosophy, Judaism*). This bewildering meeting of minds in or near the American center as of mid-2006 is one of the saddest results of 9/11 in the realm of ideas. I have polemically traced some of the pre-history of this liberal centrism in my book *The Disappearing Liberal Intellectual*, the general response to which, as was perhaps to be expected, affirmed the need for a responsible liberal alternative to my petulant, wild-eyed, self-indulgent, irrelevant radicalism. But the new speculative bubble I have come to think of as the Truman show is a bounded mental universe, as in the Peter Weir film, of self-evident Cold-War clarity that, in a time of perpetual war for perpetual peace, seems to constitute, for a great range of thinkers, the very edge of sense. In this pax fides, the Cold War is the explicit template for the war against "Islamo-fascism." The celebrated summa of the Truman show is 35-year-old former *New Republic* editor Peter Beinart's *The Good Fight: Why Liberals—and Only Liberals—Can Win the War on Terror and Make America Great Again.* That both Bill and Hillary Clinton attended the book party for *The Good Fight* (though they didn't overlap) indicates something of the weight Beinart's position already carries in Washington policy circles. That both Joe Klein (from the left, in the *Times Book Review*) and Ronald Radosh (from the right, in the *New York Sun*) reviewed the book positively suggests the ideological consensus the book has helped forge, or confirm, or both.

"In our contestation with Stalinism we never allowed to lapse, for one moment, our contestation with capitalism and with Western imperialism," wrote E.P. Thompson in *The Poverty of Theory.* You find none of this in the current Truman craze. Nor are the Cold-War words of, say, C. Wright Mills's *Causes of World War Three* taken up: "For the first time in American history, men in authority talk about an 'emergency' without a foreseeable end. For the first time in world history, men find themselves preparing for a war which, they admit among themselves, none of the combatants could win. They have no image of what 'victory' might mean, and no idea of any road to victory.... There are no terms of surrender and there is no confidence in the military means of imposing any such terms." The Islamist thugs who gave us 9/11 have among other things left us in a nostalgic intellectual muddle. The globalization that produced them and their methods has redounded to a warm U.S. embrace of the military-postindustrial nation-state. Five years after, our responses feel about half a century out of date.

Refugees and Searchers Go to the Movies

Armond White

"*Are we still alive?*" That's the line incarnating the unexpectedly avant-garde challenge in Steven Spielberg's *War of the Worlds*. It's when the film steps beyond the simple conventions of genre filmmaking—of being a movie about an invasion from Mars—and expresses our very contemporary concern with survival. Yes, this line speaks to post-9/11 consciousness. It gets said when Ray Farrier (Tom Cruise) and his two children have retreated to a basement bunker in a suburban home to escape an unseen, explosive cataclysm that comes deafeningly closer. But more than that, it's when Spielberg sublates our sophistication about filmmaking—and film watching—to address the worries that people have in their heads, even as they tell themselves they're merely seeking "entertainment."

Spielberg lets the screen go black for about five seconds. The communal experience of filmgoing then becomes a shared nightmare. With the screen unlit, the emergency lights in the theater are the only source of illumination. If you jump (as I did), you fear for a moment that the movie has stopped—the reel fallen off its plate, the fantasy interrupted by unfunny, drop-dead reality. "Are we still alive?" whispered by Farrier's daughter Rachel (Dakota Fanning) is an inquiry that invokes our own doubts about our safety, our capacity to dream, our possible awakening to dire reality. It recalls how many people felt after 9/11. Are we dreaming? Are we still alive? Bringing everyday experience and existential contemplation together so forcefully, Spielberg joins the ranks of the most audacious avant-garde filmmakers: He turns the popcorn movie experience into a consideration of the abyss.

War of the Worlds is the most powerful movie of the new century thus far. It's no surprise that many critics have been skeptical about its meaning and its effect, because it overturns every assumption that is casually held about the purpose of movies. *War of the Worlds* challenges how we reconcile our need for entertainment with our awareness of political reality after 9/11.

Let's immediately dispose of the naïve assumption that this is an entertainment about aliens—*E.T.* angrily remade by *Bad Santa*. It's something far different—not snarky but *alarmed*. Spielberg's previous film, *The Terminal*, confronted convivial, in fact benign, issues about America as an international symbol of freedom and welcome. It was a response to 9/11 that asked *Why?* Dramatizing Spielberg's (and our) bewilderment, it jumped off from the notion of America as a world helpmate—a capitalist Arcadia no one would object to but might, possibly, have underappreciated. Tom Hanks' misplaced immigrant Viktor is stuck at JFK airport while his home country undergoes a plausible eastern European revolution—thus leaving him stateless. But the naïf Viktor, doesn't simply buy into mainline America's preferred version of that utopian myth. The

Statue of Liberty idea ("Give me your tired, poor and restless, yearning to be free") was passed on to him by his ancestors—through his father's reality-based affection for American jazz music; the articulation of a downtrodden people who magically found a means of expressing their dreams in a land that formerly enslaved them. *The Terminal* examined Hope. *War of the Worlds* is the equally valid post-9/11 examination of Fear. Instead of Why?, it asks: What do we do now?

Working within the innocuous context of the science-fiction/fantasy genre, Spielberg has made a movie that, surprisingly, gets real about the need to prepare for war. (Just as *Close Encounters* contained images of awesome agape, *War of the Worlds* is filled with awesome shock.) That Pirandellian moment that wakes up viewers by blacking them out and leaving them in a felt state of emergency through the imbrication of theater houselights forces our consciousness about the cinematic and cinema-going process into moral awareness. We're not just here to be entertained but to connect our imaginative faculties to what is most important in our lives.

Spielberg is aware American popular culture cannot, conscientiously, be made the same way after 9/11. And, despite conventional critical wisdom, he's the one pop artist most alive to the profundity of the way we live now. He has remade *War of the Worlds* not simply as an homage to Orson Welles' 1938 radio spectacular or Byron Haskin's Technicolor 1955 dazzlement. Rather, Spielberg re-conceives this make-believe—internalizing the psychic trauma of 9/11—but with the faith, like Viktor's, that American art-making is a serious endeavor. Movies like *The Color Purple, Schindler's List, Amistad* and *Saving Private Ryan* were not Oscar bait but efforts of a Hollywood practitioner to contemplate the world and history more earnestly—though he proved it in the dark like a deceptively playful jazz artist.

I

Tom Cruise's father figure at *War* first becomes memorable during a moment when he is stunned, rendered helpless. After seeing the attack of the aliens first hand, his face covered in the ash of vaporized innocent citizens, Ray Farrier becomes a lightning rod for his children's awareness of the terrible state of things. How his daughter Rachel and his son Robbie (Justin Chatwin) react to the dire phenomena shows Speilberg's real-life sensitivity. Ray isn't sure what to do; yet he and his children have notions beyond the survival instinct. "Is it the terrorists?" Rachel wonders aloud. "Is it the Europeans?" Robbie asks, dredging up the recent hostility the European community has shown towards the American government.

Critics have been unwilling to see how the film plays out Spielberg's not-namby pamby, not conventionally "liberal" response to 9/11. His concern is with the younger generation's clear-eyed identification with the cause of humanity; their natural feelings and political instincts as embodied in the son's insistence that he be allow to "enlist" or at least personally observe the battle. ("You have to let me do this!" he insists to his understandably protective father. Those who think Spielberg follows the standard Hollywood-liberal line might be taken aback when they realize that Speilberg is not mocking youthful bellicosity and patriotic fervor, a young man's willingness to "sign-up.")

War of the Worlds is about fear and action. While liberal critics enthused over the nonsensical references to George Bush in *Star Wars: Revenge of the Sith* ("This is how liberty dies, to thunderous applause." And "Only a Sith believes in absolutes"), they conveniently disregard how Spielberg dramatizes war experiences: Rachel's trepidation, Robbie's eagerness to join-up and fight. This young generation's idealism takes the movie beyond their father's desperation and caution (which evokes the trepidation of the older generation and the cluelessness of the doctrinaire Left). Spielberg digs into grass roots intuition—the aggression that legendarily spurs us on. That's why the movie ends in Boston, with a shot of a Minuteman statue that illustrates the historic American struggle for freedom and independence. This piece of statuary is a startling reminder of what freedom looks like; for alert viewers it may even serve as a deliberate contrast to those famous 2003 images of Saddam Hussein's statue coming down (again and again) in that Baghdad square.

It is a sign of Spielberg's uniqueness as a pop artist that he uses avant-garde, high-tech filmmaking means to articulate what some would call a conservative patriotic message. Leftist critics insist this is proof of his non-progressive thinking (his "lack [of] self-knowledge" according to *The Nation*). But *War of the Worlds*, so kinetically adept and visually astonishing, is certainly the work of a film artist fully in-tune with his emotional responses. What left pundits don't realize is that he is also instinctively in touch with how audiences take in cinematic stimuli, aware of their subconscious response. Snob critics, satisfied with their sense of superiority, constantly relegate Spielberg to realm of non-seriousness and trivial manipulation. But it is an observable fact that audiences at *War of the Worlds* do not hoop and holler as they did at *Independence Day*, enjoying the violence, savoring the nifty death routines. That silly film (and its recent equivalent, Roland Emmerich's *The Day After Tomorrow*) wasn't concerned with "Are We Still Alive?" It was demonstrably non-political. *War of the Worlds* should be appreciated for its political sophistication and subtle power.

II

The "Are We Still Alive?" moment evokes the scene in Hitchcock's *The Birds* where a family under siege waits in their home, anticipating the worst. Spielberg recreates that ominous quiet but then extends the action-movie formula for excitation in taut, anxiety-inducing increments. After 9/11 he won't play with dread. The poetic anguish of *The Birds* is revived here but re-imagined—ready for a world in which 9/11 has stirred long-suppressed fears among Americans who had previously imagined war as something that happened elsewhere—not in one's backyard. Among the extraordinary images in *War of the Worlds* is the scene that follows that "Are We Still Alive?" blackout. As if awakening at some terrible dawn, we see an American home with its front blasted away, a downed jet-engine turbine where a dining table used to be. The juxtaposition is surreal. Farrier carefully instructs his daughter not to look, to keep her eyes on him no matter what. He doesn't want her to see the destruction, the upheaval and devastation of domesticity.

Spielberg takes audiences through precisely what parents, after 9/11, are unable to shield their children against. He treats comfortable American audiences like war-torn refugees, not sci-fi geeks. The opposite of this noble impulse can be found in Sam Mendes' *Jarhead*. Instead of addressing Operation Iraqi Freedom, Mendes goes back to the 1991 Desert Shield-into-Desert Storm. He rewrites David O. Russell's good *Three Kings*—a surprisingly thoughtful and wide-ranging observation of American power and innocence —then slickly invokes Vietnam-era skepticism that was featured in *Full Metal Jacket, Platoon* and *Apocalypse Now*. Mendes, a British citizen who has never made a movie about his home turf, is committed to the easy, supercilious tactic of satirizing the follies of the world's largest superpower. As slick as Mike Nichols, he knows this plays well among the left media. In *Jarhead* he casts a quick, lame glance at American foreign policy without risking the dissension caused by Spielberg's native understanding. Mendes commits an insulting revision of pop art and pop politics when he implicitly encourages his '05 audience to adopt a kind of unearned version of the cynicism once expressed by those who underwent the Vietnam experience. (He never evokes Oliver Stone's *Born on the Fourth of July* perhaps because

Mendes' shallow social consciousness was born no earlier than March 2003.)

War of the Worlds pushes its avant-garde political art toward a new understanding of American history—lessons derived from the most complicated, not most fashionable, cinema. Spielberg has finally made his version of that movie brat staple *The Searchers*, John Ford's 1957 western reverie of the Indian Wars that was also a revelation of the conservative and liberal split in America's consciousness. Spielberg is fully cognizant of Ford's political ambivalence; recent history has caused him to share it. Ray Farrier isn't a racist pioneer like John Wayne's Ethan Edwards but he does venture into new territory—the post-9/11 American trepidation that is not racist, nor xenophobic like Ethan Edwards', but healthily skeptical, practical and defensive.

The Searchers doesn't have a moment as stressful as Ray's conflict with Harlan Ogilvy (Tim Robbins). Probably many lefties were disturbed by Robbins' casting as a half-crazed survivalist; they expected him to personify the usual lefty positions of his own propaganda films *Bob Roberts* and *Cradle Will Rock*. But Robbins applies his full artistry to portraying a complicated, modern type—the scared American unable to rationalize his defenses. When he and Ray clash (a harrowing tete-a-tete that is also a power struggle), the shifts between heroism and cowardice, intelligence and desperation are actively visualized.

Spielberg realizes he's portraying the reality of uncertainty—the doubts about American might and right and the difficulty of determining which character ultimately represents which. But the logic of his narrative implicitly endorses Ray's will. Ray must take action he cannot fully justify to his daughter and, again, commands her not to look. The pop-wise audience is momentarily spared the sight of murder, but Spielberg subtly admits it in an ensuing moment of vicious pantomime: an alien, image-ed as a glaring eye—a nightmarish depiction of self-consciousness—is literally beheaded. The instant of Ray's inhumanity, when he submits to his own murderous impulse, is also the moment when he kills his own sleep. He is neither condoned nor condemned. By the end of the movie, Spielberg clarifies the personal consequences of the ugly act that Ray was forced to commit, acknowledging what all the movie brats from Scorsese and George Lucas to Paul Schrader and John Milius have been reluctant to admit about Ethan Edwards in *The Searchers*. Although they celebrate intransigence, they don't face up to the discomfiting reality of John Wayne's hard man. Spielberg exposes their obliviousness in the controversial final moment of *War of the Worlds*, which fools mistake for sentimentality.

In this scene Ray Farrier is excluded from his family's reunion. He is kept outside the miraculously preserved homestead in an image constructed just like the closing scene of *The Seachers*. After all he has gone through and what he has seen and done, he cannot sit easily at the American family hearth. And despite gossip column pariah Tom Cruise playing the part, the suffering of his character Ray Farrier is noble. It should not be disdained or ignored as happened with Vietnam vets. Ray must stand outside the American home—a civilian-soldier whose humanity and psychic well-being have been sacrificed. This is not standard self-reflexive, post-modern iconography but a prescient movie image built on Spielberg's familiarity with the cost of life during wartime—from pop zeitgeist (*1941*) to contemporary remembrance (*Saving Private Ryan*). The image of Ray removed from domestic idylls poetically defines the situation of citizens in crisis from the twin towers to Hurricane Katrina, from refugees to searchers. Ray's forlorn figure standing in solitary on an autumnal suburban street reveals that weight felt by every post-9/11 American desperately holding on for something to believe in, wondering "Are We Still Alive?" For some, the answer to this moral question may well be unimaginable, as if the screen of our collective consciousness has gone blank. Spielberg's final scene fills in our doubt, suggestively. It anticipates every family reunion that occurs as a result of Operation Iraqi Freedom—that is, the lucky ones.

Now Lie in It

In a time when a toney brownstone
Is worth way more than tens of thousands
Of brown skins in Iraq, sleep on a bed of straw
Or a lumpy old mattress, not a Posturepedic.

In a time when the ultimate leader
Rules that our soldiers' bodies must be broken
In the name of spreading the jam of our way
Of life on the broken crusts of Iraq,

Sleep on a hard bed to remind yourself of your luck
That you don't have to leave your spouse and kids
And ride a Humvee with your fingers crossed,
Hoping a bomb or missile won't blow you up.

In a war caused by lies lie
On your hard bed and just try to sleep.

—George Held

Part XI

Amateur Hours (or The Pity of Love)

As I was finishing up this volume, Michael Lydon sent me his latest self-published pamphlet, *A House of Books*. His subject—why/how/which books in a New England home library speak to a common reader— grabbed me because it synched up with my own task as I looked back over 10 years of *First*s trying to pick pieces for this volume.

But it wasn't only Lydon's theme that seemed aligned. His DIY aesthetic reminded me of the impulse that moved *First*'s crew to make our own tabloid. And beyond that, his latest pointed to deeper motivations that have kept us (and him) going. Like our occasional *First*s, Lydon's self-published works have been amateur creations. And the root of amateur is love as Armond White reminds us in his contribution to this final section.

I don't mean to promote "fate crap" but the message implicit in Lydon's latest pushed me to end this volume with pieces of love (and pity). There's an explicit lesson in our fellow amateur's *House* that seemed spot on too. The book-loving Lydon observes, "the more life in a book the more likely it will live." I hope *First of the Year: 2008* comes alive on every page.

Fathers and Sons

Benj DeMott

Born on Christmas Day, jazz pianist Don Pullen inspired something like faith among those who witnessed his miraculous live performances.

I got initiated back in the '80s when I was getting overpaid dispatching limos for lawyers. After an evening shift, I'd often take a free car to catch a late set at Downtown jazz clubs where I'd sniff the Cointreau and swing alone with masters like Tony Williams, Jackie McLean, Wayne Shorter, Betty Carter, Benny Carter, Max Roach, Hank Jones, Richard Davis, David Murray, McCoy Tyner. And Don Pullen who broke me out of my solitary lush life. Shaken and stirred, rolling on his rhythms like a jerking boat, I felt at sea. (But not entirely without historical coordinates since I'd been Experienced, Clash-ed and Afro-popped.) As Pullen action-painted what was dancing in his head, he made me want to socialize rather than settle for individuating pleasures provided by his jazz peers—I had to share the shock of this new music. Pullen was the one jazz artist I pressed all my intimates to hear live. I loved getting gone with them as he'd sound out of their world—hammering the keys to their hearts with the backs of his fingers, fists and elbows.

You can catch Pullen in the act of creation on the DVD *Mingus at Montreux* (1975) which documents a performance by a small group that includes drummer Dannie Richmond and saxophonist George Adams (who went on to make their own band with Pullen and bassist Cameron Brown after Mingus died). When Mingus turns the beat around (after smoking a cigar) in "Sue's Changes," Pullen takes the pick-ed up pace as a dare. Acting on his free jazz impulse, he swirls up a whirlwind. The scene/sound of Pullen's fine heedlessness on the DVD has something in common with another image—"more live-action film than snapshot"—relayed by a jazz fan replaying "what I see when I hear Don Pullen:"

> Don is at the piano playing with the repertory band Mingus Dynasty.... A few minutes into the piano solo on "Haitian Fight Song," something amazing happens. Pullen begins throwing down a series of ferocious right-hand clusters—one of his trademarks—when, shockingly, he dislocates a finger. In obvious pain he attempts to shake the throbbing digit back into place, all the while continuing the tonal barrage with his left hand. Without hesitation, Pullen completes his musical statement, then steps off stage to address the injury. This odd choreography comes off so matter of fact-ly, I get the distinct impression he's done this dance before.[1]

No doubt. But Pullen had so much time in his hands. *Mingus at Montreux* shows him treating the Tradition gentle when the band does Mingus's tribute to Lester Young, "Good-By Pork Pie Hat." Pullen lights the Montreux night with soft cascades of notes that float out over Lake Geneva before falling down around Mingus's bass tones—a tour de douceur that hints why Mingus once grabbed a microphone during another supremely tender Pullen piano solo and shouted at some loud college kids in a club: "Shut up out there. This cat's playin' his ass off."

Stanley Crouch understood that back in 1984 when he pointed out:

> Pullen is able to get effects that resemble what one would expect of a percussive harp, since he has invented for himself ways of stroking the keyboard for splashes of ideas that nearly fuse the notes together, making his variations into bursts of sound.... As you listen to Pullen you become aware of how much he knows about giving each note the color he wants it to have. If he wants a note to ping, it pings; when he wants a floating, song-like quality, the note rises from the string and curves in the air.

Pullen left his fans hanging forever when he died (young) in 1995. His music wasn't widely known while he was alive so it was gratifying when NYC's Jazz Gallery honored him in 1999 with an exhibit and solo concert series ("From Gospel to the Globe") that affirmed Pullen was *the* piano player of his generation. (The Gallery's shows seconded Stanley Crouch's judgment—"Pullen has probably done more than any other musician associated with the so-called avant-garde to make the most adventurous harmonic combinations and flat out blocks of clustered notes ... work within the forms of songs.") I can't rate Pullen as I'm no jazz expert but for years I've felt that I've owed him a piece (at least). My impulse to finally pay that debt now has something to do with the recent death of my Dad who was a writer first but always a jazz piano player too. Sharing music gave us something beyond words. Still, I'm not all clear about why his passing has sent me back to Don Pullen. One reason I'm writing this is to find out.

But I won't require immediate indulgence on that score. My first Pullen-inspired revelation isn't all about me and/or my pop.

Surfing the web last summer, I came across a German website devoted to musical file-sharing where I heard a snatch of a 17 minute track titled "Goree" that Pullen composed for *Well-Kept Secrets*—an album he made in the '70s as co-leader of The Beaver Harris/Don Pullen 360 Experience. Goree is a small island off the coast of Senegal at the westernmost point of Africa that was central to the slave trade for centuries. Thousands of slaves (over hundreds of years) suffered through their final days before the Middle Passage in dungeons on the island. I visited it once with my wife and her family. And the sample from Pullen's "Goree" made me want to hear how he'd handled the weight of the island's past.

Well-Kept Secrets isn't an easy record to find. The German webmaster at the file-sharing site didn't respond to my online enquiries. But a few weeks later I learned longtime jazz journalist Howard Mandel (who wrote liner notes for a number of Pullen's '90s CDs) had a copy of the album and he graciously agreed to let me have a listen to "Goree." When I knocked on the door of his office in the Village, Mandel seemed ready to get on with his business (though he was polite). He hadn't heard "Goree" in decades—he vaguely recalled a "blow-out"—but the track turned out to be something more considered. When the awe-full music filled up the space between us, we both faded back in time. I recalled my Senegalese mother-in-law looking at the grandest Baobab tree on Goree with an animist's eye, wondering what it had witnessed....

Pullen's composition jumps off with a puzzling jingle jangle meant (I realized when it rang my bell again later in the track) to evoke chimes on slaves' chains that Goree's wardens—Portuguese and Dutch and English and French—used to monitor their captives' movements. Pullen solos into the mix, serenely scaling up and down the keyboard until those hellish bells give his melody snake an ugly twist. That tolling underscores how slaves were regarded as livestock and "Goree" becomes a sort of horrific pastoral. It plays like an aural equivalent of "The Fall of Icarus"—the Bruegel painting depicting a tingling spring land-and-seascape "concerned with itself" as the mythic figure of Icarus drowns quite unnoticed off in the corner. Though there's more iron in Pullen's ironic approach to the nature of indifference because he's trying to get real about obliviousness on Goree—an actual blood-and-treasure island. Green and hilly like Breughel's idealized image of the natural world, it's a pretty, eerie place dotted with stone steps and ramparts that offer expansive views of the Atlantic and the city of Dakar back on the mainland. A protected, sandy beach with wavelets calls out to small children to come lose themselves by the sea....

The slavemasters found themselves a sweet spot. Though it's hard to imagine anyone taking the evening breeze or sipping their Claret while around the corner or (in some slave "castles") under trap doors in dining rooms, starving Africans were locked into cells waiting to be jettisoned through "the Door of No Return."

When the bells start tolling again after Pullen's first masterful solo in "Goree," I thought of Morgan Freeman's fearful moment in *Amistad*—Freeman plays a respectable Northern "Negro"—sure of himself and his attainments—who almost loses it when he goes down into the hold of the empty slave ship and bumps into the chains of the departed. Once "Goree's" chimes of slavery fade, Philly International style horns and a marching beat put me in mind of another pop moment that may well have had resonance for Pullen and his band-mates back in the '70s. "Goree" seems to offer an avant-garde echo of Gamble & Huff's "Ship Ahoy"—the audacious side-long "conscious" song about the slave trade those R&B auteurs composed for a hit O-Jays album in 1973. It's not a stretch to think Pullen (who played organ in R&B combos throughout the 60s) or some other pop-wise head in the 360 band picked up on Gamble & Huff's liberation orchestrations.

Pullen brings home the message in his own Black Atlantic music by playing with oceanic feeling on top of drums that snap like whips coming down. That sound is muffled though. You have to try to hear it. To get down with it as Amiri Baraka might say, instead of elevating "the intellectual process above emotions."

Baraka has visited Goree with his family and his comments on that experience provide deep background for Pullen's composition:

> My son Ras and I went up there in Goree ... and when we went to the slave castle and we sat up there in this dungeon with the door closed and everything, tears started coming out of our eyes. The two of us sitting there, father and son, not saying a word, just sitting there crying. Why? I don't know. It's just that feeling is too strong, it's too strong.... You just sit there and suddenly, psychologically you begin to feel it on you. It's something. You don't want that but you start feeling it. I remember we came out of there crying and when we came out in the open, it was a group of French tourists walking towards us, and Ras says to me, what they want? What do these White people want? That thing grips you. When you come into that, when you actually come close to slavery itself—I don't mean stories of it, but when you actually get close to it, it will do something to you. No doubt about it. They got a hole in the wall, the door of no return and if you couldn't make it they would just kick you aside into the ocean. A lot of the people had never seen the ocean, you know, because they were from inland. They had seen lakes. They might jump out there and think they could swim it, might think it was a lake, but that was the Atlantic Ocean and the sharks be circling down in there. Now when you conceive that and conceive that there were people upstairs over the prison, who lived there, who had a little hatch, a trap door in their floor where they could look through there and check on the slaves, you understand what I'm saying? You've got to be a cold mamajamma to do that. People down there [makes screaming sounds] screaming and what not, and you can pick up the door, you have your dinner and sh– upstairs and you could pick up the door and look down and see what was happening with that, well, you can't have no feeling with that. Feeling has to be abolished. That's why I'm saying they make that separation between the intellectual process and emotion. But I say, if you can't feel you can't think. That's my feeling about that. That's why we ask philosophers every morning, how you feel?

"Goree's" protest against Oblivion Wind was one of Don Pullen's numberless answers to that question. His musical conceptions always embodied felt responses. (Max Gordon, longtime owner of the *Village Vanguard*, once said of Pullen's '80s band—The Don Pullen-George Adams Quartet—"Whatever it is, at least they play with anger. I don't go to sleep when they're up there.") Pianist D.D. Jackson's recollection of his first encounter with Pullen underscores there was no disassociation of sensibility in the man's music or mind:

> Pullen was conducting a master class where he proceeded to turn the entire audience, many of whom were distinguished jazz teachers and performers as well as students, completely on its head in terms of how they thought about music. Here was somebody who instead of, for example, focusing on which scale sounded good with which chord, and on the right way to approach a voicing, was dealing with "concept" on an almost cosmic level. He talked about the relationship between playing "outside" versus "in," and how you could combine the two, not just over time during a solo, but often at the same time, between the two hands.

Jackson recalled Pullen's master class at a memorable celebration
of Pullen's life that took place at St. Peter's Church on June 11, 1995.
There were performances by dancers (including Garth Fagin's company),
singers like Amina Claudine Myers and Abbey Lincoln (whose "Down
Here Below" left us perfectly bereft and dying for more), groups led by
horn-men (Howard Johnson and David Murray) and pianists (Geri Allen
and John Hicks), Pullen's own African-Brazilian Connection with D.D.
Jackson sitting in on piano. There were also spoken tributes that echoed
Jackson's memories of his master's way into the music. One of Pullen's
sons explained his pop's Zennish method of piano instruction, remembering ruefully how Pullen let him play one note in their first lesson. Amiri
Baraka, who'd been tight with Pullen ever since their days in the Black
Arts Movement of the '60s, delivered a eulogy that reached for inspiration "like the voice of our mother the sky when she is wet and on fire"
and left off on a sustained high note of identity politics....

> Don was my Brother. He could sing to me like from a very old place and I would feel
> and hear and understand. And then we would be flying, Black up against the guinea
> blue. In my memory Don is the future waiting to say hello again. And we know life
> does not end. Don, if you dig it, is where ever Blue is light, he circles just above our
> heads, invisible and nuclear, telling quiet stories in the voice of the mother tongue,
> so we are never alone.

I was listening in the packed Church along with the woman who
would later become my wife. We hadn't been dating long, she'd never
seen Don Pullen play, wasn't familiar with jazz and (as a good Muslim)
didn't exactly share my instinct to drink whatever was flowing from the
cup. But she got the groove when the party started with her countrymen
Mor Thiam playing djembe and calling down Pullen's spirit. Thiam—a
master drummer who put the Motherland in Pullen's African-Brazilian
Connection band during the 90s—helped my future wife (and me!) by
making her feel she might be able to find her own way around my beat.
Our shared sense of possibility was amped up further when we watched
film that night of Pullen's '94 performance at Montreux with the African-
Brazilian Connection. Here again he blessed us through Mor Thiam who
sang "Kele Mou Bana"—a Senegalese folk song that my heart knew by
heart (and translated for me when she wasn't singing along)—before
Pullen took the tune to heaven. Making my partner fly and see from up
there so her homeland became the edge not the End of the Black Atlantic.
And even Allah was just another word for everything. (Peace A.B.) By
swinging the black music of two worlds into Tomorrow, Pullen and friends
proved to my amore you could have your roots and freedom too.

Their evidence, though, was inadmissible in the court of (self-proclaimed) Hanging Judge, Stanley Crouch, who wasn't trying to hear what
might extend him beyond his anti-Afrocentric comfort zone. Crouch
was a no-show at St. Peter's Church that night and he never rolled with
Pullen's spin on World-Jazz. I shouldn't have been surprised but Crouch
brought me up short one time when I brought up Pullen's African-Brazilian Connection—"You like that Afro crap?" He must have avoided the
Connection's live shows because that band could turn anyone around.

As I found out the last time they played an extended gig at a club in
New York City. I went to hear Pullen's group with a very particular woman
who was preparing to ex me out. She didn't believe in going to the West
Village on the weekend. Especially not to hang in a tourist trap with no
dance floor. Her idea of a good time dated her but it was still undeniable:
a night of disco at the Garage and then on to the beach for a morning
dip. Yet I didn't pick up when she called to cancel. I thought Pullen's
tidal waves of sound might flow her away. The morning after he took us
keyboarding, she used the L word for the first (and as it turned out) only
time. She Dear John-ed me a week or two after Pullen fast-forwarded
her. Thanks to him, though, I got all she had to give (and more).

All's fair because Pullen once made me give away more than I intended in front of another girlfriend (who stuck with me a lot longer).
That happened when he played the Vanguard with the band led by David
Murray that made *Shakil's Warrior* (1992). On that album and in the club,
Pullen played organ, returning to the instrument that was his bread and
butter in the 60s when he couldn't find steady work as a piano player.
Along with Murray, he reconceived the kind of roots music he'd played
in R&B organ trios. His blues seemed born again. Un-phased by the
organ's limitations, he took on the instrument's technical challenge with
nervy trills and soulful silences. In command of the moment, alive to
the other musicians on the stage, he played like Magic—a "point guard
of the new" to lift Baraka's phrase. (On piano Pullen was more like Jordan at his peak.) The Vanguard audience set out to clap Pullen and the
Warriors back on the bandstand after the last set. While we were urging
them to return (for the only encore I've ever seen at that club), I realized
my girlfriend was staring at me. Then I heard myself. I was wailing "I
NEED it!" over and over. Which sounded strange, of course, but my
girl was looking at me funny because she'd heard something like those
needful cries before. Back in the dawn of our relationship, all I wanted
was her sharp, baby-soft curves. I didn't like condoms so when my time
was coming I'd slide on her thigh or breast-bone. Or rub him right on

her sweetback. And when I'd finally spray, we'd hear a lion groan in relief (and frustration). Though I wasn't pouring it all out, I didn't mind because I dug the sound of my nature rising.

What's this jizz have to do with Pullen's jazz? "Don loved love," as per Baraka: "he wanted, like all of us human beings to be love, to make everything love … to make everybody whisper and scream and embrace themselves." If you doubt that, try "Andre's Ups and Downs," where Pullen referenced his son's romantic life and where his repeated transitions from regular technique to swirls seem inspired by a serial monogamist's leaps into the plenitude of love. Or jump to the Bo Diddely riff in "Big Alice" on Don Pullen/George Adams Quartet *Live at the Village Vanguard Vol. II.* Pullen and drummer Dannie Richmond rode that beast with (three into) two backs for about twenty minutes the first time I ever heard him. (What can two people do in twenty minutes?—Darling, you're gonna *need* my help—You can't make love all by yourself!) That's when I started wanting to share a Saturday Night in Pullen's Cosmos with somebody pretty or willing.

But no one was having me so I began with family—my little sis and older brother (and my sister-and-brother-in-law) were high on Pullen right away. My brother ended up bringing us all closer to our culture-hero when it turned out he was working with Pullen's son Andre in the 125th St. Post Office. One time Pullen sat down at our table after a set (avoiding a fan eager to discourse on his "intervallic concept") and we happily exchanged family anecdotes. That night was a trip for us because Pullen had just come flying home from Rio and Dakar in his first NYC performance with his African-Brazilian Connection. But the evening was daunting as well because Pullen appeared to have lost a lot of weight and we worried he might be sick. I don't know if he'd already been diagnosed with cancer at that point, but his End must have seemed close like that during his final years. Especially since two of his closest musician-friends—George Adams and Dannie Richmond—died way before their time.

Pullen's composition "George We Hardly Knew Ye" was dedicated to Adams and his second pass at that melody during the '94 Montreux show (preserved on *Live Again*) is for the Ages. In an effort to ease the pain of those who were missing "G. and Dannie," Pullen quoted these lines, which he'd read at their St. Peter's Memorial Services, in the notes to his CD *Ode to Life*:

Death is nothing at all. I have only slipped away into the next room. Whatever we were to each other, we still are. Call me by my old familiar name. Speak to me in the same easy way you always have. Laugh as we always laughed together.... Life means all that it ever meant. It is the same as it always was. There is absolute unbroken continuity. Why should I be out of your mind because I'm out of your sight? I am but waiting for you, for an interval. Somewhere very near, just around the corner. All is well. Nothing is past. Nothing has been lost. One brief Moment, and all will be as it was before—Only better. Infinitely better. We will be one, together forever.

I've found a little consolation in these lines since my dad's death. But the nothing-but-blue-sky attitude bothered me too. Something shattering was obviously missing so I googled Pullen's quotation. It comes from a 19th-century sermon titled "The King of Terrors" written by an Anglican churchman named Henry Holland who wasn't a beamish type. (Struck by the fact the "streets of London reek with human misery," he became a sort of liberation theologian who rejected Social Darwinism without denying evolution or the historical Jesus.) The point of his sermon was to help his hearers confront what surfaces at the moment of death—"so ruthless, so blundering—this death we must die. It is the cruel ambush into which we are snared. It is the pit of destruction. It wrecks, it defeats, it shatters. Can any end be more untoward, more irrational than this?" But, as we've seen, he also invoked an innerness that even "death cannot destroy."

Pullen's performances in the '90s often suggested he understood such double-truths inside-Out. Infused with faith of "black and going on" folks, his music was marked by a deep sense of continuity, yet his playing took on a new ferocity and pity. In a late live version of a song titled "Silence = Death," which he played one night at a free show in Lincoln Center's bandshell, sorrowful single notes gave away to the back of his hand and what sounded like a touch of madness. But as he swung back and forth between grief and going off, his balancing act seemed to signify sweet, bitter reason. In this version of "Silence = Death" (which took off from the one on a 1990 solo album where he tried to shame the sky with thunder-block chords), anger became an energy, a measure of love and sanity in an Age of AIDS.

Thousands of listeners were caught up in Pullen's flows that night at the bandshell. I was by myself but I didn't feel alone as the college kid next to me marveled at Pullen's technique and two elderly race men on the other side of the aisle danced in their seats, reveling in the reality their people—under the radar-screen and beneath the underdog—had produced another indisputable champ. Pullen swirled their world even though his performance was relatively restrained. He was intent (I think) on not upstaging Ahmad Jamal who followed him on the program. (Pullen played solo, Jamal had a trio.) Before his last number Pullen spoke with feeling about Jamal's influence on him. On my way out of the bandshell, I ran into a jazz critic who knows much more than I do about the Tradition and who scoffed at the notion that Ahmad Jamal might have a problem following Don Pullen. But I couldn't help noticing that he, like me, was stepping off half-way through the elder pianist's set.

My pop once had trouble getting through one of Pullen's sets. Back in the '80s, I pushed him one time to pass up Ellis Larkin's regular uptown gig at the Café Carlyle and check my man at the Vanguard. (C'mon pop, since you're down when Larkin takes "I Got Rhythm" slooooow, you'll get lifted when Pullen finds a perfect beat at warp speed.) But I shouldn't have pressed. My pop enjoyed Beatles' tunes and "Lady Jane;" he loved "I Never Loved a Man" and (Percy Sledge's) "My Adorable One"; he wrote appreciatively of Springsteen and Elvis and Marley. But he *played* jazz. It was his music—the soundtrack for his own singularity. He once said that no aesthetic experience in his lifetime beat hearing Jelly Roll Morton's "Win'ing Boy." The art in Pullen's swirling, on the other hand, was beyond his reach. My pop wasn't a moldy fig but he never needed to go past *Thelonious Monk Plays Duke Ellington*.

And who could blame him? Still we did get into it once when a particularly dissonant Pullen track got into the mix during a family occasion. My pop dissed it quick, quoting a Philip Larkin line about avant-garde jazzmen "improvising on fuck-all." Which pissed me off because I knew my pop recognized the limits of Larkin's proudly provincial approach to jazz. (Forget Pullen, no Monk need apply.) The emotion generated by our little blow-up lingered since we avoided arguments during my pop's last decade—there wasn't time enough to enjoy the frisson of contention.

But I took a little risk when I was visiting my parents during my pop's final year. One soft evening I put on Pullen's "Variations on Ode to Life" (the final track on *Ode to Life*).

Pullen knew he had cancer then and this "Life" feels like a summation as well as a provocation. You're sure he's going to leap from single notes to swirls during his first solo. His trills have you treble-ing on the edge of his keyboard. But he never turns his hands up to throw all the way down; he stays inside the Tradition. (Pullen allowed longtime listeners might find his playing "subdued" in the CD's notes.) Yet his "variation" on "Life" isn't about giving in. Pullen aims to sustain; he's carrying on and closing in (not cooling out). No longer naturally forcing the tempo, he faces the music of his mortality. His final solo takes it shimmery and slow—the pulse of his piano flickers for breath-catching moments. But his blue Clair de Lune shines on. Until his final bass chord kills the light.

My pop and I sat outside listening in the dark. We didn't speak much after Pullen finished his moonlit version of "Life" but our common sense told us the soul of the man will never die. My pop not only shared my taste, he appreciated Pullen's more than I ever could—wondering at how his fellow piano player had colored it all in with "one blue note."

That note reminds me of some blue ones my pop played when he was trying desperately to recover from the second of what became a series of heart operations. He wasn't allowed to eat or talk (or sing) and was barely able to walk on his own when he sat down at the piano for the first time in weeks to play Duke Ellington's "Lucky So and So." He'd fallen in love with that blues when he heard Ella Fitzgerald sing it, accompanied by Ellis Larkin on their (no strings!) collaboration, *Ella Sings Gershwin*. (It's the only non-Gershwin track.) My pop plays and sings his own "Lucky So and So" on a homemade CD that my brother-in-law helped him make. But he went deeper into the song when he was laid down low. He couldn't sing the springy lyrics—"the birds in every tree/ all sing so merrily/they sing wherever I go/I'm guess I'm just a lucky so and so" (and not just because his throat wouldn't let him). Without a voice, with the bad luck, he made his piano testify for a human right to good times. He swung the song's open-hearted melody with infinite care, slowing the song's mellow roll—"as I walk down the street/seems like everyone I meet/says a friendly hello"—until its final promise of happiness—"when the day is through/each night I hurry to/a love that's faithful I know/I guess I'm just a lucky so and so"—seemed so far gone. Looking back now, I guess it was his "Ode to Life."

That's a pretty thought (and the need to have it probably impelled me to write this piece). But my pop wouldn't have let me leave off there. He was wary about promoting comforting ebony-and-ivory visions of commonality. He realized (see *The Trouble With Friendship: Why Americans Can't Think Straight About Race*) the mystique of one-on-one interracial intimacy in our culture obscures a debt that must be paid even if it can't be made good. He understood, as long as obligations conferred by history (by Goree!) remain unmet, life in America won't stop breaking down to black and white.

And color lines aren't all that separate my pop's un-"Lucky So and So" from Don Pullen's graceful "Ode to Life." My pop lacked faith. Pullen played like there was something up above his head. The apple don't fall far from the tree. Yet Pullen's example might be leading me back to the future here. I'm intrigued by that Victorian theologian Pullen directed me to. In a famous long ago book *Lux Mundi*, Henry Holland argued Christianity was to be experienced, not contemplated (though faith for him wasn't blind but a matter of reason). Maybe I'll search for his *Lux*. Tis the season after all. And I'm (almost) a Christmas baby like Don Pullen.

Note

1.   Doug Schulkind's Sound Mind—www.wfmu.org.

"ALL BOY"

Fr. Rick Frechette

This piece was excerpted from e-mails Fr. Frechette sent after he and his colleagues provided disaster relief to flooded rural regions of Haiti.

June 18th (2004)

During this past week we made two trips to the impoverished flood areas. The truth is, all these towns and indeed most of Haiti would be considered a disaster even if there had not been a flood. They are terribly poor, and lack the most basic services including schools and clinics. It is impossible not to be deeply struck by the depth of poverty and hunger in this country, once you stray away from Petionville where there is an illusion of development. Many of the people who come to these various towns hoping to get a little bag of beans and rice are not from the flood areas. Hunger drives them to seek help wherever they can.

As a doctor it is easy to diagnose illnesses as you offer a little bag of food and talk for a few minutes to the people. Many are so very polite and want to show their gratitude and they stay close by to talk a little bit. I am thinking of a woman who has the bulging eyes and enlarging neck from thyroid disease. I notice she had a chain tightly around her neck, surely the attempt of the local voudou doctor to stop the growth of her thyroid gland. I see a very old thin man, groaning with bellyache, his legs discolored and ulcerated. I am sure he is diabetic. And I see a very pathetic ten-year-old albino boy. He is doing his best to keep up with all the other children, as curious as they are about us and what we are doing. He has his tee shirt pulled above his head to keep the sun off his pained eyes, since the sunlight hurts his tender retinas. His legs are red from sunburn, and dry and flakey. I can see he already has a patch of melanoma on the skin over his collarbone. How much could have been done for this boy in another setting: simple sunglasses, ultraviolet protective sun lotions, proper education and proper clothing regarding sun exposure. Instead of this, he is a small, fried boy with a deadly cancer ... but he is ALL BOY. I gave him two bags of rice, and he squealed with delight and ran off. This child haunts my sleep now.

I will go find him again and see if that melanoma can be removed and hope it hasn't spread. I will give him a big hat and sunglasses and ask the next person coming over from Miami to bring lots of 15 or higher sunblock. There is so much to do it is hard to know where to start....

July 12 (2004)

The little albino boy I mentioned in a previous report is with us now in our hospital. His name is Ronald. His grandmother wanted to just GIVE him to me, for life. It is amazing how often people offer you their children for keeps. We have Ronald outfitted now for the tropical sun ... glasses and creams for UV protection, and a big floppy hat. He will be with us for a few weeks while being evaluated by a dermatologist for removal of cancerous and precancerous skin lesions. He is a delight....

Sisterhood Is Powerful

Judy Oppenheimer

Adapted from a talk Ms. Oppenheimer gave at Ellen Willis' memorial service.

Ellen and I had a connection that began before we were born. Our mothers were sisters, and very close; we were their first pregnancies, practically simultaneous. They wrote letters to each other constantly before and after giving birth, which they did a month apart. Our earliest pictures show us in the same crib, eyeing each other warily. Ellen was the first person I knew besides my parents, and almost the first thing I remember knowing was that she was smarter than me. That, of course, was long before I knew she was smarter than anyone. I remember the time both of us, aged 4, were crayoning, and I managed to rip through my coloring book. "I hate these crayons," I cried. "Judy, don't be so sarcastic," she said coolly, a word I wouldn't understand for years (it would be even more years before I understood she was using the word incorrectly; being a typical 4-year-old, at that moment I really did hate those crayons). At the time, she simply floored me; I stared at her, awed.

As kids, we were together for holidays, vacations and most of the summer, which we spent in Ellenville, New York, the small Catskills town where our mothers had grown up. Because of the war, and our fathers' absences, Ellen and I made it to age 6 before we had to deal with siblings, first one, then two years later another, apiece (our mothers really were amazingly in sync). Becoming big sisters was a challenge. We handled it by first developing a deep yearning for a big sister of our own, and second, inventing one.

Her name was Margaret, our favorite name of the moment, and she was, we decided, away at camp—this, we figured, would explain her absence to anyone churlish enough to question her existence. We painstakingly composed a letter from her, which had her complaining about camp—Ellen thought that was a good touch, since we could then act annoyed at her complaints. We spent several days running around the small town of Ellenville, calling her name, informing anyone who looked at us quizzically that she was just up ahead, around the corner. For some reason this whole venture satisfied us.

The odd thing was it never occurred to either of us that there was no way we could have had a mutual older sister. Obviously, it had never occurred to us that we weren't sisters ourselves.

We shared many things, growing up. Books, for one. Almost every year we had a special book. We were 10 when we discovered Anne Frank. She affected us strongly, though not, I'm afraid, the same way she affected everyone else. What got to us was the fact that she had been on the spot at a particularly important time and place—and written it all down, earning eternal fame. We immediately started diaries of our own, even giving them names, silly as that seemed, since it had worked for her. We then set out to find adventures to record. It was slim pickings, back in 1950s surburbia, but we strove valiantly. One day we went for a walk and a dog followed us for an hour—Sandy, an amiable Irish setter. Thrilled, we ran home and rushed to our notebooks to record it.

We shared music, too. We were both there for that cataclysmic event, the birth of rock and roll. I remember us going to see *Blackboard Jungle*, which started and ended with Bill Haley's "Rock Around the Clock," later pinpointed by many as a primal moment. No one had to tell us that. We were so thrilled, so excited, we rushed outside feverishly, holding hands, the music ringing in our ears. Everything else was down the road—Elvis, Dylan, the Stones, all of it—but it was as if we knew it all in that one intoxicating moment, knew what was coming, felt it in the air.

Then there was sex, which fascinated us. We used to lie in bed when we were 12, planning our first honeymoon night. What would be best to wear, something sheer or maybe something flannel—that way, Ellen thought, you'd save the surprise for the end. In our 20s, our ways diverged. Ellen got married, at age 20, because (she later admitted) she wanted to go to California with her boyfriend, and no one went off with a boyfriend in 1960 without being married. It didn't last; she returned to New York and started forging her amazing career as a rock critic, then as a founder of the new feminist movement. I married and stayed home when the babies came, something she never, never made me feel bad about.

Still, she herself would never have children, she said. She needed too much time to read the papers on Sunday, and besides, changing diapers disgusted her and she would end up giving the kid a complex. I believed her, naturally; you always believed Ellen. Then one day, when we were standing in line at a supermarket and I was hugely pregnant and holding on to my 2-year-old, I thrust him at her, saying, "Here, hold this," so I could pay. After I finished I glanced at her. She was holding him so tenderly, with such a loving look on her face, I knew right then: It didn't matter what she said. Someday, someway, there would be a baby.

But before that, there was Stanley, and what everyone in our family considered the most romantic relationship of our generation. I remember them coming to visit, early on. It was a bad night; one of my kids had come down with a horrible case of stomach flu and was throwing up all over the house. I kept getting up to tend to him. I don't think either of them noticed. They were totally oblivious—so completely immersed in each other, they could have been on the moon. Finally they left, both of them glowing, under their own private glass bell.

And then, of course, there was her miracle daughter, beautiful Nona, who she adored from the moment she was born, who made her so proud. A few years ago, at one holiday or another, we were sitting around quietly, letting our kids—Nona, my nephew, one of my sons—do the talking. Ellen nudged me. "I feel like ... wow, here are these prize watermelons we grew," she said.

Ellen and I always talked nonstop when we were together, one long endless conversation, throughout our lives. But in the last few years, for some reason it seemed even more important to sit close to each other, hold hands, keep our arms around each other. Even when walking down a street or sitting at a restaurant. Just like we did when we were little, between squabbles. I have no idea why this was true, why we felt this need, but it felt so comforting, somehow. And necessary. I guess it was a way of saying without words, You know how much I've always loved you, don't you? You know how important you've always been to me, right? How much I'll miss you, forever.

Four Tough Good Byes

Amiri Baraka

Though "beginning" travels backward into the wherever, this one was Jackie Mc's. I've already written about it for some weird Spanish magazine (*Matador* ca: Jan 07). That's the way it goes in the craziness where we live, harnessed to the dead. Those who still walk around with the harshing memory of those who don't (not visibly) Right now *Little Melonnae* is playing accidentally (not) on the box. I played it, maybe, the day I got the news. Jackie's great album *Let Freedom Ring* (which really marked the high water mark of that generation's thrust to innovation). The story about how I had to curse out Clerk Eichman at the record store, even to buy the record, is in the Spanish piece. And just before I began* (*physically not philosophically) to type

Whatever this is … this piece, I picked up the old LP sitting on top of the middle aged box & put it on, not really realizing that I was going to work on this piece.

But the crown of it all is the sense of whooom, woooosh, wheeee, gone, that layers it all. Jackie Mc was one of my touchstones, as far as the developing music of BeBop. That sound and presumed whizzing hip panache were valuable to me, I guess, and in me. Jackie was also, for a minute, one of my road buddies, him and his soon to be, lovely, wife, Dolly. This just before we all made our move out of the Lower East Side, of which Slug's Dopery had get to be the white house.

To mean, I could not think of him gone. Did not want to think of him that way, because his leaving carried some of my life with him too. One cannot remember one's life as fully as one has lived it. For one reason was that Jackie was fully alive when I knew him best, and still full of all that the last time I saw him. The funeral, weirdly, confirmed that for all the other I's, entering our lives through all the eyes we looked into at Abyssinia. And ain't it funny that as unchurchly as all of us was and is most likely to be right now, how the church do seep into our STOPPED lives? (Yet, I pledge not to be buried in the church, if I have anything to say about it!)

But this is not just about Jackie, the great paradigm post Bird BeBop-per, whose sharp cutting edge, and in and out of the dope world, at full hoisted banner still wailing for the next deepness, I/WE hoped was Our own! This is about the month of death, or so it seemed. And it really was for the bare extent of my focus. Though death for my generation has been mounting like Katrina's bath. Each week some other close friend or known personality cuts out. Of the latter, in essence it didn't matter whether they were positive or negative, with news of their booking it meant still more of our world was moving away. Perhaps that is why old folks sometime seem so grumpy because, minimally, they have fewer and fewer to verify the epiphanies or even the rotten little misfortunes of their lives.

So that a few days later I thought I saw something on the net, naw, forget it, it couldn't be that. Not ... no ... what??? But a few hours later ... & I had just seen John at the Iridium, with Grachan Moncur's group. The piano seemed further away from the whole group, off to the side. It's probably always there. (It is, but this week checking out Charles Tolliver's wondrous big band, it was over there on the side but during the last intermission they changed it so the pianist's back was to the audience! What dat mean?)

After the set John and I sat at the back of the club, while he ate ice cream and I was telling him about a series we planned in Newark of solo piano concerts which wd feature John, Adegoke Colson, Hilton Ruiz, DD Jackson, Vijay Iyer, some of the badder young "Ticklers" (piano players, viz. early 20th-century hip). Talking with our usual subtle un-dergarment of humor. John was one of the subtlest and sharpest of the walking around musical minds, his casual understated persona quite the opposite of the rushing syncopation of his OH AW FUNK FUNK YEH THAT'S RIGHT! approach to the box.

John's playing, ask anyone who dug him, put him in line to cop the jazz pianist's equivalent of James Brown's "The Hardest Working Man in Show Business."

We'd known each other for many years. He and his wife, Elise, with me and my wife, Amina sat together at many sets, in many joints, in many people's houses and ran the world back and forth between us. One of the last was at a party given by another partner of mine, the painter, Emilio Cruz, who also split without notice.

I remember John was sitting at the piano and I crept up on him and challenged him to play Billy Strayhorn's *Blood Count*. Yeh, he played it straight out, with the kind of lovely lilt that Duke would give it. Or like his own marvelous *After The Morning*. Then, just to take me all the way out, he invited another fine piano player, Larry Willis, to sit down and they played it again four hands. It was an altogether spontaneous stretch of loveliness to add to that party's overall hipness.

I'd also gotten John to come over to Newark to play quite a few times. As featured pianist for our multi-arts presentations as Kimako's Blues People which went on for 15 years, or for private parties Amina and I had. Once for Amina's birthday. The last time John played here at our house, he wailed far into the night, not only the smoking tunes we know him for, but for the last hour or so he came out of the covers and instead of the constant reference to the church, he went deep into it and the whole place turned into a revival.

It was the suddenness, the it-couldn't-be quality of John's get outta here that was so devastating, disheartening. Jackie Mc's was a deep blow, like Brando hearing his oldest son getting wiped, it is a body punch that threatens to shatter even the pavement you stand on.

And then the music itself trembles, from these disappearances but also from the general dumbed down condition of the whole culture. The *New York Times Book Review* reads like the possible reject list 40 years ago, with dim-witted professors, right wing hatchet persons, and straight out hacks emboldened with dirty lucre.

Looking at New York City schedules for The Music, in the clubs and wherever, is likewise chilling. Occasionally (of which I'll speak in a minute) some brightness and actual reflection of real minds reporting, but in the main the headless whorespeepas run amuck. I've repeated myself saying that so called fusion is really social & intellectual betrayal.

But we could hear some of the greats passing among us from time to too long a time later, e.g, recently Andrew Hill, McCoy Tyner, David Murray, Abbey is not feeling well we're told and that in itself is painful. But for two greats, both warm friends, Jackie Mc and John Hicks, those are like some cruel thing going up side your head with two devastating overhand rights.

We went to Jackie Mc's funeral at the eloquent Rev Butt's, Abyssinia, where Gil Noble, the dauntless face of Afro America's television blog, *Like It Is*, and Jackie's roadie since their Harlem childhood, was a eulogist of living and instructive memory. Randy Weston evoked a similar lyrical nostalgic New York vibe to seal the blue package.

A scant few days later Amina and I went John's wake and funeral, at St Mark's Methodist Church in Harlem, successive days, plus to the tribute at St Peter's (May). Amina once had to change the title of her poem to John from "John The Baptist," once he told her to "John The Methodist." Son of a Methodist preacher! (Still sounded like a Baptist to us.)

The tribute tho it expressed our collective loss was also an expression of great love and warmth the large audience and broad list of celebrants, which included, Larry Willis, Mulgrew Miller, Joe Lovano, Mickey Bass, Lincoln Center's Todd Barkan, Amina and I accompanied by Amina Claudine Meyers, The World Saxophone Quartet, Buster Williams, Elise Hicks, and our man Cecil Taylor, so there was all that lyrical and funky love, for us to wander out of the place, still stiff with grief but at least given something of value to go with our loss.

But a few days later, was it on the net, the newspaper later, that again a big NO! flashed and fished through us at this further grimness. Again, one of the young classicists of the Music, and another close friend. How could this be? With the same incredulous terror that stalked us with news of John, unlike the funeral sadness that came with word of Jackie's going, the news of Hilton's death was punctuated with an actual terror! The word was that he had "fallen" but a cynical wonder surged across the jazz community, how could a person receive the kind of injury it was reported that Hilton had suffered—the bones in his face fractured, so badly he went into a coma, from which he never fully returned. From a Fall? So that the word "Murder!" was wrapped completely around this news. And no matter what other word came out, for those of us close to him, that lurking horror remains.

A few days before Hilton had gone to New Orleans to publicize a record he made as a benefit for the survivors of the Katrina Bushwacking, my wife and I had dug him up at Cecil's Place in Orange, NJ, a place where it's always possible to see some of the best of the Music.

We arrived mid-set and Hilton was at full smoke. A Carnegie Hall performing prodigy at 8, who studied with the great Mary Lou Williams, & made his first recording at 14, Hilton's playing was always characterized by constant melodic blues shapes driven by an engine of ever changing rhythms. Hilton would leap back and forth from deep funk blues to Afro-Latino boomaloom effortlessly, cracking himself up at the transformative hip. That night, as he finished, he went into a rap that combined peddling his most recent CD (*A New York Story* issued by the Hilton Ruiz Music Company), to serving as a jazz quiz show mc, rewarding correct answers with copies of the CD. To a question answered by some quick dude and my wife almost simultaneously "What was Clifford Brown's nickname?," Hilton laughed, not knowing I was there, "You sound like

Amiri Baraka!" At which I called out and raised my hand from the back. That cracked him and the rest of us all the way up.

Between sets we talked about his recent gigs, his sharp sense of politics, in and out of the music, and how proud he was of himself that he no longer smoked, drank or "messed around." He also had me touch his stomach, to show that now he had become a karate "black belt." Not only that, we exchanged phone calls and e-mails the next couple of weeks, as I was trying to get his schedule clear so that we might invite him again to Newark. Like John Hicks, Hilton had been to our house in Newark to play several times, in the Kimako's Blues People series and for our private sets upstairs. The last time he played here, was at a reading, at the Aljira Art Gallery downtown, featuring Amina and myself, with poets Sekou Sundiata and Halim Suliman & grand trombonist, Craig Harris on the set as well. We still have some boss flicks about that wonderful night.

After the first word came, mainly from the New Orleans police, that Hilton had accidentally fallen in front of a spot in New Orleans, which Hilton's ex-wife and daughter initially seemed to co-sign despite a swarm of queries and suspicions to the contrary (in recent days daughter Aida is now suing several folk in New Orleans citing Hilton's being beaten by some person or persons). Horrible, whatever the case, especially this great pianist was only in New Orleans to give survivors financial and spiritual aid.

We went to the New York Tribute to Hilton at LQ's on Lexington Ave. A buncha musicians played, Zon del Barrio, Willie Martinez y La Familia, Craig Harris, David Murray, Frankie Vasquez, and more, poet Papoleto Melendez fetched us from one side of the room to dig a celebrant slouched in a corner seat. It was Bill Cosby, mournfully quiet, making us remember that Hilton had provided the music from time to time for Cosby's family show and his Detective series.

But as Spike Lee showed in his powerful *When The Levees Broke*, the madness and horror in that ex-Black city, is another real terror to be attributed to the Bush'it coming from the Caucasian Crib in Washington, D.C.

I mention a generation seeming to fly out at top speed. The last of the *Goodbyes* here is the death of a close friend of ours, the poet Halim Suliman. The personal relationship I had with all these people makes this a roll call of regret. Particularly, Halim, who was for several years one of the poets on Amina and my poetry-music ensemble, Blue Ark: The Word Ship. From the earliest days of our Kimako's Blues People multi-arts series, Halim was on the set, reading and even video taping a few of the programs.

With Blue Ark, Halim traveled with us to the Berlin Jazz Festival, where we made a record, *Real Song*, plus to universities and venues across the country. He was also acted in my one act play, *Song*, and as part of the company of actor-singers in the Adegoke Steve Colson production of *A Cultural Reminiscence*, playing several parts & in a group singing the freedom songs of the Civil Rights Movement, in one act of the work, my *Dr. King and The Mountain*. The entire work features Colson's music and another act by Richard Wesley. We did that at NJPAC in Newark and also in Paris.

Halim was a poet lit up by the fire of Newark's faces and places like a rocket straight out of the Black Arts Movement. That is, he was still trying to make Cultural Revolution. He also taught at Newark's (shd be) world famous Art's High School where folks like Sarah Vaughan, Savion Glover, Woodie Shaw, Wayne Shorter, Amina Baraka went. He was the mentor for the string of State Champion Newark High School Debating victories.

But ubiquitous where ever there was a heavy reading in this city. In the Poet-On! Series, I put together, at the Newark Public Library and Public Schools, to continue "popularizing poetry" to carry out my work as New Jersey Poet Laureate in 2002, despite the attack by lying pests, Halim, as usual, was one of the stalwarts. How many folks in this city quoted one of Halim's poems to make their comments on Newark politics, viz., "James/Ain't never been Sharp!"

So the loss is up close and personal but also a continuing diminution of the forces of an advanced American art. So these sad goodbyes.

Lineaments of a Promised Land

Charles O'Brien

For a long time, "Get Up (I Feel Like Being a Sex Machine)" (*Sex Machine*, Polydor, 1970 on vinyl) has been one of my favorite pieces of music; and I sometimes wondered if there wasn't something unreasonable how much I loved it. But this was the song that was played over and over at James Brown's funeral. Judged by the title alone, it'd be hard to come up with anything more incongruous. The song as it is, though, was a great choice. "Sex Machine" is ten and a half minutes of prime JB built around practically nothing: a song called "Sex Machine" might hint at all kinds of prurience, but here it mostly just rhymes with "stay on the scene." The song begins with JB "moving these things around." Equipment, furniture, who knows? This is James Brown in the studio, "just proud and doing my thing."

The full band starts the song. The horns play eight notes for just one bar; about halfway through, they play that same bar; and the song ends with that bar. Otherwise, they're gone. The song is just guitar, bass, and drums, sticking to one chord, except for a short bridge, done twice, and a "taste of piano," JB himself for about eight bars. In performance, James Brown *poured* sweat. His music, no: it could be icy in its perfection, as it is here. At the end, he wanted to "hit it and quit."

> In other words we hit and we done.
> Hit me!

The horns, eight eighth notes worth, hit him, and us, and we *are* done, and it could not have ended better—

But first, there's a lot of ground to be covered. American music (movies, too, and literature) loves to throw out place names from around the continent. Think of Chuck Berry's songs, or Bobby Troupe's "Route 66."

> Oklahoma City looks oh so pretty

Well, *maybe* it does. The point here is that it sounds pretty. These songs are imagination taking joy in a map. James Brown's place names are realer. In "Living in America"[1] JB sings:

> You might not be looking for the promised land but you might
> find it anyway under one of those old familiar names

And he reels off some of them. But "Sex Machine" has more. When he goes to the bridge for the second time, he asks the band *where* he can go.

> We got to go to Dayton
> [Has anyone over spoken those words with such delight?]
> Atlanta GA
> Lovely Atlanta
> Atlanta GA
> (and I might go to Macon, if you don't mind)
> xxx
>
> Texas!
> Houston…
> or Dallas?
> Houston or Dallas?
> Which one?

Both of 'em!
Got to go San Antone, brother
xxx

Over to Memphis
I think I'll go to Nashville, too
By the way of Chattanooga

And on and on. All these places are lively memories, all scenes of—this is the James Brown Band!—past troubles and past good times, troubles and good times just up ahead, near enough to taste. "Night Train" is not a James Brown original, but he *takes* it. The horns come in with a swell, emulating the Doppler Effect, what anyone has heard, dreaming of being taken away. You can see the train's single light cutting through the darkness, speeding through the night. The train in Robert Johnson's "Love in Vain" and Junior Parker's "Mystery Train" had showed only their rear lights, menace and regret. The "Night Train" is full of promise, and all the places the train travels are blest with that promise.

In his recent memoir, *I Feel Good*, JB reports that Hubert Humphrey wanted him to run for Vice-President in 1968. Think of it, though. James Brown, as President of the Senate, could have turned the place around, setting bounds on windy speeches, fining members for missing votes, *running* the place. An America with James Brown as its best-known diplomatic face to the world in 1969-1972, it would have been a different America, different world, different 1969-1972. And picture him doing the ceremonial stuff, like funerals. He could put aside the flashy threads and wear a suit as well as anyone—look at the pictures of him with Richard Nixon. And he could look as solemn as anyone has ever looked.

Even though JB was best known for dance music, he kept that solemnity near at hand. "Man's World" is the obvious example. But I'd like to call attention to 1972's *There It Is* album. The hits on that album were the up-tempo numbers, "There It Is," "Greedy Man," "Talkin' Loud and Sayin' Nothing," "I Need Help." The dope raps "King Heroin" and "Public Enemy #1" are undeniably a little ridiculous and may come across as filler. But listen again. This was 1972, and amid the wreckage of the civil rights movement—and the hopes it had engendered and the music that was its twin star—there was a mournful strain of black popular music—something new in its time, and a lot of the best hip hop in years to come would draw on it. Records like the *Superfly* and *Across 110th Street* soundtracks brought the bad news to your door. But sitting inside your door, hardly noticed, and probably even more powerful, were James Brown's heavier, flawed dirges.

More often, of course, he was *up*. He recorded prolifically, and toured incessantly. On his deathbed, he was planning to see in the New Year on stage. On record, he has laughed more than even Al Green. It was notorious how he *worked* his band. There's a story about his confrontation with some Nation of Islam heavies. They were berating him for having a white bass player, Tim Drummond. JB looked and looked around the room, trying to find this white bass player. Finally, he said, "Oh, that's *my* bass player." A story about race, obviously, but also a story about *management* style. P-Funk, a mutant form of James Brown's band, has always been happy to get recognized names into the fold—Vanessa Williams, say, or Philippe Wynne. James Brown's band was filled with James Brown's players. Bootsy and Maceo could be musicians in his bands; they could become names only afterward.

His most important formal innovations were labor-intensive. Staying on one chord for ten minutes, and making it work, is a lot harder than running through a lot of changes. Stripping away (and *minimalism* doesn't feel like the right word for James Brown's music) often involves an appeal to an aural comfort zone, a false memory of past assurance. JB's basics were the opposite. Listen to the 45 version of "I Can't Stand Myself." The instrumentation is this: an organ playing the same seven-note riff throughout the song; one guitar playing an invariant *four*-note riff; another guitar playing one two-note chord, slid down a half–tone and back once; a drummer keeps the beat; only the bass player (Bootsy) goes crazy—but this was 1968, when bass wasn't received as a lead instrument, and the equipment to hear it didn't exist, at least not where JB was likeliest to be listened to. This music is not your old time used to be. It is someplace you never guessed was there, and forty years later, the strangeness in the song remains. Much of what James Brown started has become familiar, either because the songs themselves are still heard or he's been sampled[2] or the formal stuff has been assimilated by others. The newness is untouched.

Mr. Dyn-ee-mite, Hard Working has rested.

Notes

1.   *Rocky IV* is hardly a defensible movie. It has one great scene, though. Carl Weathers, as Apollo Creed, is about to fight Dolph Lundgren, playing a robotic Russian (He's *acting*). James Brown is on stage, his band, showgirls, everything cooking, doing "Living in America." The camera goes around the room, taking in Sylvester Stallone, Weathers (dressed in patriotic colors, and dancing with an Uncle Sam hat on), JB, the players and the dancers. JB ends the song throwing one arm out and shouting

I Feel Good!

Everybody feels good. A moment later, Lundgren bumps Weathers' gloves hard, and tells him, "You will lose." Weathers' face registers shock. And a moment later, Weathers, in his Stars and Stripes trunks, is carried unconscious from the ring.

However briefly, James Brown raises the movie from a delirium of silliness to a delirium of fraternity.

2. A personal favorite: the "Okay, I'll talk a little louder" sample on Technotronic's "Come Back."

Expat on Main Street

Armond White

Sting, Paul Simon, Peter Gabriel, David Byrne, Bruce Springsteen, all famously liberal pop stars, never performed at the Apollo in Harlem, yet that's where Morrissey chose to launch a concert series to promote his album *You Are The Quarry*. Another perversely provocative move from the British singer, his five-night Apollo stint last May obtruded upon the legacy of James Brown and Motown, complicating our narrow view of pop music. This was, in fact, the *ungentrification* of popular culture. And that's been Morrissey's method ever since his 1980s group The Smiths reinvigorated British pop in the aftermath of the Punk movement.

Few critics have credited Morrissey for his Punk ethic. His elegant, idiosyncratic singing and Johnny Marr's melodic, eclectic guitar-playing in The Smiths confounded most people's notions of what pop music could accomplish. Lyrics such as "England is mine/And it owes me a living" were puzzled at, or overlooked, by critics who understood them less than the average wage-earning record-buyer. Protest and distemper, an especially youthful mix, underscored Morrissey's most romantic longings. His songs made art out of coming to terms with love and sex in thorny political circumstances. (It was the era of Margaret Thatcher and the Britsh miners' strike.) He examined the most private traumas in the public arena, which Punk and folk music had usually reserved for political statement.

Pursuing Pop Star rather than Hero status, Morrissey could take a pass on showbiz self-righteousness (as when The Smiths refused to take part in Bob Geldof's Live Aid single "Do They Know It's Christmas?"). Convinced that his bottom dog's expression of lonely romanticism was worthier and truer than any top-down agit-pop, Morrissey was committed to making musical equivalents of the melodramatic social dissent in Britain's '60s Angry Young Man films. He's always sought to make contemporary pop as socially conscious and emotional as the best pop art of the past. Post-Punk acts of late-'70s and early '80s—from The Buzzcocks to The Au Pairs, X-Ray Spex to the Slits—pioneered blatantly sexual content yet none were as effectively insinuating as The Smiths' "Hand in Glove," "This Charming Man," "How Soon Is Now," or "Shoplifters of the World, Unite." That's the way Morrissey chose to emerge from specific cultural traditions—Oscar Wilde, Graham Greene, Shelagh Delaney, Elizabeth Smart, Joe Orton, The Shirelles, The New York Dolls, The Jam, etc. Only The Pet Shop Boys and Public Enemy have been as erudite and purposeful.

Each Smiths song was an outcry—though not an obvious political remonstration. Morrissey wasn't a teenager when he made those records; it is an accident of commerce that the pop market was the only place for such unusual expression. Unfortunately reviewers and some fans still view his work chiefly as adolescent petulance but *You Are the Quarry* proves there's more to it. In The Smiths, Morrissey bridged teenage impudence to adult apostasy. He confronted the insularity of teen pop and its erasure of socio-historical contexts. The commonly accepted division between white and black pop (still perpetuated in publications like *Rolling Stone*, *Spin* and *Vibe*) was exposed and exacerbated by Morrissey's infamous quote "reggae is vile" and the controversial "hang the dj" refrain of "Panic." Those alarming phrases still resonate against the dreads-wearing and pot-smoking of one-worlders who, in the face of today's global chaos, now seem especially fatuous and irrelevant.

But the Apollo appearance was more shocking. It gestured toward clarifying the pop culture paradoxes, which Morrissey has instinctively resisted in the past. Never before has he seemed so right-on. In his own version of Amateur Night at the Apollo (remember the root word of "amateur" is love), Morrissey threw down a practical challenge to those fans who might be content with their elite cult status and to the pop culture venues that promote segregation in everyday life. (Harlem's Apollo is celebrating its 70th anniversary this year.) Defying both camps by forcing them together, is a truly bold Act—the kind the mainstream press was willing to attribute to The Clash's performances at the Times Square disco Bonds in 1980. Morrissey never enjoyed such mainstream acceptance, which is why his popularity has always seemed so genuine rather than manufactured. He has been almost too successfully subversive.

Morrissey's Apollo shows didn't just play with pop conventions. He's cast himself as a perpetual outsider, an apostate who observes no cultural or social rules. Having left England (as foreshadowed in his 1992 lyric "We look to Los Angeles/For the language we use"), Morrissey proves himself an expat on main street. Hyper-aware that he's settled in the land targeted by al Qaeda, he goes on to profess a conflicted allegiance in *You Are the Quarry*'s important opening track, "America Is Not the World." Remarkably, this national yet personal love song escapes being another soundtrack for masochistic-liberal Bush-bashing. Instead, it is a model of ambivalent commentary on this political and cultural moment.

Morrissey begins "America your head is too big/Because, America, your belly's too big." But before this first arrow of imperialist critique sinks into the bullseye, he very quickly confirms "But I love ya!" Yet it's the next line that's amplified by his Apollo stint: "I just wish you'd stay where you is." This can be interpreted as a protest against the Iraq invasion—or against the global dominance that the U.S. has engineered since World War II. (In the controversial Brazil episode of *The Simpsons*, Homer sports a t-shirt depicting Uncle Sam biting into the globe as if it were a hamburger; underneath is the phrase "TRY AND STOP ME!") But Morrissey's song is extraordinary because it eschews standard politicking. The "stay where you is" line is curious—and compelling because the locution Morrissey adopts can only be defined as Black English. (Evoking the American South, it is now redolent of all urban America.) It suggests that Morrissey's Apollo stint anticipated some empathic communion with the All-American, trans-racial spirit of James Brown. Morrissey's identification with working class expression (as in 1997's daring "Ambitious Outsiders" where he sang in dialect, "And we knows when the school bus comes and goes") demonstrates that he indeed knows how malcontents are caught between the privilege and the anxiety of life in an open but troubled society.

This ambivalence and Morrissey's sincerity make "America is Not the World" the most illuminating song yet released post-9/11. Morrissey's plaint is as valid as that of a natural-born citizen. In the past, singing out his experience as an echt-Brit, Morrissey has evoked pangs of love and loyalty that came with being born in the UK as well as the reflex to be inhospitable in-country (which explains his notorious "Bengali in Platforms," a subject for further study). The felt nature of imagined communities is conveyed remarkably when the new song makes a poignant turn. Morrissey sings the words "All I have to offer you/Is a heart deep and true" with the aspiring notes of a romantic supplicant, followed by "Which you say you don't need" sung in heartbroken descent. It's a signature Morrissey sequeway. Moving from hope to despair, he twists pleading into resignation—an emotional vamp.

It is rare to find pop music of such powerful sentiment that also has political effect. Morrissey's objection to American habit is strongest when he accuses "But when the President is never black, female or gay/And until that day/You've got nothing to say to me/To help me believe." Morrissey has never before been tendentious. His outright declaration: "black, female, gay" (the first such explicitness in his career) is the sign of American candor, not his usual British discretion. He's using the language of American reproach (and of typical American identity politics), fully aware of how the society is divided between unmentionable power—the invisible hegemony of the white male elite—and easily tagged disadvantage.

The line is not a partisan rallying cry but a piteous acknowledgment of the sensibilities and histories of all those Americans who feel unrepresented.

This entreaty could easily be mistaken for a fashionable political statement, but it stands alone. Detached from today's movements of social protest, Morrissey offers an authentic expression of worldliness intersecting with individual yearning. In youth music, a turn toward social awareness usually results in shrill, partisan positions (from BRING THE BOYS HOME to NO NUKES to STOP THE VIOLENCE). But Morrissey's distrust of cliques (and the herd-like thinking of student protestors) keeps the politics of "America is Not the World" distinct—close to his vegan breast and teasingly separate from current Iraq War postures. While avoiding the patriotism of Toby Keith's "I Love This Bar" and Neil Young's "Sun Green," Morrissey posits political awareness through the sensitivity of a love song.

Individual feeling is thus made as pertinent as a manifesto, but eloquent, not strident.

There's no slyer example of Morrissey's wit and style than the verse "And if you wonder/ Why in Estonia/They say 'Hey you, big fat pig!'" The name Estonia conjures recent Eastern bloc political debacle but the word itself is also the perfect homonym to describe the anti-American itch. The phrase doesn't goad Yankee-haters; more ingeniously, it evokes America's self-consciousness about its Homer Simpson world image. Listen to that internal rhyme "stone ya," the slang expression of an enemy lobbing bitterness. It also, very importantly, points to political oppression: "Estonia." The image momentarily replaces "America." Not just a country but a state personifying misery. Morrissey has learned to articulate dissatisfaction so fluently that he transcends the song's potential offense. It is, at heart, a lament about the impossibility of an ideal society—the essence of what one awakened to on 9/12. Plus, it's an extension of that sense of dread that Morrissey has relayed even in youth-specific schooldays songs like The Smiths' great, turbulent "The Headmaster Ritual." Acknowledging the failings of his new homeland and the fears of its people, Morrissey connects with "America is Not the World" through the fidelity of true adoration. The phrase "big fat pig" is unsettling but it's also poignant because, as Morrissey sings it, it's also a cruelly intimate endearment (remember 1994's "You're the One for Me, Fatty"?). This affection is keenly voiced when Morrissey shifts into his beseeching mode. No singer makes the word "please" as heartrending as Morrissey. When he embarks upon the song's bridge—"See with your eyes/Touch with your hands/Please"—it's as trenchant as James Brown begging "Please, Please, Please." Fans of The Smiths will immediately recall the 1984 single "Please, Please, Please, Let Me Get What I Want This Time." And 20 years later, one is able to link Brown's personal agon and Morrissey's, despite differences of time, place, race. That's what the national specificity of "America is Not the World" renders ironic and undeniable. It sounds off against the distinctions and stratifications of social difference. The song feels at one with yearning, as blues-based and guttural—as classical—as Brown's.

Morrissey has never sung better. His voice has the emotional directness of Billie Holiday or Iris Dement, and the extravagance—the daring—of Sinatra or Shirley Bassey. Producer Peter Asher, who worked with James Taylor and Linda Ronstadt, knows how to cultivate vocal nuance and, in the seven years since recording his last album *Maladjusted*, Morrissey has grown on this score. He featured the word "please" very prominently in the 1997 b-side track "You Must Please Remember" but in "America" it is especially cogent. Though the song's terms are contentious (challenging the U.S.A. to live up to its ideological claims) the song is, above all, soulful. That sense of compassion is what makes *You Are the Quarry* an impressive—and a signal—achievement of this era.

"America is Not the World," with all its lovelorn loveliness, embraces the condition of a conflicted consciousness like Morrissey's. The rest of the album depends on displays of naked—yet discreet—honesty, but "America" becomes a great love song through the original, complex way that Morrissey's pledge of commitment entwines around his indissolvable core of disappointment. He scolds then caresses. His new home is as trying as a new lover; it is an uncontrollable object of affection—and a reflection of Morrissey's own spiritual ambivalence. *You Are the Quarry*'s fourth track, "Come Back to Camden" looks back to England for left-behind language and habits. An expatriate's nostalgia merges old customs with the most exquisite intimacy. ("Your leg came to rest against mine … and me and my heart/We just knew.") This same synecdotal method—eroticizing social attitudes—is what gives "America" such wit—and sex + humor trumps the song's "provocative" editorializing. By representing the romance of political identifications (not namby-pamby love in place of politics), Morrissey achieves an enhanced, thorough examination of his own state of being. Inadvertently, Morrissey articulates the West's most trenchant post-9/11 appeal.

"America" isn't an inventory of Yankee imperialism so much as it is Morrissey's assessment of the personal need that informs his search for a place to be free, a circumstance to love, a world to trust. This degree of personal accountability is rarely found in a song ostensibly about political awareness. Morrissey's incredulousness ("The land of the free they said/And of opportunity/In a just and peaceful way") is enriched by desire that is voluptuously sung. It's better than the usual snide judgments of political-pop zealots. Has any emigrant ever plighted his troth so faithfully as in that wrenching apostrophe "There is nothing I can offer you/Except a heart deep and true/Which you say you don't need"? It's an attitude that has been buried in post-9/11 anxiety—and corrupted by much war-mongering jingoism. However, pop listeners must stiffen their spines and realize "America" offers no substitute for patriotism. It stands to the side of national identity. Morrissey's clever bit of Black English proves his subconscious empathy with all Others—those it has become fashionable to loathe such as the big bad American and even Americans who themselves feel left-out. "America is Not the World" conveys both sympathy and ambivalence quite unlike an anthem. In our stunned, post-9/11 grief, it wakes us up to the longing that lies within longing.

Rainy Night in Europa

Hans Koning

This passage from the author's last novel, The Irish Deserter, *lives on in or outside the book's narrative.*

The king riding out of Brussels at dark, where had he read that? The shortness of the life of one man in time—a passage about a king, he did not know which one, leaving the town, galloping over the wet stones and then through the woods which came so close to it—in a far past, it was a year with fourteen hundred in it. He had never forgotten the sound of those words; he could not quite recall them now but he remembered sharply the emotion they had invoked in him. The Middle Ages, and then the idea of a rainy evening, so very long ago, and yet rain on the streets in which he himself had walked, a wood that still was; he had seen it, that man riding out because he wanted to think alone, the drops falling softly from the leaves of the trees, how much that evening must have seemed the now to him, how tracelessly it had vanished.

He could think about it without end, about those glittering streets and paths, the moon must have played such a part in that world of dark nights, the king looking up at it and seeing it follow him through the foliage; how to conceive of life then, an age of mystery, the ocean the border of the known, wolves in the woods around Brussels? Why this image through time, why a feeling of pity for that lonely man riding, halting to stop the sound of hoofs and listen to nothing but the silence, the dripping of the rain, the beating of his heart, four hundred years ago.

Geezer Music

Richard Meltzer

Adolphe Sax, a Belgian, created prototypes of the various members of the saxophone family somewhere around 1840, but it wasn't until the second and third decades of the 20th century that anyone anywhere would figure out how to play more than imitation animal sounds, and other co-medic "circus" effects, on a single one of them. Somewhere before 1920, New Orleans jazzman Sidney Bechet performed the deed on soprano sax, followed in the '20s proper by Coleman Hawkins on tenor.

For the next 40 years, Hawkins would be known for a sensuous (often dangerous) muscularity of tone and phrase, a signature warmth emanating from the chest and belly. He had a "sense of the ballad" as advanced, and as simple, as any hornplayer's ever, and was a majestic improviser. According to lore, he was the chronological FIRST to "tell a story" on a saxophone, and as time went by the stories got longer and more intimate. (Check the '39 "Body and Soul," the '45 "Talk of the Town," the '48 "Picasso.")

In 1966, at his last studio session, the phrases at his command for story-ing are fairly short and unmenacing, and not always perfectly formed (or even sturdy), and they end as often as not with an almost gauzy vibrato like that favored by his acolyte and rival Ben Webster. You can just about hear columns of toneless, pitchless air vibrating, and ceasing to vibrate … sound unto silence.

A minute and a half into "Time on My Hands," the rhythm section drops out, and for the next two minutes-plus, which feel to the listener like five or six or ten—time as perceived being so palpably molded, so altered—the 62-year-old Hawk delivers not so much a story as a valediction. So little breathing time remains, yet time is *his* … micro-duration is macro … all time is NOW. It's not always such a great idea to lean heavily on metaphors, but astro-time implodes, matter too, and Sirius, brightest star in the heavens, becomes a neutron star … a campfire … a matchbook aflame in a skeleton hand. All entropy, all destiny compress the final recitation to a throaty whimper … a final peep.

A poignantly MAGNIFICENT peep, but a peep … then neverending stillness.

Part XII

Unwritten Rules

It's been an elegiac time for our crew lately. In the past year, we lost (among others) Hans Koning, Ellen Willis, George Trow,[1] Kurt Vonnegut and, a year before that, Benjamin DeMott. They were *First* readers as well as writers for our tab. You could count on them to give it to you straight and there were occasions when one of their opinions could outweigh all others due to its cogency. There are no substitutes for irreplaceable elders but we'll try to sustain what they valued in *First* by finding new originals to help carry us into the future. Which, sorry to repeat myself, remains unwritten (despite the chorus of that slack Natasha Bedingfield song).

The Future Is Unwritten, the new documentary about The Clash's Joe Strummer (who died in 2002) made me feel less embarrassed about being locked on that phrase 25 years after it was first coined to cry up the Clash's album *Sandinista*. It got me thinking (again) about how we'll keep *First* burning down the road. The movie is built around blue-hours-in-the-cities scenes of Stummer's friends reminiscing around campfires with dark waters behind them. (Their lost Promethean boy apparently loved a bonfire in the night.) Those scenes evoke Strummer's attraction to social living (to use the Rastas' term for socialism) and his openness to world musics/cultures.

First of the Year will never be as punctual as a culture-hero like Strummer in his youth, but we'll always try to cultivate a timely internationalism. Some one of these days we should tell the stories of that white record producer/musicologist in Ghana who's partly responsible for the rise of Afro-pop. It's past time for us to cover Shack-Dwellers International, which has enabled thousands of dirt-poor people to own their own homes. And something real social seems to have gone down behind the election of Bolivia's first indigenous head of state, Evo Morales (though yammering by/about Chavez threatens to drown it out).

Going international is easier now because of the Internet, but the worldwide Web shouldn't screen out what's up on the block. Or at the local Cineplex. Armond White's beautiful catch of a graceful scene at the end of *This Christmas*—a formulaic holiday movie ("not-August Wilson, glib-Charles Burnett, sub-Tyler Perry") for the Afro-American market—shows why *First* must always attend to American pop life on the edge of mainline culture.

> The cast (the family) … all form a *Soul Train* dance line and boogie their own curtain call. The fact of celebration—of Black American cultural ritual—is in your face, unapologetic and joyous. The longer [director] Whitmore holds on the dance scene, the more amazing it becomes. Transcending Kubrick, past Straub and more physically beautiful than Tarkovsky, this sequence tells much about how families repair their differences and (pace Albert Murray) how Black folks "stomp the blues."
>
> It might help to know that the film is titled after Donnie Hathaway's composition, "This Christmas"—a song as traditional to contemporary African Americans as "White Christmas" is to the mainstream. But the smiles and body-work of the film's ending dance line has its own authentic meaning. And Whitmore's long-take is so bold—and so satisfying—that there isn't a single movie this year that offers more insight or greater pleasure.

White's capacity to pick up on such good (all around) times rests on a rootsy sense of his people's traditions, but he's aware millionaire authentics may be a scam in the Age of 50 Cent. (See his "Tales from Behind the Black Curtain.") It's fair to say our crew is less upbeat about the possibilities of hip-hop culture than we once were, though the future of rap remains unspoken.

Scenes from *The Future Is Unwritten* of The Clash hooking up with hip hop originators in NYC reminded me how fecund that early '80s moment was and how far gone it seems now. The social energy generated by Atlantic crossings of that period was one source of *First*'s sense of cultural possibility. But it was never the only vector that mattered. Most *First*er's are Strummer's brothers and sisters on that score. Though punk originally pogo-ed away from the rock of ages past, Strummer himself acknowledged there were always cultural continuities. "We're all hippies," he said, late in his life. (And he was pretty beat too!) *First of the Year* will continue to reflect both the breaks and bridges in radical cultural flows. I think I flashed on *First*'s place in time when I heard the ender of a prose poem Philip Levine read during his 80th birthday celebration at Cooper Union. His poem evokes romance with a Spanish tinge that becomes an academic nightmare when his post-modern dance partner—a PhD in "critical theory"—whispers in his ear:

"I *dream* of tenure."
It was the '50s all over again.

First's crew will never bow down to the weight of that past. Our felt sense
of the '60s protects us here. If *First* ever gets off track, we'll go back
with Charles O'Brien to the bridge of Aretha Franklin's 1966 recording
of "Think."

> Aretha sings "Freedom!" Now up to this point, the lyric has said essentially, Don't
> play with my love, think about what you're doing. This cry for freedom doesn't
> seem to follow. But it is not the song, "Think," subject of a copyright, somebody's
> private property, that engenders this cry. Rather the song's (and Aretha's) historical
> setting does that. Where she might have less exceptionally filled that bridge with an
> oo-whee, Aretha felt it just as natural to sing of freedom, as if oo-whee and freedom
> were interchangeable words, hitting on the truth that they probably are.

Aretha's (and O'Brien's) truth hit me all over again after Barack Obama
spoke in Washington Square Park last fall. Music played as folks filed
out or stayed inside the Park, hanging on to Obama's final riff which
he'd lifted (with acknowledgements) from a grassrootsy Southern Sister: "Fired Up!—Ready to go? Fired Up!—Ready to Go?" I hung out
for a few minutes and then stepped off, but just as I reached the street
there was a voice and song that turned me around. Aretha was singing
"Think." FREEDOM!!!

Obama, of course, isn't stuck on the '60s. He's tried to distance himself
from the decade's hotter rhetoric and pointlessly polarizing culture wars.
But the free thinking in that era will always be exemplary.

If we're lucky, historian Lawrence Goodwyn will clarify the uses of
the '60s for Obama and the rest of us. He's proposed to do a twofer for
First—a review of *Many Hearts, One Mind: SNCC's Dream of a New
America* and another important new historical work, *Unruly Americans
and the Origins of the Constitution*. Focused on lessons of the past, but
in the moment, Goodwyn's piece promises to illuminate contemporary
American politics and uphold *First*'s tradition of infusing radical imagination with historical understanding.

The past won't stay still right now. Check this passage from Jack
Kerouac's *On the Road*:

> When daylight came we were zooming through New Jersey with the great cloud of
> metropolitan New York rising before us in the snowy distance. Dean had a sweater
> wrapped around his ears to keep warm. He said we were a band of Arabs coming to
> blow up New York.

Reading this now, as John Leland notes (in *Why Kerouac Matters*), "takes
your breath away." It's "pure coincidence" but Leland points out that

On the Road parallels another road book—"the Egyptian writer Sayyid Qutb's *Milestones* based on his travels in America during the same years, which became a central text of the Islamist Jihad movement."

Sayyid Qutb's chief American critic (and mighty explainer) is Paul Berman whose accounts of the intellectual origins of Jihadism highlight Qutb's modernity. Berman once guessed *First of the Month* would be too '60s to comprehend bad new days. But I think he'd allow that *First*'s post-9/11 issues have been up to our minute. *First of the Year* will stay on time if we keep stretching radical traditions and refusing claptrap offered by the left's "anti-imperialists" or the right's fans of American hegemony. Two (ideologically incorrect) teachable historical moments come immediately to my mind here.

I learned recently from a History Channel program devoted to Saddam Hussein's Hitler fetish that one of the most revered spokesmen for the Palestinian cause—the Grand Mufti, Al-haj Amin al-Husseini—was friendly with Adolf Eichmann and visited Auschwitz, where he is said to have pushed those tending the gas chambers to work harder. Not content with propaganda activities on behalf of Nazis, he became an SS general and military units he was associated with were notorious for committing war crimes in Yugoslavia. The Mufti evaded prosecution at Nuremburg and returned to rabble-rouse in the Middle East where he ended up becoming a mentor to his nephew Yassir Arafat who celebrated him as "our hero" in a 2002 interview (though Arafat may have shortened his own name to obscure his relationship with his Nazi uncle).

John Berger—a famous writer on the left—might have had such twisted history in mind when he wrote the following excuse for Arafat after visiting the Palestinian leader's grave:

> [Arafat] was nicknamed the walking catastrophe. Are loved leaders ever pure? Aren't they always full of faults, not weaknesses, flagrant faults? Is this maybe a condition for being a loved leader?

Berger's perception that human failings in a leader encourage deep identity politics seems wasted on Arafat. But it fits the case of another Middle Eastern local hero, Mohammad Mossadegh. According to *All the Shah's Men*, Steven Kinzer's definitive account of events that climaxed in the CIA coup that ousted Mossadegh from power in 1953, the Iranian prime minister was a profoundly quirky sort who suffered from a variety of illnesses that "led to fits and breakdowns."

> Neither purely medical nor psychosomatic, [Mossadegh's illnesses] both reflected and became part of his persona. He was as dramatic a politician as his country had

ever known. At times he became so passionate while delivering speeches that tears streamed down his cheeks…. When he became a world figure, his enemies in foreign capitals used this aspect of his personality to ridicule and belittle him. But in Iran where centuries of Shiite religious practice had exposed everyone to depths of public emotion unknown in the West, it was not only accepted but celebrated. It seemed to prove how completely he embraced and shared his country's suffering.

Kinzer's story of the passion of Mossadegh is immensely pertinent today. It shows how American and British power smashed a process of democratization in Iran that went back to the beginning of the 20th century. That process has been subverted once again by the mullahs. But Americans must understand that our government's initial, indefensible assault on Iran's sovereignty means we *owe* that country's democrats even as we confront a common clerical enemy. *All the Shah's Men* earns the Harry Truman line that serves as the book's epigraph—"There's nothing new in the world except the history you do not know."

A scene in *The Future Is Unwritten* underscores how volatile history is in our post-9/11 era. A passionate interlocutor claims Joe Strummer despaired at the thought pop fans might mix up rationales for war in Iraq with the pleasure principle of the Clash's biggest hit, "Rock the Casbah." But, on the real side, Strummer had zip to apologize for. Written around the time the Ayatollah banned rock music in Iran, that novelty song hints how the Clash's engagement with their times gave this band a common touch that cut deeper than personal opinions of any individual member in the group. Thrown back on himself years later, Strummer may have wanted to disavow his prophetic lyrics about an Islamist despot who tries to ban (and bomb!) "boogie-men"—"Fundamentally he can't take it. You know he really hates it!"—but that kind of hater needs mocking now more than ever. While "Rock the Casbah" never amounted to a case for shock and awe, there seems to be a teleological truth to the Clash's old imperatives. Consider how "The Future Is Unwritten" talks back to a proverb that incarnates Arab/Islamic fatalism: "It is written." Strummer's own wishes notwithstanding, class-based clashes aren't likely to sublate the Clash of Civilizations until "moderate" Muslims stop writing off Islamist crimes against humanity.

The Future Is Unwritten, with its foregrounding of huddles around bonfires in cities that have been recent targets of bombers (New York, London, Madrid), is a bit of a tease on this front. Spectacles of provisional solidarity in these cities have an eternal charm, but in our time of danger such scenes inevitably call up memories of collective responses to terror attacks. Yet no one in the movie acknowledges that Stummer's (and so many other's) pre-9/11 ideas of "cultural revolution" need rethinking. There are other teases in the movie too. L.A. campfire scenes focus on celebs (Johnny Depp! John Cusack!) who bring nothing but star power to their interviews. And Bono gets his own campfire, though he doesn't have much to say either.

The presence of those stars highlights how hard it is to resist celeb-mongering. Walking out of *The Future Is Unwritten*, I thought of how I once wandered around the Upper West Side searching for Mick Jagger's New York City apartment so I could slip him a *First*. When I missed him there, I sent stuff to his friend Jann Wenner. Two birds at one *Stone*. I wrote Wenner (the truth) that I'd grown up reading his magazine and asked him to pass a *First* on to Jagger and take a look at our sheet himself. I'll allow I hoped he might consider investing money (as a tax-write-off?) in *First*. Wenner did the right thing by his lights. He had an assistant send on the package to Jagger and he sent me a polite note that consigned *First* to the wilderness—"*First* seems to be a worthwhile publication that ought to continue. *I didn't read it*" (emphasis added). We deserved no more particularly since *First* once published Richard Meltzer's lines on *Rolling Stone*:

> "I was done with that sorry useless publication in less than two years. People I run into still hit me with "Ooh, didn't you write for *Rolling Stone*?" "Yeah," I say, "but at least I've had the smarts never to put my prick in a garbage disposal."

First of the Year will keep providing alternatives to disposable culture. But as long as we have nothing material to offer the Meltzers of the world, real writers might be better off rolling with Mr. Wenner. He'll *pay* them after all. For their sake, let's hope *First of the Year* sells out in a way *First of the Month* never could.

Money changes everything. (Another lesson implicit in *The Future Is Unwritten* since Strummer and The Clash couldn't handle success.) But some transitions are easier than others. Whatever happens, *First*'s family will need to maintain a sense of unity that's not predicated on consensus. We're not the Movement but (as per Ella Baker) we can't eat on each other when we disagree.

Back to *The Future Is Unwritten* one more time. As Strummer's oldest, conflicted friends sat around their campfires thinking back on prickly moments with their lost comrade (who wasn't always so comradely), I was reminded of Karl Marx's line when he was asked as an elder: "What abides?" The Old Moor replied: "Struggle."[2]

If our writers (and readers) stay in struggle and think beyond the given, *First of the Year* might fire up the next left.

Notes

1. George Trow's marvelous *First* piece on Dan Rather and the decline of American journalism (which was the last essay Trow ever published) would have been in this volume, but his mother asked us not to reprint it at this time.
2. As per David Quigley's *Second Founding: New York City, Reconstruction, and the Making of American Democracy.*

Contributors' Notes

Stanley Aronowitz is a teacher, writer and activist who has been a Green Party candidate for governor of New York. He is co-founder and co-editor of the journal *Situations* and his latest book is *Against Schooling* (Paradigm Publishers).

Amiri Baraka published a collection of short stories, *Tales of the Out and Gone*, in 2007. He has two books scheduled for 2008: *Digging: The Afro American Soul of American Classical Music* (University of California) and *Razor: Revolutionary Art for Cultural Revolution* (Third World Press).

Paul Berman is a writer in residence at New York University and the author, most recently, of *Power and the Idealists*. He is the editor of *Carl Sandburg: Selected Poems* (American Poets Project, Library of America).

Grace Lee Boggs has been an organizer of multiracial progressive coalitions in Detroit for over 50 years. She is the author of *Living for Change*.

Cecil Brown is a novelist, memoirist and cultural critic. His latest books are *I, Stagolee* and *Dude, Where's My Black Studies Department?*

Jay Cantor is the author of three novels, most recently *Great Neck*, and two books of essays. He teaches at Tufts University.

Robert Chametzky is the author of two books of theoretical syntax published by SUNY Press and Blackwell.

Robert Douglas Cushman died in 2004, a few days before he completed his volume of poetry, *The City Among Us*, which remains unpublished.

Chuck D rhymes with Public Enemy, whose latest CD is *How You Sell Soul to a Soulless People Who Sold Their Soul?*

Benj DeMott is a member of First of the Month Writers' Collective. He lives with his wife and son, across the street from his brother in New York City.

Benjamin DeMott began publishing cultural criticism (and fiction) in the 1950s. He was the author of (among other works) *You Don't Say*, *Supergrow* and the "Thinking Straight" trilogy about race, class and gender. He died in 2005.

Tom DeMott worked in the Postal Service for 31 years (mostly at the 125th St. Station) and has lived since 1969 with his family in Harlem where he has collaborated with others to defend tenants' rights in hundreds of buildings. He is now working with the Coalition to Preserve Community as it battles gentrification uptown, and specifically, Columbia University's plan to replace a diverse working class community with a monolithic and exclusionary world of privilege: www.stopcolumbia. org.

Jean Bethke Elsthain's latest book, *Sovereignty. God, State, and Self*, will be published by Basic Books in 2008.

Natalie Estrellita is from Venus; everyone else is from Mars.

Nat Finkelstein has been Underground and in The Breeze. He is currently in Greenpoint, Brooklyn working on his memoirs: "The 14 Ounce Pound."

Fr. Rich Frechette is a medical doctor and Catholic priest who directs an orphanage and children's hospital located on the edge of Port-au-Prince. He also runs mobile clinics that reach the poorest of the poor in that city. You can learn more about his work (and how to support it) at www.npfshaiti.

Donna Gaines is the author of *Teenage Wasteland* and *A Misfit's Manifesto*. She lives in New York City and online at www.donnagaines.com.

Lawrence Goodwyn is the author of the classic works, *Breaking the Barrier: The Rise of Solidarity in Poland* and *Democratic Promise: The Populist Movement in America*.

William Greider is National Affairs correspondent at *The Nation*. He is currently working on a book called *Come Home America*.

George Held's latest poetry chapbook is *The Art of Writing and Others* (www.finishinglinepress.com). His poem "Aftermath" was read by Garrison Keillor on *The Writer's Almanac* in December 2007.

Wesley Hogan is the author of *Many Minds, One Heart: SNCC's Dream for a New America*. She teaches at Virginia State University in Petersberg V.A, where she is active in linking local schools with the national Algebra Project.

Richard Hoggart invented the discipline of cultural studies during the '60s when he was Director of University of Birmingham's Center for Contemporary Cultural Studies. He is the author of (among other books) the classic account of British working class life, *The Uses of Literacy*.

Irving Louis Horowitz is Hannah Arendt University Professor Emeritus of Sociology and Political Science at Rutgers. He was born and raised in Harlem, New York, and is the author of *Daydreams and Nightmares: Reflections of a Harlem Childhood*, which was the recipient in the biography-autobiography category of the National Jewish Book Award for 1991. Along the way he has kept busy with other, less interesting, professional and publishing tasks.

Bruce Jackson teaches at University of Buffalo. His most recent books are *The Story is True: the Art and Meaning of Telling Stories* and *Cummins Wide: Photographs from the Arkansas Prison*.

Charles Keil is the author of (among other works) *Urban Blues* and *Music Grooves* (with Steven Feld). He blogs at www.conserving.consensus.us and invites everyone to join the rhythm nation at www.borntogroove.org.

Benjamin Kessler is a playwright and essayist whose works for the theater include *The Professor's Daughter*, *Luv 2 H8 U*, and *Blue States*. His plays have been performed in New York City and Los Angeles.

Fred Kirshnit is classical music critic for *The New York Sun*. He worked as a studio musician for Buddha records in the 1960s and later hosted his own radio program on WWUH-FM in Connecticut. He has recently written pieces on Mahler, Elgar, Prokofiev and others for *Dialogues and Extensions*, the publication of the American Symphony Orchestra.

Hans Koning was the author of (among other novels) *An American Romance, I Know What I'm Doing, The Kleber Flight, Acts of Faith, America Made Me, A Walk with Love and Death*. He wrote non-fiction as well, including *1968: A Personal Report, The Almost World, Columbus: His Enterprise: Exploding the Myth*. Koning died on April 13, 2007. You can learn more about his work at http://www.hanskoning.net.

Tuli Kupferberg is now 84 (but doesn't look a day over 80). A born and still breathing New Yorker, he has seen tyrants come and tyrants go, and still claims to be a Fug and humorous anarcho-pacifist engagé "as the world slowly (?) burns."

George Lakey is an organizer, writer, and teacher, who has led over fifteen hundred social change workshops in 20 countries; see www.TrainingForChange.org.

Philip Levine is the author of 16 books of poetry. His most recent publication is *Tarumba: The Selected Poems of Jaime Sabines*, which he co-translated with the late Ernesto Trejo. Levine was born in Detroit.

David Levering Lewis is Julius Silver University Professor and Professor of History at New York University. His latest book is *God's Crucible: Islam and the Making of Modern Europe, 570-1215*.

W.T. Lhamon, Jr. has published books on fifties cultural style, blackface from its beginnings to hip hop, and the earliest American popular culture. In 2008, Harvard will publish a new anthology of plays—*Jim Crow, American*—and he will continue work on a book called *Secret Histories*, which traces the long meting out of cultural democracy across class, race, and place.

Eric Lott teaches American Studies at the University of Virginia. He is the author of *Love and Theft: Blackface Minstrelsy and the American Working Class* (1993) and *The Disappearing Liberal Intellectual* (2006).

Michael Lydon lives in New York City with his wife, composer Ellen Mandel. Best known for his writing on rock 'n' roll in the 1960s and his 1999 biography, *Ray Charles: Man and Music*, Lydon has published books on songwriting, jazz guitar, the art of writing, including *Writing and Life*.

Staughton Lynd is a historian and a lawyer. Together with Daniel Gross of the IWW he is bringing out a new edition of *Labor Law for the Rank and Filer*, published by PM Press.

Kanan Makiya is the author of (among other works) *Republic of Fear* and *Cruelty and Silence*. He teaches at Brandeis and is the founder of The Iraq Memory Foundation, which is based in Baghdad.

Greil Marcus is the author of *The Shape of Things to Come: Prophecy and the American Voice* (2006). He lives in Berkeley.

Timothy Mayer was a theatre director, playwright, lyricist and poet who died in 1988. His work was collected in the posthumous volume, *Running from America*.

Richard Meltzer's early work—*The Aesthetics of Rock,* etc.—helped make sense of the '60s in real time. In more recent decades, Meltzer has made himself into a writer for the Ages. Asked for an update on his latest work, Meltzer reports that "*A World That Don't Exist*, my frigging goddam masterpiece (so called), is about 11 or 12 days from being done (5-6 torturous years in the making) … whoopee."

Kate Millett's *The Politics of Cruelty* will be reprinted in 2008 and *Mother Millett* will be published in the U.K.

Bob Moses is founder/director of the Algebra Project and author of *Radical Equations*. Working with the Student Nonviolent Coordinating Committee (SNCC) in the '60s, he helped organize the Mississippi Freedom Democratic Party (and Freedom Summer).

Dennis Myers wishes he was the first to say this (but a friend beat him to it): "I wanted to be Kurt Vonnegut, Jr., but someone beat me to it."

Victor S. Navasky is Publisher Emeritus of *The Nation*, and chairman of *The Columbia Journalism Review*. He is the author of (with Christopher Cerf), *Mission Accomplished! Or How We Won the War in Iraq* (An *Experts Speak* book).

Charles O'Brien is a member of First of the Month Writers' Collective. He lives in New York City.

Judy Oppenheimer is a freelance writer who lives in Washington, D.C. She is the author of (among other works) *Private Demons: The Life of Shirley Jackson*.

Wendy Oxenhorn is Executive Director of The Jazz Foundation of America.

Charles Planck runs Wheatland Vegetable Farms in Virginia. He has written regularly for *First of the Month*.

R. D. Pohl writes on art and culture for *The Buffalo News*.

Adolph Reed teaches at the University of Pennsylvania. He is the author of many books including the definitive work, *The Jesse Jackson Phenomenon*. Reed is committed to organizing a Labor Party in the U.S. and his response to the current presidential campaign, "Sitting This One Out" is online at http://progressive.org/mag_reed1107.

Mike Rose teaches at UCLA. He is the author of (most recently) *The Mind at Work: Valuing the Intelligence of the American Worker*.

Barham Saleh is deputy prime minister of Iraq.

Lorna Salzman has worked at Friends of the Earth, the NYC Dept. of Environmental Protection and has run for public offices as a Green Party candidate. She has published many articles on the environment and evolution. Her website is www.lornasalzman.com.

Tim Shorrock writes about U. S. foreign policy and national affairs for *The Nation, Mother Jones, Salon, Harper's, The Progressive, Asia Times*, and other publications. He blogs at www.timshorrock.com and his book on the outsourcing of US intelligence, *Spies for Hire*, will be published in May 2008 by Simon & Schuster.

Fredric Smoler teaches at Sarah Lawrence College. He is Contributing Editor at *American Heritage Magazine*. He has written regularly for *First of the Month* and has been published in various other places, including *The Observer* (UK), *Dissent, The Nation*, and *The New York Times*.

Tom Smucker's mother was born and raised in Kansas and he is an Elder at Middle Collegiate Church in the East Village, NYC.

Ann Snitow teaches at the New School. She is the editor (with Rachel Blau Deuplessis) of *The Feminist Memoir Project*.

Alison Stone's poems have appeared in *The Paris Review, Poetry, Ploughshares*, and other journals. She has been awarded *Poetry*'s Frederick Bock Prize, *New York Quarterly*'s Madeline Sadin award and her first book, *They Sing at Midnight*, won the 2003 Many Mountains Moving Poetry Award.

Stephan Talty is the author of three books, including *Mulatto America* and a forthcoming work on Napoleon's invasion of Russia.

Jeanne Theoharis teaches at Brooklyn College. She is the author of (most recently) *Not Working: Latina Immigrants, Low-Wage Jobs, and the Failure of Welfare Reform* (with Alejandra Marchevsky).

Kyle Thibodo completed his second tour of duty as a medic in Iraq in the spring of 2007. He's planning a trip around the world.

Lorenzo Thomas once said, "I write poems because I can't sing." His final book of poetry, *Dancing on Main Street* (Coffee House Press) was published in 2004. He died in 2005.

Robert Farris Thompson teaches at Yale University where he is Master of Timothy Dwight College. He is author of (most recently), *Tango: the*

Art History of Love (which moved Michael Baryshnikov to comment: "Thompson … inflames us with his reverence for the form").

Harlem-born and Brooklyn-bred, **Richard Torres** has written for *Vibe, The New Yorker, Rolling Stone, XXL, Penthouse* and *The New York Times.* A former columnist for *Newsday* and *Inside Sports,* his first novel, *Freddie's Dead,* was published in 2007 by the X-Press in the U.K. and the U.S.

Kurt Vonnegut's posthumous collection, *Armageddon in Retrospect,* will be published in 2008. Vonnegut was such a large presence in the American imagination that we were a little overwhelmed when he took an interest in *First of the Month.* He cultivated a misanthropic persona, but, to *First*'s crew, he was a life-lover. He always acted like we were doing him a favor when he graced us with pieces and poems. We'd play our part in this friendly charade by mailing him classic jazz CDs. The last one we sent was *Ben Webster: King of the Tenors.* Vonnegut responded in a tone of wonder. We'll miss the sound of his voice.

Gayle Wald teaches at George Washington University. She is the author of *Shout, Sister, Shout!: The Untold Story of Rock-and-Roll Trailblazer Sister Rosetta Tharpe,* which *Vibe* dubbed "about as good as musical reparations get."

Richard Webster was born in 1950 and studied English literature at the University of East Anglia. He is the author of *Why Freud was Wrong: Sin, Science and Psychoanalysis* and is currently working on a study of the role of disgust in the evolution of culture.

Armond White is a member of First of the Month Writers' Collective. He is film critic for *New York Press* and recently wrote notes for the DVD releases of Charles Burnett's *Killer of Sheep* and Wendell Harris's *Chameleon Street.*

Ellen Willis was a writer and activist who helped inspire Second Wave feminism. She was an important editor, New Journalist and rock critic. After her death in 2006, the Ellen Willis Fund was established to support projects of the radical imagination. Contributions to the Fund may be sent c/o Stanley Aronowitz to:

Center for the Study of Culture Technology and Work
CUNY Graduate Center rm. 6115
New York, NY 10016

Peter Lamborn Wilson's last work of prose was *Green Hermeticism* (an alchemy and ecology) with C. Bamford & K. Townley. His new book of poems, *Black Fez Manifesto Etc.* will be published by Autonomedia in 2008. He is currently editing the unpublished lectures and writings of filmmaker/ethnographer/magus Harry Smith.

Sheldon Wolin's *Democracy Incorporated: Managed Democracy and the Specter of Inverted Totalitarianism* will be published in 2008.

Howard Zinn's latest book is *A Power Government Cannot Suppress* (City Lights).